The Child and Family Facing Life-Threatening Illness

Edited by

Tamar Krulik, R.N., D.N.S.

Assistant Professor and Chairperson
Department of Nursing, Tel Aviv University, Israel

Bonnie Holaday, R.N., D.N.S.

Assistant Professor
Department of Family Health Care Nursing
University of California, San Francisco

Ida M. Martinson, R.N., Ph.D., F.A.A.N.

Professor and Chairperson
Department of Family Health Care Nursing
University of California, San Francisco

with 26 contributors

Foreword by

Margretta M. Styles, R.N., Ed.D.

Professor and Dean
School of Nursing
University of California, San Francisco

The Child
and Family Facing
Life-Threatening
Illness

A Tribute to Eugenia Waechter

J.B. Lippincott Company • Philadelphia

LONDON • MEXICO CITY • NEW YORK • ST. LOUIS • SÃO PAULO • SYDNEY

Sponsoring Editor: Paul Hill
Manuscript Editor: Lorraine D. Smith
Indexer: Alberta Morrison
Design Director: Tracy Baldwin
Design Coordinator: Don Shenkle
Designer: Carl Gross
Production Manager: Kathleen P. Dunn
Production Coordinator: George V. Gordon
Compositor: TAPSCO, Inc.
Printer/Binder: R. R. Donnelley & Sons Company

6 5 4 3 2 1

Library of Congress Cataloging-in-Publication Data

The Child and family facing life-threatening illness.

   Includes bibliographies and index.
   1. Terminally ill children—Psychology. 2. Children
and death. 3. Death—Psychological aspects.
4. Terminally ill children—Family relationships.
I. Waechter, Eugenia H. II. Krulik, Tamar.
III. Holaday, Bonnie. IV. Martinson, Ida Marie, date.
[DNLM: 1. Attitude to Death. 2. Death—in infancy
& childhood. 3. Terminal Care—in infancy
& childhood. 4. Terminal Care—psychology.
WS 105.5.A8 C53615]
RJ249.C485 1987   155.9'37   86-19995
ISBN 0-397-54634-3

Contributors

Stephen Armstrong, Ph.D.

Baystate Medical Center
Springfield, Maryland

Cecily Lynn Betz, R.N., Ph.D.

Nursing Training Coordinator
University Affiliated Facility
Neuropsychiatric Institute
University of California, Los Angeles

Sandor Brent, Ph.D.

Department of Psychology
Wayne State University
Detroit, Michigan

Mary R. Crittenden, Ph.D.

Assistant Clinical Professor
Pediatrics
University of California, San Francisco

Delphine Eschbach, R.N., D.N.S.

Professor of Nursing and Health Sciences
Saddleback College
Mission Viejo, California

Bonnie Holaday, R.N., D.N.S.

Assistant Professor
Department of Family Health Care Nursing
University of California, San Francisco

Fred T. Horton, M.D.

Division of Child Psychiatry
Vanderbilt University School of Medicine
Nashville, Tennessee

Myron Karon, M.D.

Children's Hospital of Los Angeles
Los Angeles, California

Robin F. Kramer, R.N., M.S.

Clinical Nurse Specialist
Pediatric Oncology
University of California, San Francisco

Tamar Krulik, R.N., D.N.S.

Assistant Professor and Chairperson
Department of Nursing
Tel Aviv University, Israel

Lynda L. LaMontagne, R.N., D.N.S.

Assistant Professor
College of Nursing
Arizona State University, Tempe

Susan Lewis, Ph.D.

Division of Psychiatry
Vanderbilt University School of Medicine
Nashville, Tennessee

Margaret M. Malone, Ph.D.

Rockland Children's Psychiatric Center
Orangeburg, New York

Lorrie J. Maloney, M.S.

Department of Psychology
San Diego State University
San Diego, California

*Ida M. Martinson, R.N., Ph.D.,
F.A.A.N.*

Professor and Chairperson
Department of Family Health Care Nursing
University of California, San Francisco

Cynthia Mikkelsen, M.S.W. (Retired)

Department of Social Services
University of California, San Francisco

Afaf I. Meleis, R.N., Ph.D.

Professor
Department of Mental and Community
Health Nursing
University of California, San Francisco

Ida Marie Moore

Assistant Professor
Department of Physiological Nursing
University of California, San Francisco

David Rigler, Ph.D.

Department of Psychology
San Diego State University
San Diego, California

Marilyn K. Savedra, R.N., D.N.S.

Associate Professor
Department of Family Health Care Nursing
University of California, San Francisco

Lee Schmidt, R.N., M.N.

Education Counselor, Nursing Service
Center for the Health Sciences
University of California, Los Angeles
Founder, Parent Bereavement Outreach
Santa Monica, California

Mark W. Speece, Ph.D.

Department of Psychology
Wayne State University
Detroit, Michigan

John J. Spinetta, Ph.D.

Professor
Psychology Department
San Diego State University
San Diego, California

M. Colleen Stainton, R.N., D.N.S.

Associate Professor
Faculty of Nursing
University of Calgary
Calgary, Alberta, Canada

Margretta M. Styles, R.N., Ed.D.

Professor and Dean
School of Nursing
University of California, San Francisco

*Eugenia H. Waechter, R.N., Ph.D.,
F.A.A.N.*

Formerly Professor
Department of Family Health Care Nursing
University of California, San Francisco

Foreword

A Note on Eugenia Waechter

Painful memories are often exquisite in their intensity and detail. Every nerve ending snaps to attention, recreating the sights, the sounds, the smells, the minutiae of a tragic event long past. Most of us recall where we were and what we were doing and how we felt when the news of President Kennedy's assassination reached us. The radio announcement of the Japanese attack on Pearl Harbor when I was a child is more vivid to me today than yesterday's headlines.

January 12, 1982, ranks with these memories. At 10:17 A.M. I was sitting in the first row on the right in a large classroom in our school preparing to hear a lecture on professional issues when an associate came to the open doorway and signaled for me to join her in the hallway. With no preliminaries she informed me that she had just been notified by the Fire Department that Gene Waechter had died in a fire in her home in the suburbs. I could not catch my breath.

Gene would be the first to tell me to forget this dark moment and to get on with today's good stuff. But Gene is unforgettable. And her work goes on.

Gene was born in 1925 of missionary parents in Crespo, Argentina. She graduated from St. Luke's Hospital School of Nursing, St. Louis, Missouri, Class of 1947. She earned her baccalaureate in biological science and public health nursing, her master's in pediatric nursing from the University of Chicago, and her Ph.D. in child development from Stanford University. All degrees were conferred with high honors.

Gene practiced as a public health nurse in Illinois from 1948 to 1963. The remainder of her distinguished career was spent at the School of Nursing, University of California, San Francisco, where she attained the rank of full professor in 1981. At the time of her death she was acting chairperson of the Department of Family Health Care Nursing. Among other key achievements, she was very instrumental in the development of the school's Child Care/Study Center.

Gene's curriculum vitae, 44 pages in length, and other records are full and rich with references to her good works as a scholar and a humanitarian. She is best known nationally and internationally for her research with dying children and for her authoritative text, *Nursing Care of Children,* the tenth edition of which was nearing completion when she died at age 56. She served as a lecturer and consultant to schools and organizations in the United States and in other nations including Canada, Great Britain, Nigeria, Turkey, and Yugoslavia. Her curriculum vitae continues to grow through the accomplishments of her colleagues and former students, many of whom have banded together to write this scholarly tribute to Gene. It is obvious that the authors, too, share this exquisite memory and are putting it to constructive use. And Gene's work goes on.

My friend Rheba De Tornyay, Dean at the University of Washington, in describing tenured faculty, has differentiated between "stars" and "solid citizens." Gene was every dean's dream, the combination of the two. She was a super-achiever whose work was on the cutting edge of knowledge. She developed, not a retinue, but a collegial circle of scholars with the same research interests. She was committed to the University as well as her own professional and personal goals. She very quietly and competently did all that was asked of her and more in the way of University service. We all took great pleasure in her company.

Stars generally get more recognition than solid citizens. Gene's gentle, unassuming manner called forth fewer accolades than she deserved. This book is a testimony to her stellar performance. We wish to thank Gene for the gifts of the mind and gifts of the heart she bestowed upon so many of us. What greater recognition than that her work goes on!

Margretta M. Styles, R.N., Ed.D.

Preface

The purpose of this book is twofold. The first is to pay tribute to Dr. Eugenia Waechter's continuing contribution to our understanding of children with life-threatening illness. The second is to provide information that will improve the care given to children with a life-threatening illness and their families.

American nursing is just beginning to recognize the contributions of various individuals to its growth as a practice and as a scholarly discipline. This text represents another step in nursing's coming of age as it reflects on one individual's accomplishments.

We in the 1980s are practicing with increased confidence amidst the reverberations of two revolutions launched in the decade of the 1970s. As with many revolutions, the ideas were not always new, but the rapidity with which they spread through the nursing profession and society was. First, Elizabeth Kubler–Ross opened the door to let death and dying out of the closet where hospitals and modern medicine had hidden them for much of the century. The publication of her book *On Death and Dying* in 1969 marked the beginning of grief, dying, and death appearing regularly in our newspapers, books, magazines, and television. Concurrently, Dr. Waechter completed her dissertation, "Death Anxiety in Children with Fatal Illness" in 1968. In 1971 her classic paper "Children's Awareness of Fatal Illness" was published. Subsequently, practitioners began to acknowledge the fact that dying children were aware of their impending death. During the decade that followed, children were increasingly able to discuss their concerns and reach out to others for help.

Second, during the 1970s, theory emerged to permeate the field of nursing. This created new paradigms through which phenomena could be studied and treated. Dr. Waechter integrated knowledge of illness in childhood, theory of normal growth and development, and family theory to lead the way for the establishment of a body of knowledge unique to pediatric nursing. The infusion of these theories into the study and treatment of children and their families helped to strengthen nursing's claim as a profession and to revitalize nursing care.

We have acquired important new knowledge about children with life-threatening illness in recent years, and the insights of Eugenia Waechter have had a prominent role in guiding the search for that knowledge. The book is organized around three units, each of which includes some of Dr. Waechter's work. The first unit provides a review of research studies on the child's concept of death. The second unit focuses on two issues: (1) what the child with a life-threatening illness knows about death, and (2) how the child acts in response to that knowledge.

The last unit provides a review of intervention techniques for those who care for the children, siblings, and parents, or who are teaching others how to provide care. These chapters summarize almost 20 years of Dr. Waechter's work. For historical perspective we have not altered the content of these papers. Therefore, these papers should be read in the light of the prevailing health care practices.

It is eminently appropriate that half of the contributors to this volume were students of Eugenia's, for Gene excited the curiosity of her students and enticed them to be her collaborators in the quest for new knowledge. The other half of the contributors are professional colleagues who worked with Gene or shared a research interest. All proceeds from this text will be used to support faculty and doctoral student research with children with life-threatening illness and their families at the University of California, San Francisco, Department of Family Health Care Nursing, and Tel Aviv University Department of Nursing.

For assistance in preparing a text of this sort, we must acknowledge the contributions of many individuals. We are particularly indebted to each of the contributors who wrote chapters for no fee, and to all of the journals and publishing companies that waived their usual permission fees. We want to thank Paul Hill, editor, J. B. Lippincott Company, for his enthusiastic support of this project. We are especially grateful to Luther Waechter for sharing Eugenia Waechter's personal papers. We would like to express our appreciation to John Rukkila and Lorraine Smith for their editorial assistance. Our thanks goes to Diana Zielinski, administrative assistant, who typed several versions of the manuscript and whose good nature and efficiency have been many times appreciated.

Bonnie Holaday, R.N., D.N.S.
Tamar Krulik, R.N., D.N.S.
Ida M. Martinson, R.N., Ph.D., F.A.A.N.

Contents

The Child and Family Facing Life-Threatening Illness

Unit I

An Overview of the Literature and Research

1 · Death, Dying, and Bereavement: A Review of the Literature

Eugenia H. Waechter

Since the assassination of President Kennedy, the thoughts of the nation have been turned to death. This was a single death, but one that brought every individual face to face with the inevitability of his own death and of those about him. The transition from time to timelessness is always there—the only certainty.

Down through the ages people have been concerned with death. The Egyptians saw death as everpresent: "Say not I am too young for thee to carry off, for thou knowest not thy death. Death cometh and leadeth away the babe that is still in the bosom of it's mother, even as the man when he hath become old."

The kings of Babylon attempted to cheat death by having substitutes die for them. The Greeks were concerned about dying honorably; death could not be controlled, but could be met proudly. Socrates met death philosophically; "Will you not allow that I have as much of the spirit of prophecy in me as the swans? For they, when they perceive that they must die, having sung all their life long, do then sing more lustily than ever, rejoicing in the thought that they are about to go away to the God whose ministers they are. But men, because they are themselves afraid of death, slanderously affirm of the swans that they sing a lament at the last, not considering that no bird sings when cold or hungry or in pain. . . . I would not go out of life less merrily than the swans" (Sulzberger, 1961).

Other early philosophers examined death with fascination. Empedocles says, "There is no coming into being of aught that perishes, nor any end of it in boneful death; but only mingling of change of what has been mingled. Coming into being is but a name given to these by men" (Sulzberger, 1961).

Paper written in 1964.

The ancient Buddhist doctrine held that death was a punishment for sins, as did the Hebrew culture. The early Romans spoke to their dead as though attempting to recall them. In Tibet death was regarded as the work of death demons, and in the Muhammadan faith, it is believed that the exact hour of death is foreordained.

The attitudes expressed toward death have changed in Western culture in the past century. In mid-Victorian times, the drama of death was well known to every individual. People witnessed death in their homes, and cemeteries were prominent in the center of every village. Deathbed scenes were feature in the theater since death was not something mysterious to be hidden.

In 20th-century American culture there has been a switch from prudery regarding sex to hiding, negation, and denial of death. "The natural process of corruption and decay has become disgusting, as disgusting as the natural processes of copulation and birth were a century ago" (Gorer, 1960). Many sociologists believe that Americans are afraid of death and ashamed of it. Three popular books recently have accused Americans of hiding from the reality of death, as evidenced by the structure of a 9 billion dollar industry, the "undertakers." Americans are accused of paying immense sums to shield themselves from the sight of death and of employing defenses more patently magical and uncritical than in any other area of human experiences (Sulzberger, 1961). The range of knowledge in the past century has grown to encompass the origin, birth, growth, decline, death, and dissolution of the individual to such an extent that human beings have felt the need for illusion to conceal the knowledge of vital and fatal matters.

Several factors have contributed to this cultural development. With the emergence of science, society turned to scientists to find the answers for a longer and more perfect life. Instead, science labored not to perfect man, but to develop new weapons with which to destroy him. To this disillusionment was added the factor that death might be a chance encounter, survival a matter of "luck."

In addition, there has been a shift in religious beliefs. A century ago most people believed in an afterlife. Today, however, this promise of continuation into eternity is found less credible and is thought by many to be a superstition or an allowable indiscretion (Feifel, 1959). Because of this, natural death and physical decompsition have become too horrible to contemplate or discuss.

Advances in public health and preventive medicine also have contributed to this trend. The death of young people is much less common and, therefore, does not need to be faced very often in an intimate way. On the other hand, comprehension of the violent death of many young people in catastrophe and war is impeded because of sheer numbers and distance.

Yet when we deal with death, we deal with the very mystery of human beings, who alone among all creatures know they must die. With personal love we grasp other people's individualism, constitution, and uniqueness as being essentially different from ourselves. With this love, and inevitable loss, we can therefore also learn to know what death is. Landsberg states, "The awareness of death and it's necessity is only provoked by participation, by the personal love in which the whole experience is bathed. We constituted a 'we' with the dying man, and it is through this 'we,' through the very strength of this community, which constitutes, as it were, a new order of persons, that we are led into an experiential knowledge of our own mortality'' (Landsberg, 1953).

Even with knowledge, however, the fear of death, if not conscious, is part of the subconscious of all individuals and has been universal. It is not understood because it is the only one of life's experiences that cannot be shared. Not being understood, it is feared.

THE FEAR OF DEATH

There has been much speculation about the origin of the fear of death since the time of Francis Bacon, who mused, ''Men fear death as children fear to go in the dark, and as the natural fear in children is increased with tales, so is the other.''

Most of the theories concerning the origin of this fear have been advanced by investigators in the field of psychoanalysis, through the analysis of adult patients. Freud himself had quite a good deal to say about the subject. In *The Ego and the Id*, he derives the fear of death from castration anxiety and from fear of desertion of the superego—that is, a fear of losing the love object. In 1936, in *The Problem of Anxiety*, Freud again conceived of fear of death as being like the fear of conscience, which was a derivation of the fear of castration. As if to imply derivation in descending order, he gave the series: fear of castration, of conscience, and of death. He spoke of a ''death instinct'' or an ''unconscious wish to die,'' a tendency in everyone to wish for death. In *Hemmung, Symptom und Angst*, Freud implies that the death fear is one of fundamental anxiety. He believed that the greatest dynamic in the life of women was fear of loss of love which he equated to man's fear of loss of the penis. Death then would symbolize: (1) loss of love, which means separation from the parents, and (2) loss of penis (Chadwick, 1929).

Otto Rank stated in *The Trauma of Birth* (1924) that all basic anxiety, which includes the death fear, was a result of the birth trauma.

It would seem that the primal anxiety affect at birth, which remains operative through life, right up to the final separation from the outer world at death, is from the very beginning not merely an expression of the newborn child's physiological injuries, but in consequence of the change from a highly pleasurable situation to an extremely painful one, immediately acquires a 'psychial' quality of feeling. This experienced anxiety is thus the first content of perception and the first act, so to say, to set up barriers; and in these we must recognize the primal repression against the already powerful tendency to re-establish the pleasurable situation just left (Ramzy and Wallerstein, 1958).

Other psychoanalysts have advanced correlating theories or elaborated on those already given. Mary Chadwick (1929) proposed that the fear of death was connected with the awareness of helplessness in the infant who realizes the mother's absence and fears that she may not return, this fear of absence being a fundamental alliance with the realization of helplessness. Chadwick believed that death also represents helplessness—a power over which we have no control—and therefore is terrifying.

Chadwick separated death into a dual representation in the unconscious: the unwanted father-death (hostile or violent death, an action of the cruel father who slays the sons and orders the exposure of the daughters) and the desired, benign mother-death (regression to the prenatal state, which is wished for and neither unknown nor feared). Thus, in fantasy, such death is often imagined as a floating in water or drowning. Chadwick corroborates this by the fact that when the death wish in woman is carried out in suicide, it often occurs in the form of mother regression, such as by actual drowning or by suffocation with gas from an oven.

She agrees tentatively with Freud that the fear of death may be a derivative of the castration fear. However, conversely, she speculates that the castration fear may be a derivative of the more primary fear of death, which she feels is borne out by the equal prevalence of this anxiety in both men and women. She suggests that in women the fear of death is equated with loss of love because women especially learn from childhood onwards that it is their duty to please and to fear loss of life.

In 1933 Bromberg and Schilder questioned normal adults about their attitudes toward death and concluded that the actual fear of dying is uppermost, rather than the fear of death itself. They concluded that in the unconscious, death is considered a bereavement of libidinous enjoyment, and the fear of death, therefore, is less prominent in the individual who suffers a lack of libidinous enjoyment. The fear of death is thus related to the fear of losing pleasure potentialities. They suggest that, for this reason, people fear disfigurement as much as death itself, as evidenced by the prominent desire "to look nice when they die."

Some years later, Melanie Klein (1940), though referring more particularly to mourning, suggested that the primary "depressive position" is due to loss of the mother's breast and that, without that, there is also loss of love, goodness, and security. Fear of death then would be related to loss of past pleasure and security potentialities. She also concurs with Freud to the extent that "further distress about impending loss arises out of the Oedipal, which sets in so early and in such close connection with breast frustrations, that in its beginnings it is dominated by oral impulses and fears."

THE INDIVIDUAL MEANING OF DEATH

Comparatively little study has been done on normal adults to ascertain what meaning death has for the individual. One exception is the study done by Bromberg and Schilder referred to previously. In their questionnaire study they found that the occurrence of spontaneous death thoughts was a relative rarity. Most often these thoughts were brought into being by association; nonetheless, they were of unappreciated frequency in daily life. Almost three fourths of the people questioned felt their own death was definitely improbable, and a remoteness from personal death was the usual reaction. They concluded that the average person is not aware of a preconscious stream of death thoughts; that it is difficult to think of personal death, but relatively easy to think of the death of others. In the average person, thoughts of death are inadmissible in the midst of life. When such thoughts do become conscious, however, most people think of dying rather than of being dead. Conscious wishes for death are usually equated in the normal person with fantasies about causing a feeling of loss and remorse in friends and relatives or of punishing them for real or imagined withdrawal of love.

The Child's Awareness of Death

Most of the information we have concerning the construction of the concept of death in the mind of the child derives from studies done by Sylvia Anthony in prewar London in 1937–39 and Maria Nagy in Budapest in 1940.

In a longitudinal study of 117 children ranging in age from 3 to 13 years, Anthony gathered material from story completion tests performed with the children and from daily diaries kept by their parents.

Nagy, on the other hand, had single contacts with her subjects, children ranging in age from 3 to 10 years. She attempted to answer concepts of death by discussion with children under age 6 and by requesting compositions about death from the older children.

THE CHILD UNDER FIVE YEARS

Anthony (1940) disagrees with Freud's postulation that early thoughts of death in the child are derived from "death wishes." She states, "Not only are early so-called death-wishes void of any real death significance, but it is also doubtful whether they lead to the earliest apprehension of the idea. The impressions given by the behavior of the children observed during this research suggests that the idea arises independently of the earlier impulses toward aggression, and is only linked up with such impulses and flooded with the emotions connected with them at a later stage of development."

She believes that the idea of death develops in the child as intellect advances, rather than as more years increase or as personal experience teach.

This concept has also been formulated by Piaget (1962) who states that thinking processes are governed by different laws at different mental ages in an orderly progression. The construction of reality is accomplished step by step. Early concepts of cessation of life are not intelligible to very young children because their inner mental structures are not flexible enough. The outer reality is constructed only gradually, and the young child's viewpoint is controlled by the perceptual aspects of reality.

In the earliest years, Piaget says, the idea of the fortuitous does not exist, causality presupposes a "maker," God, the parents, etc. "If the child at this stage is puzzled by the problem of death, it is precisely because in his conception of things, death is inexplicable. . . . Death is the fortuitous and mysterious phenomenon par excellence. And in the questions about plants and animals and the human body, it is those which refer to death which will cause the child to leave behind him the stage of pure finalism, and to acquire the notion of statistical causality or chance" (Piaget, 1962). Anthony suggests that if the idea of death has any special importance for intellectual development at this stage, it must be because it presents itself as proof of the ultimate impotence of thought and desire.

Therefore, in line with Piaget's concept of causality, the infant must have reached the *why* stage before there is any awareness of death or the word *dead,* for it is only with this question that function becomes of interest. Thus, there must already be present in the child's mind: (1) organization of experience at a certain level, and (2) some comprehension of causation, which depends on the whole of mental development.

In children the first common factor observed to lead to the embryonic idea of the word *dead* is the attitude of puzzlement, wonder, and surprise aroused when a child sees something dead. The child realizes that there is a gap in his other experience. Piaget suggests that this earliest experience forms a link between the emotional life of the earliest period and the intellectual developments that follow that stage, to leave behind the stage of pure finalism.

In this exploration process the first experience with death leads children to equate it with: (1) separation, departure, or disappearance, (2) sleep, and (3) going into a grave, coffin, earth, or water. Many other observers, in addition to Piaget, think that children first equate death with separation.

Maria Nagy (1948) also found in her investigations that during the first stage of developing a concept of death, the child attributes life and consciousness to the dead; death was a departure, or a sleep. She believed that, for young children, the most painful thing about death was the separation itself. She also observed that young children reversed this concept—if anyone has gone away, he is dead.

This reversal was also observed by Freud and Burlingame (1943) in wartime London. In *War and Children,* they commented, "It is common knowledge that after the death of a father or mother, small children behave as if their parents had just gone away. We can certainly say that when parents have only gone away, the children behave as if they had died. This only means to say that the important factor for the small child is bodily absence or presence of the mother. The question of existence or nonexistence in the real world seems to be beyond the child's emotional comprehension."

Bromberg and Schilder (1933) in their study found that most subjects remembered first hearing the words "death and dying" sometime after the age of three. At this young age they thought the idea was inexplicable, that it meant "sleep and no return," or they "never thought that death meant any more than going away." Other ideas associated with this first knowledge were "stillness," "curiosity," "awe and wonder," "unexplained mysterious feelings," "fear inspiring," "something different and baffling," and "being far away."

Death is a mysterious absence, somehow vaguely connected with threats. Bromberg and Schilder believed a dead person's absence merges with the idea of removal of the libidinous object, that is, its nonavailability as a love object for those who remain behind.

Anthony (1940) also found that death to young children meant in death the departure context: loss of the mother, not their own death; thus, the child views death with aversion since it threatens loss of protection.

The set of notions concerned with the word "dead" must be acquired by experience. Often this means experiencing the death of animals, which later in the developing conception of death may lead to a predominating note of destruction and decay or with violence in the killing of domestic animals. Death becomes the end result of aggression, but never a natural event.

Anthony (1940) also concludes, "It is a sorrow about death conceived as separation or loneliness. The fear, on the other hand, is not simply of death; it is of an aggressive outsider (a 'burglar') breaking into the home and killing the child, and perhaps his parents too. It is a fear of death conceived as the ultimate effect of aggression, violation, and robbery. These two themes, of death as sorrowful separation and of death as the ultimate result of aggression, stand out as the main typical connotations of the idea by whatever method we have studied it."

She believes that the law of talion is also involved, the tit-for-tat, although the idea of retaliation may even derive from something more primitive, a thought complex alternately seen in primary and then reversed order—a mother loses her child by death, and then the mother herself dies; after which the child is alive again, and then the mother comes back, too.

Although, unfortunately, Schilder and Wechsler (1934) in their study did not differ sufficiently in regard to age, they do concur that the conception of death in the young child is equated with separation, sleep, and violence.

Their subjects also viewed death as a deprivation and as a result of human violence or the violence of God. Schilder and Wechsler also thought the child is led to believe in the reversibility of death because the child is alive and has not seen death or what happens to the dead. This would also be borne out by the fact that often the "separated" do return.

Nagy (1948) also observed this reversibility. In death, children under 5 years old see life. She concludes that before this age the opposition to death is so strong that children deny death because emotionally they cannot accept it.

Another aspect of the child's earliest thoughts about death are linked with magic. When the death concept is linked with the complex of birth, separation, and sleep, there may be a resulting belief that the actual pattern of life is symmetrical. This is suggested by the common association of birth and death as union with and separation from the mother. Anthony concludes that there are many similarities between the life before birth and the life after death. She states, "We begin and we end in nothingness and mystery—we begin helpless and we end helpless." Thus, in magical thinking, birth and death are identical, or death is equated with prenatal life. Thus, death may become an aspect of rebirth.

The Fear of Death in the Young Child

There is considerable difference of opinion among psychoanalysts and reseachers regarding at what approximate age anxiety about death may appear in the child and what are the precipitating factors. There is general agreement, however, that children aged 4 to 6 years think about death more than adults are willing, because of repression of their own fear, to admit. Children have an insatiable curiosity not only about "where people come from," but also about "where people go." Often this is met with evasion, subterfuge, embarrassed prudery, or frightened withdrawal.

Generally, evidence for fear of death in young children has been expected to appear after the Oedipal period, a symbolic product of the fear of castration. It is usually considered the expression of a fear of punishment for hostile thoughts toward the magic father or mother.

Other opinions, however, relate the death anxiety to other developmental periods. Wahl (1959) thinks that fear of death is frequently encountered in children as early as the third year and is manifested by obsessive blessing of persons at the end of prayers. He relates this anxiety to the formation of guilt that greatly antedates the Oedipus complex and results from intrafamilial stress or derives from the socialization process. Since the training period is painful and frustrating, no child escapes forming hostile wishes toward the parent, and therefore none escapes the fear of personal death.

Chadwick (1929) places the origins of the fear of death at an even earlier period—dawning of the visual and muscular senses, the two earliest vehicles of the emerging ego. Since, by these two senses, children first learn to control the outside world, any restraint of movement or restriction of vision leads to the conception of the fear of death. She states, "By means of the realization of pleasure through muscular movement and muscle erotism, the child learns to appreciate the power of its own ego at a very early stage of auto-erotic libido development. Muscle erotism may thus take on a very high cathexis, which would lead to a correspondingly intense reaction to muscular opposition of restraint from outside sources, so giving rise to anxiety, which expresses itself as the fear of death and causes the cry 'let go, you're killing me.' "

From her investigations, Anthony (1940) concludes that a chronic form of death anxiety may be a reaction resulting from aggressive impulses that occur before there is a clear conception of what death means. Critical anxiety may appear at a definite stage of development when death first comes into mental association with the idea of the differentiated self. At this time some children may go through a period of acute and manifest anxiety, which they may resolve by developing a belief in reincarnation.

DEATH OF A PARENT OR SIBLING

The death of a parent or sibling is a shattering experience for the child and may have far reaching effects. In analysis of adult schizophrenics, Rosenzweig (1943) found that a significant number of patients had a history of a younger-sibling death in the family before the patient had reached the sixth year of life. He suggests that because of guilt, the groundwork was laid for a disturbance of the normal transfer of social patterns from the family constellation to the extrafamilial milieu.

Other writers link this guilt to the magical thinking of the child of this age. The young, loved child has a feeling of omnipotence that he has carried over from his babyhood.

Anthony (1940) states,

To understand the conflict in the child's mind at such a time, we must take account of a factor which we have as yet overlooked: his conception of causality. It would be an over-simplification to say that the child believes in his own omnipotence, in the sense that he believes his wishes take effect automatically. Undoubtedly his mental scheme includes a variety of forms of causation, with little coordination between them. But it is a characteristic feature of the thought of the child that his own wishes have magical power to influence events. From his babyhood he preserves an impression of himself as the activating centre of his world, whose wishes are known, carried out or thwarted, even when he does not or cannot express them. So it happened with him in babyhood, apparently; so he more than half believes it continues to happen.

In the children's fantasies, therefore, they take responsibility for these wishes. If something has happened, it was because they wished it—they must have wished it. When a parent or sibling dies, the child feels like the secret slayer and, in addition, feels rage toward the deceased, if a parent, because of deliberate abandonment and deprivation.

An actual death also proves the comparative weakness of the child's own love impulses or the general malevolence of fate.

Acute anxiety at this age may be manifested by a fear of ghosts, of enclosed places, of the dark, or of being left alone. A child at the stage of talion will fear punishment or at the reparation stage may become overobedient and conscientious. Some children may strongly reject the idea of death or may take a "flight into reality." They may repress temporarily their own fantasies about death and adopt an adult attitude involving a complete rejection of the whole idea of personal responsibility for the death in question (Anthony, 1940).

This first acquaintance with death may also be crucial inasmuch as the child will be exposed for perhaps the first time to attitudes about death of the significant adults around him and of their values of life. Nagy concludes, "To conceal death from the child is not possible and not permissible. Natural behavior in the child's surroundings can greatly diminish the shock of its acquaintance with death" (Nagy, 1948).

Wolf (1938) also believes that ultimately the child's attitudes and reactions stem from parental values communicated to the child. The child's source of strength will be acceptance of his or her feelings and the need for expressing them, whether of anger, fear, or grief. When the child is very young, this communication of acceptance will be mainly nonverbal, since words are only a supplement to a deeper emotional message.

The School-aged Child

In between 5 and 6 years of age some children no longer deny the reality of death but they think of death as gradual or temporary. Attributes of life are still thought of as provisional. Thus, we see in games of "cowboys and Indians," that each side kills the other off and then all are resurrected to play another game—violent death and its undoing. The distinctions between life and death are not complete; while they acknowledge that death exists, they are still unable to accept it as a definite fact. At this time also the paraphernalia of death is noted in detail, although very often the child is unable to connect the fact of physical death with its symbolic appurtenances (Schilder and Wechsler, 1934). The quality of time can still not be completely appreciated, and therefore, completeness of death is distorted.

From her study, Anthony (1940) concludes that the year 7 to 8 is critical in the development of the concept of death. She believes that the change in thinking during this time is striking and bears out Piaget's findings about the significance of the years 7 and 8 as the turning point in development and in progressive objectification of the child's attitude to phenomena and intellectual development in general.

Anthony further believes that at this age the child has a more complete conception of time and logic. There is a connection between the concept of death and the concepts of age, time, and number. With logical thinking, children may come to associate death with themselves through the idea of old people dying, growing ever older themselves, or dying themselves. With this association between death and number, magical practices may arise out of the anxiety about death. These practices are usually associated with warding off old age.

Thus, development of the concept of death and of conscious logic and rational science are interrelated. The child now realizes the powerlessness of the individual to avert death of the loved object; he or she is not omnipotent and does not have magical powers: natural law prevails over human will.

Anthony definitely concludes that the eighth year cuts off the "infantile from the mature groups." Following this, there is a period of elaboration of the idea and the adult concept of death is reached between the ages of 11 and 13. From her findings she believes that this evolution is not affected by home teaching.

In her study of children, Nagy found that between the ages of 5 and 9 children personify death. Death either is imagined as a separate person or is identified with the dead. Thus, we hear such concepts as "The death man carries off children," or "Death lies in the coffin." Two thirds of her subjects imagined death as a distinct personality, whereas one third identified it with the dead. A significant number of these children reported thinking of death in the evening, suggesting relationships between death and darkness.

Nagy places the critical age for final comprehension of the concept of death at the ninth year, after which death is recognized as the cessation of corporeal life. At this stage, according to her view, death becomes comprehensible and it is inevitable. Not only does the child's view of death become realistic but also the child's general view of the world.

Schilder and Wechsler concluded from their study that school-aged children are filled with the idea of violence and death, and with the tendency to kill, which may come out in play. They believed that religious morality enters in the child's attitude toward death relatively rarely.

When faced with the death of a significant love object, children in latency may show a surprising indifference. Rochlin (1959) expresses the view that depressive attitudes are absent in children, although Bowlby (1960) more closely relates mourning in children to adult reactions.

Deutsch (1937) says that this apparent indifference results from the fact that the ego of the child is not sufficiently developed to bear the strain of the work of mourning and that the child therefore utilizes some mechanisms of narcissistic self-protection to circumvent the mourning process. She states, "If the ego is too weak to undertake the elaborate function of mourning, two courses are possible: first, infantile regression is expressed as anxiety, and second, defense forces intended to protect the ego from anxiety and other dangers are mobilized. The most extreme expression of this defense mechanism is the omission of affect. It is of great interest that observers of children note that the ego is rent asunder in those children who do not employ the usual defenses and who mourn as an adult does."

Shambaugh (1961) found in his analysis of a 7-year-old boy who lost his mother during treatment, that this type of object loss may disrupt remaining object relationships, at least for a time. In order to reduce anxiety, children may use surviving objects and relationships for defensive purposes.

Shambaugh also agrees with Deutsch that this reaction to loss in childhood occurs because of the child's dependency on adults, the not yet fully incorporated superego, and the relatively undeveloped ego.

Anthony (1940) expresses the opinion that when anxiety is raised in a child by death in the family circle, the child employs defenses resembling those of a maladjusted adult. The child may use the mechanism of reaction formation, an escape to the mental atmosphere of the adult where safety can be suggested by resources other than the child's. The child may also isolate the happening from consciousness, causing complete loss of memory for a portion of the experience and contributing to an often observed curious indifference to the relationship loss.

The Adolescent

Little research has been reported about adolescents' attitudes toward death in general and their own death in particular. It has been generally observed, however, that the adolescent lives intensely in the present. "Everything that is important and valuable in life lies either in the immediate life situation or in the rather close future" (Kastenbaum, 1959).

Therefore, although adolescents have an intellectual comprehension of the meaning of death, personal death is relegated to the distant future, which is indefinitely and negatively structured.

In a study of 15-, 16-, and 17-year olds, Kastenbaum concludes that remote time fields are "risky, unpleasant, and devoid of significant positive values." Thoughts of death, therefore, are generally excluded from conscious awareness, though there may be a considerable unconscius preoccupation with death.

THE DEATH OF A CHILD

From the years 1955 through 1963 five studies were reported in the literature relating to the death of a child and its impact on the family circle. The diagnosis of the children in each of these studies implied a chronic course of the illness, specifically either leukemia or neoplastic disease. No studies have been done of parental reactions to the acute illness or sudden death of a child owing to the obvious difficulties inherent in gathering such data.

In most of the studies reported the major emphasis has been placed on interviewing and/or observation of the parents concerned, generally mothers. In one study interviews were complemented by study of parental urinary 17 hydroxycorticosteriod excretion rates, as indicative of chronic stress (Friedman, Mason, and Hamburg, 1963), and in another certain projective tests were administered.

In most of these studies only incidental clinical observations of the behavior of the children involved was reported. Only a few studies have been reported that were specifically designed to ascertain the children's attitudes to their own diagnosis and impending death.

The Reaction of the Child

Specific data regarding children's reactions to their own imminent deaths is seriously lacking. Solnit and Green (1963) observe, ''Indeed, there is a notable want of reports that attempt to examine at any level this frequent and fateful clinical circumstance in childhood.''

A wealth of information is available about the reaction of the preschool child to hospitalization, illness, and separation. Knudson and Natterson (1963) also studied children less than 3 years of age and reported separation anxieties that suerseded any fear of death.

Of children approximately 4 years of age, Bozeman, Orbach, and Sutherland (1955) report that they were ''extraordinarily quiet, sometimes apathetic, either alone or in groups despite the extensive equipment and staff dedicated to their amusement.''

Although children aged 4 to 5 are generally not expected to question their own survival, Solnit and Green (1963) report that, in their experience, this question has been raised by a few children of this age, and they cite a case study in which a 4-year-old boy conveyed the knowledge of his own impending death.

Somewhat more information is available about the reactions of school-age children; however, this is also based on incidental observation.

Knudson and Natterson (1960) separate the reactions of the child into three phases: under 6, fears of separation are paramount; from 6 to 10, fears related to physical injury are foremost; and not until after 10 are children obviously fearful of their own impending death. This finding suggests to them that separation, mutilation, and death fears are separate and distinctive.

For children between 6 and 10 they believe that the manifestations of death fear are vague and evanescent. Expressed anxiety is generally related to intrusive or painful procedures.

Friedman and colleagues (1963) reported that the younger child with leukemia often rejected his parents, which was related to the parents' inability to prevent painful procedures and the child's perceived recognition of the transfer of parental authority to medical personnel. Young children often bypassed their parents, which reflected an awareness that their parents' ability to help them was limited.

Much more has been written about the general role of bodily illness in the mental life of children. Freud suggests that the child is unable to distinguish between feelings of suffering caused by the disease inside the body and suffering imposed on him from outside for the sake of curing the disease.

Other factors affecting the child of school age included the emotional climate during the illness and the child's general reaction to being nursed. Freud (1952) states, "The gradual mastering of various bodily functions, such as independent eating, independent bowel and bladder evacuation, the ability to wash, dress, undress, etc. mark for the child highly significant stages in ego development as well as advances in detaching his own body from that of the mother and possessing it at least in part. A loss of these abilities, when occasioned by the nursing procedures (or by the weakened bodily condition itself) means an equivalent loss in ego control, a pull-back toward the earlier and more passive levels of infantile development."

She further suggests that the reaction to pain is related to its psychic meaning and that any child in pain (intrusive procedures, etc.) feels maltreated, harmed, punished, persecuted, and threatened with annihilation.

All studies indicated that children over the age of 10 did manifest a fear of their own death. Different qualities of this manifestation, however, were noted by the different observers.

Natterson and Knudson (1960) believed that the fear of death communicated to personnel was urgent, pervasive, and persistent, and took definite precedent over other fears. Although the children seldom asked questions of the staff, the latter felt that the children probably knew of their own impending death. Reactions included anxiousness, depression, and withdrawal that deepened with the death of another child on the ward.

On the other hand, Richmond and Waisman (1955) reported that the children they observed rarely manifested an overt concern about death but reacted with an air of passive acceptance and resignation. "Even among adolescents, who intellectually know much about cancer, the question concerning diagnosis and possibility of death usually was not raised as it often is by the adult patient. Our suspicion is that this does not reflect an unawareness, but rather represents an attempt at repression psychologically of the anxiety concerning death."

Friedman and associates (1963) commented in relation to this that the majority of parents and adults shield the child from ever hearing the word *leukemia*, resulting in a feeling of isolation in the child, a feeling that his disease is "too awful to talk about," and that others are not aware of what the child is experiencing.

Solnit and Green (1959) also observed that children invariably sense what is happening even when a deliberate attempt is made to shield them from this tragic and frightening situation. They suggested that adults do not see fears of death in children because they are blinded by their own fears and anxieties. They concluded, "It should be the aim of future research in this area not only to examine systematically how children express their knowledge or sense that they are dying but also to determine the principles, techniques, and limitations of communicating with these children in a therapeutic manner. . . . Only through a more thorough understanding of the dying child's ways of communicating his sense of dying will we be able to know and teach how to help the dying child psychologically, and come to appreciate the limitations of our knowledge and psychological therapy."

The Reactions of Parents

The threatened or actual loss of a child is one of the most shattering and tragic experiences that can occur in the life of parents. How this contingency is met depends upon the circumstances of the child's illness and the parent's resources, both personal and environmental. "Perhaps at no other time does the previous integration of the personality of the family unit reflect itself so clearly as it does during the severe emotional stress associated with mourning" (Richmond and Waisman, 1955).

There is surprising unanimity of findings regarding the parent's general observable reactions to threatened and actual loss of a fatally ill child.

Following the diagnosis, parents felt "shocked" or "stunned." Many parents were unable to comprehend the fatal implications of the diagnosis, and they excluded it from consciousness. They behaved "in a disbelieving manner," and "as though it hadn't sunk in." Many others reported the initial reaction in terms of physical injury to themselves such as "it was a blow in the face."

The manner in which the diagnosis was imparted to parents was found to be of vital importance in determining their attitudes and relationships with medical personnel and nurses. If, because of the physician's own feelings, parents were informed in an abrupt manner or in a way that eliminated any hope, extreme hostility was aroused, which tended to become reactivated thereafter on any pretext, either realistic or distorted. The common theme in all these situations was the destruction of hope for recovery (Bozeman, Orbach, and Sutherland, 1955).

The parents were next eager to have their child hospitalized for two basic reasons: (1) frantic attempt to reverse the diagnosis, and (2) immediate treatment in order to save the child. This initial hospitalization had concomitant severe separation anxiety for both mother and child, which was reciprocal and seemed to be related to the threat of permanent separation.

Initially, all mothers attempted to deny the implications of the diagnosis, either by screening out the massive threat from awareness, or by compulsive attempts to reverse it. The latter did not extend to the fact of the child's illness itself, and often parents demanded additional consultations and diagnostic procedures from other physicians of their personal or professional acquaintance. With verification of the diagnosis, hostility was often observed. Continued denial, with lack of associated emotional response and affective experience, was also a common defense.

With the initiation of treatment, and thus a demonstration of the reality of the situation, guilt feelings were universally elicited. Parents questioned in many ways, "What could have caused it?" and "Why did this have to happen?" They blamed themselves for not recognizing the early nonspecific manifestations of the disease, for not being more appreciative of the child before the illness, for failing to care for and protect the child, or for personal failures and wrongdoing: "It's God's way of punishing me."

As one interesting sidelight to this question of causality, Greene and Miller (1958) have reported some surprising research findings about psychological factors and reticuloendothelial disease.

In their study of 33 children and adolescents with leukemia, they found that the disease was prefaced with significant frequency by losses or separations for the child (change of home, beginning school, separation or threat of separation from a significant person) and/or by depression in the mothers for weeks or months before the diagnosis of disease in the child. In addition, they found that in most of the maternal–child relationships, the mother had assigned a role to the child entirely disproportionate to his or her age.

Following the expression of guilt in the parents, overactivity continued but now was directed in a compulsive manner to learning everything they could about the disease, to reading widely and to questioning medical staff in a frantic search to find loopholes that would prove their own child was an exception to the general rule. Expressed hope during this period was nonspecific.

With knowledge of the disease and acceptance of the diagnosis, the parents begin the second phase of response described by Natterson and Knudson (1960), which is characterized by realism and continued nonspecific hope. During this phase the mother wishes to be with the child as much as possible. There is a physical clinging to the child with hostility directed at persons who threaten or interrupt this physical closeness. This phenomenon is an effort on the part of parents to master separation anxiety and guilt aroused by the diagnosis. Mothers evaluated nurses by two standards: (1) efficiency of the nurses in maintaining the physical cleanliness of the child and in clarifying procedures, which was seen positively, and (2) the assumption by nurses of maternal functions of discipline, feeding, and affection, which was evaluated in terms of whether it facilitated or interfered with the mother's continuance of these functions.

Richmond and Waisman (1955) also observed that involvement of parents in the physical care of their child facilitated parental adaptation by permitting them to feel they had done everything possible for the child, and thus relieving guilt. Retrospectively, parents were also grateful to have had the opportunity to be with the child as much as possible and to participate in measures directed toward relieving pain and discomfort. Friedman and co-workers (1963) also observed that helping in the care of the child was most supportive for parents.

During this phase, anticipatory grief and mourning was initiated and varied greatly. Emotionally, parents began to separate themselves from their children. Nonspecific hope continued, although intellectually parents no longer expected a cure to be found in time to save their child. This expectancy, though, did not extend to the emotional acceptance of the prognosis. All parents were eager to try new treatments, and all parents were retrospectively grateful for the "few months, weeks, days or even moments with their child, so long as there was hope, and so long as the child's suffering could be controlled" (Cobbs, 1956).

As the disease progressed there was a curtailment of hope, and symptoms of anticipatory grief became more prominent. These included somatic symptoms, apathy, weakness, preoccupation with the thoughts of the ill child, sighing, crying, and depression. This has been considered a healthy reaction in the stepwise preparation of parents for final separation. During this time parents also searched for a meaning for this tragic occurrence in their lives—it was intolerable that it should be meaningless.

During this stage parents also turned to former relationships for support. Bozeman, Orbach, and Sutherland (1955) found that parents expressed three needs: (1) tangible services, (2) temporary escape from the oppressive awareness of the illness and approaching loss, and (3) emotional support to bolster their functioning in the face of the horror of the situation.

The main relationship or course to which parents turned was the marriage itself. The degree to which each partner was supportive depended on the stage of the relationship and personal strength of the individuals. Cobb (1956) reported that if the marriage was a good one, the stress of long separation and illness served to draw the two partners closer together in this fight against a common enemy. This is not always true. Bozeman (1955) found that in some cases the father's reaction to the illness was more disturbed than the mother's.

A surprising finding was noted in two studies of the reactions of grandparents. Friedman and associates (1963) reported their observation that generally grandparents were even more unaccepting of the diagnosis than the parents and this theme receives elaboration in the reports of Bozeman, Orbach, and Sutherland (1955). They found that most maternal grandmothers failed to extend essential emotional support to their daughters. This lack of support was resented by daughters. It seemed to be related to mother–daughter antagonisms derived from the daughter's childhood rivalry and competitiveness with her mother over sexual and maternal prerogatives, or it was related to the mother's realistic hostility.

With this lack of support from grandparents, parents usually turned to other family members or neighbors for tangible services and to friends for escape and support. This, at times, posed problems because parents are often not allowed to express hopelessness, yet are expected to appear grief stricken. A great deal of emotional support is also derived from parents of other children with the same diagnosis.

There are conflicting reports regarding the supportive role of religion during this period. Cobbs (1956) reported that the consensus of opinion from parents in her study seemed to be that "without religion, I would not have had the courage to live on." However, Bozeman, Orbach, and Sutherland (1955) stated, "The chief value that religion or a belief in God possessed during this period of threatened loss therefore consisted largely in their possible help in saving the child's life."

During this phase of illness, all investigators report that "time stood still for families." It was considered an entity in itself divorced from the normal context of living, and long-range plans were not considered.

Several writers mention other effects of the event such as disturbed family living, including adverse effects on siblings.

The terminal or third phase of this experience is characterized by a more calm acceptance and, according to Natterson and Knudson (1960) is seldom seen before 4 months after the initial diagnosis. They report that there is an observable change in parental behavior at this time. Parents are less tense, anxiousness and denial ceases, and expressed hope for the child is more specific and often related to particular scientific efforts. Sublimation is often seen with an increase in strength and breadth of ego.

Richmond and Waisman (1955) also report that, at this stage, parents cling less to their own children and express a desire to be involved in the care of other children. They consider this a turning point in parental acceptance of the child's illness and ultimate death. There is an acceleration of grief work, and separation from the child is no longer a problem. "The death of the child, therefore, did not appear as a severe superimposed stressful situation, but rather an anticipated loss, often a very long sequence of events."

The parental response to the ultimate death of the child is considered dependent on a number of variables. Foremost, of course, are individual resources and available support. Studies cited also found that parental reactions depended on the length of time intervening between diagnosis and death. Natterson and Knudson believe that most disturbed reactions were seen if the child died within a 4-month period after diagnosis and that reactions to death were directly related to the phase of the sequence parents happened to be in at the time.

Other important factors were the number of children in the family, the age of the child, and the psychological significance the child held for the parents. Orbach, Sutherland, and Bozeman (1955) commented at length on the meaning the sex of a child holds for parents. He concluded that some play a particular psychological role for many mothers, including a recapture of the male figure as a further defiance of the maternal grandmother and a means of reversing the past. The son may then be an agent who is to reverse disappointment in the past or to fulfill incompleted goals or ambitions. Loss of a son, then, may also represent a failure to the mother because chapters in her life are reopened that she had hoped were closed.

The death of a child also reactivates maternal feelings toward the mothers' own mothers. Klein (1940) comments, "If, for instance, a woman loses her child through death, along with pain and sorrow, her early dread of being robbed by a "bad" retaliating mother is reactivated and confirmed. Her own early aggressive fantasies of robbing her mother of babies gave rise to fears and feelings of being punished, which strengthened ambivalence and led to hatred and distrust of others. The reinforcing of feelings of persecution in the state of mourning is all the more painful because, as a result of an increase in ambivalence and distrust, friendly relations with people, which might at that time be so helpful, become impeded."

GRIEF AND BEREAVEMENT

The terms *grief, bereavement,* and *mourning* are often used interchangeably in the medical and psychiatric literature. It is generally understood, however, that *bereavement* pertains to the condition of loss by death, usually applied to members of the immediate nuclear family. The term *grief* is used to describe many types of emotional suffering and can be applied in many loss situations other than actual death, as for instance in separation anxieties. The term *mourning* is usually understood to denote the behavioral aspects of expressions of grieving, and thus it may also be used to describe reactions to losses by any means, including death, of objects highly cathected by libido.

The study of behavior in the expression of grief has become of increasing interest to sociologists, psychiatrists, and psychoanalysts. Some sources have suggested that grief can be conceptualized as a disease, in that it runs a consistent course, modified mainly by the abruptness of the loss, the nature of the preparation for the event, and the significance for the survivor of the lost object. Furthermore, grief involves suffering with impairment of function for which the etiologic factor can be identified; thus, it fulfills all the criteria for a discrete syndrome (Engel, 1961).

The expression of grief, and the states of bereavement and mourning, are thus no longer irrelevant or coincidental, and they are beginning to be considered a legitimate and proper subject for study.

Factors Involved in Grief Reactions

The qualifying factors involved in the intensity of the grief reaction have been discussed by various writers in the different disciplines. One of the earliest sociologic investigators, Thomas D. Eliot (1943), writing during the last war, suggests that variations in response occur according to the situation surrounding the death: whether the death occurs at home or during a phase of separation, such as in battle. He also suggests that reactions may be modified in persons accustomed to long separations, such as wives of seamen, and that differences may correlate with cultural levels related to attitudes toward death.

Henry Stack Sullivan (Pretty, 1959) has suggested that the ability to form a concept of true grief depends on a tertiary level of abstraction and symbolization. He further relates grief responses to the satisfaction and security a person receives from interaction with another. "If then the satisfaction and security becomes to a large extent invested in one person, then the loss of that person becomes highly disrupting."

Lindemann (1944) inferred from his study of grief reactions after disasters that the type of reaction seen results from the previous personality makeup of the bereaved and the intensity of the interaction with the deceased before death. He thought severe reactions seemed to occur in mothers who had lost young children. This interaction does not necessarily have to be of the affectionate type; on the contrary, interactions can be seen in which hostile impulses are the most conspicuous feature.

The death of an individual who is a key person in a social system has also been cited as a factor, because the severe task of readjustment is involved apart from the grief reaction. This was dramatically demonstrated with the death of President Kennedy. Such deaths may involve alteration of living along with disintegration and reintegration of the social system.

Jackson (1957) believes that no grief situation can be considered without taking into account the bereaved person's attitude toward his or her own eventual death and his or her concept of the meaning of life and death; or of the meaning versus the nonmeaning.

Other factors that may influence the grief response are related to the age of the deceased, the amount of reality deprivation involved, and the conditioning of the grief response by group influence. The cultural aspects of the grief response among different peoples has been described at length in the literature and will not be further elaborated here.

Symptomatology of Grief

In the past, until the work of Lindemann in 1944, the literature regarding the symptomatology of grief has been based on general observations and is characterized by broad descriptions of behavior. In 1932, Eliot classified the immediate effects of bereavement in nine general categories:

1. Abandonment
2. Refusal or rejection of the facts
3. A detached calm
4. Shock in the neurological sense
5. Exaltation
6. Self-injury
7. Repression
8. Blame of self or others; revenge
9. The intense longing of grief

Later, in 1943, he concurred with the findings of Fulcomer in dividing the grief reaction into phases—the immediate stage, the postimmediate stage, the transition stage, and the stage of repatterning. These stages are further subdivided into descriptions of the behavior generally seen during the particular time interval, such as stoic, dazed, and collapsed in the first stage.

The first and still widely quoted study is that of Lindemann (1944) who conducted psychiatric interviews on 101 patients who had lost a relative by death in the Coconut Grove fire. He divides the grief response into two categories: the somatic and the psychic.

Somatic symptoms are usually seen as an immediate response to the object loss and are usually characterized by distress that occurs in waves lasting from 20 minutes to an hour at a time, a feeling of tightness in the throat, choking with shortness of breath, need for sighing, empty feeling in the abdomen, lack of muscular power, and an intense subjective distress described as tension or mental pain. Any of these symptoms can be precipitated by visits, by mentioning the deceased, and by receiving sympathy. The most widely seen features are (1) a marked tendency for sighing respirations that are most conspicuous during discussion of grief, (2) complaints of lack of strength and exhaustion, and (3) digestive symptoms.

All accounts of grief reactions dwell on the insistence with which behavior, thought, and feeling tend to remain oriented toward the lost person. Although intellectually, the bereaved has knowledge that the deceased is irrevocably gone, nonetheless, there is a continuing sense of presence. Commonly there is a slight sense of unreality, a preoccupation with the image of the deceased.

Along with this preoccupation is a tendency to withdraw from people, a disconcerting lack of warmth, inability to initiate any action, and lack of interest in ordinary pursuits. Coupled with this apathy, however, is a restlessness that includes a drive for activity that is complicated by a lack of patterns of conduct by which to express this drive. More than that, activities not obviously connected with the presence of the deceased have lost their meaning and are carried out only with difficulty, which often leads to strong dependency.

Often a concomitant of withdrawal is hostility aimed at others, the lost object, or the self. This hostility is surprising and quite inexplicable to the bereaved, and it appears to be spread out over all relationships. It is a general feeling expressed by such statements as "I hate everybody," or "I can't be bothered with people." Irritability is magnified. At other times the hostility may be aimed at specific people—the physician, the nurse, or the lost figure—in the form of complaints. The hostility that is directed against the self takes the form of a profound sense of guilt and unworthiness (Lindemann, 1944).

One of the greatest difficulties for the bereaved is the unaccountable oscillation of feelings from one moment to the next. Paroxysms of weeping or rage may be followed by stolidity or inability to act or move. Each act of daily routine may have to be carried out with conscious effort, and all habits of social interaction seem to have been lost.

Lindemann (1944) summarizes the most striking features of grief into five main categories:

1. Somatic distress
2. Preoccupation with the image of the deceased
3. Guilt
4. Hostile reactions
5. Loss of patterns of conduct.

These, he believes, are pathogenic for grief. Bowlby (1960) condenses these categories into the more inclusive concept of personality disorganization.

Grief Work

The duration of the grief reaction has been generally described by investigators as dependant on the bereaved's success in completing the *grief work*. This term has been defined by Lindemann as the process of "emancipation from the bondage of the deceased, readjustment to the environment in which the deceased is missing, and the formation of new relationships."

As one would expect, the phase occupied by grief work during mourning has been discussed from the differing viewpoints implied in sociology, psychiatry, psychoanalysis, and theology. Sociologists have concentrated on classification of responses of larger groups of people in terms of observed behavior, psychiatrists and psychoanalysts in terms of the individual's uses of defense mechanisms that assist in coping with stress and in terms of the relationship of the unconscious to grief, and theologists in terms of the needs of the bereaved.

In sociology, T. D. Eliot (1932) describes responses of people during grief work with the following broad categories in terms of the individual's most characteristic observed behavior:

1. Acquiescent
2. Excited
3. Protective
4. Detached
5. Despondent

He delineates time periods occurring during the grief work as previously mentioned. During the *transitional stage,* which he defines as the time between the first adjustments and the period when acceptable adjustive patterns become established and integrated into the total life pattern, he lists the following classifications:

1. Alternating activity–depression
2. Enforced–collaborative (return to necessary duties with great effort)
3. Attention seeking

During the final phase of grief work, which Eliot terms *repatterning stage,* he classifies responses into

1. Projective
2. Participative
3. Identification
4. Memory–fantasy
5. Repressive–seclusive.

Thus, the degree of the success of grief work is roughly (and perhaps subjectively) evaluated and grouped. The effect of culture is also discussed by sociologists in that the expression of grief implied in grief work is more or less standardized by acceptable group behavior. This is borne out by many published studies that demonstrate amazing differences in both the inner and the outer manifestations of grief.

Psychiatrists and psychoanalysts have discussed grief work from experience in psychiatric interviews and analysis of individuals. From many such case studies, generalizations have been drawn that throw light on the mental processes involved in grief work leading to reintegration of the personality of the bereaved.

With object loss, deep emotional forces come into being. To understand the human suffering that is implied in grief work, these deeper factors of the personality that become operative must be taken into account. Old childhood ways of solving problems may be revealed and old insecurities made manifest. Aggressions that have been buried in the unconscious may come to the surface, previous methods employed in coping during crisis may again be used, and unconscius forces may be demonstrated in overt behavior.

One of the largest tasks involved in grief work is the testing of reality. Freud (1957) in *Mourning and Melancholia* states, "Reality passes its verdict that the object no longer exists upon each single one of the memories and hopes through which the libido was attached to the lost object, and the ego, confronted as it were with the decision whether it will share this fate, is persuaded by the sum of its narcissistic satisfactions in being alive to sever its attachment to the nonexistent object. Because of the slowness and the gradual way in which this severance is achieved, the expenditure of energy necessary for it becomes somehow dissipated by the time the task is carried through."

In this crisis, the manner of coping that the bereaved uses is dependent on former defense mechanisms available to the ego and on the availability of environmental support as related to the relative strength of the ego.

One of the most common defense mechanisms seen in bereavement is identification. To make the experience tolerable, the lost object is incorporated or internalized. One outward universal sign of this mechanism is the employment of mourning clothes, which has symbolic value in relation to the shroud. The mourner may also temporarily take on characteristics of the deceased. Consolation is derived from the thought that now "I carry him within myself and can never lose him." The object of identification is to hasten the emancipation from the deceased. Penichel states, "Apparently, for a normal person it is easier to loosen the ties with an introject than with an external object. The establishment of an introjection is a means of facilitating the final loosening. Mourning consists of two acts, the first being the establishment of an introjection, the second the loosening of the binding to the introjected object" (Jackson, 1957).

Exaggeration of identification sometimes occurs that may endanger the ego by continued enslavement to the deceased. This is an aspect of abnormal grief that will be discussed in a later section of this paper.

Regression is also commonly seen, especially early in the grief work. Early infantile modes of possessing objects through the alimentary canal again may come into force.

Denial is often seen, also early in the grief work, particularly if the relationship between the bereaved and deceased was very intense. This mechanism is often seen in women who have lost children by sudden death.

There is a certain amount of substitution in all grief reaction as the bereaved attempt to separate themselves from the deceased. It is a type of exteriorization, expressed in clearing up the deceased's affairs. Exaggerations of this mechanism may also be seen in fetishism or the binding to an object or behavior pattern that exerts an undue influence in the life of the bereaved.

In almost every human relationship there is a quality of ambivalence, consisting of the love–hate polarity. At the death of an object highly cathected with libido, therefore, the bereaved may experience intense feelings of guilt. These are complicated by a regression to an earlier childhood pattern in which the feelings of parent–child exerted an influence. If there was a rarity factor of neglect in the relationship between the deceased and the bereaved, the grief work may be complicated or intense, or may take on a pathologic character. Working off this debt to the deceased may involve compulsive talking or idealization.

Unconscious forces of the mind are also a large part of the process known as grief work. From the time of Freud, psychoanalysts have speculated about the relationship between early experience and the adult concepts of death, dying, and bereavement.

Melanie Klein (1964) believes that there is a close connection between reality testing in normal mourning and early processes of the mind. She states, "My contention is that the child goes through states of mind comparable to the mourning of the adult, or rather, that this early mourning is revived whenever grief is experienced in later life. The most important of the methods by which the child overcomes his states of mourning is, in my view, the testing of reality; this process, however, as Freud stresses, is part of the work of mourning."

Klein makes clear the relation between the infantile depressive position and normal mourning by commenting, "In short persecution (by 'bad' objects) and the characteristic defense against it, on the one hand, and pining for the loved (good) object, on the other, constitute the depressive position."

She believes that the poignancy of the loss of a loved person is increased by the mourner's unconscious fantasies of having lost his internalized "good" object as well. Therefore, his internal "bad" object may be predominating and may threaten disruption of the inner world. She relates this to the defense mechanism of identification by commenting, "We know that the loss of a loved person leads to an impulse in the mourner to reinstate the lost loved object in the ego. In my view, however, he may not only take into himself the good person whom he has just lost, but also reinstates his internalized good objects (ultimately his loved parents) who become part of his inner world from the earliest stages of his development onwards."

Thus, part of the grief work related to reality testing is to continuously reexperience the loss and by this means to rebuild with anguish the inner world that may be in danger of deteriorating and collapsing. Aside from the defense mechanisms discussed previously, other methods may be employed in order to reintegrate the personality in a world without the loved object.

Greene (1958) suggests that many persons may use a vicarious object in the adaptation to loss. By the use of someone in the environment, who has suffered the loss of the same person as the adjustive individual, adaptation is made by the use of "proxy mechanisms." Usually, the adjustive individual succors the vicarious object.

Resolution of the grief work implies acceptance of the pain; review of the relationship; acquaintance with the alternations in the personal modes of emotional reaction; and working through of fear of insanity, hostility, and changes of feeling. This involves expression of the sorrow, sense of loss, and guilt felt by the bereaved, who must also find an acceptable formulation of his future relationship to the deceased.

Grief work is completed and successful when the mourner feels more strongly that the life inside and outside will go on after all and that the lost loved person is preserved within as a reinstatement not only of the deceased, but also of the loved parents. With this rebuilding of the inner world, the state of mourning has been resolved.

Abnormal Grief

Morbid grief reactions may be produced when the relationship to the deceased has been of an ambivalent or hostile nature or if earlier severe unresolved conflicts in the bereaved come to the surface.

These abnormal reactions may be characterized by a delay or postponement of grieving, or by an exaggerated or distorted reaction in conduct. Lindemann (1944) classifies the following types according to the behavior seen, conditions produced, or emotions felt by the bereaved:

1. Overactivity without a sense of loss
2. Acquisition of symptoms belonging to the last illness of the deceased
3. A recognized medical disease, as ulcerative colitis, rheumatoid arthritis, asthma, etc.
4. Alteration in relationship to friends or relatives
5. Furious hostility against specific persons
6. Affectivity and conduct resembling schizophrenia caused by hiding hostility
7. Loss of patterns of social interaction
8. Engagement in activities most of which attain a coloring detrimental to the patient's own social and economic existence, such as generosity, stupid acts, etc.
9. Agitated depression

Deutsch (1937) is convinced that:

1. The death of a beloved person must produce reactive expression of feeling in the normal course of events
2. Omission of such reactive response is to be considered just as much a variation from the norm as excess in time or in intensity
3. Unmanifested grief will be found expressed to the full in some way or other.

She concludes, "In any case the expediency of the flight from the suffering of grief is but a temporary gain, because, as we have seen, the necessity to mourn persists in the psychic apparatus."

Freud (1957) comments in regard to this, "The conflict of ambivalence colors pathologically the process of mourning, and forces the afflicted person to manifest itself in the form of self reproaches to the effect that oneself has caused the loss of the love object, that means that oneself has wished it."

Klein (1940) is convinced that the greatest danger for mourners comes when they turn their hatred against the lost person. One of the ways in which this hatred may express itself is in feelings of triumph over the dead person. She believes that infantile wishes are actually fulfilled whenever a loved person dies; thus, death is a victory, increasing guilt. Furthermore, the hatred of the loved person is increased by the fear that by dying the loved one was seeking to inflict punishment and deprivation, thus reactivating the infantile feelings of separation from the maternal figure.

In his analysis of patients with disturbed reactions, Anderson (1949) found mainly four types of neuroses: anxiety states, hysterias, obsessional tension states, and manic-depressive responses.

In the anxiety states, the patients were despairing and assailed by nightmares in which they were confronted with the images of the injured and avenging objects. The patients were tense and restless, anxious, fearful, and afraid to sleep for fear of encountering internal persecutors in their dreams. There were outbursts of rage against being alive while somebody they cared for was dead. Suicide was a prevailing theme and seemed to stem from persecutory demands of the deceased.

Of the reactions to death by persons previously suffering from melancholia, Freud (1957) states, "The melancholiac who either in reality or in fantasy has suffered the loss of a beloved object is unable to free his libido from the object and its association. Owing to the prevalent type of narcissistic object choice, the lost object of the melancholiac becomes introjected. Furthermore, in melancholia regression has taken place to the oral–sadistic phase, so that ambivalence, and with it sadism, are pronounced. The aggression directed against the original object becomes directed against the individual's self or rather against the introjected object. Owing to the severity of the super-ego, in which destructive impulses are prevalent, the patient is forced to destroy himself."

Bereavement and Cultural Role

The topic of death is just beginning to be significantly investigated by social psychiatry. Some contributions have already found their way into the literature, and other studies are now in progress.

The concept of *role* has been largely explored by the discipline of sociology. The roles of the bereaved are determined by the culture in which they live, and overt behavior is heavily saturated with cultural assumptions.

In American society, the extended family is fading from significance, and much emphasis is placed on the nuclear family. Thus, relationships within this small group are intensified, and the range of interactions are limited. Both children and adults find their most intense satisfactions and frustrations here. This situation tends to maximize ambivalence, repressed hostility, and guilt in connection with authority figures.

Volkart (1957) states that one of the difficulties in bereavement is that the bereaved must assume a new social role that varies widely cross-culturally. New obligations exist for the bereaved in the form of expectations, demands, and pressures from others. The role requirements are often painful and difficult to learn because they are not often encountered. When it is remembered that the bereaved may be apathetic, restless, and withdrawn, it is understandable that problems in this sphere may be intensified.

In the United States, the role of the bereaved places emphasis on the expression of grief that may not be psychologically functional. For instance, men may experience a role conflict when expected to express open emotion. The role of the bereaved in the United States provides no discharge for hostility and guilt, which may create mental health problems of which we are only dimly aware.

Since the relationships are intense in the nuclear family, loss of a member may change the entire structure. Eliot (1943) summarized the changes that may occur in the family as follows:

1. The role of a family member exists in relation to the configuration and functioning of the family as a unit. A death tends to disturb this unity. The shifting of the roles of the various members under bereavement represents a reshaping of the configuration.
2. The consensus of the family in respect to these roles, i.e., in respect to its own pattern may result, or family conflict may develop as a sequence to incompatible conceptions of the role of certain members under new conditions.
3. Such conflicts or jealousies or the lack of a common personal or domestic object or symbol of affectional attachment (conditioning stimuli) may result in decreased family solidarity.
4. Acceptance of new interpersonal responsibilities may increase family solidarity.
5. Removal of authority, of habit-stimuli, of home, or of support may lead to revision of family folkways.
6. Maturity of children who lost their parents may lead to individualism or turning to their own families.
7. The will, or personality, of the deceased, acting psychologically as a dynamic complex in each member's memory, and re-enforced by consensus, may activate the behavior of the entire family.

Bereavement and Religion

One of the outcomes of the nuclear age is a return to the tenets of religion for large numbers of people. Churches report better membership and attendance than at any time in recent years. People are actively looking for answers to the eternal mystery of life, in the feeling of "being-no-more."

Theology deals with extending of the boundaries of consciousness to this problem of being and not being. It is actively involved in helping people find answers to the age-old questions, "From whence did I come?" "Where am I going?" and also "Why am I?"

With these questions people must come to grips with the meaning of life itself and with individual values. The purpose of existence must be answered by every individual in finding his own answers to these questions. When the answer is found as to the purpose of life, then a reflection is also seen in the purpose and meaning of death.

That man is more than a composite of experiences and instincts, of breath and mere existence, is hinted at, even by the skeptical Freud, who wrote in his last work:

Although I do not wish to retract anything I have said before, I cannot help feeling that it is somehow not altogether satisfactory. The cause does not, so to speak, accord with the result. The fact we are trying to explain seems to be incommensurate with everything we adduce by way of explanation. Is it possible that all our investigations have so far discovered not the whole motivation, but only a superficial layer, and that behind this lies hidden another very significant component? Considering how extraordinarily complicated all causation in life and history is, we should have been prepared for something of that kind (Freud, 1939).

Individual dogmas of theology are not within the scope of this paper, except as they relate to teachings of survival after death and religious rites for the dead and bereaved.

The doctrines of survival after death console the believer because they provide a concrete image of the dead that the bereaved can follow in imagination. Perhaps the anguish of death is more comprehensible in the fundamental structure of being which includes the existential postulate of something beyond.

Although religious rites and practices surrounding the process of mourning have received much attention and criticism, yet they also have positive value. The symbolic rituals speak to the more primitive aspects of being, invite participation, and point to the philosophy of life. The mourner is encouraged to express feelings and is supported by the other members of the church community. Also religion gives consolation for feelings of guilt when the dead can no longer forgive, an oversoul who is capable of forgiving is a source of release and comfort.

The activities that engage the bereaved at the time of death encourage a firm grip on reality and prepare the individual for the departure of the body of the loved one. Jackson (1957) states, "the surrounding of death with rituals and practices that fortify the reality of death make it easier for time to saturate the unconscious with the awareness of emotional amputation and the need for the adjustments that relate it to reality." These practices also reenact a previous death of religious significance 2000 years ago, which speaks of the continuous rhythm of life and death.

Perhaps we can concur with the thought that whereas biology describes life it does not define it, and although psychology illuminates the life of the psyche, it does not confine it.

CONCLUSION

Although death, dying, and bereavement have concerned mankind through the ages, it is only within recent years that reseachers in the various disciplines have been actively involved in gathering concrete data that are beginning to throw light on the concept and fear of death in man.

Sociologists and anthropologists are concerning themselves with reporting the rites and rituals surrounding death in various cultures, in cultural connotations of expressions of grief, and in social role assumptions of the bereaved as well as in role changes caused by the death of a member of the small and larger group. Social psychiatrists are also beginning to view death and bereavement as a legitimate field for research.

Psychiatrists and psychoanalysts have long been interested in death, although few organized research studies have been reported in the literature. Both disciplines provide much information about methods used in coping with the crisis of death and bereavement and about the origins and meaning of the concept and fear of death in the unconscious. Most of this information has been derived from psychiatric interviews and from analytic studies of adult patients.

The disciplines of theology, medicine, and nursing have characteristically been focused on the needs of the dying and bereaved person. It has been pointed out by various writers that physicians and nurses, in particular, must face this issue more squarely in order to be of maximum assistance, both to the dying child and adult and to the bereft. As more information becomes available and educators are able to be of greater assistance to students who are meeting with death in hospital rooms and wards, it is hoped that such denial and avoidance as is seen currently in hospital personnel will be lessened.

Perhaps those of us in the helping professions, along with the American people in general, may have grown up a little since the death of President Kennedy left a mark on our group consciousness. Perhaps we have begun to acquire what the rest of the world has known all along—a sense of the tragic that is neither morbid nor fatalistic, but more mature and accepting of human limitations.

REFERENCES

Anderson G: Aspects of pathological grief and mourning. Int J Psychoanal 30:48–55, 1949
Anthony S: The Child's Discovery of Death. New York, Harcourt, Brace & Co, 1940
Bowlby J: Grief, mourning in infancy and early childhood. Psychoanal Study Child. 15:9–52, 1960
Bozeman M, Orbach G, Sutherland A: The adaptation of mothers to the threatened loss of their children through leukemia. Part I. Cancer 8:1, 1–19, 1955
Bromberg W, Schilder P: Death and dying: A comparative study of the attitudes and mental reactions towad death and dying. Psychoanal Rev 20:133–185, 1933
Chadwick M. Notes upon fear of death. Int J Psychoanal 10:321–334, 1929
Cobb S, Lindemann E: "Neuropsychiatric Observations after the Coconut Grove fire." Ann Surg, June 1943
Cobbs B: Psychological impact of long-term illness and death of a child on the family circle. J Pediatr 49:746–751, December 1956
Deutsch H: Absence of grief. Psychoanal Q 6:12–22, 1937
Engel GL: Is grief a disease? Psychosom Med 23:18–22, 1961
Eliot TD: Of the shadow of death. American Academy of Political and Social Sciences, Annals, pp 87–99, 1943
Eliot TD: The bereaved family. American Academy of Political and Social Sciences, Annals, pp 1–7, March 1932
Feifel H: The Meaning of Death. New York, McGraw-Hill, 1959
Freud A: The role of bodily illness in the mental life of children. Psychoanal Study Child 7:69–81, 1952
Freud A, Burlingame D: War and Children. New York, International University Press, 1943
Freud S: Mourning and Melancholia, Stand Ed LV. London, Hogarth Press, 1957
Freud S: Mores and Monthesism. New York, Knopf, 1939
Friedman SB, Chodoff P, Mason JW: Behavorial observations in parents anticipating the death of a child. Pediatrics 32:610–625, 1963
Friedman SB, Mason JW, Hamburg DA: Urinary 17 hydroxycorticosteroid levels in parents of children with neoplastic disease: A study of chronic psychological stress. Psychosom Med 25:364, 1963
Gorer G: The pornography of death. In Stein M, Vidich A, White D (eds): Identity and Anxiety. Glencoe, IL, Free Press, 1960

Greene WA: The role of a vicarious object in the adaptation of object loss. Psychosom Med 20:344–350, 1958

Greene WA, Miller G: Psychological factors and reticuloendothelial disease. Psychosom Med 20:124, 1958

Jackson E: Understanding Grief. Nashville, Abingdon Press, 1957

Kastenbaum R: Time and death in adolescence. In Feifel H (ed): The Meaning of Death. New York, McGraw-Hill, 1959

Klein M: Mourning and its relation to manic–depressive states. Int J Psychoanal 21:125–153, 1940

Klein M: Contributions to Psychoanalysis. New York, McGraw-Hill, 1964

Knudson GG, Natterson JM: Participation of parents in the hospital care of fatally ill children. Pediatrics, 26:482, 1960

Landsberg L: The Experience of Death. London, Lockliff, 1953

Lindemann E: Symptomatology and management of acute grief. Am J Psychiatry 101:141–148, 1944

Nagy M: The child's theories concerning death. J Genet Psychol 73:3–29, September 1948

Nagy M: The child's view of death. In Feifel H (ed): The Meaning of Death. New York, McGraw-Hill, 1959

Natterson J, Knudson A: Observations concerning fear of death in fatally ill children and their families. Psychosom Med 22:456–465, 1960

Orbach C, Sutherland A, Bozeman M: The adaptation of mothers to the threatened loss of their children through leukemia, Part II. Cancer 8:1, 20–33, 1955

Piaget J: The Language and Thought of the Child. Kegan Paul, 1962

Pretty LC: Ministering to the bereaved and dying. Nebr Med J 44:5, 243–249, May 1959

Ramzy I, Wallerstein R: Pain, fear and anxiety—A study in their inter-relationships. Psychoanal Study Child 13:147–189, 1958

Richmond JB, Waisman HA: Psychological aspects of management of children with malignant diseases. Am J Dis Child 89:42–47, 1955

Rochlin G: The loss complex. J Am Psychoan Assoc 7:11–15, 1959

Rosenzweig S: Sibling death as a psychological experience with special reference to schizophrenia. Psychoanal Rev 30:177–186, 1943

Schilder P, Wechsler D: The attitudes of children toward death. J Genet Psychol 45:406–451, 1934

Shambaugh B: A study of loss reactions in a seven year old. Psychoanal Study Child XVI, 1961

Solnit, AJ, Green M: Psychologic considerations in the management of deaths on pediatric hospital services. Pediatrics 24:106–112, 1959

Solnit AJ, Green M: The pediatric management of the dying child: Part II. The child's reaction to the fear of dying. In Solnit A, Provence S (eds): Mod Perspect Child Dev, 1963

Sulzberger C: My Brother's Death. New York, Harper & Brothers, 1961

Volkart EH: Bereavement and mental health. In Leighton AH, Clausen JA, Wislon, RN (eds): Exploration of Social Psychiatry. New York, Basic Books, 1957

Wahl CW: The fear of death. In Feifel H (ed.): The Meaning of Death. New York, McGraw-Hill, 1959

Wolf A: Helping Your Child to Understand Death. New York, The Child Study Association of America, 1958

2 · Death, Dying, and Bereavement: A Review of Literature, 1970–1985

Cecily Lynn Betz

Your children are not your children
They are the sons and daughters of Life's longing for itself.
They come through you but not from you,
And though they are with you yet they belong not to you.
· *Kahlil Gibran, 1923*

Gibran's admonition evokes a sense of harmonious accord when read in an unencumbered spirit. However, such platitudes do not rest easy for the parents, family members and health professionals involved with the child who is dying. As this paper will address, the experience of witnessing a child's death is at best the most difficult and trying of human experiences.

The purpose of this paper is to review the research and theory generated in the field of pediatric thanatology during the last decade and a half. The four major areas of inquiry that will be reviewed are children's conceptions of death, children and parental bereavement responses, and the fatally ill child.

CHILDREN'S CONCEPTIONS OF DEATH

Since Nagy's (1948) and Anthony's (1940) classic studies on children's conceptions of death, there has been a dearth of empirical studies on the topic until the last decade. Renewed interest in the area has been stimulated by both clinical and theoretical inducements. It is argued that knowledge of a child's conception of death provides additional insight and understanding about the child's cognitive capacities related to emotionally laden and abstract concepts (Childers and Wimmer, 1971; Koocher, 1971; White, Elsom and Prawat, 1978), bereavement reactions (Bowlby, 1961; Furman, 1970; Wolfenstein, 1966), as well as developmentally appropriate grief counseling and intervention (Alexander and Alderstein, 1973; Furman, 1974; Kane, 1979; Koocher, 1974; Lonetto, 1980; Plank and Plank, 1978; Salladay and Royal, 1981). Furthermore, the recent studies have overcome the methodological limitations of earlier studies in relation to design instrumentation and use of theoretical frameworks, thereby providing more reliable and valid data in this area of inquiry.

Researchers have primarily used Piaget's (1960) theory of cognitive development as the conceptual framework for investigations of children's conceptions of death. In Koocher's study (1973), 75 children recruited from summer camps in a midwestern university community, ranging in age from 6 to 15 years, were asked four questions to ascertain their understanding of death. These questions were: "What makes things die?", "How do you make dead things come back to life?", "When will you die?", and "What will happen then?" Children's responses to these questions were associated with their level of cognitive development. Preoperational children were more likely to provide concrete, egocentric answers in response to questions, whereas children of higher cognitive functioning (concrete and formal levels) provided responses that were more sophisticated and reality based.

For example, the preoperational child has magical beliefs about death. Seemingly illogical reasoning is used to explain and describe death. In the transition from preoperational to concrete stage, the child uses more logical forms of reasoning to explain death. In the concrete stage, the child comprehends the concept that body and organ systems are finite. In formal operations, concepts of death have attained mature dimensions. Unlike Nagy's (1948) finding that younger children personify death, these findings were not supported in Koocher's study (1973).

Building upon this cognitive approach, Portz (1972) speculated that a child's concept of death had not fully reached mature abstraction until comprehension of the component features of death had been acquired. This included the child's ability to make distinctions between the following pairs: immobility vs. mobility; permanent vs. temporary absence; irreversible vs. reversible change; insensibility (cessation of physiologic functioning) vs. immobilization by constraints; and natural vs. magical events.

White's investigation (1978) tested children from kindergarten through fourth grade (N = 170) using vignettes to assess understanding of three death-related concepts: irrevocability, cessation of bodily processes, and universality based upon Portz's conceptualization. This study found that children's understanding of universality of death was associated with level of cognitive development. The two remaining concepts were not attributable to cognitive developmental levels. These findings support the Piagetian contention that universality is a spontaneous concept, whereas the other two concepts must be learned.

A study by Childers and Wimmer (1971) examined the relationship between awareness of universality and irrevocability of death in 75 children from 4 to 10 years of age. Although a developmental framework was not used in this study, the age-specific results support the findings of White's study (1978) and further support Portz's (1972) contention.

Kane (1979) interviewed 122 children about their understanding of death as well as the impact of personal experience upon that understanding. The resulting findings supported previous studies (Childers and Wimmer, 1971; Koocher, 1971; White, 1973), which found that acquisition of the concept of death was age related. More specifically, a sequenced progression was found in children in the acquisition of the conceptual components in gaining understanding of death. The acquisition of death-related concepts was as follows: age 3, realization; age 5, separation and immobility; age 6, irrevocability, causality, dysfunctionality, and universality; age 8, insensitivity; and age 12, appearance.

Kane found that children as young as 3 have some concept of death. Differences in acquisition patterns of death conception were found among children ages 3 to 6 who had experienced a death as compared to those who had not; these differences were not apparent in the older children. According to Kane's findings, children progressed through three stages of death concept development roughly equivalent to the levels of cognitive development.

In Stage 1 (preoperational), the child held a magical, egocentric attitude toward death. The child fantasized that he or she could make someone dead by his or her behavior or wish. Death was associated with only the immediate here and now; the idea of permanency was not evident. The child's concept of death was constituted of the following components: realization, separation, and immobility without being integrated or interrelated to one another.

The child in Stage 2 (concrete) conceived of death primarily in terms of functioning. Dysfunction was associated with death, the most obvious being the inability to eat or hear. Conceptions became reality oriented; logical thought emerged. The child gained in understanding of the components of the concept of death. Initially during this stage causality was attributed to external factors; later, understanding of internal factors was achieved. Finally, in Stage 3 (formal), the abstract concept of death is achieved. Again the findings of this study did not support Nagy's (1948) as children were not found to personify death at any age.

Reilly (1983) investigated the association between conception of death and personal mortality in 60 children ages 5 through 10. Findings revealed that most children 6 years and older possessed some understanding of the universality of death. This finding lent further support to White's study (1978) that a dramatic shift in understanding the universality of death occurs between the ages of 6 and 7 years.

Reilly's study suggested that a child's understanding of personal mortality is related not only to level of cognitive development, but to death-related experiences as well. That is, children who had experienced the death of a significant other (parent, sibling, close relative, or peer) were found to have a greater awareness of their own personal mortality when compared to children who had no such previous experiences.

Lonetto (1980) sampled 201 children ranging in age from 3 years, 5 months to 13 years to elicit their perceptions of death. Data were collected by asking the children to draw their idea of death and to discuss their drawings as well as their feelings about death. Results of this study demonstrated the conceptions of death were age related.

As the results of Lonetto's investigation revealed, children from 3 to 5 comprehended death as a living state but under a different set of circumstances, such as "standing up." Death also represented separation, especially as it related to the mother. As in Nagy's study (1948), children ages 6 through 8 personified death. Death was conceptualized as an external agent such as a ghost or monster. Metaphors were used to symbolize the nature and meaning of death such as "getting sick" and "being scared." Death was associated with the cessation of bodily functions. Children 9 years and older demonstrated adultlike understanding of death. Concern about death expressed by this age group centered on the funeral and what happens to the body following death. Again, Lonetto's research supports the findings of previous research (Childers and Wimmer, 1971; Kane, 1979; Koocher, 1973; Reilly, 1983; White, Elsom, and Pravat, 1978), that children's conceptions of death became progressively more abstract as they grew older. Unlike these more recent studies, however, this study supported the finding of Nagy that children in the age range from 5 to 9 years personified death.

As with the earlier classic studies (Anthony, 1940; Nagy, 1948) there were methodological limitations associated with the aforementioned studies that must be considered in the interpretation of findings. Several of the studies (Kane, 1979; Koocher, 1973; Lonetto, 1981) used convenience samples without randomization procedures (selection/assignment) included. The generalizability thus becomes a question, perhaps a factor contributing to inconsistency in findings (i.e., children's personification of death). A potential biasing factor of the sample itself must be considered in the interpretation of findings. As has been discussed previously in critique of Nagy's work (1948), the cultural factors of the postwar era were suggested as confounding effects on the results of that study. So, too, must the cultural and social influences affecting the subjects selected for study (Kane, 1979; Koocher, 1971; Lonetto, 1980) be considered in the more recent investigations.

THE FATALLY ILL CHILD

Beginning with Waechter's hallmark study (1968, 1971) of the fatally ill child's awareness of death, researchers have attempted to explore this sensitive yet profoundly relevant area of inquiry. Prior to Waechter's work, experts (Knudsen and Natterson, 1960; Natterson and Knudson, 1960; Morrissey, 1963a, 1963b, 1965; Richmond and Waisman, 1955) argued convincingly that children younger than 10 years, having no cognitive grasp of the meaning of death, were not capable of experiencing or expressing feelings about death. However, the research of Waechter (1968, 1971) and subsequently of others (Bluebond–Langner, 1978; Easson, 1970; Leyn, 1976; Raimbault, 1973, 1981; Spinetta, Rigler, and Karon, 1972,

1973; Spinetta, 1972) refuted this contention and have demonstrated that younger children who are fatally ill have an understanding of the meaning of dying and death.

In Waechter's studies (1968, 1971) using both projective drawings and interviews, responses of fatally ill children reflected their concerns about death. Stories as told by children with poor prognoses centered more often on themes related to loneliness, separation, and death. Sixty-three percent of the stories included death themes. Strong feelings of anger and hostility were intertwined with the projections of feelings expressed by children in their stories.

Spinetta's study (1972) replicated Waechter's drawings with 25 leukemic and 25 chronically ill children. Findings of this study supported those from Waechter's (1968, 1971). The results demonstrated the leukemic children related stories indicating greater preoccupation with threats to body integrity and functioning than those related by chronically ill children. Although the children did not make any overt references to death in their story-telling, the leukemic children expressed a greater degree of both hospital and non–hospital-related anxiety than the chronically ill children.

Using a three-dimensional replica of a hospital room, Spinetta (1972) assessed the fatally ill child's sense of interpersonal distance. Using the placements of human figures as a measure of psychological distance, Spinetta tested the hypothesis that the fatally ill child would place the human figures (nurse/doctor, parents) at a distance further away than the chronically ill child as a measure of his or her growing sense of isolation as death approached. The results of the study supported this hypothesis. The fatally ill children placed the figures significantly greater distances away than the chronically ill children. Fatally ill children with repeated admissions placed figures at distances further away than children during their first admission. The findings of this study suggest that, on some level, the child's awareness of death precedes their ability to discuss it.

Other investigators (Raimbault, 1973, 1981; Vernick, 1973) interviewed children themselves to elicit their feelings and concerns about death and dying. Raimbault found that fatally ill children's understanding of death was not age dependent but rather corresponded to those of adults. Their greatest expressed concern was that of loneliness and isolation as death approached. They expressed the need for someone's continued presence to cushion the effect of the imposed loneliness and isolation.

Vernick's investigation (1973) indicated that dying children were more fully aware of the diagnostic meaning and prognostic consequences of their disease than previously credited as being. Vernick (1973) found that children were knowledgeable about their diagnoses although they were not directly discussed with them. As these findings reveal, children interpreted changes in parental and adult behavior, such as overindulgence and discomfort, as a reaction to their fatal condition. The child's most significant concern was fear of not having control as death approached.

Bluebond–Langner (1978) provided an anthropological perspective of the fatally ill child's growing recognition that his or her condition was terminal. Employing a field-study approach in the gathering of data, Bluebond–Langner formulated a schema of stages to describe the child's evolving awareness of his or her terminal illness. As the model (below) demonstrates, the child's evolving awareness of the diagnostic implications and prognostic consequences of the disease is a mirror of its progression and concomitant treatment therapies. That is, the child learns, through the experience of being seriously ill and subject to a multitude of medical treatment and diagnostic modalities, the profoundness of his or her clinical status whether directly informed or not. The disease-related experiences become the source for gathering information that is used in developing a self-concept that excludes the normality of wellness and health previously associated with oneself.

Easson (1970) also formulated a stage framework as a means of describing the child's evolving understanding of death and dying. Supporting Bluebond–Langner's contention, Easson asserted that children's understanding of death and dying is contingent upon related experiences to add meaning to the concept of death as a phenomenon. Easson identified five stages that children progress through in their understanding of death. Stage 1 refers to the period of infancy

Bluebond–Langner Stage Model

Stage One (Diagnosis)

> Learns disease is serious.
> Begins development of an image of self as "sick."
> Learns information about action and side effects of prescribed medications.

Stage Two (Remission)

> Discovers there is a relationship between medications and clinical status.
> Learns that relapse is a serious problem.
> Learns that adults are uncomfortable with child's relapse.
> > Discussion of relapse is taboo.
> > Adults avoid discussion of the topic.
> > Complete explanation of treatment and prognostic implications are judiciously avoided.

Stage Three (Relapse)

> Child's sense of well being diminishes with repeated/extended relapse as well as complications.
> Child's world becomes increasingly centered upon medical treatment and hospital.
> Child becomes increasingly aware of differences that separate him from others.
> Child becomes increasingly more knowledgeable of treatments and medications.

Stage Four

> Illness is accepted as a permanent condition.
> Child does not believe he will get better.
> Child realizes that death may and does occur (as expressed directly/indirectly).
> Child realizes that medical treatment and drugs are not working.

---

during which time no understanding of death exists. Stage 2 (1–2 years) refers to the the child's conception of death as it relates to their own physical pain and discomfort. During the third state (3–4 years) the child develops the awareness that being and nonbeing are separate and distinguishable processes. By the fourth stage (4–5 years) the child becomes capable of understanding the implications of a fatal prognosis. Finally, in the fifth stage (5–7 years) the child is able to comprehend the finality associated with the dying process and death itself.

As these studies suggest, the child comprehends the seriousness and even fatal nature of their condition although it may be beyond his or her ability actually to discuss it. The dying child's evolving awareness is not age dependent, but rather the outcome of the progressive as well as cumulative effects of the disease and concomitant medical treatment (Bluebond–Langner, 1978; Easson, 1970; Raimbault, 1973, 1981; Spinetta, Rigler, and Karon, 1972, 1973; Spinetta, 1972). As these studies revealed, the dying child feels a sense of isolation (Spinetta, 1972; Raimbault, 1981; Vernick, 1973; Waechter, 1968, 1971) and sense of separation (Raimbault, 1973, 1981; Waechter, 1968, 1971) as death approaches. The question remains, however, what the child actually comprehends and anticipates in terms of approaching death. Although these (Bluebond–Langner, 1978; Easson, 1970; Raimbault, 1973, 1981; Spinetta, Rigler, and Karon, 1972, 1973; Spinetta, 1974; Waechter, 1968, 1971) suggest the child understands the concept of his or her forthcoming death, few of the studies were actually able to elicit this fact from children explicitly. The question remains whether the child actually understands the concept of finality and life cessation as associated with the impending progression of his or her condition, or whether the child is reacting to the circumstances with the diminished capacities and resources the child possesses. Again, this warrants further investigation.

Although substantive attempts have been made to elicit data directly from the child with objective measures (Spinetta, Rigler, and Karon, 1973; Spinetta, 1974; Waechter, 1968, 1971), further development of tools and use of valid and reliable tools is needed. Several studies used tools with no reportable scores attesting to validity and reliability (Spinetta, Rigler, and Karon, 1973; Spinetta, 1974), thereby casting some question on the generalizability of findings. Other studies (Easson, 1970; Raimbault, 1980, 1981) relied upon anecdotal and unstructured data collection techniques in reporting of findings. Although much progress has been made in gaining knowledge and insight into the world of the dying child, much remains to be accomplished in this area of investigation as well.

PARENTAL BEREAVEMENT RESPONSE

Actually few studies (Cook, 1984; Cown and Murphy, 1985; Kaplan, Grobstein, and Smith, 1976; Kerner, Harvey, and Lewiston, 1979; Krell, 1979; Lansky, et al, 1978; Pozanski, 1972; Rando, 1984; Spinetta, Swarner, and Sheposh, 1981; Tietz, McSherry, and Britt, 1972) have been conducted to explore the consequent effects of the child's death upon the family. Despite the paucity of empirical studies conducted, much literature based upon clinical experience has been written (Adams, 1980; Easson, 1970; Fischoff and O'Brien, 1976; Fulton and Fulton, 1971; Futterman, Hoffman, and Sabshin, 1972; Guylay, 1978; Hamovitch, 1964; Hefler and Schneider, 1978; Kagen–Goodheart, 1977; Kellerman, 1980; Martinson, 1976; Schiff, 1977; Schulman and Kupst, 1980; Schoenberg, et al, 1974; Sourkes, 1977). As these seminal studies reveal, loss of a child has pervasive, lasting, and complex effects upon the entire family.

Several studies have demonstrated that bereaved parents manifest more intense symptomatology and sequelae following the death of a child than those who have lost a parent or spouse (Owen, Fulton, and Markusen, 1982, 1983; Sanders, 1979, 1980; Williams and Polak, 1972). Sander's study revealed that bereaved parents experienced greater somatization, depression, anger, guilt, and despair than other groups of bereaved. Miles (1984) found that intense grief may continue for months and even years following the child's death regardless of the cause.

Kerner et al (1979) interviewed families following the death of a child from cystic fibrosis. Data were collected from families approximately $2\frac{1}{2}$ years following the child's death. Findings revealed that families experienced a variety of post-mortem sequelae. Psychiatric care was required in 25% of the families. In three of the families, one or more of the parents sought counseling. In four other families, parents demonstrated sleep problems, overwhelming sadness, and increased irritability. One parent in five developed medical problems. In two of the families, the parent's health improved. Spousal relationships remained intact in 14 families; one divorced and one separated.

Fifty percent of the families continued to maintain the deceased child's room as a shrine; 50% of the families visited the gravesite on a weekly basis. Of the 16 families, 11 reported no anniversary reaction on the occasion of the deceased child's birthdate or date of death. Overall, researchers reported that the symptomology demonstrated by parents was less severe than reported in previous investigations (Binger et al, 1969; Futterman and Hoffman, 1973).

Bereaved parents were interviewed following their child's death by drowning (Nicon and Pearn, 1977). Findings revealed that parents experienced a variety of bereavement reactions which included marital, sleep, and drinking problems, as well as feelings of guilt.

Miles (1985) compared the emotional symptoms and physical health of bereaved and nonbereaved parents. Results demonstrated that bereaved parents differed from nonbereaved parents in greater frequency of symptoms and overall emotional state. Bereaved parents reported greater incidence of emotional symptoms including depression, anxiety, somatization, and obsessive–compulsive behavior. Bereaved parents reported a higher frequency of sleep and appetite changes than nonbereaved parents. Miles (1985) also found that parents from lower socio-economic status (SES) were at greater risk for emotional distress following the death of their child than parents from higher SES groups. No difference was found in parents' bereavement reactions based on cause of death (child died from accidental or long-term illness).

Tietz et al (1972) interviewed nine families following the death of their child from leukemia and solid tumors. Results revealed that parents demonstrated a variety of psychological problems following the child's death. Researchers found that families had particular difficulty acknowledging that their child was dead. Families demonstrated symptoms of chronic grief, which included depression, hypochondriasis, and the development of psychosomatic illness. Thirty percent of the families experienced significant marital difficulties after the child's death: one family separated and two families reported constant quarreling.

As in the Tietz study (1972), Spinetta et al (1981) found that few families were functioning adaptively following the child's death according to predetermined criteria. Findings revealed that parents continued to exhibit feelings of sadness and crying spells for as long as 3 years following their child's death. Few of the parents interviewed were able to discuss comfortably their feelings about the deceased child. Age, sex, and length of parental grieving were not related to postdeath adaptation. Of the 23 sets of parents interviewed, two were divorced and one separated. Variables that accounted for parental postdeath adaptation were positive life meaning, social support, and open communication.

Rando's study (1983) gathered data from 26 sets of parents through use of interviews and questionnaires to investigate the variables affecting parental grief and subsequent adaptation. Findings revealed significant differences between mothers' and fathers' bereavement responses. As indicated on the grief experience inventory (Sanders, Maeyer, and Strong, 1978), mothers experienced more intense emotional bereavement reactions than fathers. Fathers scored higher in measures of adjustment than mothers.

This investigation (Rando, 1983) found an association between optimal preparation time for the child's anticipated death and postdeath adjustment. Parents who demonstrated the highest levels of adjustment following the death were those whose predeath preparation ranged between 6 and 18 months. Conversely, parents whose postdeath adaptation was problematic had one of two predeath preparation intervals: less than 6 months or greater than 18 months. The length of the child's illness was associated with a higher incidence of hostile and atypical responses postdeath. That is, the greater the duration of the child's illness, the more likely the parent would report more frequently problematic postdeath responses. Finally, postdeath adaptation was positively related to the amount of support received during the terminal stages of the child's illness. These findings support Spinetta's (1981) study, which found a positive correlation between social support and postdeath adaptation.

One hundred forty-five bereaved parents (90 mothers, 55 fathers) participated in Cook's investigation (1984) to explore differences in mothers' and fathers' adaptation during their child's fatal illness. Mothers identified the following as the most difficult problems encountered during their child's fatal illness: shielding others, marital problems, concerns for the child's morale, and emotional strain.

More specifically, mothers reported stress associated with their attempts to shield the child from learning the diagnosis as well as prognosis of his or her disease. This shielding of information extended to parents, relatives, and friends as well. Marital problems, if preexistent, were further aggravated by the child's condition. Conflicts between spouses centered on differences in allocation of time and priorities. The mother's need and felt obligation to be at the dying child's bedside were often in conflict with the needs of the husband. Fathers were reported to express resentment over the amount of time mothers spent with the child.

Mothers reported expending energy and efforts to buoy the child's morale in the face of the ravages of the fatal disease. Lastly, mothers reported the tremendous emotional strain imposed by the persistent and unyielding fear of their child's approaching death. Combined with the unpredictable progression of the disease, mothers reported experiencing the rollercoaster of emotional highs and lows during their child's illness.

Fathers identified a different set of pressing problems experienced during the course of their child's terminal illness. These problems included responsibility for work and family, exclusion from family, the wife's overinvolvement with the ill child, and desire to be with the child and wife. Fathers reported increased amounts of pressure due to assumption of additional responsibilities at home. Fathers reported feeling as though they were a "forgotten entity" as they were excluded from the majority of daily events and decisions associated with their fatally ill child. This feeling was further exacerbated by the wife's continual vigil at the child's bedside.

Together, 50% of the parents reported experiencing three or more major problems during the terminal phase of their child's illness. The problems most frequently cited by parental respondents were feeling helpless (87%); fear of being unable to cope with death (74%); finances (58%); having to comfort others (51%); and denial by family members (50%).

As Cook's study (1984) demonstrated, mothers and fathers reported differing sources of stress during the terminal phase of their child's illness. The focus of the mother's problems were associated with nurturant and caretaking activities associated with the child. In contrast, fathers reported that sources of stress were associated with activities and role responsibilities not directly associated with the dying child. Both parents reported problems related to the spousal relationship. The findings suggest that the shift in the father's role serves as a mechanism for anticipatory grieving by separating the father from the child's bedside. In contrast, the mothers invested greater amounts of emotional involvement and time during this difficult period. This differential shift in parents' roles may account for subsequent differences in adjustment postdeath (Rando, 1983).

As these studies demonstrate, the bereavement responses of parents are associated with a variety of predeath variables such as social support, spousal relationship, and positive life philosophy. Differences in postdeath adaptation were also noted in mothers and fathers (Cook, 1984; Rando, 1984). Further parental reactions manifest a diverse as well as dramatic range reflecting the profound and pervasive effects of bereavement. Although the research to date has provided insight and understanding into the bereavement reactions of parents, many questions remain. Questions that warrant further investigation include the identification of risk factors associated with maladaptive bereavement responses, identification of therapeutic strategies to facilitate adaptation following the child's death, and the relationship between anticipatory grieving and bereavement responses.

CHILDREN'S BEREAVEMENT RESPONSES

Much has been written about the process of mourning and bereavement in adults (Clayton, 1968; Engel, 1964; Glick, 1974; Lindemann, 1944; Parkes, 1972; Raphael, 1983); in contrast, scant literature exists describing this phenomenon in children (Albin, 1971; Archibald, 1962; Balk, 1983; Betz, 1984; Cain, 1964; Davies, 1984; Elizur and Kaffman, 1982; Furman, 1973; Harrison, Davenport, and McDermott, 1967; Kaffman and Elizur, 1979, 1983; McCown, 1981; Salladay and Royal, 1981; Willis, 1974). Areas of research in childhood bereavement have primarily focused on three areas of inquiry: long-term consequences of parental loss (Bendiksen and Fulton, 1975; Birtchnell, 1970a,b, 1972, 1975, 1978; Brown, Harris, and Copeland, 1977; Lifshitz, 1976; Tennant, Bibbington, and Hurry, 1980); the immediate and short-term effects of parental loss (Elizur and Kaffman, 1982, 1983; Kaffman and Elizur, 1983; Tooley, 1975; Van Eerdewegh et al, 1982); the sibling death (Balk, 1983; Betz, 1985; Binger, 1973; Davies, 1985; Furman, 1970; Kerner, Harvey, and Lewiston, 1979; McCown, 1981; Tietz, McSherrY, and Britt, 1972). This section will provide a review and critique of the major studies conducted in this area of research.

The findings of studies examining the long-term consequences (Bendiksen and Fulton, 1975; Birtchnell, 1970a,b, 1972, 1975, 1978; Brown, Harris, and Copeland, 1977; Lifshitz, 1976; Tennant, Bibbington, and Hurry, 1980) are inconclusive and contradictory. Several studies (Birtchnell, 1970a,b, 1972; Brown, Harris, and Copeland, 1977) demonstrate a gender-associated reaction to parental loss. That is, the longitudinal data revealed greater pathological consequences for females than males. Other studies (Lifshitz, 1976; Ray, 1978; Birtchnell, 1972) do not provide supporting evidence for this finding.

Retrospective studies examining the long-term sequelae of parental loss have revealed a higher incidence of psychiatric disturbances in persons who experienced early parental loss as compared to matched groups who did not (Bendiksen and Fulton, 1975; Birtchnell, 1970a,b, 1972). Other investigations report conflicting results suggesting no differences between matched, experimental, and control groups (Brown, Harris, and Copeland, 1977; Ray, 1978).

A variety of negative consequences have been associated with early parental loss, including increased dependency (Birtchnell, 1975, 1978), hypochondriasis (Birtchnell, 1975, 1978), greater incidence of illness (Bendiksen and Fulton, 1975), constriction of attention (Lifshitz, 1976), reduced social interaction (Lifshitz, 1976), and greater anxiety (Lifshitz, 1976).

The findings of these studies (Bendiksen and Fulton, 1975; Birtchnell, 1970a,b, 1972, 1975, 1978; Brown, Harris, and Copeland, 1977; Lifshitz, 1976; Tennant, Bibbington, and Hurry, 1980) do not provide conclusive support for the long-term detrimental effects of early parental loss. The contradictory findings suggest that the results may be attributable to uncontrolled confounding variables, an obvious methodological limitation of retrospective longitudinal design (Bendiksen and Fulton, 1975; Birtchnell, 1970a,b, 1972, 1975, 1978; Brown, Harris, and Copeland, 1977; Lifshitz, 1976; Tennant, Bibbington, and Hurry, 1980). Other limitations that must be taken into consideration of interpretation of findings in these studies are biased sample (Birtchnell, 1970a,b, 1972; Roy, 1978), case study approach (Birtchnell, 1970a,b, 1972), use of self-reports (Bendiksen and Fulton, 1975), and lack of control groups (Lifshitz, 1976).

However, it must be noted that even with the most rigorous of matching procedures used, no conclusive association has been demonstrated between early parental loss and subsequent adult morbidity. Few areas of consistency in findings have been demonstrated between or among diagnostic groups studied.

Several studies (Elizur and Kaffman, 1982, 1983; Kaffman and Elizur, 1983; Tooley, 1975; Van Eerdewegh et al, 1982) have been conducted to investigate the immediate and short-term effects of parental loss. As these studies (Elizur and Kaffman, 1982, 1983; Kaffman and Elizur, 1983; Tooley, 1975; Van Eerdewegh et al, 1982) indicated, children manifest a spectrum of reactions to the death of a parent that is significantly influenced by a constellation of psychosocial variables.

Several studies (Elizur and Kaffman, 1982, 1983; Kaffman and Elizur, 1983) reported the findings of longitudinal research conducted with 25 bereaved kibbutz and nonkibbutz children. These studies revealed that bereaved children manifested multiple and enduring symptoms of such severe degree as to be considered handi-capping. In the early months of bereavement, children demonstrated a preponder-ance of affective responses that included sobbing, crying, and expressions of sad-ness (Elizur and Kaffman, 1982). Other initial reactions to the death included longing for the deceased, denial of the death, preoccupation with the idea of death, avoidance of the subject of death, and search for a father substitute (Elizur and Kaffman, 1982). During this time approximately 25% of the sample demonstrated increased incidence of eating problems, enuresis, and regressive tendencies (thumbsucking). These behaviors decreased in frequency during the following years of the study except for the search for a substitute father (Elizur and Kaffman, 1982).

Although findings did not indicate any significant association between symp-toms of pathology and variables of age and sex, a significant correlation was associated with the interaction of age and sex (Elizur and Kaffman, 1983). A higher incidence of pathology (70%) was noted among boys ages 3 to 6 as compared to girls (20%). Other differences in manifest though not pathological bereavement symptomology were noted according to age groups. Increased restlessness, aggres-siveness, and "exemplary behavior" were noted more frequently among older children. In contrast, preschoolers exhibited a higher frequency of night fears, separation difficulties, overdependence, and increased demandingness. Re-searchers (Kaffman and Elizur, 1983) also found that younger children were more likely to spontaneously share anecdotal accounts about the deceased father than were the older children. Instead, older children appeared more reluctant to share the details of their grief.

In assessing differences between the bereavement responses of kibbutz and nonkibbutz children a year and a half following the father's death, several trends were evident (Kaffman and Elizur, 1983). Nonkibbutz children demonstrated a greater frequency of bereavement reactions, which included night fears and ter-rors, increased dependency, and increased clinging and attention-seeking behav-iors. Both groups of bereaved children were found to exhibit similar patterns of grief: saddened affect, recurrent periods of moodiness, tendency to cry, feelings of longing and remembered experiences with spouse (Kaffman and Elizur, 1983).

Finally, associations were found between pathological responses in children and selected variables (Elizur and Kaffman, 1983). Pathological reactions were found to be associated with children typified as having "high-intensity" temperaments (Thomas and Chess, 1977). These children were characterized as having poor impulse control, being emotionally labile, and overreacting to frustrations. Children described as inhibited and withdrawn exhibited significant symptomatiology during the second and third stages of bereavement. Their behavior was characterized as being overdependent and exhibiting high levels of motor activity.

In a prospective study (Van Eerdewegh et al, 1982), 105 children ages 2 to 17 years were followed at 1 and 13 months following the death of a parent. Significant behaviors noted in children 1 month postdeath were dysphoric mood, sleep difficulties, decreased appetite, and withdrawn behaviors. Other behaviors noted included temper tantrums, resurgence in bedwetting, and decline in school performance. At 13 months, the following behaviors were reported in the bereaved children: decrease in dysphoric mood, complaints of abdominal pain, increased frequency of fights with siblings, and waning interest in school with concomitant increase of interest in nonacademic activities. The findings of the study indicate that the most immediate and profound reaction to parental death is mild and short-lived. Furthermore, the most severely depressed group of children were adolescent boys. The older the child, the more likely the expression of grief will be comparable to that of adults.

Other researchers investigating children's bereavement reactions (Balk, 1983; Betz, 1985; Binger, 1973; Britt, 1972; Davies, 1985; Furman, 1970; Kerner, Harvey, and Lewiston, 1979; McCown, 1981; Tietz, McSherry, and Britt, 1972) have examined the child's reaction to the death of a sibling. Based upon parental reports (Tietz, McSherry, and Britt, 1972) of 26 surviving siblings, the following changes were noted in children after the death (death due to leukemia or solid tumor). Eight of the siblings developed school achievement problems and 15 developed behavior problems. These problems included delinquency, aggressive acts and poor relationships with parents. Lastly, six of the surviving siblings were reported to have psychosomatic problems.

Binger (1973) reported similar findings on sibling's bereavement reactions. Parents reported the following disorders noted in siblings after the child's death (due to leukemia): enuresis, headaches, poor school performance and school phobia, depression, severe anxiety, and persistent abdominal pain. In addition, several factors were identified as mediating the sibling's bereavement reactions. These factors included stage of development, familial response, natural history of illness, and extent to which the illness was intertwined with family conflicts. Other variables affecting the child's response were the preexisting relationship with the sibling, extent of involvement in sibling's death, and the parent's handling of the sibling's response. Again, reports of sibling reactions were gathered during interviews with parents.

Kerner's study (1979) of 33 surviving siblings of cystic fibrosis children revealed that this group manifested fewer and less intense bereavement reactions than those of siblings of leukemic children. According to parental reports, three children demonstrated difficulty in adjustment postdeath. One child required psychiatric care to deal with excessive guilt; another required special school placement for academic problems, and one developed excessive concerns about mucous production. No other significant problems were reported. All siblings shared feelings of being neglected; however, they demonstrated understanding of the problem in this regard.

Balk (1983) sampled 33 teenagers following the death of their sibling. The teenagers reported a multitude of responses in reaction to their siblings' death. Shock, confusion, depression, anger, and fear were the most frequently cited emotional reactions by the bereaved teenagers. Nearly all of the siblings (30) reported difficulty eating after the death with subsequent improvement by the time of the interview. Thirty percent (11) of the siblings had thoughts of suicide immediately after the death, whereas 9 reported such thoughts at the time of the interview.

Initially, nearly all of the teenagers (31) reported problems with academic studies. In 23 cases, the study habits worsened; in 19 cases the grades had declined. By the time of the interview, only 9 reported continued problems with academic performance. Twenty-one of the teenagers reported changes in their relationships: 7 improved and 10 worsened. Teenagers identified several lessons learned from the death, including ways to cope with adversity and the value of human life.

Other researchers (Betz, 1985; Davies, 1985; McCown, 1981) found associations between the child's bereavement response and selected variables. Results of two studies (Davies, 1985; McCown, 1981) indicated that bereaved children were reported to have significantly more behavior problems than the standardized norm as obtained on the Achenbach Child Behavior Checklist. Closeness in age to the deceased child was not reported as a significant variable in bereavement behavior on data compiled from the Achenbach Checklist (Davies, 1985). The results from interview data indicated that closeness of the predeath relationship with the deceased was related to sibling's subsequent bereavement responses (Davies, 1985).

In a study (Betz, 1985) of 32 bereaved children ranging in age from 2 to 19 years, data were obtained from parents and children concerning their reactions following the death of their siblings. Findings revealed that significant differences in reactions were associated with age. Lack of feeling exhibited, remembering the deceased, noncommunicativeness and acknowledged spiritual presence were reported most often by the school-age child. Adolescents reported avoidance behavior and decline in school performance most frequently in comparison to the other ages. Significant differences were reported in relation to months since death. Avoidance and beliefs in spiritual presence were reported more frequently during the first year postdeath than at other time periods. Withdrawal behavior was reported more frequently 2 years or more following the death.

These investigations have used a retrospective approach in the collection of data (Balk, 1983; Betz, 1985; Binger, 1973; Davies, 1985; Elizur and Kaffman, 1982, 1983; Furman, 1970; Kaffman and Elizur, 1983; Kerner, Harvey, and Lewiston, 1979; McCown, 1981; Tietz, McSherry, and Britt, 1972; Tooley, 1975; Van Eerdewegh et al, 1982). Observations of children's behaviors were based primarily on anecdotal accounts from third-party observers such as physicians and nurses (Archibald, 1962; Furman, 1964; Willis, 1974). In several studies, interview data on children's behavior were collected from parents (Betz, 1985; Binger, 1973; Elizur and Kaffman, 1982, 1983; Furman, 1970; Kaffman and Elizur, 1983; Kerner, Harvey, and Lewiston, 1979; Tietz, McSherry, and Britt, 1972; Tooley, 1975; Van Eerdewegh et al, 1982). Factors that warrant consideration in terms of eliciting interview data from parents include memory distortion, parental bias in reporting information, and limitations imposed by the pervasive mourning effects on the part of parents in identifying accurately their child's grief response. Few studies collected data from the children directly (Balk, 1983; Betz, 1985; Davies, 1985). Factors that must be weighed in the interpretation of data from children's interviews are (1) children are less likely to communicate honestly and openly with a researcher than is an adult; (2) children younger than school age have difficulty communicating their feelings accurately; and (3) children may feel inhibited in reporting feelings for fear of retribution and for need of maintaining status quo.

Direction for future research might investigate longitudinally the child's response to loss of a family member. In this manner, short- and long-term effects of grieving—the direct and indirect effects as well as the positive outcomes associated with the child's resolution of the loss—could be investigated. Additionally, the use of standardized measures with qualitative data would strengthen the validity and reliability of findings.

SUMMARY

This chapter has reviewed the literature in the field of pediatric thanatology over the past 15 years. As this review has demonstrated, despite the scant amount of research that has been conducted, important questions have been raised and pertinent issues have begun to be addressed. The seminal beginnings have laid the foundation for further research that will continue to provide insight and understanding in the provision of care to bereaved families.

REFERENCES

Ablin A, Binger C, Stein R, Kushner J, Zager S, Middelson C: A conference with the family of a leukemic child. Am J Disab Child 112:362–364, 1971
Adams D: Childhood malignancy: The psychosocial care of the child and his family. Springfield, IL, Charles C Thomas, 1980
Alexander I, Alderstein A: Affective responses to the concept of death in a population of children and early adolescents. In Fulton R (ed): Death and Identity, New York, Wiley, 1973
Archibald H, Bill D, Miller C, Futterman R: Bereavement in childhood and adult psychiatric disturbance. Psychosom Med 24(4):344–359, 1962
Balk D: Effects of sibling death on teenagers. J Publ Health 53(1):14–18, 1983
Bendiksen R, Fulton R: Death and the child: An anterospective test of the childhood bereavement and later behavior disorder hypothesis. Omega 6(1):45–59, 1975

Betz C: Children's bereavement reactions to death of a family member. Paper presented to Children and Death Conference, King's College, London, Ontario, June 2–5, 1985

Binger C, Ablin A, Feuerstein R, Kushner J, Zagin S, Mikkelsen C: Childhood leukemia: Emotional impact on patient and family. N Engl J Med 28:414–418, 1969

Binger C: Childhood leukemia: Emotional impact on siblings. In Anthony C, Koupernik C (eds): The Child in His Family: The Impact of Disease and Death, pp 195–208. New York, Wiley, 1973

Birtchnell J: Sibship size and mental illness. Br J Psychiatr 117:303–308, 1970a

Birtchnell J: Depression in relation to early and recent parent death. Br J Psychiatr 116:299–306, 1970b

Birtchnell J: Early parent death and psychiatric diagnosis. Soc Psychiatr 7:202–210, 1972

Birtchnell J: The inter-relationship between social class, early parent death, and mental illness. Psychol Med 2:166–175, 1972

Birtchnell J: The personality characteristics of early bereaved psychiatric patients. Soc Psychiatry 10:97–103, 1975

Birtchnell J: Early parent death and the clinical scales of the MMPI. Br J Psychiatr 16:97–103, 1978

Bluebond–Langner M: The private worlds of dying children. Princeton: Princeton University Press, 1978

Brown G, Harris T, Copeland J: Depression and loss. Br J Psychiatr 130:1–18, 1977

Brown G, Harris T: Social origins of depression: A study of psychiatric disorder in women. London, Lavistock, 1978

Cain A, Fast L, Erickson G: Children's disturbed reactions to the death of a sibling. J Orthopsychiatry 3:443–447, 1964

Clayton P, Desmarais L, Winokur G: A study of normal bereavement. Am J Psychiatr 125:168–178, 1968

Cook J: Influence of gender on the problems of parents of fatally ill children. J Psychosoc Oncol 2(1):71–91, 1984

Davies E: Shared life space and bereavement responses in children. Paper presented to The Western Council on Higher Education for Nursing. The Eighteenth Annual Communicating Nursing Research Conference: Influencing the Future of Nursing Research Through Power and Politics. Seattle, WA, May 1–3, 1985

Easson W: The dying child: The management of the child or adolescent who is dying. Springfield, KL, Charles C Thomas, 1970

Elizur E, Kaffman M: Children's bereavement reactions following death of the father. II. J Am Acad Child Psychiatr 2:474–480, 1982

Elizur E, Kaffman M: Factors influencing the severity of childhood bereavement reactions. Am J Orthopsychiatr 53(4):668:677, 1983

Engel G: Grief and grieving. Am J Nurs 64:93–98, 1964

Fischoff J, O'Brien N: After the child dies. J Pediatr 88:140–146, 1976

Fulton R, Fulton J: A psychological aspect of terminal care: Anticipatory grief. Omega 2: 91–99, 1971

Furman R: The child's reaction to death in the family. In Schoenberg B, Carr A, Peretz D, Kutscher A (eds): Loss and grief: Psychological Management in Medical Practice, pp 70–86. New York, Columbia University Press, 1970

Furman R: A child's capacity for mourning. In Anthony EJ, Koupernik C (eds): The Child in His Family: The Impact of Disease and Death. New York, John Wiley & Sons 1973

Furman R: A Child's Parent Dies: Studies in Childhood Bereavement. New Haven, CT, Yale University Press, 1974

Futterman E, Hoffman I, Sabshin M: Parental anticipatory mourning. In Schoenberg B, Carr A, Peretz D, Kutscher A (eds): Psychosocial Aspects of Terminal Care. New York, Columbia University Press, 1972

Futterman E, Hoffman I: Crisis and adaptation in the families of fatally ill children. In Anthony E, Koupernik C (eds): The Child in His Family: The Impact of Disease and Death (Yearbook of the International Association for Child Psychiatry and Allied Professions, Vol. 2). New York, John Wiley & Sons, 1973

Glick I, Weiss R, Parkes C: The First Year of Bereavement. New York, John Wiley & Sons, 1974

Guylay J: The Dying Child. New York, McGraw–Hill, 1978

Hamovitch M: The Parent and the Fatally Ill Child. Los Angeles, Delmar Publishing, 1964

Harrison S, Davenport C, McDermott J: Children's reactions to bereavement. Arch Gen Psychiatr 17:593–597, 1967

Hefler D, Schneider C: Interpersonal methods for coping with stress: Helping families of dying children. Omega 8(4):319–331, 1978

Hofer M, Wolff C, Friedman S, Mason J: A psychoendocrine study of bereavement, Part I: 17 hydroxycorticosteroid excretion rates of parents following death of their children from leukemia. Psychosom Med 34:481–502, 1972

Kaffman M, Elizur E: Bereavement responses of kibbutz and non-kibbutz children following the death of a father. J Child Psychol Psychiatr 24:435–442, 1983

Kagen–Goodheart L: Re-entry: Living with childhood cancer. Am J Orthopsychiatr 47:651–658, 1977

Kane B: Children's concepts of death. J Gen Psychiatr 134:141–153, 1979

Kaplan D, Grobstein R, Smith A: Severe illness in families. Health Soc Work 1:72–81, 1976

Kellerman J (ed): Psychological Aspects of Childhood Cancer. Springfield, IL, Charles C Thomas, 1980

Kerner J, Harvey B, Lewiston N: The impact of grief: A retrospective study of family function following loss of a child with cystic fibrosis. J Chron Dis 32:221–225, 1979

Knudson A, Natterson J: Participation of parents in the hospital care of their fatally ill children. Pediatrics 26:482–490, 1960

Koocher G: Talking with children about death. Am J Orthopsychiatr 44:404–411, 1974

Lansky S, Cairns N, Hassamin R, Wehr J, Lowman J: Childhood cancer: Parental discord and divorce. Pediatrics 62:184–188, 1978

Leyn R: Terminally ill children and their families: A study of the variety of responses to fatal illness. Matern Child Nurs J 5:179–188, 1976

Lifshitz M: Long range effects of father's loss: The cognitive complexity of bereaved children and their school adjustment. Br J Med Psychol 49:189–197, 1976

Lindemann E: Symptomatology and management of acute grief. Am J Psychiatr 101:141–149, 1944

Martinson I (ed): Home Care for the Dying Child: Professional and Family Perspectives. New York, Appleton–Century–Crofts, 1976

Miles M: Helping adults mourn the death of a child. In Wass H, Carr C, (eds): Children and Death, pp, 219–241. New York, Hemisphere, 1984

Miles M: Emotional symptoms and physical health in bereaved parents. Nurs Res 34(2):76–81, 1985

Morrissey J: A note on interviews with children facing imminent death. Soc Casework 44:343–345, 1963

Morrissey J: Children's adaptations to fata illness. Soc Work, 8(4):81–88, 1963

Morrissey J: Death anxiety in children with a fatal illness. In Pared HJ (ed): Crisis Intervention, pp 324–338. New York, Family Service Association of America, 1965

Natterson J, Knudson A: Observations concerning fear of death in fatally ill children and their mothers. Psychosom Med 22:456–465, 1960

Nixon J, Pearn J: Emotional sequelae of parents and siblings following the drowning or near drowning of a child. Austral N Zeal J Psychiatry 11:265–268, 1977

Owen G, Fulton R, Markusen E: Death at a distance: A study of family survivors. Omega 13:191–224, 1982–1983

Parkes C: Bereavement: Studies of grief in adult life. New York, International Universities Press, 1972

Plank E, Plank R: Children and death. In Solnit AJ (ed): The Psychoanalytic Study of the Child. New Haven, CT, Yale University Press, 1978

Pozanski E: The "replacement child": A sign of unsolved parental grief. J Pediatr 81(6):1190–1193, 1972

Raimbault G: Psychological problems in the chronic nephropathies of childhood. In Anthony J (ed): The Child and His Family, pp 65–74. New York, John Wiley & Sons, 1973

Raimbault G: Children talk about death. Acta Paediatr Scand 70:179–182, 1981

Rando T: An investigation of grief and adaptation in parents whose children have died from cancer. J Pediatric Psychol 8(1):3–19, 1983

Raphael B: The Anatomy of Bereavement. New York, Basic Books, 1983

Richmond J, Waisman H: Psychological aspects of management of children with malignant diseases. Am J Dis Child 89:42–47, 1955

Roy A: Vulnerability factors and depression in women. Br J Psychiatr 113:106–110, 1978

Salladay S, Royal M: Children and death: Guidelines for grief work. Child Psychiatr Hum Dev 11(4):203–212, 1981

Sanders C, Maiyer P, Strong P: The Grief Experience Inventory. Charlotte, University of North Carolina, 1979

Sanders C: A comparison of adult bereavement in the death of a spouse, child and parent. Omega 13:227–241, 1979–1980

Schiff H: The Bereaved Parent. New York, Crown, 1977

Schoenberg B, Carr A, Kutscher A, Peretz D, Goldberg I (eds): Anticipatory Grief. New York, Columbia University Press, 1974

Schulman J, Kupst M (eds): The Child with Cancer: Clinical Approaches to Psychosocial Care, Research in Psychosocial Aspects. Springfield, IL, Charles C Thomas, 1980

Sourkes B: Facilitating family coping with childhood cancer. J Pediatr Psychol 2:65–67, 1977

Spinetta J: Death, anxiety in leukemic children. Dissertation Abstracts International 33:1807–1808, 1972

Spinetta J, Rigler D, Karon M: Personal space as a measure of a dying child's sense of isolation. J Consult Clin Psychol 42(6):751–756, 1972

Spinetta J, Rigler D, Karon M: Anxiety in the dying child. Pediatrics 52(6):841–844, 1973

Spinetta J, Swarner J, Sheposh J: Effective parental coping following the death of a child from cancer. J Pediatr Psychol 6(3):251–263, 1981

Tennant C, Bibbington P, Hurry J: Parental death in childhood and risk of adult depressive disorders: A review. Psychol Med 16:289–299, 1980

Thomas A, Chess S: Temperament and Development. New York, Brunner, Mazel, 1977

Tietz W, McSherry L, Britt B: Family sequelae after a child's death due to cancer. Am J Psychother 26(3):417–425, 1972

Tooley K: The choice of a surviving sibling as "scapegoat" in some cases of maternal bereavement—a case report. J Child Psychol Psychiatr 16:331–339, 1975

Van Eerdewegh M, Bieri M, Parrilia R, Clayton P: The bereaved child. Br J Psychiatr 140:23–29, 1982

Vernick J: Meaningful communication with the fatally ill child. In Anthony E, Koupernik C (eds): The Child in His Family: The Impact of Disease and Death, pp 105–119. New York, Wiley, 1973

Waechter E: Death anxiety in children with fatal illness. Doctoral dissertation, Stanford University. Ann Arbor, MI, University Microfilms 69–310, 1968

Waechter E: Children's awareness of fatal illness. Am J Nurs 71:1168–1172, 1971

Williams W, Polak P: Crisis intervention in acute grief. Omega 3:67–70, 1972

Willis D: The families of terminally ill children: Symptomatology and management. J Clin Child Psychol, pp 32–33, Summer, 1974

Wolfenstein M: How is mourning possible? Psychoanal Study Child 21:93, 1966

3 · Children With Life-Threatening Illness: Change and Continuity in Research

Eugenia H. Waechter

Until 10 years ago, no systematically controlled research had been done directly with children. Former conclusions about the impact of the illness on children were based on observation of them and on indirect evidence drawn from anecdotal data provided by hospital personnel.

This lack of research resulted largely from the taboo surrounding death, not only in the larger society, but also in our health institutions. Feifel (Quint, 1967) reported that his attempts to interview dying adults were unsuccessful over a period of years even though he found that such conversations were therapeutic to the patient. He concluded that death was a dark symbol not to be stirred or even touched, an obscenity to be avoided.

In 1967 my own attempts to gain access to children with life-threatening illness reflected those of Feifel and others. Researchers were considered somewhat odd and pathologically morbid if they were interested in conducting systematically controlled studies to broaden our knowledge about the impact of death and dying on patients and families. Talking about death with dying patients was considered more than ill-advised since it would "raise the patient's anxiety."

Educational institutions at that time paid scant attention to how death and dying related to the human condition and professional care. Death as a work problem for nurses was extensively explored by Quint–Benoliel (1967) who con-

Speech given at workshop on the Advances in Pediatric Nursing, San Francisco, California, March 19, 1978.

vincingly portrayed the difficulties that nurses have when there is a lack of planned experiences in the educational preparation and in their ongoing professional experience. Investigation of faculty teaching methods indicated that emphasis was focused largely on the nurses' life-saving goals and relatively little on death.

This neglect is understandable because nurses and physicians are also products of their culture—a culture that was charged with attempting to deny death through socially sanctioned conventions of avoidance, through circumvolution, through complicated measures to protect the young from contact with terminal illness and death, and through disguising the reality of death whenever possible.

It was also true then, and is today, that health practitioners often see death as a personal challenge. The health professions exist for the purpose of extending life—to cheat death. Death can thus have special meaning to physicians and nurses and may become reinforced as the symbol of professional and personal failure. These professionals also value alert consciousness, control, and autonomy which is the antithesis of death.

Nurses, along with other professionals and the general public, however, are now showing significant growth in their interest and awareness of the many complexities and issues surrounding life and death. The advent of organ transplants, population control methods, and life-support systems constantly forces us to face questions about who shall live, when does death occur, and who has the ultimate responsibility for making such decisions. The concepts of "quality of life" and the rights of individuals to influence the manner of their dying are now openly discussed in public and professional circles and in all public communication media.

Nurses are greatly involved with these issues naturally because they are physically present and responsible when questions of life and death arise but also because they must cope with philosophical questions and value judgments in order to come to terms with their own concerns about death. Nurses are now indicating their wish and need to explore these issues through demands for educational experiences, through massive attendance at symposia about death and dying, through increased planning for ongoing ward conferences, and in many other ways.

Although there appears to be a melting of the death taboo, the concept of death, particularly death of the young, continues to be a problem for nurses and other professionals who often become highly irrational and emotional when contemplating working with dying patients and their families. In a recent study, Hurley (1977) used retrospective reports, interviews, and questionnaires to determine that 78% of 122 practicing nurses employed used avoidance and evasion as their preferred coping strategy when patients introduced or alluded to the subject of dying, either verbally or nonverbally.

This "psychological disinheriting" of the dying patient while being attentive to bodily needs occurs even more frequently with pediatric patients. In a 1975 survey by a nursing journal (*Nursing '75*) more than half of the respondents reported having very uncomfortable feelings when caring for terminally ill children, adolescents, and mothers with young children. The statistical findings showed nurses in general can more easily cope with dying patients who are at the two extremes of the lifespan—the newborn and the elderly. The discomfort, however, was found to be more pronounced in older nurses and in those with the least educational preparation.

This would indicate that within the past 10 years nursing education has made great strides in integrating death education into the curriculum. In a recent survey for the foundation Thanatology, Drs. Schoenberg and Carr (1971) found that in the schools they contacted, the curricula almost universally included some consideration of the nurse's responsibility toward the dying patient and the relatives who attend him. Still, most of the schools were not entirely satisfied with their coverage of death problems and more than half reported plans to make curriculum changes on the care of the dying patient.

On the other hand, in a survey of medical schools, Drs. Schoenberg and Carr found that even the requirements for a diagnosis of death are not formally included in the medical curricula in almost half of the schools they queried. About a third offered no coverage of the doctor's responsibilities toward families of dying patients. Although faculty members expressed some dissatisfaction with the state of affairs, less than a third of them indicated any plan to change their curricula in order to include training on the care of the dying patient, although two thirds of the students wanted curriculum changes. Perhaps yet more startling was the fact that hardly any departments conducted discussions with medical students about the controversial issues connected with the care of dying patients—euthanasia, definitions of death, ethics of organ transplantation, and the possible consequences of narcotic addiction.

Much more hopeful is the tremendous increase in controlled research in the areas of both adult death and pediatric death, although the latter is still somewhat lagging in the research arena. Death, while virtually ignored by child developmentalists and psychologists a decade ago, is now becoming quite fashionable, and studies are proliferating on the development of the concept of death and death education for well children. These disciplines along with those of the health professions are also taking a closer look at the many unresolved issues relating to how children adapt to life-threatening illness.

CHANGES IN PROBLEMS AND ISSUES RELATED TO CANCER

Since the time I began studying children with cancer and leukemia 10 years ago, the definitions and prognoses have altered considerably. The diagnosis of cancer no longer automatically means impending death. Because of major successes in medical treatment of some kinds of childhood cancer, more and more children have the chance to become adults. At least half of the 6000 children expected to develop cancer in the United States next year are likely to survive many years, thanks to improved radiation and chemical therapy.

These illnesses, which were once acutely fatal, have now become chronic life-threatening conditions. Despite the positive success of increased life spans, these children and their families now have entirely new sets of problems which they have never had to face before. Formerly, there was not ambiguity involved in the impact of cancer on the family. Cancer meant the death of the child within a period of 2 to 3 years. At that time, parents and society did not worry so much about quality of life or of integrating the child into the mainstream of the community because the child was not going to be around to integrate. Parents were not required to worry greatly about the problems of education or the long-term effects of treatment on their child's physical and psychosocial development.

Today, there is much more ambiguity, which parents are called upon to face. These children and their parents now sit under a modern sword of Damocles, not knowing whether to engage in anticipatory grief or to devote their energies toward the issues of life and hope for prolonged remission or "cure." Long-term survival of the child is offered to parents as a distinct possibility. On the other hand, they are told, "We will work toward your child's survival; but we do not know if he will survive. According to statistics you have a right to hope. You may get to keep your child around permanently. But we may not know that for 2, 3, 4, or 5 or more years." This is, understandably, a powerful source of stress and ushers in an entirely new set of problems, both for the child and for his family that involve issues related to prolonged medical supervision as well as to the long-term quality of family life.

DECISION MAKING

Parents often have more decisions to make currently about the treatment regimen than they did in the past. Much research on chemotherapy and radiation therapy combinations is now being done on hematology–oncology services in major medical centers throughout the country. At the time of diagnosis parents are often asked to choose whether their child receives routine treatment or treatment under a system of research protocols. This decision is often difficult, even for the sophisticated parent, because if they elect to join the experimental group they cannot be given a choice as to which combination of chemotherapy and radiation they want their child to have.

The term *research* often implies to parents that their child will become an experimental object. Even though parents wish the newest and best for their child, they may be apprehensive because experimental protocols often entail widespread or full-body radiation that can have long-lasting effects on development. Even for parents who have little knowledge of the medical world, the forced choice between "experimental" and "routine" can be agonizing—perhaps more so if they experience no subtle pressures toward either alternative.

As the disease progresses and all means of controlling the condition have been exhausted, parents often face another serious treatment decision. At this stage they are frequently told that all conventional means for controlling the disease have been exhausted and the death of their child now seems inevitable. Options are then often given for further chemotherapy with a research drug or for discontinuation of treatment. Further treatment may entail considerable suffering for the child, whereas cessation of the treatment implies abandonment of all hope. In many centers children who are old enough are also confronted with this decision. When the decisions of the physician, parents, and child concur, planning can be harmonious; nevertheless, this is a difficult task for parents. While coping with their own feelings, they must respect their child's desire. At the same time they must evaluate the impartiality of medical advice.

STIGMA

Despite our society's greater openness to death, the social stigma of cancer does not seem to have altered substantially in the past 10 years. Cancer is still seen as a mysterious, often fatal disease, and the parents as well as the child may be shunned by friends and relatives. In my past and current studies, parents have complained of the treatment they received from former associates. Recently one mother stated, "My neighbor, Marge, used to be a good friend of mine. Then Gloria got leukemia. You should have seen Marge run! She didn't come over for a long time. Then she convinced herself that Gloria has anemia and would be all right after a while. She won't talk to me about leukemia at all. I think parents should be told that they're apt to get some pretty funny reactions from their friends and relatives."

Such response may still be due to fear of contagion. More frequently it results from continuing unease with what to say and uncertainty about the child's future. Such unease is also still encountered among physicians and nurses when dealing with leukemia children, as previously stated. Spinetta, Rigler, and Karon (1973) measured the sense of isolation in leukemia children by having them place dolls representing doctor, nurse, mother, and father in a replica of a hospital room. They reported that the scores of patients' interpersonal distance as measured by this projective technique were significantly greater than the scores of the controls. They hypothesized that this was due to a decrease in the frequency, intensity, and quality of adult physical and verbal contact with the child. This isolation also became more intense as death drew near.

COMMUNICATION WITH THE CHILD

Until recently it was assumed that until the age of 9 or 10, healthy children do not approach a realistic understanding that death is permanent and inevitable; therefore, children with life-threatening illness could not deal with feelings about death. This widely held belief was the basis for many clinicians' practices of shielding the young patient from any knowledge of his disease. In my first study (Waechter, 1971) only 2 children of 16 with fatal illness had discussed their imminent deaths with their parents, 6 had received little realistic information regarding their illnesses, and 8 had been informed that their illnesses were temporary or trivial.

Many of the parents were deeply troubled as to the best procedure to follow with their child—would it be in the child's best interests to withhold the diagnosis or would it be more helpful to answer questions frankly and completely? They received little help from their medical advisors in dealing with their child's questions since during the 1960s a "protective" approach was widely advocated.

My study used a modified thematic apperception test with the children. The dichotomy was striking in the degree of the child's awareness, as derived from his imaginative stories, and in the parent's knowledge about the child's awareness. Although only two of sixteen children in the fatal group had discussed concerns about death with their parents, the percentage of death imagery in stories containing threat was found to be 63%.

The correlation between the child's opportunity to discuss the illness and the child's total score on the projective test was .633, which is significant at the .01 level. This finding indicated that children with a fatal illness who expressed less specific death anxiety were those who had had a greater opportunity to discuss their fears and concerns about their present and future body integrity.

These findings were supported by Spinetta's later study (1974), in which it was concluded that many young patients are aware of the threat of death, even though they may not be able to express their awareness in adult terms. Spinetta also encouraged health professionals to answer all children's questions simply, directly, and honestly, thus setting the stage for all members of the family to share their grief and anxiety and offer one another support in facing their fears.

In the early '70s, the open approach to death and dying began gaining ground and is now widely accepted, in theory if not in practice, which now often relieves parents of bearing a secret burden. It also helps children, who formerly learned not to ask disturbing questions and as a result become increasingly frightened and withdrawn.

In my current study of 52 children with life-threatening or other chronic illness, all but a few of the parents responded that they felt they should be open with their children. All discussed aspects of treatment with their children, although some parents, particularly those with very young children, were more guarded in discussing the prognosis. However, if the child asked questions about death, no parent stated that they avoided or refused to discuss them. Most of these children were under medical care that espouses the open approach, and many were included in the conferences physicians held with their parents.

Almost all parents stated that their children over 5 years of age also learned much about their illness from other children and from professionals on the wards and outpatient clinics. The amount learned and quickness of learning appeared to be related to age, the acuteness of the illness, and the degree of openness espoused by the particular medical setting. Older children with an illness having a faster course who were treated in an open setting were able to answer most questions in greater detail about tests, symptoms, and diagnosis. Most of this knowledge stemmed from the induction phase of the illness. These children, however, did not necessarily also speak freely about their prognosis. Some children talked openly about their possible deaths, whereas others felt that they would rather not know too much about the future since it would cause them to worry more. Almost all children over 6 years of age stated that their mothers worried about them, whereas only a few felt that they could or should share their own worries freely with their parents. When they did so, the content of their worries was sometimes startling to parents. One 7-year-old girl whose mother questioned her about her obvious concern stated her worry that it would be many years after she died and went to heaven that her mother would arrive. She worried that her mother would have changed so much that she would not recognize her. Her mother allayed her fear by answering, "Honey, I'll call your name."

EDUCATION

As the rate of survival has increased in the past 10 years, so also the focus has changed from death to life for the child patient, and increased attention is being paid to quality of life. The ambiguity in prognosis now makes it particularly difficult for parents to cope with the area of education. Ten years ago, when there was less ambiguity, parents and professional personnel were less concerned about the time the child missed from school. Parental concerns about education at that time seemed to stem more from the need to provide normality for their child during a limited life span. This need for normality is also stressed today inasmuch as school is the main arena for the child's social relationships; however, now added to this is concern for the child's need for education in an uncertain future.

The need for long-term medical supervision in inpatient and outpatient settings results in the loss of 4 to 6 weeks of school time within a year for many children. Academic difficulties imposed by this loss time may be compounded by the child's reluctance to attend school because of negative changes in appearance which have resulted from treatment and because both the child and his parents fear separation. Parents are often uncertain whether to encourage education, and this may also create difficulties with the child's attitude about going to school. This attitude is further influenced by the ambiguity of others in the community, particularly peers and teachers. There is often much teasing and many negative reactions to the child from peers, which increases the child's reluctance to attend school. In addition, teachers are often ill-prepared to deal with these children, both on an emotional and on a knowledge level. Many simply don't know what to expect from a child or how to react. Some teachers may create dual standards for the child with cancer as opposed to his peers, thus enhancing the child's sense of inadequacy. Others may hold the child to inflexible and unattainable standards.

Problems of reintegration after a prolonged absence may be particularly difficult. Many parents are now counseled about the positive value of school in the child's overall adjustment to the illness. Yet their need to protect the child, both physically and psychologically, may be in conflict with this goal. In schools where psychological consultation is available, children have less difficulty. In these instances, reintegration of the child can be facilitated by involvement of the school, the parents, and the child in preparation for his return.

BODY IMAGE

The increased emphasis placed on the child's involvement with peers and school often compounds the child's concern about his appearance. The longer-term, chronic nature of the illness also contributes to the anxiety of the child and of his parents. The more vigorous, aggressive therapy used now also often produces side-effects of a more drastic nature than was seen formerly. Loss of hair, jaundice, stunted growth, obesity, or amputation are sources of great distress for the child. For younger children, peers may not have reached the level of development where they are able to demonstrate a great deal of empathy. For older children approaching adolescence, appearance and the need to be like others is all consuming. Our body-conscious society, which elevates appearance as a major value, contributes to these problems.

The isolation of children with cancer is a major concern. In my study and in others, four out of five children were isolated to some extent, and some were severely withdrawn to the point that they had little contact with peers and others in the community. What this can mean for emotional and social development is obvious.

In addition to withdrawal from others, some children may use their illness to become manipulative with peers and teachers. Others, however, with help, are able to accept their situation and lay the groundwork for their friends' acceptance of them.

In my current study a grandmother described her grandson's response to his loss of hair:

Monday his hair started coming out. The next day there was more and by Wednesday morning, he was completely bald, and believe me, that was a trauma! That really was. So we decided a little wig would help a lot, you know. Of course, after we explained to him how it had to come out and it would grow back, and when he saw that it didn't show too much under the cap, it wasn't too bad. But then he didn't want us to see him when I put him to bed. He didn't want grandpa to see him. So I said, "You know, Steven, that Grandpa will not love you any less without your hair." And then I explained to him, "You know, Steven, if you will not take off your cap and show the kids, they're going to call you baldy and they're going to try to knock your cap off." So, I said, "If one of them calls you baldy, you just take off that cap right away and show it to him and then you tell him that it was because of your radiation and your illness and so on," and I said, "He'll never ask you again."

"Well, the funny thing was, he's got these two little boys next door that he plays with and he just loves them. One is about two years older and the other is about two years younger. So he was playing with them and had his little cap. So when he came in to eat his dinner he said, "Grandma, I showed Mike and Jeff my head." I said , "What did they say?" He said, "They didn't say anything. They wanted to know how come I was bald and I told them it was because I had leukemia."

DISCIPLINE

Parents have always had concerns about disciplining their children who have life-threatening illness. Previously, when life expectancy was relatively brief, parents could rationalize indulging their ill children by arguing that they wished their child to be as happy as possible in the short time available. Even then, however, they encountered problems with their other children, who tend to get caught in the cycle of jealousy and guilt, which was exacerbated when relatives bestowed special presents and favors on the ill child.

Currently, when life expectancy is much more ambiguous, parents are regularly counseled at the onset of the illness to maintain normalcy within the home in order to (1) support the ill child's positive view of the future, (2) prevent sibling problems and family disruption, and (3) avoid creating a "social tyrant" who will have difficulties relating to others in the future, should the child become a long-time survivor.

This is a very difficult area for parents, since the young cancer patient tends to be manipulative with parents because of hospital experiences and may be difficult to discipline. This difficulty is increased because of the parents' sense of guilt for the illness. Most parents are able to deal with the period of self-blame. Others, however, unable to resolve their guilt and engrossed in anticipatory grief, may abdicate the parental responsibility of providing normalcy both for the ill child and for his siblings. When this period of time extends to 5 years or longer, severe family problems are usually inevitable. In a recent retrospective study, Gogan and colleagues (1977) reported that 5 or more years after diagnosis of cancer in a child who is still alive, problems with siblings included intensified rivalry, inappropriate feelings of guilt, and a sense of exclusion from a significant family crisis.

In my own current study that included 14 children with leukemia and other forms of cancer, all but two parents reported problems with disciplining their ill child. Of those children who had siblings, all parents except one reported sibling problems ranging from mild to severe. These problems ranged from somatic complaints to difficulties with school, peers, family, and other relationships. Most parents felt concern and, except for mild problems, most felt the need for help or intervention.

PARENTAL COPING

In facing an ambiguous future, many parents today are subjected to greater stresses in relation to coping than were families even a decade ago. The shock of the initial diagnosis sets in motion the process of anticipatory grief, despite a more hopeful prognosis. Through uncertain times of remission and relapse, family members experience fear, guilt, anger, and sorrow. Very often the patient and various members of the family are out of synchrony with one another in these emotional phases.

Because of the possibility for long-term survival, parents in some centers are now counseled to put anticipatory mourning into cold storage for the postmortem period lest there be premature distancing from the child, thus increasing the child's sense of loneliness and isolation. This may be difficult for the parents to do though they respond positively to the more hopeful aura surrounding the child's medical experience.

Parents now are in somewhat of a dilemma. Anticipatory grief is a coping process that allows the family to prepare for the child's death gradually through the illness. When death comes, they thus are not faced with an overwhelming number of grieving tasks and may even greet death with relief. This is now, however, a double-edged sword. It may be helpful for the future of the survivors, but harmful to the child. The child may survive but may return to the family almost as a stranger among strangers. This is particularly true if there has been a lengthy separation with diminished hope of reunion and the family has learned to live without the child. Easson (1972) has termed this the *Lazarus syndrome.* On the other hand, if the child dies and the parents have not prepared themselves for this event, grief tasks may be overwhelming.

Another problem that families face today is the long-term nature of this crisis. Whereas previously, family disruption did occur, it usually followed the death of the child. During the shorter time period of the illness, parents were more able to maintain their marital relationship, despite severe stress, tending to live "one day at a time." Currently, with the longer period of illness and chronic stress, some medical centers, including the one from which my sample was drawn, are seeing more marital breakdowns during the course of the child's illness. The increased ambiguity and uncertainty about the future undoubtedly contributes to marital problems. And marital breakdown undoubtedly adds to stress for the entire family.

PROBLEMS RELATED TO HEALTH SUPERVISION

With the current long-term nature of most life-threatening illnesses, parents also have additional problems because the nature of our health care delivery system in the United States is ill equipped to provide all the supportive services required. Children and parents now need a host of ongoing services including community agencies, health centers and mental health centers, family service associations, school psychological services, and children guidance clinics in addition to inpatient and outpatient services. Because of the episodic nature of stress points for families, which are often unpredictable, they also need continuity of contact with an interested and emphathetic health professional they can trust and call on in periods of uncertainty.

Unfortunately, such services are not always available for a large proportion of families that may live far from medical centers. In addition, medical priorities have often relegated mental health care to the bottom rung of the ladder of the limited resources allocated for the care of children and families.

DEATH OF THE CHILD

Most terminally ill children spend their last days and weeks in hospitals, where they are greatly dependent on the professional staff caring for them to maintain their right to "live until they die," to die in the manner they choose and with the dignity they deserve. Death today is still seldom private, though it is often a lonely business. And it is still true that families are often abruptly abandoned after the death of the child.

New trends in some medical centers in various parts of the country, however, provide hope that the loneliness of death can be lessened for children in the future. The hospice movement is gaining ground and spreading throughout the country. The positive findings of Dr. Martinson's study (1976) at the University of Minnesota are receiving widespread attention. Other centers are also studying the values for both children and families, of dying at home. Eighty percent of the children who are terminally ill at the medical center from which the sample in my current study was drawn now die at home. Though much more evaluation of the child's experiences and the problems encountered in providing the necessary support for families is necessary, the efforts being made are hopeful and indicative of renewed professional concern for providing the quality of care we wish for children and families presently and in the future.

REFERENCES

Dealing with death—Thanatology looks at the doctor and the dying patient. Med World News, pp 31–36, 1971
Easson W: The Lazarus syndrome in childhood. Med Insight, pp 44–51, 1972
Frequency and Feelings. Nursing '75, pp 17–24, August 1975
Gogan J, O'Malley JE, Foster D: Treating the pediatric cancer patient: A review. J Pediatr Psychol 2:42–46, 1977
Hurley B: Problems of interaction between nurses and dying patients. Precis, WICHE, 9th Nursing Research Conference, Seattle, WA, 1977
Martinson I: Home care for the dying child. New York, Appleton–Century–Crofts, 1976
Quint JC: The nurse and the dying patient, New York, Macmillan, 1967
Spinetta J: Personal space as a measure of a dying child's sense of isolation. J Consult Clin Psychol 42:751–756, 1974
Spinetta J, Rigler D, Karon M: Anxiety in the dying child. Pediatrics 52:841–845, 1973
Waechter E: Children's awareness of fatal illness. Am J Nurs 71:1168–1172, 1971

4 · Distress in Fatally and Chronically Ill Children: Methodological Note

Susan Lewis, Fred T. Horton, and Stephen Armstrong

Abstract

This report concerns the important empirical question of measuring distress experienced by a child who is coming to terms with his or her own life-threatening illness. Nineteen fatally and chronically ill outpatient children were assessed in seven areas of personality functioning with seven different measurement methods. Inspection of the multitrait–multimethod correlation matrix indicates that there are important differences in measures of distress that are thought to be roughly the same and that, in general, the most common empirical methods are poorly fitted to the task of understanding the distress of fatally or chronically ill children.

INTRODUCTION

Starting with the early World War II studies, psychoanalytic investigators of children's attachment behavior have concentrated on the effects of interrupting the mother–child bond, e.g., in orphaned children [1,2], and in children separated by war from parents [3]. Children are thought to be vulnerable to negative psychological consequences of interrupted attachments [4–8] and "work them through" in a phasic coping process of protesting the loss of the parent, despairing over the loss, and, finally, psychological detachment itself [4,7,9]. The psychological importance

The data analysis was supported by a faculty grant from the Vanderbilt Computer Center. Reprinted from Omega 12(4):293–306, 1981–1982.

of separation and detachment has not been ignored by physicians who treat children [10–13]; clinical experience in this area has sparked several fine studies on the management of detachment in dying children [14–17]. Despite these excellent descriptive studies, however, there is relatively little quantitative research into the measurement of separation, detachment, or psychological distress in fatally or chronically ill children, excepting studies by Waechter [18]; Spinetta [19]; Spinetta, Rigler, Karon [20]; and Spinetta and Maloney [21]. We have questioned how much psychological distress a fatally or chronically ill child experiences, and which measures of distress accurately and validly reflect the distress of detachment.

The first step in answering these questions is to collect data on children's distress in a "multitrait–multimethod" correlational design [22]. To answer the question of whether or not various measurement methods converge independently on the stages of protest, despair and detachment, the areas of personality functioning which we selected to measure are those characterizing these stages: anxiety, anger/aggression, denial, sadness/depression, reality-contact, object relatedness and interpersonal withdrawal.

METHOD

Subjects in this study were nineteen 5 to 12 year-old children being treated at Vanderbilt University Hospital for severe chronic or fatal childhood illnesses. Ten children had a diagnosis of acute lymphocytic leukemia, five children had cystic fibrosis, three children had hemophilia and one child had diabetes. There are twelve boys and seven girls in the sample, who came to us through the Vanderbilt Pediatric Clinic. Parents of children with these four diagnoses were approached by their primary physician and the first author who asked them to participate with their children in a study on how children who had a serious illness fare psychologically. They were told that their participation would involve approximately one hour of their time plus travel time. Fifty-one parents were approached and twenty-eight agreed to participate, but only nineteen followed through by bringing their child at the appointed time for the interview and assessment procedures. Informed consent was obtained in writing from the parents and each child. No payments or other promises were used.

MEASURES

Since the purpose of the study is to validate the presence of particular psychological characteristics, seven data collection methods were used to assess seven specific areas of personality functioning. These areas include anxiety (through six methods), anger and aggression (five methods), reality contact (two methods), object relatedness (two methods), and interpersonal withdrawal (five methods). The seven data collection methods are: a behavior rating scale filled out by parents; two types of ratings by a child psychiatrist following a brief interview with the child; an examiner-administered anxiety scale; a differential personality inventory to which the child responded; and, finally a projective measure which yields an interpersonal distance score, and two stories which are content analyzed. The child came to the Child Psychiatry offices, which are located in a different building than the main hospital, on a day other than their regular clinic visit. This was to minimize effects of the medical procedures on the child. It was explained to the child that we wanted to ask him or her to help us understand how a child feels, so that the doctors and nurses at the hospital could care for them better. The child was interviewed briefly by the child psychiatrist and then spent approximately 30 minutes with a second-year medical student, who administered the three measures described more fully below.

Burk's Behavior Rating Scale (BRS)

The BRS for grades 1–8 is a 116-item rating on 10-point scales of the child's behavior in a variety of situations. The items are summed into twenty scales of childhood prsonality functioning [23]. Six of the twenty scales are included in this study: excessive anxiety, poor reality contact, poor anger control, excessive aggressiveness, excessive withdrawal, and excessive suffering. The parent accompanying the child did the ratings.

Interview with the Child Psychiatrist

The child psychiatrist (the second author) was not told the child's diagnosis prior to this interview. He was instructed to interview the child in his office for approximately fifteen minutes and was given a list of general questions which he might want to use as a guide. Most of the questions were derived from standard interviewing questions for a brief psychiatric evaluation, but several questions were aimed at exploring the child's understanding of and reaction to his or her illness. Following the interview, the psychiatrist filled out 5-point rating scales on the content of the child's communications, and, second, on his clinical impressions of the child. The rated content areas, based on the conversation itself, were: anxiety, anger–aggression, sadness–depression, pessimism, optimism, and isolation–withdrawal. The clinical impressions, based more on the psychiatrist's judgment were: anxiety, anger, depression, denial, apathy, reality testing, and object relatedness. Ratings of content and impression ratings are regarded as two distinct methods in this study.

General Anxiety Scale for Children (GASC)

The GASC is a 45-item scale which measures a child's anxiety level in several types of situations [24]. This measure has two anxiety scores, one of which (the "Positive Anxiety" score) is used in this study. This instrument was used in Waechter's studies [18,25]. In the present study, the questions were read aloud to the child by the experimenter.

Missouri Children's Pictures Series (MCPS)

The MCPS consists of 238 simple line drawings, each on a 3 by 5-inch card. Each picture shows a child of indefinite age and of sometimes unclear gender in an activity. The child is given the set of cards and asked to sort each picture into a pile that looks like fun, or another pile that does not look like fun. This personality test yields a profile of scores on eight scales [26]. Four of these characteristics are included in this study: aggression, activity level, sleep disturbance, and somatization.

Doll-House Measure

The doll house measure used here is a modification of Spinetta's 3-D test [19]. Because the subjects in this study are out-patients, it was felt children would be more responsive using a home scene, rather than a hospital scene. Thus a three-dimensional replica of a living room was used, which featured sturdy doll house furniture glued to a square grid floor for accurate measurement. A doll representing the child was placed on a couch at one end of the room. A mother, father and sibling (opposite sex) doll were handed to the child, who was asked to place them in the living room scene where they "usually" are. The child was then asked to tell a story about the scene. The stories were tape-recorded and the distance of each doll from the child doll was recorded. Then the mother, father, and sibling doll were removed and the child was handed a friend (same sex) doll and asked to place the friend doll in the living room and tell a story as before. The physical distance between the child doll and another doll is taken to be a measure of the child's perceived interpersonal distance from the figure whom the other doll represents. Finally, as a last measurement source, the transcribed stories were coded by the third author, who was blind to diagnosis, using a psychoanalytically oriented process code [27]. The codes are for five dynamic interpersonal themes (hostility, affection, dependency, affective distress, and death or mutilation themes), and in this study have a code–recode agreement from .52 to .74, which is acceptably above the chance level [28]. Since the variable of the number of codable sentences was low, no independent control for productivity is required [29,30].

FINDINGS

The data are analyzed within a multitrait–multimethod product moment correlation matrix [22]. The measurement task, first, is to demonstrate, in terms of seven areas of personality functioning, convergent validity by independent methods of measurement. A second task is to assess the suitability of particular measures of constructs in terms of the psychoanalytic theory of loss and detachment. Does the method of measurement make a difference?

For each of the seven areas of personality functioning for which there is more than one method of measuring, there is little agreement among methods. In terms of anxiety, for example, the range of correlation is from −.272 (GASC with expressions of anxiety in the family story) to .575 (MCPS "activity level" with the psychiatrist's ratings of anxious interview content), with a mean correlation between methods of .057 (Table 4-1). A child's expressions of anger and aggression elicit comparable measures only from the child psychiatrist's ratings of interview

(Text continued, p. 67.)

Table 4-1. Correlations of Six Methods of Assessing Anxiety

				Method			
	1. BRS Rating of Anxiety	2. Psychiatrist Rating of Content	3. Psychiatrist Impression of Child	4. GASC Anxiety Scale	5. MCPS "Activity Level" Scale	6. Family Story Codes	
						Expressing Anxiety	Denying Anxiety
1. BRS rating of anxiety	1.000	.036	−.107	.137	.094	.076	.351
2. Psychiatrist rating of content		1.000	.067	.251	.575*	−.029	.248
3. Psychiatrist impression of child			1.000	.349	.062	.087	−.050
4. GASC anxiety scale				1.000	−.109	−.272	.042
5. MCPS "activity level" scale					1.000	.185	−.004
6. Family story codes Expressing anxiety						1.000	.003
Denying anxiety							1.000

* p < .05, two-tailed test

Table 4-2. Correlations of Five Methods of Assessing Anger and Aggression

	1. BRS Rating		2. Psychiatrist Rating of Content	3. Psychiatrist Impression of Child	4. MCPS "Aggression" Scale	5. Family Story Codes	
	"Poor Anger control"	"Excessive Aggression"				Expressing Anxiety	Denying Anxiety
1. BRS							
"Poor anger control"	1.000						
"Excessive agression"	.551	1.000					
2. Psychiatrist rating of content	-.040	.062	1.000				
3. Psychiatrist impression of child	-.010	-.090	.893*	1.000			
4. MCPS "aggression" scale	-.453	-0.355	.215	.164	1.000		
5. Family story codes							
Expressing anxiety	-.079	.005	-.123	-.183	.396	1.000	
Denying anxiety	.311	-.205	.098	.036	-.324	-.249	1.000

Method

* p < .01, two-tailed test

Table 4-3. Correlations of Two Methods of Assessing Denial

| | *Method* | | | | |
| | 1. MCPC | | 2. Family Story Codes | | |
	Disturbance Scale	Somaticization Scale	Denying Anxiety	Denying Aggression	Denying Depression
1. MCPS					
Sleep disturbance scale	1.000	−.598	−.158	−.092	−.143
Somaticization scale		1.000	−.131	.079	−.358*
2. Family story codes					
Denying anxiety			1.000	−.068	.254
Denying aggression				1.000	−.008
Denying depression					1.000

* $p < .10$, two-tailed test

content and diagnostic impressions (Table 4-2), which are maximally similar methods, and, hence, is a "weak" finding. The two methods of measuring denial are not similar at all. There is a slight tendency for children whose story themes deny depression to not use somatic defenses (Table 4-3), but an explanation for this finding is not immediately apparent. As Table 4-4 indicates, there is a negative agreement among independent methods of measuring reality contact. Finally, there is little inter-method agreement on assessment of object relatedness and interpersonal withdrawal (Table 4-5). The single psychological construct that is measured in a similar fashion across several methods is the child's expression of sadness and depression (Table 4-6), in which the psychiatrist's ratings of pessimism and depression appear to conform appreciably with the child's thematic imagery in family stories.

Table 4-4. Correlations of Two Methods of Assessing Reality Contact

| | *Method* | |
	1. BRS Reality Contact	2. Psychiatrist Impression of Child Reality Testing
1. BRS Reality Contact	1.000	−.467
2. Psychiatrist Impression of Child Reality Testing		1.000

* $p < .10$, two-tailed test

(*Text continued, p. 70.*)

Table 4-5. Correlations of Five Methods of Assessing Object Relatedness and Interpersonal Withdrawal

Method

	1. BRS Excessive Withdrawal	2. Psychiatrist Content Isolation	3. Psychiatrist Impression Object Relatedness	4. Doll House Distance Measures				5. Family Story Codes		
				Patient to Friend	Patient to Mother	Patient to Father	Patient to Sibling	Affectionate Impulses	Hostile Impulses	Death Impulses
1. BRS excessive withdrawal	1.000									
2. Psychiatrist content isolation	.105	1.000								
3. Psychiatrist impression object relatedness	-.089	.730	1.000							
4. Doll house distance measures										
to Friend	.162	.186	.142	1.000						
to Mother	-.080	-.015	-.257	-.075	1.000					
to Father	-.558	.041	.099	-.173	.394	1.000				
to Sibling	.036	.140	.210	.125	-.083	-.137	1.000			
5. Family story codes										
Affectionate impulses	-.023	.002	-.057	-.216	-.006	.367		1.000		
Hostile impulses	.004	.136	-.062	.506*	.260	.002		-.561*	1.000	
Death imagery	.247	-.398	-.142	.003	-.193	-.234		.222		1.000

* p < .05, two-tailed test

Table 4-6. Correlations of Four Methods of Assessing Sadness and Depression

	Method					
	1. MCPS "Self Blame" Scale	2. Psychiatrist Rating of Content		3. Psychiatrist Impression of Child Depression	4. Family Story Codes	
		Sadness	Pessimism		Express Depression	Deny Depression
1. MCPS "self blame" scale	1.000					
2. Psychiatrist rating of content						
Sadness	.167	1.000				
Pessimism	−.309	.282	1.000			
3. Psychiatrist impression of child Depression	−.228	−.035	.271	1.000		
4. Family story codes						
Express depression	.159	1.53	.462	.517*	1.000	
Deny depression	−.356	−.349	.562*	.636*	.316	1.000

* $p < .05$, two-tailed test

DISREGARDING METHOD, ARE THESE CHILDREN DISTRESSED?

If one disregards the part of the ratings or scores that are due to differences in method, the question arises about whether or not these chronically and fatally ill children are acutely or severely distressed. One BRS Scale ("excessive anxiety"), three MCPS scales ("activity level", "sleep disturbance", and "somaticization"), and the GASC anxiety measure all have mean values near their respective normative means (t-test, p < .05; [31]). The child psychiatrist rated the children, on the average, as "moderately" sad or depressed, but not more so than other children who come to the clinic for psychiatric problems. It is important to note, however, that, even though the mean values of these measures are not far from the population means, the variances are quite high, often one-half to two-thirds of the possible range, which suggests that there are selected, individual children who are quite anxious or sad.

The finding that chronically and fatally ill children in this study are not, as a group, acutely or severely distressed is similar to that of other studies in this area. Although Waechter [18,25] reported high anxiety levels in the fatally ill group, only two of the fatally ill children had spoken with their parents about their disease, and, hence, the high measured anxiety levels may have been appropriate. The children in Spinetta's series [19–21] were not so acutely distressed as those in Waechter's studies, and the mean value of the anxiety measure of out-patient children is near the population mean. (For all of his groups, the mean anxiety level in the children was between the 48th percentile, not a finding of "high anxiety"). A very recent multimethod study of four groups of children with chronic disease (asthma, diabetes, cystic fibrosis, and hearing impaired) reports a parallel result [32]. Five psychological measures were used (Piers–Harris Self Concept Scale; Nowicki–Strickland Locus of Control Scale; the Junior Eysenck Personality Inventory; Missouri Children's Picture Series; and the Psychological Screening Inventory), and the chronically ill children were measured, on the average, very close to mean normative values. The present study findings could be understood in light of the fact that the nineteen subjects are relatively "healthy" at the time of measurement, all the leukemic children were in their first remission, and the chronically ill children were being managed successfully; and, finally, all children were outpatients.

DISCUSSION

This research uses many of the same methods that previous studies have used, and finds that the method of assessing distress in ill children has a great impact on the results. In contrast to Spinetta's work with a hospital room scene, this study does not support the notion that severely ill children perceive greater interpersonal distance between family members. Moreover, other measures of detachment or withdrawal fail to agree with the doll distance measures. Additionally, one notes that there is not previous work that validates the use of doll techniques in assessing withdrawal, despite the intuitive clinical appeal of the measure. In fact, one reason for the poor agreement of this method may be that there is only a small amount of research on "personal space" with children, and a recent review concluded that "children develop spatial norms which have a regular sequence with the onset of personal-space behavior at about age 12" [33]. A second reason for the poor intermethod agreement may be the fact that clinical observers characteristically have a hard time agreeing [34]. One study compared three ratings of anxiety in pediatric clinic and psychiatric clinic children, and found the highest correlation to be among the mother's and father's ratings (r = .53) [35], and the lowest being parent–child ratings. The fact that observers do not agree does not necessarily invalidate a measure, but it does indicate that multiple measures must be taken [36], which is not the usual case in this area.

An alternative explanation for the lack of agreement between methods may be that the psychological constructs may be somehow defective. It had been hypothesized initially that protest–despair–detachment is a cyclical and phasic process, and therefore had been asserted that chronically or fatally ill children could be sampled at any cross-sectional point in the disease process. If, however, the detachment and loss process is not recurrently phasic or if the children are not distressed, then certainly the methods could be unlikely to agree, or each method could capture a different part of the protest–despair–detachment process. While this may be the case, it does seem clear that the methods used here do not capture the subtleties of the protest–despair–detachment process, nor, indeed, whatever distress the child may be feeling. Indeed, this study of children in remission and other well managed children may indicate, more clearly than before, that protest–despair–detachment can be interrupted with a supportive environment.

CONCLUSIONS

The method of assessment contributes significantly to measures of distress in chronically and fatally ill children. It seems reasonable to conclude that these methods, and the constructs they bear, are not sufficiently sensitive to warrant the common use of these empirical measures. Furthermore, proposed studies, e.g., Wright, [37] should steer away from the usual application of these empirical methods.

Second, even though some children in this series are quite distressed, the group as a whole does not differ much from normative populations of well children. Thus, chronically and fatally ill children, who are not in acute physical distress and who receive appropriate outpatient support, may not be particularly disturbed. There may be a tendency to think of these children as more upset than they, in fact, are.

Finally, a methodology for empirical investigation into the upset of fatally and chronically ill children is required, apart from the usual "test-" and factorially-oriented designs used heretofore. The subtle process of detachment may be lost to straightforward methods that do not include a relationship with the child. Thus, a longitudinal, qualitative psychodynamic methodology seems most appropriate, which includes detailed observations across time. There have been important recent additions to the capacity of researchers to formulate testable psychodynamic propositions [37,38], and this type of investigation can be subtly tuned to the form and course of individual differences of children that may "wash out" in other designs. Finally, there are now available appropriate statistical treatments for the kind of study proposed here [39,40] and the type of rich relationship data described by Heinicke and Westheimer [41] and James and Joyce Robertson [42] can be used fully.

REFERENCES

1. Spitz RA: Hospitalism. Psychoanalyt Study Child 1:53–74, 1975
2. Spitz RA, Wolfe KM: Analclitic depression. Psychoanalyt Study Child 2:312–342, 1946
3. Burlingham D, Freud, A: Young Children in Wartime. London, Allen & Unwin, 1942
4. Bowlby J: Grief and mourning in infancy and early childhood. Psychoanalyt Study Child 15:9–52, 1960
5. Bowlby J: Process of Mourning. Int J Psycho-anal 42:317–340, 1961
6. Green M, Solnit AJ: Reaction to the threatened loss of a child: A vulnerable child syndrome: Pediatric management of the dying child, Part III. Pediatrics 34:58–66, 1964
7. Robertson J: Some responses of young children to loss of maternal care. Nurs Times 49:382–386, 1953
8. Solnit AJ: A study of object loss in infancy. Psychoanalyt Study Child 25:257–272, 1970
9. Bowlby J: Attachment and Loss, Vol 1, Attachment. New York, Basic Books, 1969
10. Bozeman, MF, Orbach CE, Sutherland AM: Psychological impact of cancer and its treatment, III: The adaptation of mothers to the threatened loss of their children through leukemia, Part I. Cancer 8:1–19, 1955
11. Eissler K: The Psychiatrist and the Dying Patient. New York, International Universities Press, 1955
12. Knudson AG, Natterson JM: Participation of parents in the hospital care of their fatally ill children. Pediatrics 26:482–490, 1960
13. Morrissey JR: Children's adaptation to fatal illness. Soc Work 8:81–88, 1963
14. Binger CM, Ablin AR, Fuerstein RC, Kushner JH, Zoger S, Mikkelsen D: Childhood leukemia: Emotional impact on patient and family. N Engl J Med 280:414–418, 1969
15. Easson WM: Care of the young patient who is dying. JAMA 205:203–207, 1968
16. Kubler–Ross E: The language of dying. J Child Clin Psychol 3:22–24, 1974
17. Richards AI, Schmale AH: Psychosocial conferences in medical oncology: Role in a training program. Ann Intern Med 80:541–545, 1974
18. Waechter EH: Death Anxiety in Children With Fatal Illness. Doctoral Dissertation, Stanford University, University Microfilms, Ann Arbor, Michigan, No. 69-310, 1968
19. Spinetta JJ: Death Anxiety in Leukemic Children. Doctoral Dissertation, University of Southern California, University Microfilms, Ann Arbor, Michigan, No. 72-26,056, 1972
20. Spinetta JJ, Rigler D, Karon M: Anxiety in the dying child. Pediatrics 52:841–845, 1973
21. Spinetta JJ, Maloney LJ: Death anxiety in the outpatient leukemic child. Pediatrics 56:1034–1037, 1975
22. Campbell DT, Fiske DW: Convergent and discriminant validation by the multitrait-multimethod matrix. Psychol Bull 56:81–105, 1959
23. Burks HF: Manual for Burks Behavior Rating Scales. Huntington Beach, CA, The Arden Press, 1971
24. Sarason SB, Lighthall FF, Davidson KS, Waite RR, Rasbush BK: Anxiety in Elementary School Children. New York, John Wiley & Sons, 1960
25. Waechter EH: Chilren's awareness of fatal illness. Am J Nurs 71:1168–1172, 1971

26. Sines JO, Pauker JD, Sines LK: The Missouri Children's Picture Series Manual. Iowa City, Psychological Assessment and Services, 1971
27. Mann RD: Interpersonal Styles and Group Development. New York, John Wiley & Sons, 1967
28. Tinsley JEA, Weiss DJ: Interrater reliability and agreement of subjective judgments. J Counsel Psychol 22:358–376, 1975
29. Cronbach LJ: Statistical methods applied to Rorschach scores: A review. Psychol Bull 46:383–429, 1949
30. Marsden G, Kalter N, Ericson WA: Response productivity: A methodological problem in content analysis studies in psychotherapy. J Consult Clin Psychol 42:224–230, 1974
31. Bruning JL, Kintz BL: Computational Handbook of Statistics. Glenview, IL, Scott Foresman & Co, 1968.
32. Tavormina JB, Kastner JS, Slater PM, Watt SL: Chronically ill children: A psychologically and emotionally deviant population. J Abnorm Child Psychol 4:99–110, 1976
33. Evans GW, Howard RB: Personal space. Psychol Bull 80:334–344, 1973
34. Garfield SL, Prager RA, Bergin AE: Evaluation of outcome in psychotherapy. J Consult Clin Psychol 37:307–313, 1971
35. Hafner AJ, Quast W, Speer DC, Grams A: Children's anxiety scales in relation to self, parental, and psychiatric ratings of anxiety. J Consult Psychol 28:555–558, 1964
36. Fiske DW: The shaky evidence is slowly put together. J Consult Clin Psychol 37:314–315, 1971
37. Wright L: An emotional support program for parents of dying children. J Child Clin Psychol 3:37–38, 1974
38. Malan DH, Health ES, Bacal HA, Balfour FHG: Psychodynamic changes in untreated neurotic patients. Arch Gen Psychiatr 32:110–126, 1975
39. Hersen M, Barlow DH: Single Case Experimental Designs: Strategies for Studying Behavior Change—1975. New York, Pergamon Press, 1977
40. Gottman JM, McFall RM, Barnett J: Design and analysis of research using time series. Psychol Bull 72:299–306, 1969
41. Heinicke CM, Westheimer IJ: Brief Separations. New York, International Universities Press, 1965
42. Robertson J, Robertson J: Young children in brief separation: A fresh look. Psychoanal Study Child 26:264–315, 1971

5 · Children's Understanding of Death: A Review of Three Components of a Death Concept

Mark W. Speece and Sandor B. Brent

Abstract

This review of the empirical literature on the development of the concept of death focuses on three components of that concept: irreversibility, nonfunctionality, and universality. These findings overall suggest that the majority of healthy children in modern urban-industrial societies achieve an understanding of all three components between 5 and 7 years of age. Since this is also the age at which most children make the transition from preoperational to concrete-operational thinking, some relationship between these two processes seems likely. However, attempts to validate that relationship empirically have thus far yielded ambiguous results. Possible reasons for this ambiguity are suggested.

In recent years there has been steadily increasing interest in the psychological aspects of death and dying in children. This article reviews selected aspects of the empirical literature regarding healthy children's understanding of death.* This

Preparation of this manuscript was supported in part by NIMH Research Training grant MH-14603-05 to the first author. We wish to thank Carolyn U. Shantz for her helpful comments on an earlier draft of this paper. Portions of this article we presented at the Foundation of Thanatology Symposium Children and Death, New York, June 1983. Reprinted from Child Development 55:1671–1686, 1984.

* For a discussion of dying children and their understanding of death, see Bluebond–Langner (1978) and Spinetta (1974).

literature is interesting not only for what it reveals about the development of the concept of death itself, but also for what it reveals about the difficulties one encounters in attempting to use a general theory of cognitive development like Piaget's as the basis for understanding the development of a specific abstract concept such as the concept of death.

BACKGROUND

The study of healthy children's understanding of death began in the 1930s with two investigations (Anthony, 1939, 1940, 1972; Schilder & Wechsler, 1934), followed by two more in the 1940s (Gesell & Ilg, 1946; Nagy, 1948, 1959), and one the next decade (Alexander & Adlerstein, 1958). Since that time children's understanding of death has become the focus of a rapidly increasing body of research, with eight studies reported in the 1960s, and at least 27 from 1970 to the present. Thus, to date there have been at least 40 studies in all.

Despite this substantial and growing body of information, no exhaustive review of this literature has yet appeared. Kastenbaum and Aisenbery (1972) reviewed many of the conceptual and methodological issues raised by this research. However, more than two-thirds of the studies now available have been reported since their review. Even a more recent review of Lonetto (1980) included only 13 of these 40 studies. The present paper reviews all of the available data concerning three of the most widely studied components of the "mature" concept of death: irreversibility, nonfunctionality, and universality (see Beauchamp, 1974; Kane, 1979).

DEFINITIONS

Irreversibility refers to the understanding that once a living thing dies, this physical body cannot be made alive again (e.g., Hornblum, 1978). Terms such as *death as final* (e.g., Gartley & Bernasconi, 1967), *death as irrevocable* (e.g., Childers & Wimmer, 1971), and *death as permanent* (e.g., Koocher, 1972/1973, 1973, 1974) have also been used to refer to this basic concept. The question of whether the physical body itself can come back to life after death is separate from the belief in a spiritual afterlife. In the present review we will only address the former question.

Nonfunctionality refers to the understanding that all life-defining functions cease at death. Alternate terms include *dysfunctionality* (Kane, 1975, 1979) and *cessation* (e.g., Nagy, 1948).

Universality refers to the understanding that all livings things die (e.g., Childers & Wimmer, 1971). Other terms used for this general notion include *death as an immediate possibility* (e.g., Gartley & Bernasconi, 1967), *death as a personal event* (Swain, 1973/1976, 1979), and *inevitability* (Bolduc, 1972).

RATIONALE

We decided to focus on these three components for two reasons. First, each has been a focus of more than 20 studies, and a total of 35 studies examined at least one of the three components (see Table 5-1).* Thus, these components are the most widely investigated aspects of children's understanding of death. Second, since each is considered part of a mature adult's conceptualization of death, each has a well-defined developmental end state against which children's notions can be readily compared (Brent & Speece, Note 1).

FOCAL QUESTIONS

In reviewing this literature, we focused on four questions: 1) How was each component measured? 2) How do young children view death before they achieve a mature understanding of the component? 3) At what age do the majority of children appear to achieve such a "mature" understanding? and 4) Is the understanding of each component related to a child's overall level of cognitive development?

POPULATION CHARACTERISTICS

With the exception of age, sample size, and gender, this literature is strikingly incomplete in its reporting of the demographic characteristics of the populations investigated. Despite this scarcity of information, these data appear to represent primarily white, urban, middle-class children of average or above intelligence. There are, however, several clear exceptions: Zweig (1976/1977) studied mostly lower-class black children. Orbach and Glaubman (1978, 1979) also studied lower-class children; Sternlicht (1980) studied retarded individuals; Bolduc (1972) studied only females; and Hansen (1972/1973), Peck (1966), Portz (1964/1965), and Safier (1964) studied only males.

Although these studies included subjects from 2 to 20 years of age, about half of the studies examined ages 5 through 12, while children younger than 5 and older than 12 have received considerably less attention (see Table 5-1).

METHODOLOGY

Let us turn next to the methods used in these studies. All but four studies used interviews (many were not standardized) with children as their primary source of data. The four exceptions are Anthony (1972), who had children define the word "dead"; Bolduc (1972), who had them write an essay about what death meant to them; Pitcher and Prelinger (1963), who had them write stories and then analyzed the story themes (some children wrote about death spontaneously); and Zweig

---

* The remaining five studies did not examine any of the components and are not included in this review (Alexander & Adlerstein, 1958; Koocher, O'Malley, Foster & Gogan, 1976; Menig–Peterson & McCabe, 1977–78; Tallmer, Formanek & Tallmer, 1974; Wass & Scott, 1978). Two additional studies (Reilly, Hasazi, & Bond, 1983; Walco, 1982) reported since the completion of this review are also not included.

(1976/1977), who gave children a written questionnaire concerning their understanding of and attitudes toward death.

Some of the investigators who used interviews also used other techniques as well. These included drawings (Childers & Wimmer, 1971; Lonetto, 1980; Nagy, 1948), descriptions of death-related pictures (Schilder & Wechsler, 1934; Steiner, 1965), written compositions (Childers & Wimmer, 1971; Nagy, 1948), spontaneous play (Rochlin, 1967), directed play (Hansen, 1972/1973; Weininger, 1979) and nonverbal tasks (Hornblum, 1978). Because most of these additional techniques involve some methodological difficulties, the results we report here are based primarily on information gained from interviews.

Specific Questions*

The specific interview questions used to elicit information regarding each component varied somewhat among these studies. We will consider the components one at a time.

IRREVERSIBILITY

Of the 21 studies that provided their specific questions, 13 used a variation of "Can a dead person come back to life?" Of the remaining seven, three (Koocher, 1973; Sternlicht, 1980; Weininger, 1979) asked the question, "How can you make dead things come back to life?"; two (Lonetto, 1980; Steiner, 1965) simply asked about what happens after death; one (Nagy, 1948) asked the general question, "What is death?";[†] and one (Beauchamp, 1974) asked a series of questions that focused on whether children thought specific actions (e.g., giving medicine, magic words) could bring things back to life.

NONFUNCTIONALITY

Of the 15 studies that provided their specific questions, 12 asked a variation of "Can a dead person do X?" where X was some specific life-defining function. However, those 12 studies showed considerable variability in the types and number of life-defining functions they each used to concretize the notion of nonfunctionality. The functions included moving, growing, eating, heart beating, knowing, hearing, feeling, seeing, thinking, dreaming, and talking. For example,

(*Text continued, p. 80.*)

---

* Seven studies failed to provide the specific questions for some or all of the components (Gesell & Ilg, 1946; Kane, 1979; Melear, 1973; Safier, 1964; Schidler & Wechsler, 1934; Swain, 1979; White, Elsom & Prawat, 1978). Kane (1979), Melear (1973), and White et al. (1978) are based on earlier dissertations (Kane, 1975; Melear, 1972; White 1976/1977).

† Although Nagy apparently followed this general question with probes, it is unclear whether she consistently focused her probes specifically on irreversibility. She used the same general question for nonfunctionality and universality, and it is also unclear whether she used consistent probes for them as well.

Table 5-1. Age of Acquisition

Study	Ages	Sample Size	Irreversibility*	Nonfunctionality	Universality†
Anthony, 1972	3–13	128‡	10; 60%	>11; 40%	—
Beauchamp, 1974	3, 5	90	5; 60%	—	5; ≥50%§
Blum, 1975/1976	7, 9, 12–13, 18–20	155	7; 83%	—	7; 78%
Bolduc, 1972, (pilot study)	6–11	249	10; 65%	6; 100%	10; 65%
Caustim, 1977	5–7	57	—	—	5; P, 64%; G, 57%
Childers & Wimmer, 1971	4–10	75	10; 63%	—	7; 61%
Gartley & Bernasconi, 1967	5–5 to 13	60	5.5; 100%	5.5; ≥50%	5.5; 100%
Gesell & Ilg, 1946	5–10	?350	6; ≥50%	9; ≥50%	9; ≥50%
Hansen, 1972/1973	4.6 to 5.6; 6–0; 7.6 to 8.6; 11.6 to 12.6	36	7.6; 92%	7.6; 66%	7.6; 92%§
Hornblum, 1978	4,7,10	60	7; 58% (avg. over 3 tasks)	7; 73% (avg. over 3 tasks)	7; (est) 60% to 100%‖ 7; P, 100%; G (est), 85% to 90%
Kalmbach, 1978/1979	5–11 (est, K–6)	140	6; (est) 55% to 95%	7; (est) 50% to 95%	5; (est) 70% to 100%
Kane, 1979	3–12	122	4; 58%	7; 58%	5; 64%
Koocher, 1973	6–15	75	7; (est) 63% to 100%	—	6; 91%
Lonetto, 1980	3–12	201	Cnbd	6–8; ≥50%	6–8; P, 82%; G, 91%
McIntire, Angle & Struenmpler, 1972	5–17	648	5; 80%	7; 55%	—
McLear, 1973	3–12	41	Cnbd (but 100% by 7)	Cnbd	Cnbd
Nagy, 1948	3–10	378	4; 50%	10; 78%	10; 78%

Study	Age	N			
Orbach & Glaubman, 1978	10–12	21	Cnbd*	—	—
Orbach & Glaubman, 1979	10–12	27	—	10–12; 59%	3.6; 83%
Peck, 1966	3.6 to 9.6	144	Cnbd	4.7; 63%	Cnbd
Pitcher & Prelinger, 1963	2–5	137	Cnbd	Cnbd	—
Portz, 1964/1965	3, 5, 8	90	—	Cnbd	6–8; P, 83%; G, 79%
Robinson, 1976/1978	6–8; 10–12	61	Cnbd	Cnbd	Cnbd
Rochlin, 1967	3–4	?	—	—	10; ≥50%‖
Safier, 1964	4–5, 7–8, 10–11	30	7; ≥50%	6; 100%	>8; P, ?%; 6; G, ≥50%
Schilder & Wechsler, 1934	5–15	76**	6; 71%	7; 95%	7; P, 75%; G, 55%
Steiner, 1965	4, 7, 11	60	7; 95%	—	Cnbd††
Sternlicht, 1980	11–20	14	Cnbd††	2–4; 92%	5–7; 58%
Swain, 1979	2–16	120	5–7; 88%	Cnbd	—
Townley & Thornburg, 1980	6–12	260	Cnbd*	—	—
Wass et al., 1979	10–11	403	10–11; 56%	—	—
Wass & Towry, 1980	9–12	158	>9–12; 45%	—	—
Weininger, 1979	4–9	60	>9; 44%	4; 82%	—
White et al., 1978	5–10	170	>10; 40%	>10; 43%	7–3; 67%
Zweig, 1976/1977	8–12	138‡‡	>8–12; 18%	8–12; 77%	8–12; 76%§

* In the columns for each of the components the following abbreviations will be used: "≥50%" = percentage not reported and assumed to be at least 50%; "(est)" = percentage estimated from the available data; "Cnbd" = could not be determined from information in the published report.

† When studies provided information about both personal universality and general universality the abbreviations "P" and "G" refer to each aspect.

‡ Educationally subnormals excluded (N reduced to 70).

§ Includes the universality of animal death as well.

‖ Includes the universality of animal and plant death as well.

* They confounded irreversibility with a belief in an afterlife.

** The component entries are based exclusively on a discussion of the 5–8 year-olds (N = 16).

†† Since his sample was composed entirely of retarded individuals, determination of an age of acquisition is inappropriate.

‡‡ Information is available only for the blacks in her sample (N = 115).

Steiner (1965) asked about feeling and talking, while Hansen (1972/1973) asked about moving, growing, eating, and feeling. Of the remaining three studies, both Lonetto (1980) and Orbach and Blaubman (1979) asked a general question dealing with what happens after things die, while Nagy (1948) asked the still more general question, "What is death?"

UNIVERSALTIY

Twenty studies provided the specific questions they used regarding universality. Although most of these were interested only in human death, four were also interested in animal death (Beauchamp, 1974; Hansen, 1972/1973; Zweig, 1976/1977) or animal and plant death (Hornblum, 1978). Seven of the studies concerned with human death (Beauchamp, 1974; Childers & Wimmer, 1971; Hansen, 1972/1973; Kalmbach, 1978/1979; Beck, 1966; White et al., 1978; Zweig, 1976/1977) asked about human death in general (e.g., "Does everybody die?"), five (Gartley & Bernasconi, 1967; Koocher, 1973; Rochlin, 1967; Sternlicht, 1980; Weininger, 1979) asked specifically about the child's personal death (e.g., "Will you die?"),* and six (Caustin, 1977; Hornblum, 1978; Lonetto, 1980; Robinson, 1976; Schilder & Wechsler, 1934; Steiner, 1965) asked both types of questions. With two exceptions (Blum, 1975; Nagy, 1948), these studies asked whether living things (people, animals, etc.) *would* die. Blum, on the other hand, asked, "Can you think of someone who might not die?" while Nagy asked the general question, "What is death?"

CHILDREN'S EARLY VIEWS OF DEATH

Despite the variations in methodology, these data suggest certain general conclusions concerning how children view death before they have achieved a mature understanding of the three components. In undertaking this summary it is important to bear in mind that even very young children, as young as 18 months of age, appear to have some concept of death long before they achieve the normative adult conceptualization (see Brent, 1977–78; Kastenbaum & Aisenberg, 1972; Speece, 1983).

Before Irreversibility

Before they understand irreversibility, young children often view death as temporary and reversible. For these children dead things can become alive again spontaneously (Nagy, 1948), as the result of medical intervention (Beauchamp, 1974; Hansen, 1972/1973; Kane, 1979; Lonetto, 1980; Rochlin, 1967; Steiner, 1965; Stermlicht, 1980; Weininger, 1979), after eating (Hansen, 1972/1973; Koocher, 1973), after drinking water (Beauchamp, 1974; Hansen, 1972/1973; Sternlicht, 1980), by magic (Schilder & Wechsler, 1934), through wishful thinking (Hansen,

---

* Apparently these researchers assumed that children would be most likely to think that they themselves would not die. That assumption will be examined later.

1972/1973), and by praying (Sternlicht, 1980; Weininger, 1979). These young children tend to see death as sleep (from which you wake up) or like a trip (from which you return). In addition, the fact that a large number of children mention medical intervention (e.g., going to a hospital, getting a shot) as a method for reversing death also suggests that some children see death as similar to being sick.

However, a cautionary note is needed here. Although there are examples in which children clearly show their belief in a reversible death with statements that dead things will "come alive again" (e.g., Beauchamp, 1974), the conclusion that young children view death as reversible comes primarily from affirmative responses to questions such as "Can dead things come back to life?" The concept of reversibility logically implies that the same referent is alternately in one and then in another of two distinct states at different times, that is, that dead and alive are mutually exclusive states of being. However, only two researchers—Kalmbach (1978/1979) and Steiner (1965)—attempted to first determine whether children did in fact view "dead" as distinct from "alive." All of the others seemed to have assumed that children already saw life and death as distinct states.* For this reason it is possible that some of the affirmative responses to the typical question, "Can dead things come back to life?" resulted from a belief that some things can be both dead *and* alive at the same time. Thus, the conclusion that young children view death as reversible may credit some children with more knowledge (i.e., sufficiently differentiated concepts of alive and dead) than they actually possess (see Brent & Speece, Note 1).

Before Nonfunctionality

Before children understand that death involves a cessation of all life-defining functions (nonfunctionality) they often answer "Yes" to such questions as "Can a dead person feel?" and "If someone died, could he still breathe?" Thus, it appears that for many of these children death is viewed as somewhat different from life in that either dead things do not possess all of the functional capabilities of alive things, or dead things have diminished capabilities for specific functions (e.g., feeling, moving) they asked about. Kane (1979) suggested that children realize certain functions cease at death before they realize that other functions cease. She separated cognitive aspects of functioning (e.g., knowing, feeling) from other, noncognitive aspects (e.g., heart beating, breathing) and investigated them separately. She found that children were more likely to attribute continued cognitive functions to dead things than they were the other type of functioning. Kane explained her findings in terms of the differential visibility of these two types of functioning: Children first understand the cessation of the most visible aspects of nonfunctioning such as eating and speaking and only later recognize that more subtle, cognitive aspects such as dreaming and knowing also end with death.

---

* Few studies have examined the concepts of alive and dead in the same sample of children. Six that did are reviewed here (Caustin, 1977; Hornblum, 1978; Kalmbach, 1978/1979; Orbach & Glaubman, 1979; Safier, 1964; Steiner, 1965).

Here again, most interpretations of these findings assume that these children already understand the states of alive and dead as mutually exclusive, and therefore that their principal difficulty in understanding nonfunctionality is their uncertainty about which functions continue after death. However, as we already noted, for at least some children dead and alive may not be viewed as distinct states. Therefore, concluding that young children think dead things are functional may credit some of them with more differentiated concepts of alive and dead than they actually possess (Brent & Speece, Note 1).

Before Universality

Before children understand that death is universal and inevitable, they often believe that there are certain actions that can be taken to avoid death, or that certain "special" classes of people do not die. For example, Nagy (1959) reported that young children think death can be avoided by being clever or lucky. People thought to be excluded from dying included teachers (Beauchamp, 1974), the child's immediate family (Swain, 1979), children in general (Peck, 1966; Robinson, 1976/1978), and the individual children themselves (Hornblum, 1978).

Schilder and Wechsler's data (1934) suggest that children understand that others will die before they understand that they themselves will die. This idea is also implied in those studies that only asked whether the child itself would die, using such questions as "Will you die?" Without a doubt most children understand that *some* people die before they understand that they themselves will die. However, the suggestion that children extend the possibility of death to *all* other humans prior to extending it to themselves has not been supported. Six studies (Caustin, 1977; Hornblum, 1978; Lonetto, 1980; Peck, 1966; Robinson, 1976/1978; Steiner, 1965) indicate that very few children exclude only themselves from death. Thus, if children exclude themselves from dying they usually exclude other individuals as well.

An additional point is worth noting. Many children who apparently understand the inevitability of their own deaths have a tendency to say that their death will occur only in the remote future when they get old (e.g., Lonetto, 1980). For many children this statement will turn out to be true. However, apparently these children do not seem able to grasp the possibility that their own deaths can occur at any time.

AGE OF ACQUISITION

Having examined how children view death before they have achieved a mature conceptualization of the three components, let us now turn to the age at which each component is typically acquired.

DEFINITION OF AGE OF ACQUISITION

Two problems arise in the attempt to determine the age at which children can be said to understand a component. First, the studies varied widely in the statistical criteria which they used to determine that age. For example, Hansen (1972/1973) appears to have used at least a 60% criterion, Hornblum (1978) a 75% criterion, and Childers and Wimmer (1971) close to a 100% criterion. In other words, they required, respectively, that 60%, 75%, or 100% of the children of a given age demonstrate an "adult" understanding of a component in order to specify a particular age as the age of acquisition. Thus, a common criterion was necessary in order to meaningfully compare the results of these studies. Second, five studies (Beauchamp, 1974; Gartley & Bernasconi, 1967; Gesell & Ilg, 1946; Safier, 1964; Schilder & Wechsler, 1934) did not indicate their criterion for the age of acquisition they reported, and their published data did not allow us to determine the percentage of children who understood each component. Therefore, for these studies we made the conservative assumption that at least 50% of the children at the age given by the author had achieved that understanding. In order to deal with these two problems, we settled on a simple-majority criterion—the age at which at least 50% of the children of a given age showed an adequate understanding of a given component.

Table 5-1 lists the ages studied, the sample size, and the age of acquisition for each component, as well as the actual percentage of children demonstrating an understanding of each component at the indicated age. For example, the entry for Anthony (1972) under irreversibility is "10; 60%." This means that 60% of the 10-year-olds in this study understood this component. By our 50% criterion, these data indicate that the age of acquisition for irreversibility is age 10. On the other hand, only 40% of the 11-year-olds in this study understood nonfunctionality. Since this was the oldest group in this study, we interpret these data as indicating that the age of acquisition for this component must be older than 11 years of age. Thus, the entry for Anthony (1972) for nonfunctionality is ">11; 40%." Table 5-1 also shows that Anthony did not investigate universality.

Most of the ages and percentages shown in Table 5-1 were derived directly from data or statements published by the authors in their reports. There were, however, two additional problems in six studies that resulted in estimated ages of acquisition. First, Anthony (1972), Bolduc (1972), and Nagy (1948) each reported a developmental sequence for children's understanding of death. Therefore, in order to compare their results with those of the other studies, we had to identify the particular level of their sequences at which children were said to understand the component of interest. We then determined the percentage of children of each yearly age who had attained that level. Finally, we selected the youngest age where at least 50% of children had achieved that level of understanding. Second, some of the data presented by Hornblum (1978), Kalmbach (1978/1979), and Koocher (1973) did not permit us to determine the exact percentage of children who understood a component. In these cases we estimated the percentage of children understanding each component.*

---

* In making these estimates we made the tenable assumption that the proportion of children who understand each component will increase with advancing age. Details of the procedure used in making these estimates are available from the authors.

In addition to these estimates, six additional studies did not provide sufficient information for us to even estimate an age of acquisition for at least one component (Lonetto, 1980; Melear, 1973; Pitcher & Prelinger, 1963; Portz, 1964/1965; Rochlin, 1967; Townley & Thornburg, 1980). Finally, because Orbach and Glaubman (1978) confounded the irreversibility of physical death with belief in an afterlife, we could not determine the percentage of children who understood irreversibility alone, as we have defined it; and since Sternlicht (1980) only studied retarded individuals, determination of an age of acquisition would be inappropriate.

Despite these difficulties, however, this body of data collectively yields a median and a model age of acquisition of 7 years for each component. Further, about 60% of these studies found the age of acquisition to be between 5 and 7 years of age for each component. In order to highlight the range of ages of acquisition found in the different studies, we divided them into three groups: a 4-or-younger, a 5–7, and an 8-or-older group. Table 5-2 shows the status of each study in Table 5-1 for which an age of acquisition could be determined.*

One of the problems with summarizing the data using this "scoreboard approach" in Tables 5-1 and 5-2 is the implication that all the studies are equally valid. Although the studies are clearly not equally valid, overall the findings for the age of acquisition for each component are unequivocal.

In order to provide a feel for our general conclusion, we will briefly present the study by Kane (1975, 1979). Kane studied 122 middle-class, white children aged 3 through 12 years. There were at least 10 children at each yearly age. Kane used an open-ended interview, but she did not provide her specific questions. However, she clearly focused on a number of components of a death concept, including irreversibility (which she termed irrevocability), nonfunctionality (termed dysfunctionality), and universality. Data provided in her dissertation (Kane, 1975) permit a determination of the ages of acquisition.

While only one of 10 3-year-olds understood irreversibility, 58% of the 4-year-olds (7 of 12) understood the component. Only 18% of 3- and 4-year-olds (4 of 22) and 46% of 5- and 6-year-olds (11 of 24) understood nonfunctionality, while 58% of the 7-year-olds (7 of 12) understood it. Although none of the 3-year-olds and only 42% of the 4-year-olds (5 of 12) understood universality, 64% of the 5-year-olds (7 of 11) understood it.

SEQUENCE OF ACQUISITION

In general, the sequence in which various forms of cognition are acquired plays a particularly important role in our understanding of the processes by which chil-

---

* Zweig (1976/1977) did not study children younger than 8. However, we placed her study in the 5–7 group because it seemed reasonable to assume from her data that, if they had been included, most 7-year-olds would in fact have understood nonfunctionality. We made the same assumption in interpreting Zweig's data for universality. Schilder and Waechsler's (1934) study was placed in the 8-or-older group because the universality of personal death was not understood by age 8, even though at least 50% of their 6-year-olds understood the universality of human death in general.

Table 5-2. Age of Acquisition Status for the Studies

Status	Irreversibility	Nonfunctionality	Universality
4 or younger	Kane Nagy	Peck Swain	Peck Weininger
5–7	Beauchamp Blum Gartley & Bernasconi Gesell & Ilg Hanse Hornblum Kalmbach Koocher McIntire et al. Melear Safier Schilder & Wechsler Steiner Swain	Bolduc Gartley & Bernasconi Hansen Hornblum Kalmbach Kane Lonetto McIntire et al. Schilder & Wechsler Steiner Zweig	Beauchamp Blum Caustin Childers & Wimmer Gartley & Bernasconi Hansen Hornblum Kalmbach Kane Koocher Lonetto Robinson Steiner Swain White et al. Zweig
8 or older	Anthony Bolduc Childers & Wimmer Wass et al. Wass & Towry Weininger White et al. Zweig	Anthony Gesell & Ilg Nagy Orbach & Glaubman (1979) White et al.	Bolduc Gesell & Ilg Nagy Safier Schilder & Wechsler

dren develop intellectually. In the present case, the question of sequence concerns whether the three components of the mature concept of death are acquired concurrently as a result of a more general underlying cognitive achievement, in an invariant sequence, or independently of each other. While these data cannot resolve this issue conclusively, the fact that the age range 5–7 is also the time when most children can be expected to make the transition from preoperational to concrete–operational modes of thinking (e.g., Piaget, 1976) suggests that all three components may indeed be concurrent acquisitions. We return to an examination of that possibility below.

SUMMARY AND DISCUSSION

These data suggest that (a) the majority of children achieve at least some understanding of all three components—irreversibility, nonfunctionality, and universality—and (b) all three components are understood at about the same time—between age 5 and 7. However, in addition to this strong central tendency, there is also a wide range of ages of acquisition found across these studies. This suggests that population and procedural differences among them may also play a role in determining each specific result. As we indicated earlier, so many of these studies failed to provide adequate information on their subject samples that a meaningful evaluation of the effects of population differences among them was impossible. We were thus limited to looking for procedural differences that might account for some of the differences in ages of acquisition.

The approach we took involved an examination of each 8-or-older study (see Table 5-2) for any procedure that may account for the older age of acquisition compared to the majority of studies: 1) task difficulty, 2) task specificity, and 3) leading questions. Each of these three dimensions will be discussed briefly.

TASK DIFFICULTY

Most studies only required children to make simple verbal responses. In many cases all that was required was a yes/no response to such questions as "Does everybody die?" However, Anthony's (1972) task involved definitions of the word "dead," Bolduc's (1972) an essay about death, and White et al.'s (1978) required children to logically justify their responses. Each of these three tasks appears to make considerably more nontarget demands (see Flavell, 1970, 1977) than was generally required.

TASK SPECIFICITY

The questions used by most studies requested specific information regarding the component of interest, for example, for universality the question "Does everybody die?" However, six of the 8-or-older studies (Anthony, 1972; Bolduc, 1972; Lonetto, 1980; Nagy, 1948; Orbach & Glaubman, 1979; Steiner, 1965) asked general questions that did not require children to comment on a specific component. For example, Anthony (1972) only had children define the word "dead"; Nagy (1948) only asked the general question, "What is death?" and Orbach and Glaubman (1979) only asked, "What happens to things when they die?" for nonfunctionality. These less specific tasks and questions appear better suited to measure what children of different ages spontaneously say about death (i.e., the most salient aspects) than they are at tapping what children actually understand about each specific component.

LEADING QUESTIONS

The wording of several questions used by some of the 8-or-older studies may have led some children to deny the relevance of a particular component that they would otherwise have endorsed as being an essential characteristic of death. This appears to be the case for Wass, Guenther, and Towry (1979) and Wass and Towry (1980), who asked, "Can dead people and animals ever come back to life?" and for Zweig (1976/1977), who had children respond to the statement, "When a person dies he can never come back to life." In these cases the words "ever" and "never" may have suggested to some children the possibility of exceptions to the general irreversibility of death.*

These three procedural differences account for approximately two-thirds of the 8-or-older studies. However, this a posteriori analysis also yields several inconsistencies. For example, while White et al.'s (1978) use of more difficult task may account for the 8-or-older age of acquisition for both irreversibility and nonfunctionality, it cannot at the same time account for the 7-year age of acquisition of universality. Clearly, further research is needed to validate our suggestions.

Thus far we have focused primarily on the age at which children typically appear to understand each component of the concept of death. Age has traditionally been interesting as a developmental variable because it is presumed to provide a useful index of overall physical and psychological maturity. However, we turn next to a psychologically more interesting variable—the effects of cognitive development on children's understanding of each component.

COGNITIVE DEVELOPMENT

Children's understanding of death does not exist in isolation from other developments taking place in their cognitive life in general. It is reasonable to assume that a child's conceptualization of death will vary with his or her overall level of cognitive development. Indeed, Kastenbaum (1967), among others, has held that children's understanding of death cannot be fully understood without a full appreciation of their cognitive development. It is, therefore, not surprising to find that after age, cognitive development is the variable that has been studied most often. Twelve studies (Anthony, 1972; Blum, 1975/1976; Hansen, 1972/1973; Hornblum, 1978; Kalmbach, 1978/1979; Kane, 1979; Koocher, 1973; Robinson, 1976/1978; Safier, 1964; Steiner, 1965; Townley & Thornburg, 1980; White et al., 1978) suggested a relationship between cognitive development and the understanding of death. All used a Piagetian approach to cognitive development.† Let us now examine them in more detail.

---

* Children's understanding of irreversibility may be further confused by the fact that all children are exposed to many stories about presumedly dead people subsequently coming back to life. Such stories occur in both traditional religious contexts (e.g., the resurrection of Jesus) and in news accounts of certain contemporary deaths in which a person who appears to be dead is subsequently revived. Adults frequently interpret these contemporary instances of reversibility as merely reflecting the inadequacy of our current legal–medical definitions of death. These instances are rationalized by assuming that such people were not really dead. They were just thought to be dead because we have not yet achieved precise enough scientific criterion for when living beings are in fact dead. However, many children (and many adults as well) may interpret these same instances as bona fide exceptions to the general irreversibility of death (see Moody, 1975, 1977).

† Piaget himself never specifically studied the development of children's understanding of death. He appears to have only mentioned the subject of death once (Piaget, 1959, p. 178). Here he suggested that children's discovery of, puzzlement over, and questions about death are an impetus for the development of an understanding of physical causality.

Anthony (1972), Kane (1979), Robinson (1976/1978), Safier (1964), and Steiner (1965) all concluded that the development of an understanding of death parallels Piaget's (e.g., 1976) sequence of stages for cognitive development at a macroscopic level. They did not, however, explicate at a microscopic level the specific ways in which children's ability to conceptualize death is related to the different modes of cognitive functioning associated with each Piagetian stage. In addition, while they drew logical parallels between children's conceptions of death and their general cognitive development, they did not examine those parallels empirically. Seven others (Blum, 1975/1976; Hansen, 1972/1973; Hornblum, 1978; Kalmbach, 1978/1979; Koocher, 1973; Townley & Thornburg, 1980; White et al., 1978) have been somewhat more explicit in specifying those logical relationships at a microscopic level and have also examined those relationships empirically by comparing children at different Piagetian levels. The specific cognitive achievements that have been suggested as essential for understanding these components include classification abilities (Hansen, 1972/1973), the ability to focus on transformations as well as on states (Hansen, 1972/1973), a linear notion of time (Hansen, 1972/1973; Hornblum, 1978), the ability to perform reversible operations (Hansen, 1972/1973, Hornblum, 1978; Kalmbach, 1978/1979; Townley & Thornburg, 1980), those reciprocity skills that enable children to learn from the experience of others (Blum, 1975/1976; Koocher 1973), increased objectivity and decreased egocentrism (Blum, 1975/1976; Hansen, 1972/1973; Hornblum, 1978; Townley & Thornburg, 1980), and the universal application of rules (White et al., 1978). Although these authors identified these specific achievements, their rationale for doing so was not always clear.

Since preoperational children by definition lack all of these specific cognitive abilities, they should be unable to understand any of the three components. On the other hand, since within Piaget's system these abilities are achieved with the advent of concrete operations, children who have achieved that stage should then be able to understand all three components. All of these authors except White et al. (1978) concur with that conclusion. White et al., however, took a different approach by suggesting that, while an understanding of universality should be related to the advent of concrete–operational thinking, an understanding of irreversibility and nonfunctionality should be unrelated to cognitive development. However, the basis for this suggestion is unclear from their presentation.

Because the general cognitive abilities thought to be prerequisite for understanding these components are achieved only during the concrete–operational period, the comparison between preoperational and concrete–operational children is particularly interesting. Five of the seven studies that compared children at different cognitive developmental levels differentiated preoperational and concrete–operational children directly through the use of classical Piagetian conservation tasks (Hornblum, 1978; Kalmbach, 1978/1979; Koocher, 1973; Townley & Thornburg, 1980; White et al., 1978). One of these, Hornblum (1978), also used Piagetian time-concept tasks to assess the children's level of cognitive development independently of their conservation performance. The remaining two studies (Blum, 1975/1976; Hansen, 1972/1973) did not independently determine the children's actual level of cognitive development, but rather inferred that level from the children's chronological age. Let us consider each of these three assessment procedures separately.

STUDIES USING CONSERVATION TASKS

The results of the studies using conservation tasks have yielded ambiguous results.

IRREVERSIBILITY

Three studies, Hornblum (1978), Kalmbach (1978/1979), and Koocher (1973), found a relationship between the understanding of irreversibility and general cognitive development, while two, Townley and Thornburg (1980) and White et al. (1978) did not. Further, Kalmbach (1978/1979) found that 73% and Koocher (1973) found that 63% of preoperational children understood irreversibility. This suggests that preoperational thinking alone may be sufficient for understanding irreversibility. On the other hand, White et al. (1978) found that only 33% of concrete–operational children understood irreversibility. This suggests that concrete–operational thinking by itself may not be sufficient for understanding this component.

NONFUNCTIONALITY

Three studies, Kalmbach (1978/1979), Townley and Thornburg (1980), and White et al. (1978) found no relationship between the understanding of nonfunctionality and cognitive development. Further, Kalmbach (1978/1979) found that 84% of preoperational children understood nonfunctionality, suggesting that preoperational thought may be sufficient for understanding this component. On the other hand, White et al. (1978) found that only 32% of concrete–operational children understood nonfunctionality, suggesting that concrete–operational thought by itself is not sufficient for understanding nonfunctionality.

UNIVERSALITY

Two studies, Hornblum (1978) and White et al. (1978) found a relationship between children's understanding of universality and their level of cognitive development, while Kalmbach (1978/1979) found no such relationship. Further, Kalmbach (1978/1979) and Koocher (1973) found that over two-thirds of their preoperational children understood this component, suggesting that preoperational thought may be sufficient for understanding universality. On the other hand, White et al. (1978) found that only 38% of preoperational children understood universality. This suggests that concrete–operational thinking may be necessary for an understanding of this component.

The variability in these results, represented most clearly and consistently in comparing the studies conducted by Kalmbach (1978/1979) and White et al. (1978) may be due in part to differences in the assessment of an understanding of each component. Specifically, White et al. used a procedure that we presented as being more difficult than most since it required that children logically justify their responses. Thus, even if Kalmbach and White et al. assessed level of cognitive development identically (which is not the case), White et al. would be expected to find fewer children of a given cognitive level understanding each component. Still further, there were also clear differences in the procedures used by different reseachers to assess conservation. These procedures varied along a least four dimensions: 1) the specific tasks employed (e.g., number, area, volume), 2) the number of trials per task, 3) whether the criterion for achievement of conservation was based on correct judgments alone or whether an adequate explanation for that judgment was also required, and 4) the overall number of correct judgments (and explanations) required for a child to be classified as a conserver.* In addition, a definitive statement of the relationship between general cognitive development and children's conceptualization of death cannot be made since cognitive development was in every instance confounded with age. Hornblum (1978), the only investigator to have been concerned with this issue, found that when she partialed out age effects, cognitive development was no longer related to an understanding of any of the components.

TIME–CONCEPT TASKS

Hornblum (1978) also assessed the children's level of cognitive development independently of conservation by using Piagetian time–concept tasks (Piaget, 1969). She argued that children's ability to understand the irreversibility of death should be related to their conceptualization of time, since during the course of their development they shift from a cyclical notion of time, typical of preoperational thought, to a linear notion of time, achieved during concrete operations. She described an operational notion of time as understanding time as linear and continuous, and being able to understand and integrate ideas of temporal succession, duration, and simultaneity (nonsuccession and nonduration). Here Hornblum took the achievement of an operational notion of time to be indicative of concrete–operational thinking.

Hornblum found that children who had achieved an operational notion of time were more likely than nonoperational children to understand both irreversibility and nonfunctionality. However, since at least 40% of children who had not yet achieved an operational notion of time also understood both components, she concluded that such an operational notion of time was not necessary for the understanding of both components. Furthermore, here again, when Hornblum partialed out the effects of age, the relationship between children's concepts of time and their understanding of both irreversibility and nonfunctionality no longer held.

STUDIES THAT ASSUME CHILDREN'S LEVEL OF COGNITIVE DEVELOPMENT

Blum (1975/1976) found that 83% and 78% of 7-year-olds (his youngest children, and presumed by him to be at the level of concrete operations) understood irre-

---

* While it is beyond the scope of the present paper to discuss this issue further, the interested reader is directed to Uzgiris (1968) for some of the issues in the assessment of conservation, and to Flavell (1970 and 1977, especially chapter 7) for the assessment of concepts in general.

versibility and universality, respectively. He therefore concluded that the level of concrete–operational thought is sufficient for understanding both of these components. However, there is the possibility that younger children (presumedly pre-operational) also understood those components.

Hansen (1972/1973) found that irreversibility, nonfunctionality, and universality were understood by 92%, 92%, and 66%, respectively, of her children aged 7–6 to 8–6. Since this age group was presumed to have already achieved concrete operations, she concluded that this level of thought was sufficient for understanding all three components. Hansen studied younger children as well, but we could not determine the actual percentage of children understanding each of the components since she did not ask all of the younger children about these components.

DISCUSSION

Several investigators, and Hansen (1972/1973) in particular, presented a logical rationale for expecting that a mature understanding of each component would be achieved with the advent of concrete–operational thinking. However, those empirical studies that specifically looked for a relationship between children's cognitive development and their conceptualization of death have yielded mixed results. And the results of even those investigations that reported such a relationship are ambiguous, since age was confounded with level of cognitive development in every case.

The evidence concerning the level of cognitive development (if any) that is necessary and/or sufficient for such an understanding is also ambiguous. This ambiguity may be due in part to differences in the subject populations investigated in different studies, and in part to differences in the procedures used to assess both the children's understanding of each component and those used to assess the level of cognitive development of the children.

At a more theoretical level, the relationship these authors inferred between the cognitive operations associated with each Piagetian stage and the logical operations necessary to understand each component, as well as the means used to assess the children's level of cognitive development, may reflect an overreliance on Piagetian stages as unified structure (what Piaget termed *structured d'ensembles*). If, however, it is the case that Piaget's stages are not the unified structures, as is generally believed (see Flavell, 1977), then such an inquiry as we described may be misdirected. In that case the results of even those studies that found a relationship between cognitive development and the understanding of death may be limited to the achievement of a specific ability, such as conservation ability, or time–concept ability, rather than to the achievement of concrete operations in general.

A still broader theoretical problem concerns the difficulty one encounters in attempting to determine the specific implications of Piaget's general theory of cognitive development for the development of specific abstract concepts such as the concept of death (see Bibace & Walsh, 1979). To be sure, the relationships that various authors have inferred between children's cognitive development and their understanding of each component are generally consistent with Piagetian theory. Despite this general consistency, however, they still lack sufficient specificity to allow us to understand why the achievement of a particular Piagetian stage is of necessity a prerequisite for the achievement of a particular level of understanding of a concept such as death. What is missing in these formulations is a detailed description of the specific cognitive abilities that are logically implicit in a "mature" understanding of each individual component of a death concept, and that are, therefore, logically necessary for the achievement of that understanding. Such a model is being developed (see Brent & Speece, Note 1) and hopefully will permit us to explore the development of children's understanding of death in greater detail.

However, Piagetian theory is unlikely in principle to provide a complete picture of children's conceptions of death since it emphasizes the development of context-independent reasoning abilities. It has been shown that performance on Piagetian tasks often depends on the individual's knowledge of the specific subject matter (e.g., Flavell, 1977). In the present case, differences in individual children's experience with death may affect their responses on death-concept tasks. Children's experiences with death, including their experiences with actual death as well as what they have been told about death, are probably crucial to their understanding of death.* If so, then the study of children's understanding of death, as well as that of cognitive development in general, needs a model of development that simultaneously accounts for both increases in subject-matter knowledge and the development of context-matter knowledge and the development of context-independent reasoning abilities.

CONCLUSION

The findings we have reviewed here suggested several ways in which younger children's understanding of death differs from that of older children and adults. Under at least some circumstances, young children think death is reversible; they attribute various life-defining functions to dead things; and they think that certain individuals (often including themselves) will not die. More important, the age-of-acquisition data suggested that irreversibility, nonfunctionality, and universality are understood by most children by age 7. These general findings can serve as rough guidelines concerning what children of various ages can be expected to understand about death. There are, however, at least seven general suggestions for future research regarding these specific components.

1. We need a clearer picture of the relationship between general cognitive development and an understanding of each specific component. A useful approach appears to be a more elaborate discussion of the specific cognitive prerequisites of an understanding of each, followed by an empirical investigation of those logical analyses.

2. Children's understanding of these components (and of the concept of death in general) needs to be explored in relation to other closely related concepts,

---

* The effects of children's experiences with death were not included in this review for two reasons. First, the relationship between children's death experiences and their understanding of death was rarely studied in the context of our three focal components. Second, "death experience" has been defined very narrowly in the current literature—often being limited to parent and sibling death. For a further discussion of children's death experiences, see Speece (1983).

especially the concepts of "alive," "inanimate," and "sick." It is particularly surprising that only a very few reseachers (only seven of the studies we reviewed here) examined both the concepts of alive and dead in the same sample of children.

3. Alternate tasks would aid our understanding of the components. For example, Hornblum (1978) used nonverbal tasks involving pictures to assess irreversibility. Her task had the advantage of making less demands on children's verbal abilities than is true of the typical interview techniques. While it is correct that there is no "true" measure of a concept, alternate tasks do enrich our understanding of the circumstances that enable children to express their abilities.

4. Further information regarding the order of acquisition of these components would be useful for understanding how children's concepts of death develop. At present, the most that can be said is that all three components appear to be understood at roughly the same time, for most children between 5 and 7 years.

5. The reasons for the range of ages of acquisition across studies need to be explored. In particular, the procedural differences we identified (task difficulty, task specificity, and leading questions) need to be validated as reasons for some of the variance in ages.

6. In general, the study of the three components was concerned with human death, and consequently we said very little about the findings regarding animal and plant death. Both Hornblum (1978) and Steiner (1965) also investigated plant death and suggested that irreversibility and universality were harder to understand for plant death than for human death. The explanation of their findings is not clear, but Hornblum suggested the difficulty was probably due to the fact that most children had witnessed wilted plants reviving after being watered. Thus, that event may have suggested to children that dead plants can be made alive again and/or that dead plants do not die. Future studies should examine the relationship between children's understanding of plant death and human death.

7. There is little information regarding the effects of various socioexperiential variables, such as gender, death experiences, and religious experiences, on children's developing understanding of the components. Such variables have sometimes been examined, but primarily in relation to an overall concept of death and not very often in terms of the three components. As we noted earlier, the effects of experience with death on children's understanding of death are particularly interesting.

In conclusion, the decision to subdivide the concept of death into three of its components has been useful in highlighting some general age trends regarding children's understanding of death. In particular, our review of the available data suggests that irreversibility, nonfunctionality, and universality are understood by most children by age 7.

REFERENCE NOTES

1. Brent SB, Speece MW: A microanalysis of the transition from animistic to post-animistic thinking in children's conceptualization of life and death. Paper presented at the Thirteenth Annual Symposium of the Jean Piaget Society, Philadelphia, June 1983

2. Speece MW, Brent SB: Irreversibility, nonfunctionality, and universality: Children's understanding of three components of a death concept. Paper presented at the Foundation of Thanatology Symposium Children and Death, New York, June 1983

REFERENCES

Alexander IE, Adlerstein AM: Affective responses to the concept of death in a population of children and early adolescents. J Genet Psychol 93:167–177, 1958

Anthony SA: A study of the development of the concept of death. Br J Educ Psychol 9(Abstr):276–277, 1939

Anthony S: The child's discovery of death. New York, Harcourt, Brace, 1940

Anthony S: The discovery of death in childhood and after. New York, Basic Books, 1972.

Beauchamp NW: The young child's perceptions of death. Doctoral dissertation, Purdue University, 1974. Dissertation Abstracts International 35:3288A–3289A, 1974. University Microfilms No. 74-26,684

Bibace R, Walsh ME: Developmental stages in children's conceptions of illness. In Stone GC et al (eds): Health psychology—A handbook. San Francisco, Jossey–Bass, 1979

Bluebond–Langner M: The private worlds of dying children. Princeton, Princeton University Press, 1978

Blum AH: Children's conceptions of death and an afterlife. Doctoral dissertation, SUNY at Buffalo, 1975. Dissertation Abstracts International 36:5248B, 1976. University Microfilms No. 76-9032

Bolduc JA: A developmental study of the relationship between experience of death and age and development of the concept of death. Doctoral dissertation, Columbia University, 1972. Dissertation Abstracts International 34:2758A, 1972. University Microfilms No. 72-30,311

Brent SB: Puns, metaphors, and misunderstandings in a two-year-olds conception of death. Omega 8:285–293, 1977–1978

Caustin KC: An exploration of the effect of three variables on children's concepts of aliveness. Unpublished master's thesis. Wayne State University, 1977

Childers W, Wimmer M: The concept of death in children. Child Devel 42:1299–1301, 1971

Flavell JH: Concept development. In Mussen P (ed): Carmichael's Manual of Child Psychology, vol 1. New York, John Wiley & Son, 1970

Flavell JH: Cognitive Development. Englewood Cliffs, NJ, Prentice–Hall, 1977

Gartley W, Bernasconi M: The concept of death in children. J Genet Psychol 110:71–85, 1967

Gesell A, Ilg FL: The Child from Five to Ten. New York, Harper & Brothers, 1946

Hansen Y: Development of the concept of death: Cognitive aspects. Doctoral dissertation, California School of Professional Psychology, 1972. Dissertation Abstracts International 34:853B, 1973. University Microfilms No. 73–19,640

Hornblum JN: Death concepts in childhood and their relationship to concepts of time and conservation. Doctoral dissertation, Temple University, 1978. Dissertation Abstracts International 39:2146A, 1978. University Microfilms No. 7817306

Kalmbach CA: The relationship between the cognitive level of the child and his/her conception of death. Doctoral dissertation, Florida State University, 1978. Dissertation Abstracts International 39:5518B, 1979. University Microfilms No 7909770

Kane B: Children's concepts of death. Doctoral dissertation, University of Cincinnati, 1975. Dissertation Abstracts International 36:782A, 1975. University Microfilms No 75–16,803

Kane B: Children's concepts of death. J Genet Psychol 134:141–153, 1979

Kastenbaum R: The child's understanding of death: How does it develop? In Grollman EA (ed): Explaining Death to Children. Boston, Beacon Press, 1967

Kastenbaum R, Aisenberg R: The Psychology of Death. New York, Springer, 1972

Koocher GP: Childhood, death, and cognitive development. Devel Psychol 9:369–375, 1973

Koocher GP: Talking with children about death. Am J Orthopsychiatr 44:404–411, 1974

Koocher GP, O'Malley JE, Foster D, Gogan JL: Death anxiety in normal children and adolescents. Psychiatr Clin 9:220–229, 1976

Lonetto R: Children's conceptions of death. New York, Springer, 1980

McIntire MS, Angle CR, Struempler LJ: The concept of death in Midwestern children and youth. Am J Dis Child 123:527–532, 1972

Melear JD: Children's conceptions of death. Doctoral dissertation, University of Colorado, 1972. Dissertation Abstracts International 33:919B, 1972. University Microfilms No 72-22,411

Melear JD: Children's conceptions of death. J Genet Psychol 123:359–360, 1973

Menig–Peterson C, McCabe A: Children talk about death. Omega 8:305–317, 1977–78

Moody RA Jr: Life After Life. New York, Bantam, 1975

Moody RA Jr: Reflections on Life After Life. New York, Bantam, 1977

Nagy M: The child's theories concerning death. J Genet Psychol 73:3–27, 1948

Nagy M: The child's view of death. In Feifel H (ed): The Meaning of Death. New York, McGraw–Hill, 1959

Orbach I, Glaubman H: Suicidal, aggressive, and normal children's perception of personal and impersonal death. J Clin Psychol 34:850–857, 1978

Orbach I, Glaubman H: Children's perception of death as a defensive process. J Abnorm Psychol 88:671–674, 1979

Peck R: The development of the concept of death in selected male children. Doctoral dissertation, New York University, 1966. Dissertation Abstracts International 27:1294B, 1966. University Microfilms No 66-9468

Piaget J: The Language and Thought of the Child. trans Gabain M. London, Routledge & Kegan Paul, 1959

Piaget J: The Child's Conception of Time. New York, Ballantine, 1969

Piaget J: The Psychology of Intelligence. Totowa, NJ, Littlefield, Adams, 1976

Pitcher EG, Prelinger E: Children Tell Stories: An Analysis of Fantasy. New York, International Universities Press, 1963

Portz AT: The meaning of death to children. Doctoral dissertation, University of Michigan, 1964. Dissertation Abstracts International 25:7384–7385, 1965. University Microfilms No 65-5364

Reilly TP, Hasazi JE, Bond LA: Children's conceptions of death and personal mortality. J Pediatr Psychol 8:21–31, 1983

Robinson RA: The development of a concept of death in selected groups of Mexican American and Anglo American children. Doctoral dissertation, California School of Professional Psychology, 1976. Dissertation Abstracts International 38:4478B, 1978. University Microfilms No 7732510

Rochlin G: How younger children view death and themselves. In Grollman EA (ed): Explaining Death to Children. Boston, Beacon Press, 1967

Safier GA: A study in relationships between the life and death concepts in children. J Genet Psychol 105:283–294, 1964

Schilder P, Wechsler D: The attitude of children towards death. J. Genet Psychol 45:406–451, 1934

Speece MW: Very Young Children's Experiences with and Reactions to Death. Unpublished master's theses, Wayne State University, 1983

Spinetta JJ: The dying child's awareness of death: A review. Psychol Bull 81:256–260, 1974

Steiner GL: Children's concepts of life and death: A developmental study. Doctoral dissertation, Columbia University, 1965. Dissertation Abstracts International 26:1164, 1965. University Microfilms No 65-8864

Sternlicht M: The concept of death in preoperational retarded children. J Genet Psychol 137:157–164, 1980

Swain HL: The concept of death in children. Doctoral dissertation, Marquette University, 1975. Dissertation Abstracts International 37:898A–899A, 1976. University Microfilms No 76-16,880

Swain HL: Childhood views of death. Death Educ 2:341–358, 1979

Tallmer M, Formanek R, Tallmer J: Factors influencing children's concepts of death. J Clin Child Psychol 3:17–19, 1974

Townley K, Thornburg K: Maturation of the concept of death in elementary school children. Educ Res Q 5:17–24, 1980

Uzgiris IC: Situational generality of conservation. In Sigel I, Hooper F (eds): Logical Thinking in Children. New York, Holt, Rinehart & Winston, 1968

Walco GA: Children's Concepts of Death: A Cognitive Training Study. Columbus: Ohio State University, 1982 ERIC Document Reproduction Service No ED 222 282

Wass H, Guenther ZC, Towry BJ: United States and Brazilian children's concepts of death. Death Educ 3:41–55, 1979

Wass H, Scott M: Middle school student's death concepts and concerns. Middle School J 9:10–12, 1978

Wass H, Towry BJ: Children's death concepts and ethnicity. Death Educ 4:83–87, 1980

Weininger O: Young children's concepts of dying and dead. Psychol Rep 44:395–407, 1979

White EA: A description of kindergarten through fourth grade student's conceptions of death. Doctoral dissertation, Oklahoma State University, 1976. Dissertation Abstracts International 37:5721A, 1977. University Microfilms No 77-5208

White EA, Elsom B, Prawat R: Children's conceptions of death. Child Devel 49:307–310, 1978

Zweig AR: Children's attitudes toward death. Doctoral dissertation, Northwestern University, 1976. Dissertation Abstracts International 37:4249A–4250A, 1977. University Microfilms No 77-1393

Commentary

Waechter's Influence on Literature and Research

Ida M. Martinson and Ida Marie Moore

This commentary discusses Dr. Waechter's contributions to our knowledge in the field of children and death and closes with future directions for research in the area.

In the early 1960s Eugenia Waechter had developed a major course entitled Death, Dying, and Bereavement: A Review of the Literature. The table of contents included five major substantive categories, two of which concerned the child. In the major category of the child's awareness of death, the developmental age groups of the child under 5, the school age child, and the adolescent were the divisions under which she discussed the fear of death and the death of a parent or a sibling. Her review of the literature was extremely thorough and yet today is worth reading, for either the novice or expert can gain from her critical critique of the literature. In this review, Waechter describes the evolution of the child's understanding of death from the initial and immature notion of death as departure or sleeping to the intellectual but negative conceptions of the teenager. Her description of the manifestations of death anxiety are particularly useful for those caring for children with life-threatening illness or who have experienced the death of a family member.

In the second major content area regarding the child, she speaks to the reaction of the child who is dying and the reaction of the parents to the death of a child. Again she begins with a review of the literature, and it is in this area that Dr. Waechter's work is most well known. For many years it was assumed that fatally ill children under the age of 10 are not afraid of dying, although they may be concerned with separation from parents and loved ones. This often held belief was the basis for many clinicians' practice of shielding the young patient from knowledge that he or she had a life-threatening illness. Against the odds of the time, Waechter obtained consent from the parents and worked directly with children who had a serious illness using projective techniques with pictures she developed. Waechter found that although children hospitalized with a fatal illness were not directly informed as to the nature of their illness, they demonstrated considerable preoccupation with death in fantasy, with feelings of isolation and loneliness, and with a sense of lack of control over what was happening to them. These same children told stories relating to death, and in this study loneliness, separation anxiety, and threats to body integrity constitute anxiety in relation to death. The conclusion drawn by Waechter is that the children with a chronic illness for which death was predicted were more preoccupied about their future.

Waechter also used the General Anxiety Scale for Children and found that fatally ill children had higher scores than other hospitalized and nonhospitalized children. Her research demonstrated the use of multiple techniques when investigating complex phenomena.

The pictures developed by Waechter induce thoughts of sadness and loneliness. Children under stress can easily portray their own situation and experiences in the stories they tell in response to the projective stimulus. The child's frame of reference, that is, the picture, becomes the mechanism for expression of underlying fears and concerns.

As a result of Waechter's findings, it became apparent that the dilemma of whether or not to tell the child that he has a potentially fatal illness was meaningless. Her research, then, was a major impetus for the advocation of a more open approach to treatment, one that encouraged young patients to express their concerns and answered their questions openly and honestly.

At one level, Waechter's studies attempt to more rigorously test awareness of prognosis. Her contributions provide the basis for future research in the field. The development of a theoretical model articulating the variables that influence the child's awareness of his or her prognosis would provide a more systematic framework for helping families and professionals to communicate with the child with a life-threatening illness. As a result of the more open communication patterns during the past 10 to 15 yeas, the question can again be raised whether children with life-threatening illness suffer more anxiety. Very little is known about the types of resources and social support mechanisms for helping children with a serious illness and their family to cope with stress. The diagnosis of cancer in a child affects the entire family. Research on the impact of the crisis at the level of the family, and how this influences coping effectiveness, is desperately needed. The impact the family has on the child's level of understanding of and anxiety about the illness must also be carefully examined.

Unit II

Life-Threatening Illness in Children

6 · Children's Awareness of Fatal Illness

Eugenia H. Waechter

No one's emotions are left untouched by the death of a patient, but the death of the very young is particularly poignant because it speaks silently of unfulfilled promise and destroyed hopes. To defend ourselves, we may unconsciously avoid children with fatal illness and leave them largely alone to deal with their fears and anxieties at a time when comfort, nearness, and sympathetic understanding are most important to them.

Researchers have been reporting that fatally ill children do not, as a rule, experience or express anxiety about death until after the age of 10, and they infer that until then children are not aware of what is happening to them.[1,2,3,4]

I didn't believe them.

TESTING

To test my own hypothesis I set up a study based on the assumption that, despite widespread efforts in our society to shield children with fatal illness from awareness of their diagnoses or prognoses, the anxiety of meaningful adults is conveyed to them through an altered emotional climate in their homes and through the false cheerfulness or evasiveness of those around them. The child might believe that if he expresses fear of death openly, he may risk loss of human contact. Therefore, research that relies on a child's overt expression of anxiety or fears about death, mutilation, or separation might get an incomplete or distorted picture of the actual concerns of the seriously ill child.

The subjects for my study were 64 children between the ages of 6 and 10, divided into four groups matched for age, race, social class, and family background. In one group were three children with leukemia, six with neoplastic diseases, six

Reprinted from Am J Nurs 71:1168–1172, 1971.

with cystic fibrosis, and one with progressive septic granulomatosis. In the second group were children with a chronic disease, but good prognosis; in the third, children with a brief illness. These groups were tested in the hospital. Testing of the fourth group, nonhospitalized children, was carried out at an elementary school selected after the data had been completed for the three groups of hospitalized children.

A General Anxiety Scale for Children (reproduced below) that measured concerns in many areas of living was administered to each hospitalized child.[5] Each child was also shown a set of eight pictures and asked for stories about the pictures to elicit indirect and fantasy expression of the child's concerns related to present and future body integrity. Four of the pictures were selected from the Thematic Apperception Test and four were specifically designed for the study.[6]

The General Anxiety Scale for Children

1. When you are away from home, do you worry about what might be happening at home?
2. Do you sometimes worry about whether your body is growing the way it should?
3. Are you afraid of mice and rats?
4. Do you ever worry about knowing your lessons?
5. If you were to climb a ladder, would you worry about falling off it?
6. Do you worry about whether your mother is going to get sick?
7. Do you get scared when you have to walk home alone at night?
8. Do you ever worry about what other people think of you?
9. Do you get a funny feeling when you see blood?
10. When your father is away from home, do you worry about whether he is going to come back?
11. Are you frightened by lightning and thunderstorms?
12. Do you ever worry that you won't be able to do something you want to do?
13. When you go the dentist, do you worry that he may hurt you?
14. Are you afraid of things like snakes?
15. When you are in bed at night trying to go to sleep, do you often find that you are worrying about something?
16. When you were younger, were you ever scared of anything?
17. Are you sometimes frightened when looking down from a high place?
18. Do you ever worry when you have to go to the doctor's office?
19. Do some of the stories on radio or television scare you?
20. Have you ever been afraid of getting hurt?
21. When you are home alone and someone knocks on the door, do you get a worried feeling?
22. Do you get a scary feeling when you see a dead animal?
23. Do you think you worry more than other boys and girls?
24. Do you worry that you might get hurt in some accident?
25. Has anyone ever been able to scare you?
26. Are you afraid of things like guns?
27. Without knowing why, do you sometimes get a funny feeling in your stomach?

The General Anxiety Scale for Children (*Continued*)

28. Are you afraid of being bitten or hurt by a dog?
29. Do you ever worry about something bad happening to someone you know?
30. Do you worry when you are home alone at night?
31. Are you afraid of being too near fireworks because of their exploding?
32. Do you worry that you are going to get sick?
33. Are you ever unhappy?
34. When your mother is away from home, do you worry about whether she is going to come back?
35. Are you afraid to dive into the water because you might get hurt?
36. Do you get a funny feeling when you touch something that has a real sharp edge?
37. Do you ever worry about what is going to happen?
38. Do you get scared when you have to go into a dark room?
39. Do you dislike getting in fights because you worry about getting hurt in them?
40. Do you worry about whether your father is going to get sick?
41. Have you ever had a scary dream?
42. Are you afraid of spiders?
43. Do you sometimes get the feeling that something bad is going to happen to you?
44. When you are alone in a room and you hear a strange noise, do you get a frightened feeling?
45. Do you ever worry?

Adapted from Sarason SB et al: Anxiety in Elementary School Children. New York, John Wiley & Sons, 1960)

Interviews with the parents of each hospitalized child were tape-recorded to gather data on the variables that I believed would influence the quality and quantity of fatally ill children's concerns related to death. These were the child's previous experience with death, the religious devoutness within the family, the quality of maternal warmth toward the child, and the opportunities the child had had to discuss his concerns or the nature of his illness with his parents, professional personnel, or other meaningful adults.

Analysis of the results of the General Anxiety Scale showed that the total scores of the children with fatal illness were twice as high as the scores of the other hospitalized children, supporting the prediction that, although only 2 of the 16 children had been told their prognoses, the generalized anxiety was extremely high in all cases.

Children with poor prognoses told substantially more stories relating to threat to body integrity than did the comparison groups, indicating that they were more preoccupied with death, and suggesting that the denial may not be an effective or complete defense in blocking awareness and in minimizing fear and anxiety in such an extreme situation.

Those children who were threatened with death discussed loneliness, separation, and death much more frequently in their fantasy stories, although none of them did so directly either to me or to other hospital personnel.

A most striking finding was the dichotomy between the child's degree of awareness of his prognosis, as inferred from his imaginative stories, and the parent's belief about the child's awareness. As mentioned previously, only 2 of the 16 subjects in the fatally ill group had discussed their concerns about death with their parents, yet the proportion of stories related to death told by these children was 63 percent. The children often gave the characters in the stories their own diagnoses and symptoms; they frequently depicted death in their drawings; and occasionally they would express awareness of their prognoses to persons outside their immediate family. This dichotomy suggests that knowledge is communicated to the child by the change in affect which he encounters in his total environment after the diagnosis is made and by his perceptiveness of other nonverbal clues. It also implies a deepening of isolation when the child becomes aware of the evasiveness which meets expression of his concerns.

I found a highly significant correlation between the total score on the projective test and the degree to which the child had been given an opportunity to discuss his fears and prognosis. This supports the prediction that giving the child such opportunity does not heighten death anxiety; on the contrary, understanding acceptance and conveyance of permission to discuss any aspect of his illness may decrease feelings of isolation, alienation, and the sense that his illness is too terrible to discuss completely.

The degree of awareness, as influenced by the opportunities the child has had to discuss his illness with his parents, is influenced by the immediacy of the threat of death, or the chronicity of the disease, and by the extent to which the cooperation of the child is necessary in the treatment regimen. The immediacy to parents of the threat of the child's death affects both the intensity of anxiety communicated to the child and the quality of his particular concerns. Children with illnesses which run a fairly rapid course are not often allowed to learn of their diagnoses (adults consider this a protective measure), whereas children with cystic fibrosis or other chronic handicapping conditions may become more aware of and knowledgeable about both their medical regimens and their ultimate prognosis.

Many parents are deeply troubled about the best procedure to follow with their child. Frank discussion with their child about the possibility of imminent death would arouse, they believe, feelings they couldn't cope with. Although my purpose in the interview with the parents was to elicit specific information, it also gave parents an opening to discuss their feelings and concerns about their child's prognosis. Many parents asked for further interviews. They needed to discuss these questions with an empathetic counselor.

The data about religious instruction and previous experience with death lacked a variability suitable for drawing conclusions about specific effects of either. Trends, however, indicated that both influences do affect the response of children with fatal illness. The religious devoutness of parents does not seem to affect the quantity of anxiety as expressed by children, but does influence the quality of their concerns and the manner in which they cope with their fears. Previous experience with death may also influence children's fantasy about their own future, depending on the manner in which they were supported during the former incidents.

Some illustrations from the data may highlight these children's awareness of their diagnoses and prognoses and their fears of the future.

One six-year-old boy in the terminal stages of leukemia had discussed his illness with his parents in terms of "tired blood." He told me the following story after looking at a picture of a woman entering a room with her face in her hands:

This is about a woman. She's somebody's mother. She's crying because her son was in the hospital, and he died. He had leukemia. He finally had a heart attack. It just happened . . . he died. Then they took him away to a cemetery to bury him, and his soul went up to heaven.

The woman is crying. But she forgets about it when she goes to bed. Because she relaxes and her brain relaxes. She's very sad. But she sees her little boy again when she goes up to heaven. She's looking forward to that. She won't find anybody else in heaven—just her little boy that she knows.

This story illustrates this boy's awareness of the present and probable future, the influence of religious instruction on his fantasy and ways of dealing with his concerns, and the quality of loneliness and separation he is experiencing. His sense of helplessness to alter events and certainty about an inevitable future are apparent.

One eight-year-old girl with cystic fibrosis told the following story after examining a picture of a small child in bed with a nurse standing nearby:

One girl was reading a book in the hospital. The nurse was over by the bed. The girl's name was Becky. She had the bad coughing. She had trouble with her lungs. She had lung congestion. The nurse is looking at her chart. Becky is thinking they're going to do an operation. Becky is only 8 years old. She thinks they're going to hurt her and she doesn't want it. And they did give the operation. They gave her a sleeping shot. She didn't like shots. The same nurse always came in, because she knew what to do. Becky died. Then her mother came to see her and they told her she died. But the mother didn't like to hear that.

This story illustrates further the identification which was apparent as the children viewed the pictures, and in this case, the child's projection of her feelings onto the mother. In many instances, though the clues were purposely vague, the children attributed their own diagnoses and symptoms to the characters in their story and thus communicated their concerns and fears. Again, a sense of helplessness is apparent in this story—of inability to alter events, fear of mutilation and pain, certainty about an inevitable future, sadness and separation, yet reliance on those in her environment as giving the only assistance available to her.

Some comments in the stories not only indicated the helplessness a child may feel, but also reflected the view of an environment which is nonsupportive and in some occasions actively hostile, punishing, and impeding anxiety reduction and recovery of a sense of body integrity. A seven-year-old boy with cystic fibrosis commented in a story:

The little boy had to stay in the hospital because the doctor wanted it. He got a shot in the back; a big needle. He was scared of shots, and didn't want it. And the doctor did it hard. His lungs are gone—he can't breathe. His lungs got worse and he didn't get well. He died and he was buried with a big shovel.

These statements also communicate the child's fear, his perspective regarding treatment procedures, his sensing that body integrity and intactness cannot be regained, and his feeling of incompleteness in body image. Despondency regarding the future is poignant, and loneliness is apparent in the concluding sentence.

In other stories, this boy made statements such as, "They (hospital personnel) put a tent on him and freeze him, too." "The nurse turned off the lights and the door was closed, and he was lonesome and scared." "The little boy's very sick—he's mad too, because he wanted to go home." Statements like these illustrate some children's real concern about what they see as unsupportiveness in an environment they are incapable of escaping. They may not appreciate the therapeutic intent of hospital personnel and are preoccupied with fear, loneliness, and anger. Other statements this boy made, such as, "The boy is thinking he hopes he gets well—he's thinking he might not get well and die," highlight very real anxiety about nonbeing, though he had never discussed this overtly with anyone. When coupled with the loneliness he also expressed, it is possible to imagine his fear that he might die in an alien and hostile environment, separated from all those who care about him.

The sense of loneliness is accentuated because of the young child's sense of time as stretching interminably between parental visits. One six-year-old girl commented, "She has to be in the hospital for long days and never gets to see her Mommy and Daddy. She's very lonesome." She also said in one of her stories that the child character "got sick by not coughing up the mucus," which tells us not only that she has received instruction about her condition (cystic fibrosis), but also that young children often assume responsibility for the causality of their illness whether warranted or unwarranted and may feel guilt in addition to their many fears.

Strong feelings of anger and hostility may also accompany the loneliness associated with the question, "Why did this have to happen?" And these feelings may be accentuated by sensed prohibitions against revealing suspicion or knowledge of the diagnosis. An eight-year-old girl who had very recently been diagnosed as having a malignant tumor of the femur and whose mother was determined that she should never be told the diagnosis, nevertheless indicated preoccupation with death in all eight of her stories, angrily concluding almost every story with the death of the main character and remarking, "And nobody cares—not even her mother!" Another story ended with the statement, "She was very lonesome before she died, because nobody cared." Such statements give us insight into the manner in which evasiveness or uneasy cheerfulness may be interpreted by children. That this girl was aware of the meaning of the alterations in the emotional climate surrounding her can be seen in this story:

She's in the hospital, and the doctor is talking to her mother and father. She's sick—she's got cancer. She's very, very sick. She's thinking she wishes she could go home. She had an operation at the hospital, but she didn't want it because she wanted to get out of the hospital. This little girl dies—she doesn't get better. Poor little girl. This girl at the hospital —she has cancer. Her hip is swollen and her bone's broken. This little girl in the picture died, and then they buried her. And then she went up to heaven. She didn't like it there— because God wasn't there.

CONCLUSION

It seems clear that frequent denial or the protectiveness of adults may not be entirely effective in preventing children with fatal illness from experiencing anxiety or in keeping awareness of their diagnoses and probable prognoses from them. The question of whether a child should be told that his illness is fatal is meaningless; rather questions and concerns which are conscious to the child threatened with death should be dealt with in such a way that the child does not feel further isolated and alienated from his parents and other meaningful adults. There should be no curtain of silence around his most intense fears. These feelings of isolation may also be relieved by efforts designed to keep the child closer, both spatially and emotionally, to others on pediatric wards.

Support must also be made available for them during and following actual encounters with death on pediatric wards. They need support that allows introspective examination of attitudes and fears related to death in general and to the death of children in particular.

REFERENCES

1. Knudson AG, Natterson JM: Participation of parents in the hospital care of their fatally ill children. Pediatrics 26:483–490, 1960
2. Morrissey JR: Death anxiety in children with a fatal illness. In Parad HJ (ed): Crisis Intervention, pp 324–338. New York, Family Service Association of America, 1965
3. Natterson JM, Knudson AG: Observations concerning fear of death in fatally ill children and their mothers. Psychosom Med 22:456–465, 1960
4. Richmond JB, Waisman HA: Psychologic aspects of management of children with malignant disease. Am J Dis Child 89:42–47, 1955
5. Sarason SB et al: Anxiety in Elementary School Children. New York, John Wiley & Sons, 1960
6. Murray HA: Thematic Apperception Test. Cambridge, MA, Harvard University Press, 1943

7 · Children's Reactions to Fatal Illness

Eugenia H. Waechter

Recent proliferation of knowledge and progress in medical research has resulted in concerted and successful efforts toward prolongation of life in the elderly and toward preserving life in the very young. Recently, psychological research interests have also focused on the understanding of mental processes underlying the development of a concept of death, in investigating the universal fear of death and in studying the components of the grieving process.

Though the importance of providing an atmosphere which lends comfort and dignity to approaching death is generally recognized, many conflicts and uncertainties still exist related to the compassionate management of the dying person, in determining methods and content of communication with the terminally ill, and in determining the sources of comfort most important to the person undergoing this tragic and incontrovertible fact of existence.

Death in itself can be seen as an enemy to those professions dedicated to preserving and extending life. Death of the very young is particularly poignant because it implies unfulfilled promise and destroyed hopes. Thus, children with fatal illness often find themselves largely alone with their fears, anxieties and uncertainties at a time when comfort, nearness and sympathetic understanding is most important to them. Fear, isolation and fantasy can be more painful than physical death and loss of human communication may accompany and exaggerate fear and physical discomfort.

The often debated question, "Should a child be told the truth?" may be an unnecessary one. Rather, the question could be stated, "How and what do children with a fatal disease tell and reveal regarding their fears and anxieties?"

The purpose of this study was to determine whether anxiety related to death is present in the school age child despite lack of overt communication with them

Reprinted from Godin A (ed): Death and Presence. Brussels, Lumen Vitae, 1972.

related to their diagnosis and prognosis. A further aim of the study was to discover ways in which such children communicate their needs and fears.

It was felt such knowledge would be helpful to clergymen, educators, physicians, nurses and others who have the opportunity to assist dying children to traverse their final days and hours with more comfort and dignity.

RELATED RESEARCH

Few studies pertaining to the school aged child's reaction to his own imminent death have been reported in the literature.

Knudson and Natterson (1966) separated the reactions of the children they studied into three phases: Under six years of age they felt that fears of separation were paramount; from six to ten, fears related to physical injury were foremost, and not until after ten years of age were children obviously fearful of their own demise. They suggest that separation, mutilation and death fears are separate and distinctive. Similar conclusions were reached by Morrissey (1965), though relatively few of his subjects were between the ages of six to ten years.

From his clinical experience, Solnit (1963) disagrees with the above studies and observed that his young patients invariably sensed what was happening, even when deliberate attempts were made to shield them from this tragic and frightening situation. He suggests that adults are blinded to the fears of dying children because of their own anxiety. He further suggests that the aim of research should be to examine systematically how children express their knowledge. From such studies, principles, techniques and limitations of communicating with these children in a therapeutic manner can be determined.

METHODOLOGY

Subjects and Sampling Method

The subjects for the study were 64 children between the ages of six and ten years inclusive. These children were divided into four groups: 1) children with chronic disease for which death was predicted; 2) children with chronic disease with a good prognosis; 3) children with brief illness; and 4) non-hospitalized, well children. Children between groups were matched as to age, race, social class and family background. Children within the fatal group fell into four categories by diagnosis: 1) leukemia, 3 subjects; 2) neo-plastic disease, 6 subjects; 3) cystic fibrosis, 6 subjects; and 4) progressive septic granulomatosis, 1 subject.

The study was carried out while the first three groups were hospitalized for treatment or diagnosis. Following completion of the data collection from the child and his parents within the fatal group, the subject was matched according to the previously mentioned criteria with children subsequently admitted to the same hospital with chronic and brief illness. Testing of the non-hospitalized children was carried out at an elementary school selected after the data had been completed from the three hospitalized groups of children.

Instruments

PROJECTIVE TEST
A set of eight pictures was shown individually to each child and stories requested in order to elicit fantasy expression of the child's concern regarding present and future body integrity

and functioning. Four of the pictures were selected from the Thematic Apperception Test and four were specifically designed for the study. Table 7-1 presents a description of the pictures, giving code letter and source.

The stories were scored with attention to content related to threat or fear of death, body mutilation or loneliness, on the methods used in the story to cope with threat and on the problems anticipated in reduction of security. The measurement of fear was based on the same general rationale utilized in the scoring of other motives under the view that fear of bodily harm is a motive. The stories were scored independently by two judges and reliability of total score and subcategories were determined. Reconciled scores were subsequently used in analysis of data.

THE GENERAL ANXIETY SCALE FOR CHILDREN
The General Anxiety Scale for Children as designed by Sarason and associates (Sarason, Davidson, Lighthall, Waite, Ruebush, 1960) was administered to each hospitalized child in the study. Previously determined normalized scores for well children were used for comparison with the scores received by the hospitalized groups.

THE MATERNAL INTERVIEW
A tape recorded, semi-structured interview was held with the parents of each hospitalized child in the study. The purpose of the interview was to elicit information regarding the following variables deemed significant to the amount of death anxiety expressed by the child: 1) the amount of verbal interaction with the ill child as to his diagnosis and prognosis; 2) the child's previous experience with illness and death; 3) the religious training which the child had received; and 4) the warmth of the mother–child relationships.

RESULTS

Interjudge Reliability

A Spearman rank ordered correlation on total scores on the projective test (termed the *Fear Related Motivation Score*) run on a randomly selected sample of 25 percent of the total number of protocols, was found to be .903.

Percentage of agreement between the pair of judges was defined as the number of agreements on a category or subcategory divided by the sum of the frequencies with which

Table 7-1. Projective Test Pictures

Code	Description	Source
Form A	Two boys in adjoining beds	Designed for the study
Form B	Small child in hallway outside closed door to Intensive Care Unit	Designed for the study
Form C	Boy in front of mural depicting operation	TAT 8 BM
Form D	Small child in bed, nurse nearby with back turned	Designed for the study
Form E	Figure outlined in open window	TAT 14
Form F	Child in bed, parents and doctor outside door	Designed for the study
Form G	Woman entering room, hand on face	TAT 3 GF
Form H	Small child sitting in doorway of cabin	TAT 13 B

each judge scored the given category or subcategory. The percentage agreement on decisions as to whether a story contained threat was 97.77 percent. Average interjudge agreement on categories and subcategories was 89.54 percent. Interjudge reliability on ratings of the variables in the maternal interview ranged from .96 to .99 percent.

Analysis of the General Scale for Children

The score on the General Anxiety Scale for Children was computed by addition of the items to which subjects admitted a degree of concern, and was administered to all hospitalized children. The highest possible score on this test is 45. Table 7-2 presents the range, mean score and standard deviation of the four groups.

Analysis of the data indicated that the mean score on the G.A.S.C. for subjects within the fatal group was almost double that of the two comparison groups of hospitalized children and three times the score of healthy children as presented by Sarason. This finding supported the prediction that children aged six to ten years with a diagnosis for which death is predicted will express significantly more generalized anxiety than will children who do not have a poor prognosis. Insignificant differences between the scores of the remaining hospitalized groups may reflect the concern of children facing a new and strange experience for the first time, as opposed to those who have greater knowledge of the hospital environment, but with the added concern of long term limitations.

The Projective Test

Stories told by the children were analyzed and scored for type of anxiety expressed; whether of separation, mutilation or death, for patterns of adaptation to stress, for causality as viewed by the child, for obstacles in regaining body integrity as seen by the narrator, for affect expressed by the subject and for outcome of the stories. The total score, or Fear Related Motivation Score, represents the total number of categories and subcategories scored in each protocol. Table 7-3 presents the range, mean and standard deviations of the four groups:

Analysis of this data also supports the prediction that children between the ages of six and ten years with fatal illness express more anxiety specifically related to death, mutilation and loneliness than do children with a more positive prognosis. The scores of subjects with fatal illness showed considerably more variability than did any of the comparison groups. The distribution was bimodal, reflecting

Table 7-2. G.A.S.C. Scores

Group	Range	Mean	Standard Deviation	p[†]
Fatal	31–43	36.50	3.87	.01
Chronic	12–27	18.56	4.12	N.S.
Brief	12–28	19.44	4.81	N.S.
Normal		12.00*		

* From Sarason.
† Kolmogorov–Smirnov: nonparametric test between groups.

Table 7-3. Means, Standard Deviations, and Difference: Projective Test

Group	Range	Mean	Standard Deviation	p*
Fatal	33–65	53.31	10.29	.01
Chronic	5–36	17.75	7.87	N.S.
Brief	8–29	18.19	5.94	.05
Normal	1–29	11.06	8.92	

* Kolmogorov–Smirnov: Test of significance of difference.

lower scores for children with cystic fibrosis. This finding may be due to the fact that for these children, death was not as immediately imminent, and also because of more intensive supportive professional efforts directed toward their parents in the hospital in which these children were studied.

The results of further analysis to determine variability of total scores within the fatal group by diagnosis is given in Table 7-4.

A test of significance was not done because of the small numbers of subjects involved. Examination of scores for sex differences proved to be negative, as did examination for differences relating to the hospital in which the children were receiving treatment. Analysis of total scores in relation to age indicated that although the youngest children did not express as much total concern in their imaginative stories as did the older children, this difference was not marked or significant.

Each threat related story was also scored once for each category and subcategory (affect, coping responses, etc.) appearing in the story, irrespective of the number of times the subject employed the designated category. It was found that children with fatal illness told substantially more stories relating to threat to body integrity than did the three comparison groups. A Chi Square test of significance between proportions of the groups telling unrelated stories was found to be greater than .01. This finding further supports the prediction that children with fatal illness are more pre-occupied with threat to body integrity, since they did more readily perceive and utilize the clues in the pictures presented to them, thus suggesting that the defense of denial was not totally effective in blocking preception of clues of threat.

It was noted, however, that children with a diagnosis of fatal illness displayed more symptoms of stress than did subjects in the comparison groups while telling stories, as indicated by long hesitations before beginning a threat related story, delays and blocking while narrating an imaginative episode and other behavioral manifestations of tension.

Table 7-4. Analysis of Means by Diagnosis with Fatal Group

Diagnosis	No. of Subjects	Mean
Cystic fibrosis	6	48.33
Progressive septic granulomatosis	1	53.00
Cancer	6	55.50
Leukemia	3	59.00

Analysis of Threat Imagery

A story was scored for threat imagery when it contained references to death, mutilation or loneliness. It was scored as a specific threat theme when the entire tale revolved around such fears and feelings.

Previous research (Knudson and Natterson, 1960; Morrissey, 1956) has emphasized the distinctiveness of reaction of the child with fatal illness according to age, indicating that separation, mutilation and death fears were separate and distinctive. On this premise, death anxiety was found to be present mainly when the children were over ten years of age.

The rationale of the present study, however, assumes that concern with non-being may be displaced to concern with threat from without and that concern with loneliness may be an expression of concern with the ultimate separation of death. Moreover, fears of separation, intrusive procedures and pain may substitute for an underlying general apprehensiveness about survival.

The data was therefore examined to determine whether children between the ages of six and ten years were indeed predominately concerned with physical injury rather than with non-being. Table 7-5 presents the results of this analysis relating to content of threat related imagery, comparing the subjects' use of imagery by content and group.

The test of significance of differences of proportions of subjects using fear related imagery in their scorable stories indicated that the children with fatal illness used both loneliness and death imagery more frequently than all comparison groups at a significance level of .001. It does seem possible, therefore, that concern with loneliness may also be related to concern about death. Although all groups of children did show concern in fantasy expression about mutilation, it may be that threats to body intactness involving intrusion into the body are not viewed uniformly as part of death anxiety by children with fatal illness. Such children who were anticipating major surgery did express more fears of mutilation of this type, indicating that in such cases, fear of mutilation may be closely related to death anxiety in that the surgery may be in itself life threatening. Mutilation imagery may have two components for children with fatal illness: procedures involving intrusiveness into the body which are seen as anxiety relieving and body mutilation related to major surgery which is related to concern about survival.

Table 7-5. Analysis of Imagery

Group	Mean % of Subjects' Use of Imagery in Scorable Stories			Mean % of Subjects Using Imagery at least Once in Protocol		
	Separation	Mutilation	Death	Separation	Mutilation	Death
Fatal	27.73	54.62	63.03	87.50	100.00	100.00
Chronic	6.76	35.13	17.57	31.25	75.00	50.00
Brief	6.76	35.13	17.57	25.00	81.25	56.25
Normal	1.64	44.26	6.56	6.25	81.25	25.25

The analysis of data related to themes parallels that for imagery, and a comparison of proportions between groups yielded essentially the same results as that for imagery.

THE CAUSALITY OF THE THREAT

In examining the children's perception of causality of the threat in their imaginative stories, it was found that the groups with fatal illness and with brief illness spontaneously volunteered more impressions of causality. All of the children perceived the threat to proceed more often from the environment than it did from the person involved in the threat. This suggests that externalization of threat may be fairly general in children and these data do not indicate that the trend is intensified in children with a diagnosis of fatal disease.

Another indication of the child's tendency to externalize threat was thought to be the child's perception of those obstacles hindering the regaining of body integrity or in reducing threat. Children with fatal illness more often spontaneously expressed statements to the effect that the heroes in their stories met with obstacles in achieving recovery or reduction of threat to a significant degree. These blocks were frequently described in relation to the neglect, hostility or inadequacy of attending personnel. Such findings also suggest that these children expressed more depressive feelings in fantasy regarding the subjects of their imaginative stories.

WAYS TO RELIEVE THREAT

The term *adaptive maneuvers* was given to those various methods which the narrator described as used by the subject in his story to relieve threat and included: wishfulfillment, instrumental activity and general dependency on others.

Wishfulfillment was scored when a statement was made which reflected a desire for reduction of anxiety without indication of personal or environmental effort. Subjects within the fatal group made such statements more often than did subjects in comparison groups at a significance level of .001. This fantasy expression for wish for recovery would correspond to intensification of need.

Analysis of the stories for *use of instrumental activity* revealed differences between groups only in that children within the fatal group more often saw the personal efforts of the threatened individual as unsuccessful or doubtful ($p = .02$).

A notation of *dependency* was made whenever a statement occurred to the effect that the subject in the story received nurturance by someone in the environment or relied on others to reduce threat and anxiety. No differences were found between groups in this respect, indicating that most children view this as a major method of relieving internal and external stress.

Affect and Negative Anticipations

When *affect* was expressed in the story, it was noted and examined for valence (positive or negative) as well as whether it was ascribed to the threatened individual or to others. Findings indicated that it more frequently occurred to subjects with fatal illness to mention how the threatened individual felt and to report that he was pleased when the threat was removed or anxiety reduced. Children with a poor prognosis ascribed negative affective states to the threatened individual in their stories more often at a significance level of .01. Content of the affect related principally to sadness related to separation, anticipatory worry regarding possible procedures and pain and immediate fear of pain and death. It is interesting that feelings of anger were almost nonexistent in the protocols, once more underlining the submissiveness and powerlessness in the feelings of these hospitalized children.

Negative anticipations of future outcome by threatened individuals in the imaginative stories were predominantly ascribed by the children with fatal illness, as were the actual outcomes, or endings of the stories. Although more children with a poor prognosis designated a fatal outcome for the main character significantly more often ($p = .001$), this was not invariably true. Examinations of the protocols revealed definite differences between subjects with fatal illness in the consistency with which they ascribed hopeful or pessimistic outcomes. Some of the subjects pronounced death to their main characters consistently with a quality of hostility or defiance, whereas others repeatedly lifted this sentence, almost at the conclusion of the tale with minimal indications of manner of resolution of threat. It appeared that here again was expression of the quality of wish fulfillment for some subjects.

The Maternal Interview

All interviews with the parents of these subjects were rated on four variables felt to affect fear motivation, although correlations were done only within the fatal group.

1. THE AMOUNT OF RELIGIOUS INSTRUCTION

One of the hypotheses of the study predicted that the amount of religious instruction which the child had received both prior to the diagnosis and current religious activity of the family would *not* significantly decrease the amount of anxiety which the child himself expressed relative to non-being or body integrity, as measured by the G.A.S.C. and total Fear Related Motivation Score.

It was felt that non-religious subject would be more prone to use repression, speaking and thinking less about death, whereas religious subjects would more consciously speak of an after-life following death. Since the instruments utilized such expressions as an indication of preoccupation with the ending of life, it was expected that significant differences between groups would not occur.

Examination of the protocols did indeed reveal that a minimal relationship existed between religious devoutness as expressed by the parents and child, in these 16 subjects, and total anxiety scores. However, the number of subjects was small and the correlation insignificant. The majority of families in this study did profess a religious belief and acknowledged membership in an organized church body.

Examination of the individual protocols in the projective test indicated that children who had received considerable religious instruction, and whose families professed a devout reliance on religion, expressed considerably more religious themes in their imaginative stories. This did not occur among the children who belonged to non-religious families. It was also more pronounced among the children within the fatal group than among the subjects in the comparison groups. These religious themes focused on an after-life with both positive and negative affect, and appeared as a continuation of the story following the death of one of the imaginative characters. Several protocols, however, had a number of stories with main themes related to religious subjects. Elaborations of the theme included both positive affect to the effect that Heaven was a desirable place, and qualifications of negative affect with such statements as "God was not there," or that the deceased person would rather return to earth. Such statements were seen as expressions of loneliness in leaving known and beloved persons along with some subtle indications of anger that "Nobody cared, not even God."

Further review of the protocols revealed that these children generally expressed the belief that life continued subsequent to death in an altered form and suggested the efficacy of religious belief as a coping method. In none of the protocols was there a mention of Hell as an alternative destination. It appeared, therefore, that to these subjects also, death implied departure to another world, a concept which had been instilled in them by their parents and religious instructors.

Review of the taped interviews also revealed that for those parents who expressed a devout reliance on religion, there were statements that they had received considerable support and comfort, either from their personal beliefs, or more directly from religious figures. Such statements generally included expressions of belief in the helpfulness of the prayers of others for recovery or reliance on the will of God as to the future fate of their child.

Another hypothesis of the study predicted that those children within the fatal group who had experienced a death in the immediate family or who had had other significant death experiences would express more anxiety and concern about body integrity in fantasy stories. It was not possible to test this hypothesis adequately, since only one child within the fatal group had a previous intense death experience and none of the children within this group had lost a member of the immediate family. It is possible that with a larger sample and with more variability in the subject's experience, such a relationship might be found.

The quality of maternal warmth toward the subject was ascertained both from the answers to a number of specific questions and from impressions gained from the total interview, including spontaneous comments of the parents related to their relationship with their child. Although inter-judge ratings correlated highly and all efforts were made to convey a nonjudgmental attitude on the part of the interviewer, nonetheless, this area could be assumed to be more threatening to parents, both in terms of expressing negative attitudes toward their child verbally and in recognition of personal attitudes in this respect. Parents who were threatened by the loss of their children indicated more positive feelings toward them than did the parents of other hospitalized children. It was also found that where the threat of loss of the child was more imminent, parents were judged as conveying more warmth of feelings for the child. The consistently positive appraisal was also retrospective, extending throughout the entire life of the child. This suggests that a halo effect may occur, which obscures some of the reality factors for parents, both in the child's behavior and in their attitudes toward the child. Certainly, it is possible that in the anticipatory grieving process, it may be necessary for parents to repress hostile or ambivalent feelings both currently and retrospectively.

Although a correlation between the Fear Related Motivation Score on the projective test and the rating of maternal warmth was found to be insignificant, correlation with the G.A.S.C. score was found to reach the level of significance of .05. This implies that although the degree of security gained from a positive relationship with parents may not reduce specific anxiety related to the possibility of imminent death, it does affect more generalized anxiety in the direction of greater feelings of security relative to the environment in general.

2. DISCUSSING THE NATURE OF THE ILLNESS

Judgments were also made on the basis of the maternal interview regarding the opportunities the child had had to discuss the nature of his illness with parents or professional personnel. The dimension of awareness–nonawareness appeared as a continuous range both of degree of awareness on the part of the child and in the degree to which the parents permitted or engaged in discussion with their child about his illness, diagnosis and prognosis. Parents felt very strongly about this question. Some felt that their child should know as much as possible about his illness, whereas others went to great lengths to insure that the diagnosis would not be mentioned to their child by hospital personnel. Many parents felt unable to cope with the feelings which a frank discussion about the possibility of imminent death would arouse.

Only two children with fatal illness had discussed their imminent death with their parents; six had received little realistic information regarding their illness, and the remainder had been informed that their illness was temporary or trivial.

Many of the parents were deeply troubled as to the best procedure to follow in this respect, i.e., whether it would be to the best interest of their child to withhold the diagnosis, or whether it would be more helpful to him to answer questions frankly and completely. The imminence of death in time appeared to be important, along with the degree to which the cooperation of the child was important in treatment aspects. Parents of children with leukemia or other malignant conditions were reluctant to allow the child to hear the words "leukemia" or "cancer." Some parents expressed the awareness that these words continue to hold a negative and almost shameful connotation in western culture, along with the sure implication of certain death. Several parents volunteered that they wished to protect their child from the avoidance responses of their friends and acquaintances if the diagnosis became common knowledge.

Many parents asked for assistance in making the decisions of the manner in which they should deal with this problem, and others stated that although they themselves felt incapable of coping with such a discussion, they felt that the child's question should be answered by professional personnel or religious figures.

The dichotomy in the degree of awareness on the part of the child as inferred from his imaginative stories and the parent's belief as to the child's awareness was often striking. Although only two out of the 16 subjects within the fatal group had discussed their concerns about death with their parents, the percentage of death imagery in stories containing threat was found to be 63 percent. Many of the children who had not been told their diagnosis nevertheless indicated awareness of knowledge of the diagnosis or symptoms in their imaginative stories. In all of the protocols, the degree to which the characters in the story were given the subjects' personal diagnosis and symptoms was striking.

The correlation between the child's opportunity to discuss his illness, and the Fear Related Motivation Score was found to be $-.633$ which is significant at the .01 level. This finding indicated that those children with fatal illness who had a greater opportunity to discuss their fears and concerns about their future and present body integrity expressed *less* specific death anxiety. This finding supports the hypothesis that understanding acceptance or permission to discuss any aspect of his illness may decrease feelings of isolation, alienation and the sense that his illness is too terrible to discuss.

DISCUSSION

In a rapidly changing and increasingly scientifically oriented society, lengthening of the life span has been accompanied by threats of mass annihilation which is unprecedented in human history. Although death has always represented the ultimate mystery, it has now become an eventuality which can rarely be consciously faced or calmly contemplated.

A "taboo" against speaking of death has grown within this century which is transmitted to children during the socialization process, frequently resulting in an inhibition against speaking directly of concerns and fears when prolonged illness occurs.

The findings of this study indicate that despite efforts to protect children from knowledge of their prognosis, they do indicate a considerable preoccupation with death in fantasy when given the opportunity, along with feelings of loneliness and isolation and a sense of lack of control of the forces impinging on them. The dichotomy seen between the parent's perception of the child's awareness and this demonstration of anxiety on the part of the child suggests that he perceives the threat through the altered affect in his total environment and from parental anxiety communicated in non-verbal ways. It also suggests that adults may be blinded to the child's anxiety because of personal fears and concerns and a sense of helplessness related to the diagnosis. Professional personnel attending ill children may be unaware of the child's concern due to personal defenses against the anxiety stimulated by professional helplessness to alter the course of events, personal affect related to death, previous failure experiences and because the child himself rarely communicates an overt fear of death to medical and nursing staff.

This study has supported other research reports of the therapeutic effectiveness of efforts toward communication with parents undergoing this acute and chronic stress and also has supported the hypothesis that children benefit from a permission to acknowledge their fears openly and from more frank discussions with them related to their questions and concerns about their body integrity.

However, this study also suggests that many parents may feel incapable of dealing directly with the child's questions, of coping with their own anxiety raised by these questions, and may feel a need for knowledge of the methods and words to utilize which would be most supportive to the child. This again suggests that a continuing relationship with a clergyman or with professional personnel could be helpful to them in anticipation and in meeting this situation constructively. It further suggests that some parents may not have the personal resources for this type of discussion with their fatally ill child. Certainly, such parents should not be further subjected to pressures to do so. On the other hand, a sympathetic religious or professional person—clergyman, doctor, nurse or social worker—who has himself faced his own anxiety related to death could well assist both parents and child when such a need is communicated.

From this study, the dichotomy often expressed: to tell or not to tell a child that he has a fatal illness appears to be a meaningless question. Rather, it seems clear that the questions and concerns which are conscious to the child should be dealt with in such a way that the child does not feel further isolated and alienated from his parents and other meaningful adults by a curtain of silence around his most intense fears.

REFERENCES

Knudson A, Natterson J: Participation of parents in the hospital care of their fatally ill children. Pediatrics 26:482, 1960
Morrissey J: Death anxiety in children with a fatal illness. In Parod H (ed): Crisis Intervention. New York, Family Services Association of America, 1965
Sarason S, Lighthall F, Davidson K, Waite R, Ruebush B: Anxiety in Elementary School Children. New York, John Wiley & Sons, 1960
Solnit A, Green MP: The pediatric management of the dying child, Part II. The child's reaction to the fear of dying. In Solnit A, Provence S (eds): Modern Perspectives in Child Development. New York, International Universities Press, 1963

8 · Anxiety in the Dying Child

John J. Spinetta, David Rigler, and Myron Karon

Abstract

*Twenty-five leukemic children aged 6 to 10 years related significantly more
stories that contained elements of preoccupation with threat to their body
integrity and functioning than did 25 control children with nonfatal chronic
illnesses. Although they made no overt reference to the concept of death, the
children with fatal illness showed an awareness of intrusion into their body
integrity and functioning and expressed a greater degree of both hospital-related
and nonhospital-related anxiety than did the children in the control sample.*

*The fatally ill child of 6 to 10 years appeared to be aware of the
seriousness of his illness, even though he may not yet be capable of talking
about this awareness in adult terms.*

Despite efforts to shield children with fatal illness from awareness of their prognosis, it has been claimed that the anxiety of well-meaning adults is conveyed to the children through the altered emotional climate around them.[1] How true is this? How anxious is a young child with a fatal illness, specifically a child with leukemia? The present study is an attempt to answer this question with quantified measures.

Previous studies, reviewed by Spinetta,[2] indicate the concern of authors for the parents, nurses, and physicians dealing with the child,[1,3–11] but few or no objectively based data have been gathered from the younger child himself on what he knows about his illness or what his psychological reactions are to it. Worse still, unsupported positions and opinions have been stated as objective fact.[12–16]

The question of whether or not there are any psychological accompaniments of fatal illness is particularly unsettled in the child 6 to 10 years of age. According to Schowalter,[17] in this age period the concept of terminal illness first makes its

Reprinted from Pediatrics 52:841, 1973.

impact on the dying child and death anxiety may then be greatest because death is still so poorly understood at this age.

Most studies seem to agree that the child over 10 can be aware of and anxious about his impending death, whether he is told directly about his illness or is kept from open communication about it for whatever intention of those around him.[3-10,18-21] For the fatally ill child under 5, anxiety takes the form of separation anxiety, fear of abandonment, and loneliness. Many investigators who approach the subject from the conceptual level conclude that the fatally ill child from 6 to 10 years of age lacks sufficient intellectual ability to formulate a concept of death and, therefore, is not aware of what impends. Others, more attuned to the child's emotional state, draw equally strong conclusions that many fatally ill children of 6 to 10 years, if not conceiving of their own impending death, are aware at least that something very serious is happening to them.

Investigators with these two views relied for the most part on interviews with the parents or on observation of the children, until Waechter recently used the interpretation of pictures to elicit indirect and fantasy expression of fatally ill children's concern regarding present and future body integrity and functioning.[22,23] In four otherwise matched groups from the controversial 6 to 10 year-old age level (fatally ill children, children with nonfatal chronic illness, children with brief illness, and normal nonhospitalized children), Waechter found a higher degree of overtly expressed death themes and concerns than of mutilation or separation concerns among the fatally ill. She measured objectively a higher degree of concern with intrusion into body integrity and functioning in her fatal group than in any of the three others. This strongly suggests that children aged 6 to 10 not only can be aware that they are dying, but also can express that awareness by actual and overt use of words relating to death.

The present study of 6- to 10-year old fatally ill children attempts to clarify the issue of overt expression of death concerns.

It was predicted (a) that anxiety, though not an overt expression of death, would, if present, be real, measurable, and very much related to the seriousness and fatality of the illness experienced; and (b) that from awareness of the seriousness of their illness, fatally ill children, without mentioning death overtly, would show a much greater preoccupation with threat to body integrity and functioning, and a greater overall anxiety relative both to the hospital and to nonhospital-related situations than would a control group of hospitalized children.

METHOD

Subjects

A battery of tests was administered to 50 children from 6 to 10 years of age, all hospitalized on the same ward of Childrens Hospital of Los Angeles between May 1971 and February 1972. Parental permission was obtained in writing before each child was tested and parents were very cooperative and willing to allow their child to participate in the study. Of the 50 children, 25 were hospitalized with a diagnosis of leukemia, while the remaining 25 were children with chronic but nonfatal illnesses, matched to the fatally ill in age, sex, race, and grade in school. The children also were matched as closely as possible in terms of seriousness and amount of medical intervention, as well as number of times in the hospital. Of the 25 children in each of the two groups, 9 were newly diagnosed while 16 were in the hospital for a subsequent admission for the same illness.

Procedure

The study consisted of three parts given in the following order:

1. Pictures (PIX): A set of four pictures of hospital scenes was shown individually and in the same order to each child in the study. Stories were requested in an attempt to elicit indirect and fantasy expressions of the child's concern regarding present and future body integrity and functioning, in the manner used by Waechter in her study.
2. Objective Test, Three-Dimensional (3D): A three-dimensional replica of a hospital room at Childrens Hospital of Los Angeles was specially designed for the study in a further attempt to elicit indirect and fantasy expressions of the child's concern regarding present and future body integrity and functioning. Magnetized dolls representing significant figures in the child's life (mother, father, doctor, nurse—all of appropriate race) were given to the child to place in the room. The child was asked to tell stories about each of the dolls as he placed them in the room.
3. Hospital-Anxiety (HOSP) and Home-Anxiety (HOME): The 40 questions of the two-part questionnaire were adapted from the State–Trait Anxiety Inventory for Children (STAIC) of Spielberger.[24] Each child was asked to respond to the State Anxiety questions regarding his feelings while in the hospital and to respond to the Trait Anxiety questions regarding his feelings while not in the hospital.

The entire protocol was administered in one sitting lasting from 20 to 30 minutes to each of the children individually by the same examiner. The use of a separate testing room was designed to eliminate at least the gross effects of medication, for the children would refuse to leave their room to come and "play the games" when they were feeling tired, depressed, or listless. All of the stories in parts 1 and 2 were recorded on tape and later transcribed and scored. No time limit was set for the child in any portion of the story telling and, other than prescribed instructions, no prompting was given. The scoring system used in parts 1 and 2 was based on that adapted by Waechter from McClelland et al.[25]

RESULTS

A multivariate analysis of variance for the scores was performed, and the results are summarized in Table 8-1. The cell means for the four measures are summarized in Table 8-2.

Table 8-1. Analyses of Variance for the Dependent Measures*

Source	df	PIX MS	F	3D MS	F	HOSP MS	F	HOME MS	F
Regression	2	135.5	6.35†	71.7	4.26‡	3.1	0.10	248.6	7.01†
L									
Leuk/Non-Leuk	1	614.8	28.82§	547.4	32.53§	1239.4	39.83§	300.4	8.47†
V									
First/Subsequent	1	7.1	0.33	1.5	0.09	95.9	3.08	3.3	0.09
LXV	1	8.2	0.38	0.9	0.05	160.1	5.15	1.2	0.03
Error	44	21.3		16.8	—	31.1	—	35.3	—

* Compared to the nonleukemic control group, the leukemic children told significantly more anxiety-filled stories relating to PIX ($p < 0.001$) and to 3D ($p < 0.001$), and exhibited significantly greater hospital-related ($p < 0.001$) and nonhospital-related ($p < 0.001$) anxiety.
† $p < 0.01$ ‡ $p < 0.05$ § $p < 0.001$

The scores for the four measures were covaried for age and grade in school. The age and grade made a significant difference in the scores (regression analysis $p < 0.021$). The main hypothesis was supported by the four measures of anxiety taken as a whole. That children 6 to 10 years of age with a fatal prognosis would relate stories indicating significantly greater preoccupation with threat to body integrity and functioning, and would exhibit a significantly greater anxiety both in hospital-related and non-hospital-related questions, than the control group of chronically ill children, was supported by an F of 21.32, $p < 0.001$. In their story telling, none of the children made overt references to the concept of death.

The fatally ill children both at initial hospital entry and at their subsequent readmissions related stories in response to PIX that showed a greater preoccupation with threat to their body integrity and functioning than did the control group ($F = 28.82$, $p < 0.001$) (Table 8-1). Similarly, in response to the 3D test, the F of 32.53 indicated a probability of $p < 0.001$. Table 8-1 further shows F of 39.83 (p

Table 8-2. Cell Means for Dependent Measures of Anxiety in Total Scored Items

	Leukemic 1st Admission	Subsequent Admissions	Chronic 1st Admission	Subsequent Admissions
PIX	10.67	10.25	2.44	3.81
3D	9.11	8.94	2.00	2.44
HOSP	23.33	16.75	8.33	9.19
HOME	14.56	15.00	9.67	9.56

< 0.001) for anxiety related to hospital situations and of 8.47 for feelings when not in the hospital but while at home (HOME scale) (*p* < 0.006).

DISCUSSION

If, as the parents of the 25 leukemic children maintained, their child did not know that his illness was fatal, and if the chronically ill children generally received the same number and duration of hospital-related treatments, there should have been little or no difference between the scores of the fatally ill children and the scores of the otherwise chronically ill. But the greater anxiety and preoccupation with threat to body integrity and functioning of the fatally ill, present even at the first admission to the hospital and carrying over into the home, indicates, despite efforts to keep the child with leukemia from becoming aware of his prognosis, that he somehow picks up a sense that his illness is very serious and very threatening. The fatally ill child is aware that his is no ordinary illness.

It seems clear both from the present study and from the Waechter study,[22,23] the two rigorously designed studies on the issue, that even though the concern of the 6- to 10-year-old leukemic child may not take the form of overt expression about death, the more subtle fears and anxieties are nonetheless real, painful, and very much related to the seriousness of the illness. Whether or not one wishes to call this nonconceptual anxiety about the child's own fatal illness "death anxiety" seems to be a problem of semantics rather than of fact. To equate awareness of death with the ability to conceptualize it and express the concept in an adult manner denies the possibility of an awareness of death at a less cognitive level. If it is true that the perception of death can be engraved at some level that precedes a child's ability to talk about it, then a child might well understand that he is going to die long before he can say so.

REFERENCES

1. Binger CM, Ablin AR, Feuerstein RC et al: Childhood leukemia: Emotional impact on patient and family. N Engl Med 280:414, 1969
2. Spinetta JJ: Death Anxiety in Leukemic Children. Doctoral dissertation, University of Southern California, 1972 Ann Arbor, Mich. University Microfilms
3. Easson WM: The Dying Child: The Management of the Child or Adolescent Who is Dying. Springfield, IL, Charles C Thomas, 1970
4. Yudkin S: Children and death. Lancet 1:37, 1967
5. Kliman G: Psychological Emergencies of Childhood, pp 26–43. New York, Grune & Stratton, 1968
6. Richmond JB, Waisman HA: Psychological aspects of management of children with malignant diseases, Am J Dis Child 89:42, 1955
7. Knudson AG, Natterson JM: Participation of parents in the hospital care of their fatally ill children. Pediatrics 26:482, 1960
8. Natterson J, Knudson A: Observations concerning fear of death in fatally ill children and their mothers. Psychosom Med 22:456, 1960
9. Morrissey JR: A note on interviews with children facing imminent death. Soc Casework 44:343, 1963

10. Morrissey JR: Children's adaptations to fatal illness. Soc Work 8(4):81, 1963
11. Friedman SB, Chodoff P, Mason JW, Hamburg DS: Behavioral observation in parents anticipating the death of a child. Pediatrics 32:610, 1963
12. Howell DA: A child dies. Hosp Top 45(2):93, 1967
13. Evans AE, Edin S: If a child must die. N Engl J Med 278:138, 1968
14. Editorial: The dying child. Med J Aust 1:1011, 1968
15. Debuskey M: Orchestration of care. Debuskey M (ed): In The Chronically Ill Child and His Family, Springfield, IL, Charles C. Thomas, 1970
16. Sigler AT: The leukemic child and his family: An emotional challenge. In Debuskey M (ed): The Chronically Ill Child and His Family. Springfield, IL, Charles C Thomas, 1970
17. Schowalter JE: The child's reaction to his own terminal illness. In Schoenberger B, Carr A, Peretz D et al (eds): Loss and Grief: Psychological Management in Medical Practice. New York, Columbia University Press, 1970
18. Furman RA: Death and the young child: Some preliminary considerations. Psychoanal Stud Child 19:321, 1964
19. Maurer A: Maturational concepts of death. Br J Med Psychol 39:35, 1966
20. Von Hug–Hellmuth H: The child's concept of death. Psychoanal Q 34:499, 1965
21. Vernick J, Karon M: Who's afraid of death on a leukemia ward? Am J Dis Child 109:393, 1965
22. Waechter EH: Death Anxiety in Children with Fatal Illness. Doctoral dissertation, Stanford University, 1968. Ann Arbor, Mich. University Microfilms
23. Waechter EH: Children's awareness of fatal illness. Am J Nurs 71:1168, 1971
24. Speilberger CD, Edwards ED, Montnoci J et al: Children's State–Trait Anxiety Inventory. Palo Alto, CA, Consulting Psychologist Press, 1972
25. McClelland DC, Atkinson JW, Clark RA et al A scoring manual for the achievement motive. In Atkinson JW (ed): Motives in Fantasy, Action and Society: A Method of Assessment and Study. Princeton, NJ, D. Van Nostrand Co., 1958

9 · Death Anxiety in the Outpatient Leukemic Child

John J. Spinetta and Lorrie J. Maloney

Abstract

Awareness of the seriousness of their illness seems to persist with fatally ill children, even when they are not in the hospital. As did the fatally ill hospitalized children in previous studies, so too, the fatally ill outpatient children in the present study related significantly more stories that contained elements of preoccupation with threat to their body integrity and functioning than did the control group of children with nonfatal chronic illnesses. Not only did they express a greater general anxiety and greater anxiety in relating the stories, but, in contrast to their chronically ill counterparts, the leukemic children exhibited a lack of adaptability to the necessity of clinic visits, becoming increasingly more anxious about the clinic both as visits became more frequent and as their illness became of longer duration.

The children continue to dwell on their illness, even when treated as outpatients.

The fatally ill child of 6 to 10 years appears to be aware of the seriousness of his illness, even though he may not yet be capable of talking about this awareness in adult terms. This was the conclusion reached by Spinetta and associates[1,2] in their study of hospitalized leukemic children. Using projective measures to elicit stories from the children, the authors found that the fatally ill children were significantly more preoccupied with threat to their body integrity and functioning than were the chronically ill children in the control group. The fatally ill children also expressed a greater degree of anxiety both hospital-related and non-hospital-related than did the controls.

Reprinted from Pediatrics 56:1034–1037, 1975.

Using as a further projective measure a three-dimensional replica of a hospital room in an analysis of interpersonal distancing, the authors found that the fatally ill children in the study placed each of four figures in their hospital life (nurse, doctor, mother, father) at a distance significantly greater than did the matched control group of chronically ill children. This distance increased even further with subsequent hospitalizations. It was inferred that the placement of the dolls by the dying children was reflective of a growing sense of psychological separation of the dying child from the hospital, both people and circumstances, for reasons specific to each child's reinforcement history.[2]

The question arises: how much of this awareness is hospital-related? Does awareness of the seriousness of their illness persist with the fatally ill children when they are not in the hospital? Do the children continue to dwell on their illness, or are they able, when in remission, to live a normal life, free from concerns about their illness?

The present study was undertaken to clarify these issues. The identical age group of 6 to 10 years was chosen for this study because of the difficulties involved in measuring communications at this age and because of the conflicting reports on whether or not fatally ill children this young are aware of the seriousness of their illness.[3] The instruments used were the same as in the previous studies.[1,2] The major difference was that the children in the present study were examined not while inpatients about to leave the hospital after a period of treatment, but as outpatients in remission who had come to the hospital clinic for a check-up and treatment.

Given the results of previous studies,* it was predicted that the fatally ill children would continue to be aware of the seriousness of their illness even while in remission: 1) that the fatally ill outpatient children, aged 6 to 10 years, would relate stories showing a greater preoccupation with their illness than would a matched control group of chronically ill outpatient children; 2) that the fatally ill children would exhibit a greater overall anxiety relative both to the hospital and to home than would the controls; and 3) that the fatally ill children would place significant hospital figures at a greater interpersonal distance than would the controls.

METHOD

Subjects

A battery of tests identical to the tests used in the previous studies was administered to 32 children aged 6 to 10 years who were being treated in outpatient clinics in three local children's facilities. Of the 32 children, 16 were being treated for a diagnosis of leukemia, while the remaining 16 were being treated for illnesses that

---

* See Spinetta et al[1,2] for further background and bibliography. A thorough review of the literature may be found in Spinetta.[3]

were chronic but not fatal: rheumatoid arthritis, renal dysfunction, hemophilia, osteogenesis imperfecta, and anemia. The chronically ill children were matched as closely as possible to the fatally ill in age, duration of illness, and number of times hospitalized. Written parental permission was obtained before each child was tested, and parents were very cooperative and willing to allow their child to participate in the study.

Procedure

The study consisted of three parts, given to each child in the following order:

1. Pictures (PIX)—A set of four pictures of hospital scenes was shown individually and in the same order to each child in the study. Stories were requested in an attempt to elicit indirect and fantasy expression of the child's concern regarding present and future body integrity and functioning, separation, and loneliness as an indirect measure of the child's awareness of the seriousness of his illness.
2. Three-Dimensional Test (3D)—A three-dimensional replica of a hospital room was used in a further attempt to elicit stories from each child as an indirect measure of his awareness of his illness. Magnetized dolls representing significant figures in the child's life (nurse, doctor, mother, father) were given to the child to place into the room, both where they usually were and where the child would most like them to be. The child was asked to tell stories about each of the dolls in turn as he placed them into the room. The stories were recorded on tape and later transcribed. The distance placement was recorded on a separate scoring page.
3. Anxiety Scales (STAIC)—A children's anxiety scale (the Children's State–Trait Anxiety Inventory, or STAIC, of Spielberger et al[4]) was administered to each child. The child was asked to respond to the 20 State Anxiety questions regarding his present feelings while in the hospital outpatient clinic, and to respond to the 20 Trait Anxiety questions about his usual everyday feelings.

The entire protocol was administered in one sitting lasting from 20 to 30 minutes to each of the children individually by the same examiner, in a room on the same floor as the clinic treatment rooms. No time limit was set for the child in any portion of the story telling and, other than the prescribed instructions, no prompting was given. The scoring system used with the stories was based on that adapted by Waechter[5] from McClelland and colleagues[6] and identical to that used by the present authors in their earlier studies.

Although the testing took place in the outpatient clinics of three different hospitals, analysis of the data revealed that there were no significant effects due to the difference in facilities. Further analysis revealed no significant effects due to the sex of the child.

Table 9-1. Measures of Preoccupation with Illness

Measure	Leukemic	Chronic
PIX Ratio	8.61	4.34
3D Ratio	9.01	4.64

Results

An analysis of variance was performed on each of the measures comparing the leukemic to the chronically ill children. Results are as follows:

HYPOTHESIS 1

The scores for the stories related regarding both the pictures and the three-dimensional test were divided by the number of words used in telling the story, in order to control both for age and for the effects of verbosity on the anxiety score. Cell means are given in Table 9-1. Using the resultant PIX Ratio and 3D Ratio scores for analysis, it was shown that the leukemic children related stories both about the pictures and about the figures in the three-dimensional hospital room replica, indicating a significantly greater preoccupation with loneliness and with threat to body integrity and functioning than did the control group of chronically ill children. (PIX: $F = 18.5, p < .001$; 3D: $F = 26.5, p < .001$). The first hypothesis that the fatally ill outpatient children would relate stories showing a greater awareness of their illness than would a control group was sustained at a significant level.

HYPOTHESIS 2

That the fatally ill children would exhibit a greater overall anxiety than the control group was evidenced by the Trait scale of the STAIC ($F = 2.98, p < .09$), suggesting that the leukemic children are more anxious about their life generally than are the chronically ill children. The cell means are given in Table 9-2.

Although there was no significant main effect observed in the State scale of the STAIC regarding the child's anxiety during his outpatient visits, there were several interaction effects observed.

Table 9-2. Measures of Anxiety

Measure	Leukemic	Chronic
STAIC State	36.1	34.5
STAIC Trait	39.5	35.2

Table 9-3. Effects of Age of Child on STAIC State

Age	Leukemic	Chronic
Oldest	38.4	30.8
Youngest	33.7	38.7

1. When the data were analyzed comparing the scores of the eight oldest children in each group with the scores of the eight youngest in each group, there was a significant interaction ($F = 10.42$, $p < .01$). The younger chronically ill children had a level of anxiety relative to the outpatient clinic that diminished with age, whereas the leukemic children's anxiety relative to the outpatient clinic increased with age at a significant level. As the leukemic child becomes older, his anxiety toward the clinic increases. Cell means are given in Table 9-3.
2. When the data were analyzed comparing the scores of the eight children visiting the clinic most frequently, a similar interaction effect was observed ($F = 6.56$, $p < .025$). As frequency of visits increased for the chronically ill children, anxiety decreased. The opposite was true for the leukemic children: as frequency of clinic visits increased, so did the anxiety regarding feelings relative to the clinic. Cell means are given in Table 9-4.
3. When the data were analyzed comparing the scores of the eight children with the longest duration of illness in each group with the scores of the eight children with the shortest duration, there was a significant interaction ($F = 7.23$, $p < .025$). Anxiety was least for those chronically ill children whose illness was of long duration. The opposite was true for the leukemic children: the longer the duration of the illness, the higher the anxiety. Cell means are given in Table 9-5.

HYPOTHESIS 3

Finally, regarding the measures of interpersonal distance, differences between leukemic and chronically ill children were not found to be significant. Cell means for the measure of usual distance are given in Table 9-6.

Table 9-4. Effects of STAIC State of Frequency of Clinic Visits

Frequency	Leukemic	Chronic
Most visits	38.4	30.6
Fewest visits	34.9	37.5

Table 9-5. Effects of Duration of Illness on STAIC State

Duration	Leukemic	Chronic
Longest	38.3	30.8
Shortest	34.5	37.9

DISCUSSION

It is clear from the data of the present study that, like the leukemic child who is hospitalized, the leukemic child in remission and being treated at an outpatient clinic is aware that his is no ordinary illness. Even though the concerns of the fatally ill child may not take the form of overt expression about death, the more subtle fears and anxieties are nonetheless real, painful, and very much related to the seriousness of the illness. Although the leukemic children in the present study had not been hospitalized more frequently nor for greater periods of time than the chronically ill children, the leukemic children manifested a greater preoccupation with their illness than did their chronically ill counterparts. This was clear both in the story telling and in the objective anxiety scales. The leukemic children exhibited a greater preoccupation with threat to their body integrity and functioning (PIX Ratio and 3D Ratio scores), greater anxiety in their general out-of-hospital life (Trait scores), and a lack of adaptability to the necessity of clinic visits (State scores). Whereas the chronically ill children seem to adapt to the necessity of the visits to the clinic, the leukemic children do not. The longer the duration of their illness, the more frequent their visits to the clinic, and the older the leukemic children, the more anxiety-provoking the clinic becomes.

The major difference between the present study of the outpatient child and the earlier studies of the inpatient child is the lack of contrast in interpersonal distance between the leukemic and the chronically ill children. Whereas in the study of the inpatient children interpersonal distances were greater for the leukemic children and increased with subsequent hospitalizations, this did not remain true for the outpatient children. There were no main effect differences between the groups in the present study. Although the leukemic child in remission is still very aware of the seriousness of his illness, his concern does not take the form of separation from

Table 9-6. Measures of Interpersonal Distance

Figure	Leukemic	Chronic
Nurse	1.85	1.47
Doctor	1.47	1.45
Mother	2.88	2.56
Father	2.72	2.16

the significant figures in his hospital life. Observations of three of the outpatient children when they subsequently became hospitalized and died while in the hospital indicated a depression and separation of their feelings from those around them that increased as the children neared death. The growing separation from family and staff seems to be a phenomenon very much related to hospitalization and the nearness of death.

Although the present study is cross-sectional in nature and was conducted in a different locale from the previously reported studies, the consistency of the findings of the high level of anxiety of the leukemic children and their awareness of the seriousness of their illness points to a need to help the children cope, not only when they are being treated in the hospital, but also when they are living at home and being treated in outpatient clinics.

REFERENCES

1. Spinetta JJ, Rigler D, Karon M: Anxiety in the dying child. Pediatrics 52:841, 1973
2. Spinetta JJ, Rigler D, Karon M: Personal space as a measure of a dying child's sense of isolation. Consult Clin Psychol 42:751, 1974
3. Spinetta JJ: The dying child's awareness of death: A review. Psychol Bull 81:256, 1974
4. Spielberger CD, Edwards ED, Montuori J et al: Children's State–Trait Anxiety Inventory. Palo Alto, CA, Consulting Psychologists Press, 1972
5. Waechter EH: Children's awareness of fatal illness. Am J Nurs 71:1168, 1971
6. McClelland DC, Atkinson JW, Clark RA et al: A scoring manual for the achievement motive. In Atkinson JW (ed): Motives in Fantasy, Action, and Society: A Method of Assessment and Study. Princeton, NJ, D. Van Nostrand, 1958

10 · Loneliness and Social Isolation in School-Age Children With Chronic Life-Threatening Illness

Tamar Krulik

The on-going advances in medicine and related sciences have changed dramatically the trajectory and prognosis of most childhood malignancies and other serious illnesses such as cystic fibrosis. These diseases, once considered fatal, are now regarded as chronic life-threatening illnesses.

The purpose of this chapter is to report a study on loneliness (see page 10) in school-age children living with chronic life-threatening illness (Krulik, 1978) and discuss its implications for practice.

Great numbers of ill children may enjoy long periods of remission and good health, and for many children long-term survival and cure become a reality. Thus, professionals working with these children and their families focus on helping the child and family adjust to the diagnosis and adapt to living with chronic illness (Koocher and O'Malley, 1981; Spinetta and Spinetta, 1981; Waechter, Phillips, and Holaday, 1985).

One of the most important challenges to this team is to ensure the child's normal development and enhance the actualization of his potential. Learning to socialize in the world outside the home and family is one of the main developmental tasks of the school-age child. Success in making friends and gaining peer acceptance is essential for the child to maintain and continue to develop his self-esteem, self-concept and social skills. School age is the first developmental period during which the child can measure comprehensively his capabilities against an accepted external standard.

Chronic life-threatening illness in school age may impede the sick child's social development, and also lead to experiences of isolation and loneliness. Instead of acquiring a sense of "mastery," the child may end the school-age period with various degrees of "inferiority." Prolonged social isolation, loneliness, and inferiority in the school-age child may have very serious consequences for him in adolescence and later in adult life, that is, difficulties in establishing intimate relations, hampered mental health, and suicidal tendencies (Stengel, 1971; Cowen et al, 1973; Moore, 1974). The quest of understanding loneliness is relevant to a child's quality of life in the present. It is also relevant to his future mental health.

BACKGROUND LITERATURE

The following literature review will cover the definition and experiences of loneliness, origins of loneliness in childhood, and origins of loneliness in the experience of a child with chronic life-threatening illness.

The Definition and Experience of Loneliness

On a "voyage" through the literature to discover the mystery of loneliness, I found as many versions of loneliness as the number of writers who wrote about it. Peplau and Perlman (1982) cite 12 different definitions of loneliness. With that they identify "three very important points of agreement in the way scholars view loneliness. First, loneliness results from deficiencies in a person's social relationship. Second, loneliness is a subjective experience; it is not synonymous with objective social isolation. Third, the experience of loneliness is unpleasant and distressing." (Writers such as Fromm–Reichmann [1959], Sullivan [1953], Weiss [1973], and Clancy and McBride [1975] suggest that loneliness and social isolation can occur from infancy throughout life.)

The chronically ill child may, however, suffer from both the subjective distressing experience of feeling lonely, apart from others, unable to communicate fears and feelings and/or the objective experience of social isolation, of having very few social contacts, especially with peers (Krulik, 1978). Loneliness can be accompanied by social isolation, but loneliness can be experienced also in the middle of a group (Leiderman, 1969). It is important to note that the loneliness mentioned above is different from the existential loneliness that can be a very positive experience (Moustakas, 1961). In writing his memoires, Jung (1963) refers to his experience with childhood loneliness, illustrating the preceding statements: "As a child I felt myself to be alone, and I am still, because I know things and must hint at things which others apparently know nothing of, and for the most part do not want to know. Loneliness does not come from having no people about one, but from being unable to communicate the things that seem important to oneself, or from holding certain views which others find inadmissible" (Jung, 1963, p 356). The research reported in this chapter focuses mainly on the experience of loneliness in children.

Hymel and Asher (1977) maintain that there are two important elements in defining a lonely, socially isolated child. "One is that the child lacks friends and the other is that the child is not generally accepted by peers" (p 23). The lonely child can be actively rejected or be unnoticed and ignored by his peers. As a result the child may engage in solitary play, watch other children play from the side, or seek adults' attention (Moustakas, 1972; Wayne, 1968). The lonely child is often characterized by poor academic performance (Bonney, 1971). Rubin (1982) adds that "like adults who lack a satisfying social network, children without friends can experience painful feelings of malaise, boredom and alienation" (p 266).

ORIGINS OF LONELINESS IN CHILDHOOD

Loneliness may originate in infancy. The infant's unmet needs for contact and warmth, or a parent's (especially the mother's) inappropriate response to the infant's needs over a period of time, will lead to a state of loneliness and social isolation (Sullivan, 1953; Clancy and McBride, 1975). Prolonged impaired contacts and communications between the child and his parents contribute to the child's loneliness throughout childhood and adolescence. Loneliness in the child tends to be identified when the child enters the school-age period. This period is characterized developmentally by a great need for peer group and peer acceptance. The importance of peer group acceptance for the normal development of the school-age child stimulated research in the areas of the development of social cognition and social skills (Shantz, 1975); the phenomenon of peer relations in childhood (Campbell, 1964); and methods for identiciation and modes of intervention with socially isolated children (Bonney, 1971; Hymel and Asher, 1977; Wanlass and Prinz, 1982).

In an extensive review of research literature on peer group relations in childhood, Campbell (1964) points to the role of the broader social context of children's peer groups. Broad cultural, subcultural, and family variations influence the atmosphere, values, and practices of the peer group. These variations also influence the individual child's approach to the peer group. Salient for the reported research is that these differences play a major role in the acceptance, rejection, separation, and ostracism of different children. (For example, the public notion that cancer or cystic fibrosis may be contagious will influence the peers and their parents to reject the ill child in the neighborhood.)

Campbell calls attention to another issue highly relevant to this study: what are the criteria for acceptance or rejection in the peer group? He differentiates between criteria related to personality and social characteristics and those related to skills and abilities. Campbell reports on research findings that show friendliness and sociability to be associated with high acceptance in the group, and social indifference and withdrawal to be attributes of children who have been rejected or who maintain a low status within the group. Other criteria are good physical appearance, muscular strength, and athletic ability, which are important for popularity, especially among boys.

Reese (1961) adds that there is a relationship between the child's self-concept and sociometric choices. He concludes that highest acceptance in the group is related to moderate self-concept scores and lowest acceptance in the group to low self-concept scores. Horowitz (1962) also reports that in the middle grades of elementary school the less popular children tend to think less well of themselves.

Sullivan (1953) maintains that illness in the very young child is one of the common causes leading to loneliness. It evolves from retardation in interpersonal relations that the child carries with him to the juvenile (school-age) era. Furthermore, when the child is ill during the school-age period, he is apt to develop social handicaps due to school absences and his inability to participate competently in games and competitions. The underlying theme to the process of developing loneliness as a result of illness is the child's being different both physically and emotionally from his healthy peers. To be different is to be a target for ridicule and discrimination (Peplau, 1966). Moustakas (1961) lays stress on the loneliness of the hospitalized child, who may feel abandoned by his parents and separated from his social milieu.

It appears that in order for the school-age child to be accepted and popular in the peer group, he needs to be physically well, be appealing, be able to compete, have high levels of self-esteem, possess social skills, and tend to use them in peer interaction.

In conclusion, loneliness belongs to the experience of living and growing up. However, some children may be lonelier than others. The identified factors conducive to loneliness in childhood are unmet needs for warmth and contact, lack of genuine interest in the child, impaired communications between the child and significant others, lack of social skills, and being different from one's siblings and peers.

ORIGINS OF LONELINESS IN THE CHILD WITH CHRONIC LIFE-THREATENING ILLNESS

Perlman and Peplau (1982) raise questions about the causes of loneliness; Do they reside within the person or within the environment? Do they stem from contemporary, or developmental influences on behavior? (p 123). It seems that loneliness in the child with chronic life-threatening disease can be caused by both the child's (internal) characteristics as a result of his development, but more often is caused by the characteristics of the situation/environment and is temporary and transient.

In different reports on children with chronic illness, children are identified as displaying anger, fear, depression, guilt, anxiety reactions, acceptance, and even hope (Burgert, 1972). In addition, the concept of loneliness is mentioned as part of the child's experience with the disease (Burgert, 1972; Northrup, 1974; Tropauer, Franz, and Dilgard, 1970; Waechter, 1968); the experience of loneliness *per se* has not been studied in children with chronic life-threatening illness.

Based on literature on the origins of loneliness in childhood, and the experience of children with chronic illnesses, I have identified four major origins for potential loneliness in the sick child:

1. The difference between the sick child and his siblings and peers (this origin applies also to chronic non–life-threatening illness)

2. The matrix of impaired communications that characterizes the experience of a child living with chronic life-threatening illness
3. The tendency of parents and significant others toward withdrawal and distancing from the sick child
4. The sick child's death anxiety

The Difference Between the Sick Child and His Siblings and Peers

The chronically sick child must deal with the fact that he is neither healthy nor can live a normal life in a world that admires physical health and normalcy (Cytryn, Moore, and Robinson, 1973). The difference is inherent in the nature of the illness. The illness imposes changes in energy for physical activity, changes in appearance, and changes in daily routines (diet, exercises, medications), and at times poses restrictions on contacts with others to avoid contagion or in an attempt to keep the condition secret (Cytryn, Moore, and Robinson, 1973). Unfortunately, data on how the sick child views himself and his differences are scarce and scattered.

Cytryn, Moore, and Robinson (1973) evaluated children with cystic fibrosis. The children in their study expressed concern about their self-concept and body image in different ways and in different contexts. In their human figure drawings there were in some cases clear indications of concerns about body disfigurements, for example, disproportionately large and detailed chest area or small, constricted figures. Other children produced fantasy material in response to Rorschach tests that suggests that they saw themselves as younger than they were, dependent, and inadequate. Tropauer, Franz, and Dilgard (1970) studied 20 children with cystic fibrosis and 23 mothers. They report that the younger children "complained frequently about interruption of play, dietary deprivations, or the physical limitations which prevented them from keeping up with others" (p 208). In addition, seven mothers voiced strong concerns about the child's impaired social adjustment, for example, "lost initiative to make friends," "avoids close friends."

Children with cancer were evaluated by their teachers and compared to their healthy peers on ordinary school-related behaviors, in a 3-year project (Deasy–Spinetta, 1981). There were 127 evaluations for the student–patients and 122 for a matched control from the same classroom. Deasy–Spinetta states that there were areas in which children with cancer differed significantly from their healthy controls. Children with cancer have more absences and more learning disabilities; they did not initiate activities or try new things but were instead underactive and lacking in energy. The student–patients were also different in their social skills. They were more self-conscious and self-centered, less concerned with others, and had fewer friends. (Note: if a child was diagnosed early in life, he may never have had the chance to develop social skills by interacting with peers without adult supervision.)

Besides the nature of the illness and its side effects, there is another major source for the child to feel different. Parents of children with chronic life-threatening illness tend to treat the sick child in a way different from before diagnosis (Easson, 1970) and different from his siblings (Lascari, 1969). They will adopt what

Boone and Hartman (1972) identify as the *benevolent overreaction.* This term reflects parental actions that include overprotection, overindulgence, and permissiveness. It is clinicians' opinion that the *favorite child syndrome* (Benoliel, 1972) results at first in the child's confusion and anxiety and in the long run causes lack of self-esteem, initiative, and self-control (Boone and Hartman, 1972). Favoritism and overprotection of the sick child may generate sibling jealousy and anger (Burgert, 1972).

In conclusion, although much of the findings are based on clinical experience rather than research findings, the pattern in the literature suggests that the major contributors to the child's being and feeling different are (1) the nature of the illness and side effects that result in alterations in physical appearance, physical and social competence, and self-image, and (2) the change in parent expectations and disciplining, which result in anxiety, lowered self-esteem, and possible friction with siblings.

Impaired Communications with the Sick Child

Waechter (1968), Singher (1974), and Northrup (1974) identify lack of or restriction of open communication between different family members or medical personnel and the sick child about the nature and impact of the disease as one of the major sources for potential experience of loneliness. Alteration in communications might be the result of parents' and medical personnel's adoption of the *protective approach* (Share, 1972). In order to maintain the protective approach parents and medical personnel are required "to avoid subjects that might lead to the child's questioning of the illness, ignore some of the child's overt or covert clues regarding his serious concerns, or denying the child's expressed concerns by brushing them aside or giving false reassurance. Sometimes it requires physically distancing oneself from the child to avoid difficult encounters" (p 194).

The child who soon learns that his communications are not welcomed, that discussion is taboo, and who turns adults away from him, may isolate himself and indulge in private fears and fantasies (Northrup, 1974; Singher, 1974; Vernick, 1973). The end result of such communication processes is that the child feels lonely and abandoned, believing that others are not aware of what he is experiencing at the very time when he is most in need of meaningful communication with a trustworthy adult (Vernick and Karon, 1965).

Lack of meaningful communication with the child occurs not only as a result of the belief in shielding the child. Most parents and medical personnel who adopt this approach feel helpless, inadequate, and too anxious to talk openly with the child (Northrup, 1974; Vernick, 1973; Vernick and Karon, 1965; Waechter, 1968). Vernick (1973) writes "On the whole we tend to decide for ourselves what the child needs to talk about purely on the basis of what we feel would be most comfortable for us to discuss with him" (p 106).

The *open communication* approach has many strong proponents (Ablin et al, 1971; Singher, 1974; Vernick, 1973). They propose that the often expressed dichotomy of "to tell or not to tell" appears as a meaningless question (Waechter, 1968). Rather, they agree that efforts should be geared to create a supportive environment in which the child will feel safe to ask any and all questions, share his concerns, and manifest his anxieties. Honesty and frankness are most important for reaching the child and maintaining the supportive environment.

Vernick and Karon (1965) report on a 2-year program at the National Cancer Institute that included 51 children from the ages of 9 to 20, hospitalized for leukemia. The authors utilize life space interviews with children and weekly group meetings with children, parents, and staff. Their goal was to develop the supportive environment. Every child was told his diagnosis and at the same time an outline for a potentially helpful therapeutic regimen was discussed. "On the basis of observations and discussions with these children, the authors conclude that there were no significant adjustment problems in any of the 51 patients" (Share, 1972, p 200). Most children used the opportunities to ask relevant questions about their illness and treatment and to share their intense concerns (Vernick, 1973).

Bluebond–Langner (1974) concludes a discussion on communication and terminally ill children: "Dying is difficult to do alone, and yet in so many ways it cannot be shared. If anyone is aware of this, it is the dying child. He knows and observes the restrictions against speaking about death. If he tries to break taboos, he rarely does so directly and then, perhaps, only in a highly symbolic manner" (p 180). Therefore, "giving a child such an opportunity (for discussion) does not heighten death anxiety: on the contrary, understanding acceptance and conveyance of permission to discuss any aspects of the illness may decrease feelings of isolation and alienation" (Waechter, 1971, p 1170).

Parents' and Significant Others' Anticipatory Grief

Diagnosis of life-threatening illness in a child may generate anticipatory mourning processes in parents and medical personnel. There are dysfunctional consequences of anticipatory grief for the chronically ill and dying child, his family, and the medical treatment team (Benoliel, 1974). Isolation and alienation of the sick child as a result of the anticipatory grief (Benoliel, 1974; Easson, 1970; Spinetta, Rigler, and Karon, 1974) can be considered a major dysfunctional aspect of the grieving process. Parents' behavior often demonstrates (1) intermittent clinging as well as distancing from the sick child (Futterman and Hoffman, 1973); (2) gradual detachment of emotional investment in the child and redirection of energies toward other relationships or "replacements" for the dying child; (3) completion of the mourning process and withdrawal of emotional investments from the dying child before his death. This situation results in the *living dead syndrome.* The child may be dead as far as the emotions of the family are concerned while he is still physically alive (Easson, 1970). "Because the family members have mourned him too early and too completely, the child may find himself isolated and alone. He has been mourned and laid to rest even before he is dead" (p 79). Unfortunately, there is little systematic research to support any of these statements.

Similar features characterize the dysfunctional facet of the anticipatory grief that the medical team may also display. Physicians and nurses may (1) get involved in distancing behavior, place the dying child in a distant and remote room

(Northrup, 1974), or make only quick contacts with him from the doorway (Glaser and Strauss, 1965); (2) avoid patients and parents out of feeling inadequate and helpless in supporting the sick child and family (Burgert, 1972; Singher, 1974); (3) react with sadness and depression (Burgert, 1972) when death is imminent. These behaviors enhance loneliness in the child and his family.

Spinetta, Rigler, and Karon (1974) used interpersonal distance measures in an attempt to objectify the sense of isolation said to be present in a school-age child with fatal illness. Their sample consists of 25 hospitalized leukemic children aged 6 to 10 and a matched group of 25 chronically ill children. When asked to place significant figures (father, mother, doctor, nurse) in a hospital room replica, the leukemic children placed the figures at distances significantly greater than did the matched group. For both groups the distance of placement increased in subsequent admissions; the leukemic children, however, increased the figures' distance significantly more than did the chronically ill. Based on social learning theory and interpersonal distance theory, the authors infer that the placement of the figures by the leukemic children is reflective of a growing sense of isolation. They conclude that the children react to significant adults who tend to reduce the quality and quantity of interaction with them.

Avoidance and distancing from the sick child and his family may also be a part of teachers' reactions to diagnosis and treatment effects of life-threatening disease in the child (Kaplan, Smith, and Grobstein, 1974). Rejection, withdrawal, avoidance, and distancing from the sick child are potential origins for loneliness.

The Sick Child's Death Anxiety

Mijuskovic (1977) and Waechter (1968) emphasize the link between death anxiety and loneliness in the sick child.

Children are not, at least at first, afraid of death, because they cannot comprehend or imagine what a permanent loss of consciousness might mean. . . . They are, however, terrified of the dark because it symbolizes aloneness. Thus, they are often afraid of going to sleep at night, not because they fear never awakening again, but rather because they are horrified by the prospect of being conscious and alone. We do not fear death, we fear loneliness. . . . What horrifies us concerning death is the possibility that our consciousness will continue but that it shall be the only one. We imagine ourselves . . . existing alone within a dark . . . universe, wandering the solitary, limitless expanses of space (or blackness) and time, in absolute desolation (Mijuskovic, 1977, pp 118–119).

Mijuskovic sheds light on two issues: (1) full comprehension of death is not prerequisite to the experience of death anxiety; and (2) death anxiety evolves from the perceived loneliness in separation from the known, secure world to an unknown, lonely space. These two issues are crucial in discussing death anxiety in the fatally ill child and its relatedness to loneliness.

Evans and Edin (1968), Debusky (1970), and Sigler (1970) claim that the child under 10 lacks the intellectual ability to formulate the concept of death and therefore is not aware of his own impending death. Natterson and Knudson (1960), Morrissey (1965), Spinetta (1974), and Vernick (1973) nevertheless report on some children experiencing and expressing death anxiety as early as age 4. Waechter's 1968 classic study on death anxiety in fatally ill school-age children represents a turning point to rigorous and systematic research on this subject. Her subjects are 64 children between 6 and 10. There are 4 groups of 16 subjects each—children with fatal illness, children with chronic nonfatal illness, children with brief illnesses, and healthy children. All children were asked to respond with stories to a set of projective pictures. In the findings, Waechter reports that the fatally ill children express significantly more imagery relating to death, separation, loneliness, and body integrity than the comparison groups. She concludes that concern with loneliness may be related to concern about death.

Kastenbaum (1967), Koocher (1975), and Wiener (1973) maintain that the maturing school-age child who moves into the concrete operational stage of cognitive development acquires an increasingly accurate understanding of death and dying.

A story of a 6-year-old with leukemia cited by Waechter (1968) summarizes the relationship between death anxiety and loneliness: "This is about a little boy. He looks very lonesome, all by himself. Maybe he is sick. Maybe he wishes somebody would take care of him. And that's why he is sad. He gets very sick all alone and he dies and he goes to heaven" (p 151).

In summary, the literature reviewed varies in depth and methodologies. It provides an overview of some of the salient variables related to loneliness in childhood (e.g., impaired communications, the child being different from his siblings and peers, unmet needs for warmth and contact) and points to the direction these variables may take in the experience of a child with chronic life-threatening illness.

STUDY QUESTIONS

1. Do children with chronic life-threatening disease differ in their loneliness manifestations from healthy children? Three hypotheses derived from this research question:

   a. Children with chronic life-threatening disease will respond with more loneliness themes (i.e., aloneness, separation, death anxiety, threat to body integrity, suicide) than will healthy children to a set of projective pictures.

   b. Children with chronic life-threatening illness will be more adult oriented in their choices than will healthy children on a scale measuring preference for interpersonal interaction.

   c. Children with chronic life-threatening disease will place human figures at a further distance from one another than will healthy children on an interpersonal distance scale.

2. What strategies do parents of children with chronic life-threatening illness use to deal with the problems of communication with the child, side effects of illness and treatment regimen, and death anxiety in the child?

THE STUDY SAMPLE

The sample of the study consisted of 20 children with chronic life-threatening illness and their mothers and a comparison group of 20 healthy children and their mothers. The criteria for sample selection for both groups were

1. Children aged 6 to 10
2. Child and family (Caucasian)

In addition, there were criteria for the children with chronic life-threatening disease:

1. Children with chronic disease for which a 10-year survival rate of 50% or less is predicted.
2. Disease onset—diagnosis was made at least 2 months prior to the study; it takes an average of 2 months of intensive medical treatment before a child can usually resume his regular activities.
3. The child is under follow-up in an outpatient clinic.
4. The child is not hospitalized at the time of the study in order to avoid anxieties related to present hospitalization.

The sick children were selected from the following outpatient departments of a large western university medical center:

Pediatric, Hematology, and Oncology
Cystic Fibrosis Clinical Center
Radiation Therapy
Pediatric Immunodeficiency Clinic

A convenience sample was obtained by contacting parents of sick children through the departments until a sample of 20 sick children was reached. The healthy children who served as a comparison group were selected by age, sex, marital status of mother, and social class to match the sample of sick children. A convenience sample was obtained by contacting parents of healthy children through the investigator's acquaintances until there were 20 children in the comparison group.

There were 14 girls (35%) and 26 boys (65%) in the sample. The number of boys almost doubled the number of girls. This finding is in line with the incident rates reported by the National Cancer Institute (1975). The age range of the children was from 6 to 10 years. The mean age was 6 years and 9 months. The number of siblings ranged from none to five, with a mode of one sibling. All families were white and low-to-middle class, resident in a metropolitan area in the United States. Sixty percent of the children came from intact families. In 16 families (40%) the mother was separated from the child's father. Chi square cross-tabulations of parent's education, occupation, and work status showed no significant difference between the parents of the children with chronic life-threatening illness and parents of healthy children.

Of the group of sick children, four suffered from cystic fibrosis, eight from acute lymphocytic leukemia and the rest from other forms of malignancies. The duration of illness ranged from 2 to 90 months. At the time of the interview, 10 out of the 20 children presented visible side effects, e.g., hair loss, weight gain, small stature.

All families of the sick children were first contacted by health professionals from the clinics and the families of healthy children were contacted through acquaintances only after the mothers gave their permission. The investigator contacted them, explained the nature of the research, and set a date for data collection. It is important to note that there was no single refusal from either parents or children to participate in the study. All mothers signed a consent form and the children gave verbal agreement to take part in the study.

All interviews were done by the investigator and took place at the family's homes. Mothers and children were interviewed separately. Interviews lasted from 1 hour, mainly with mothers of healthy children, to 5 hours with several mothers of sick children. Administration time for the study instruments to the children was 20 to 35 minutes. Data were collected during 6 months in 1977.

STUDY INSTRUMENTS

The study instruments included a set of tools for the children and maternal interview schedule for the mothers.

A thorough review of tests and measurements for adults and children, as well as the relevant literature in child development, was unproductive in finding an instrument for measuring degrees of loneliness in childhood. Sociometric measures are commonly used in research on children's friendships and peer relations (Hymel and Asher, 1977), or for identifying isolated children (Bonney, 1971; Wanlass and Prinz, 1982); however, their implementation involves testing whole classes, a costly and impractical tool to gain information about one specific child, and they are inappropriate to tap the subjective experience of loneliness.

Because of the lack of instruments for the direct measurement of loneliness in children, the three instruments used in the present study serve as proxy measurements of loneliness.

The WHO Scale

I designed the WHO scale for the present study as a measure of the child's preferences in interpersonal interactions. (For detailed description of tool development refer to Krulik, 1978). Social learning theory (Rotter et al, 1972), personal space theory (Hall, 1964), and Sullivan's (1953) interpersonal theory were used as the theoretical framework for the scale.

The assumption underlying the WHO scale is that the preference the child shows in choosing different figures (or no one) for interaction or communication is reflective both of his degree of sociability/loneliness and of the zone in which the proposed interaction is most likely to take place. The more social school-age child will choose more peers for interactions in the public domain, fewer in the semi-intimate and intimate domain. In moving from sociability to loneliness, the child will choose in a descending order fewer peers, then fewer sibs, then will turn to his parents, and further in various situations only to self. The lonelier the child is, the less apt he is to choose peers even in situations occurring in the public domain zone.

THE SCALE

The WHO scale (Appendix 10-1) is a paper and pencil measure. The scale is composed of 17 stimuli—typical situations in which the child is the main actor. The subjects were instructed to pick their choice for each situation as to the person(s) with whom they would like to interact or communicate. The choices were people with whom the child is most likely to interact (i.e., father, mother, siblings, friend, or someone else). An "only me" choice was added to give space for a subject's possible preference not to interact. The simulated situations were drawn from realistic situations common to children, representing a modified version of Hall's three zones.

VALIDITY

The three theories included in the framework provided theoretical validation. Six experts in child development, psychology, and child psychiatry were used to obtain face validation. Content validity was also established through judgments of another five experts in child development. Kerlinger's (1973) method was used.

RELIABILITY

Test–retest reliability was established by testing 12 healthy school-age children twice in a period of 3 weeks. The percentage of test–retest agreement for the 16 item scale was 80.2%.

Comfortable Interpersonal Distance (CID) Scale

The Comfortable Interpersonal Distance (CID) scale is a modified and improved version of previous measures of interpersonal distance (Duke and Nowicki, 1972). Duke and Nowicki (1972) adopted from Sommer (1959) the term *personal space* for the interpersonal distance phenomenon. In 1974 Spinetta used personal space as a measure of a dying child's sense of isolation as a part of a larger study on death anxiety in fatally ill children. Using measures of personal space, different experimenters devised the concept of psychological/psychosocial distance (Spinetta, 1974). This concept pertains to individual differences in the degree of desired interpersonal intimacy or dissociation. The assumption underlying the personal space measures is that "the amount of physical distance placed between human figures is reflective of psychological distance . . . [and therefore] psychological closeness is related to physical proximity" (Tolor and Donnon, 1969, p 851). Duke and Nowicki (1972) concluded from their data that interpersonal distance is the result of an interaction between an individual's prior history of reinforcement *vis à vis* others, as well as the context in which the behavior occurs. Integration of interpersonal distance behavior into Rotter's (1972) social learning theory, which emphasizes these two factors, provided the theoretical framework for the scale.

THE SCALE

The CID scale is a paper-and-pencil measure in diagram form that can be conceived as a plane with eight radii emanating from a common point. The length of each radius is 80 mm. The diagram is presented to the subjects as an imaginary round room in which the end of each radius represents an "entrance" to the room. The subjects were asked to imagine themselves standing in the middle of the diagram room, while different stimuli–persons approached them along the radii, starting from the different entrances. By making a mark on the appropriate radius indicating where they would like the person to stop, the subjects revealed their preferable physical distance from the approaching stimulus person. The stimuli–persons can vary among studies, depending upon the content of each study. Prior to specific experimental stimuli, one should begin with an "anchor–stimulus": (1) a person whom the subject likes very much to whom he wants to be very close, (2) a person whom the subject dislikes very much and from whom he wishes to be far away.* Since the chronically sick child's interactions with parents, siblings, and peers have been identified as a potential source for loneliness (Northrup, 1974; Share, 1972; Singher, 1974; Waechter, 1968), I chose them as the appropriate experimental stimuli for the present study.

VALIDITY

To establish validity the construct validation method was used. Martin (1972) and Johnson (1972), who were two students of Duke and Nowicki's, correlated distances on the CID to actual behavior (i.e., preferred distances from real life stimuli). Martin (1972) reported correlations of .65 to .71 in a group of white college students, and Johnson (1972) reported correlations of .83 and .84 in a sample of black college students.

RELIABILITY

There are no reliability studies for the 6- to 10-year age group for this instrument. Although the lack of established reliability is a serious limitation, there is enough collateral evidence to support its use. In an extensive review of the literature on

---

* Personal communication with Duke, March 7, 1977.

personal space research, Evans and Howard (1973) cited 73 studies dealing with the various aspects of the personal space phenomenon. Ten of the cited studies reported using children as young as 4 years of age as their subjects. The tools used in these studies were either measures of distances from real-life figures or a paper and pencil task with figures shown in silhouette. However, the CID scale is based on the same principles and theory of interpersonal space. King (1966), in a study of preschool children, and Meisels and Guardo (1969), in a study of the development of personal space in which third graders were included, showed that their young subjects were able to exhibit comprehension of the phenomenon and presented negative correlation between amount of personal distance and degree of liking and acquaintance. These results support the use of interpersonal distance measures with children.

I am aware of the need for sound reliability studies for the 6- to 10-year age group; unfortunately, such a study was beyond the scope of this research.

Projective Pictures

A modified Thematic Apperception Test was employed to elicit children's indirect and fantasy expressions of loneliness. The set of eight projective pictures used in this study consisted of four pictures from the Thematic Apperception Test (Murray, 1943) and four pictures designed by Waechter (1968) for a study of death anxiety in children with fatal illness. The set was used by Waechter in this study of hospitalized children aged 6 through 10 years in order to elicit content related to illness and hospitalization. In her results Waechter reported on a number of loneliness imageries in the children's responses.

THE SET

The pictures, listed in the order in which they were presented to each child, were:

1. Two boys in adjoining beds (Waechter)
2. Small child in hallway outside closed door to ICU (Waechter)
3. Boy in front of mural depicting operation (TAT 8BM)
4. Child lying in bed and a nurse standing nearby with her back turned (Waechter)
5. Figure outlines in open window (TAT 14)
6. Child in bed and three adults, one wearing a white coat and standing outside the door (Waechter)
7. Woman entering room, hand on face (TAT 3GF)
8. Small child sitting in a doorway of cabin (TAT 13B)

(Waechter's pictures were used with her permission.)

The pictures were shown individually to each child and were always presented in the same order. The child was requested to tell a story about each picture. He was asked to include in the story what he thought was happening in the picture, what the people were thinking about, how they were feeling, and how he thought the event would end. The child was assured that there were no correct or incorrect responses. Nondirective encouragement was supplied if a child had difficulty continuing a story he had started (e.g., it is good, it is your story). If a story contained a reference to illness but the child did not indicate its nature, a question eliciting the nature of the illness was asked.

The stories were recorded on tape. Each child told a story about each picture and all pictures were administered in a single session.

Scoring Scheme

I devised the scoring scheme shown in Appendix B (following the final chapters in this text) for analyzing the children's responses. Each story was analyzed for its main theme, its affect, and its outcome. The content analysis method was used to determine the categories for the themes, affect, and outcome.

Validity

Unfortunately, validity for this instrument has not been established. As a clinician, I believe that the set has content validity and is one of the best existing instruments for eliciting loneliness themes. Since 1968, the same set of projective pictures has been used by investigators studying hospitalized and non-hospitalized fatally ill and non–fatally ill school-age children (Parkas, 1974; Peters, 1975; Spinetta, 1972). This set consistently elicited themes related to a wide variety of illness concerns, loneliness and separation being part of them.

Inter-Rater Reliability

Every fifth protocol (eight subjects) was examined by an independent coder, a psychiatric nurse specialist, using the scoring theme. The degree of agreement on themes, affect, and outcome for each protocol was computed. For the eight protocols there was 97% agreement on themes, 93% on affect, and 97% on outcome. The differences were discussed and the two coders arrived by agreement at one score.

Maternal Interview

A maternal interview schedule was developed for this study. The data were gathered to provide background information as to what strategies were used by both parents and medical personnel in handling the child's illness. The interview included both structured and open-ended questions* covering demographic data and information on variables thought to be associated with loneliness. The following

---

* Some of the interview questions were taken with permission from Waechter's (1968) parental interview schedule.

variables have been identified in the literature as potential sources or influences on loneliness in childhood:

1. Parent–child relationships
2. Child–sibling relationships
3. Child–peer relationships
4. Child at school
5. Child's experience with present illness
6. Child's previous experience with illness, loss, and separation
7. Child–parent communication
8. Family communication
9. Family handling of the child's "being different"

Questions related to the life-threatening illness were eliminated from the interview with mothers of healthy children.

The interviews with the mothers of the sick children were analyzed according to the variables listed. The analysis identified the strategies used by both parents and medical personnel in handling the problems of communication, side effects of illness and treatment regimen, death anxiety of the child, and the parents' anticipatory grief. The interviews with mothers of the healthy children were not analyzed in the present study and will serve as a data bank.

RESULTS

The hypotheses derived from the first study question were partially supported. The first hypothesis was that children with chronic life-threatening disease will respond to a set of projective pictures with more loneliness themes (i.e. aloneness, separation, death anxiety, threat to body integrity, and suicide) than healthy children. The results show that children with chronic life-threatening disease responded to the projective pictures with more loneliness themes within the aloneness subcategory ($p < .03$).

Responses to a picture that showed a small child in a hallway outside a closed door to an intensive care unit read: "I think the father is in there in the Intensive Care Unit and she has nobody to turn to, so she is just waiting alone in the hall and just thinking about her daddy." Another child said: "She doesn't look like she want to be there. She wants her mother. She feels terrible she's all alone. There's no one around." To another picture a 9-year-old girl responded: "He is just sitting there, he doesn't have no one to play with. He is sad watching all the kids playing and they didn't ask him to play, maybe they don't like him. Maybe he goes after this and play with them."

In the responses depicting other subcategories, threat to body integrity, death anxiety, and suicide, there was no significant difference between sick and healthy children.

For the whole group the analysis of their stories produced 101 loneliness themes in descending order:

37 threat to body integrity themes
17 death anxiety themes
12 aloneness themes
 7 suicide themes

Tests of significant difference for the affect and outcome of the story responses show no significant difference between stories of children with chronic life-threatening disease and stories of healthy children.

The third hypothesis was that children with chronic life-threatening disease will place human figures at a further distance from one another than will healthy children on the CID scale. The results show that the mean distance of all figures for the children with chronic life-threatening illness was not significantly different than the mean distance of all figures for the healthy children. However, they tended to place their mothers and one friend at a further distance than did healthy children.

ANALYSIS OF MATERNAL INTERVIEWS

A certain degree of loneliness in the child was reported by nine mothers. Although they had frequently communicated openly with the ill child, they realized that he was keeping "a lot of things to himself," mainly about his illness trajectory and possible death. Three mothers were sure that his illness and possible death frightened the child more than he was willing to talk about. Two parents felt that the child was not sharing the fears because he wished to protect them. "She must have fears of death, but she never told me about them. She is protecting me."

Some children didn't want their friends around because of lack of energy or shame due to changes in their appearance. Some mothers related the child's loneliness to him being rejected by others. Three children were rejected by their friends. Other mothers felt that different members of the extended family were also actively avoiding or distancing the child and the immediate family.

In relation to the second study question, content analysis of the interviews with the mothers of the children with chronic life-threatening disease revealed the following strategies:

STRATEGIES RELATED TO COMMUNICATION WITH THE CHILD

All parents and involved medical personnel adopted the open approach to communications. The degree of openness and amount of communication varied according to the specific communication topic (i.e., the nature of the illness, treatments, side effects of illness and treatment, and prognosis) and the recipient of the communication.

In order to maintain channels for open communication between the child and significant others in his social milieu, the mothers initiated open communications with the child's siblings, teachers, classmates, peers, extended family, and family friends.

Communication to the Child

Some mothers believed that the child should be told the "whole truth" on all topics immediately after diagnosis. Others thought that the child should have an overview of his illness and prospective treatments at the beginning and then deal with the questions as they arise (in most of these families the child was diagnosed before his fifth birthday). Only five mothers felt that the child should be spared from some parts of the truth, mainly the burden of fatal prognosis (Table 10-1). All mothers perceived medical personnel to be supportive of their particular stance. Medical personnel shared with the child his progress and treatment schedule, and answered all his questions with sincerity.

Of the 20 children, 17 knew the name of their illness. Most mothers thought the child should hear the name from them to eliminate the possibility of a child's friend revealing to the sick child "You are sick with leukemia and you are dying." All 16 children received explanations as to the nature of their illnesses. All children with cystic fibrosis knew about the genetic aspect of the illness and understood to some extent the degree of lung and intestinal involvement. Children with malignancies knew of "a fight between good cells and bad cells" and of "a tumor—a growth that was growing with no control."

All parents were very open about check-ups and treatment procedures. They always prepared the child a day in advance as to what was going to happen in the clinic. While carrying out the procedures the doctor and nurse explained to the child every step and how much pain to expect. Mothers thought that the preparation and knowledge helped the child to express his feelings about these treatments, to gain some control over what was happening to him, and especially to establish trust relationships with parents and medical personnel.

All children were told about the chronic aspect of the illness, "an illness that you will have to live with and get treatment for all your life" (Table 10-2). The prognosis of possible death was discussed with ten children. All children were aware that the medications were keeping the disease from relapse and four children were also aware of the possible failure of medication and subsequent death. Most mothers thought they were very open and honest with the child, allowing him to ask any question and to express his feelings about the illness, treatment, and side effects. No parent regretted any degree of openness. In general, mothers

Table 10-1. Number of Mothers According to Degree of Open Communication

Variable	N	%
Child should be told the "whole truth"	10	50
Child should be told only when he asks and then the "whole truth"	5	25
Child should be spared from some part of the truth (fatal prognosis)	5	25

Table 10-2. Children's Knowledge of Various Aspects of Illness According to Mothers' Report

	Number of Children		
Variable	Yes	No	Not Sure
Diagnosis	17	3	
Nature of illness	15	4	1
Procedures and treatment schedules	18	1	1
Side effects of illness and treatment	18	1	1
Fatal prognosis	12	6	2

felt that keeping open communication drew the family closer together than it had been before the illness.

Communication to Siblings

Parents and medical personnel communicated to the child's siblings in a way similar to the way they did to the sick child himself. As a result, in seven families the siblings got involved in the sick child's care and helped him, especially toward the outside world. Three mothers knew the child shared with his siblings feelings and concerns that he had never before shared with them. Open communication with siblings was considered by several mothers the only way to reduce potential feelings of isolation and rejection for the siblings.

Communication to Teachers, Classmates, and Peers

All mothers contacted the teacher and discussed with her the child's illness, treatment, possible side effects, and limitations. Fourteen teachers discussed the child's illness with the class, mainly to prepare the children to accept the sick child's side effects and possible school absences. Some teachers also encouraged the children to keep contact with the sick child by sending him cards or going to visit in his home.

Only a few mothers initiated communications with the child's peers. One mother always explained to new friends about the child's illness, treatments, and side effects. Another mother called her child's friends' mothers and asked them to talk to their children about the child's illness. All of these mothers felt that informing the child's friends reduced the amount of teasing and increased understanding.

Communication to Extended Family and Family Friends

All mothers told members of the extended family and close friends about the child's illness and its progress. Communication between the child's parents and their ability to communicate openly with the sick child, the siblings, extended family, friends, teachers, and the child's peers was a crucial element in enhancing family unity.

STRATEGIES RELATED TO MANAGEMENT OF THE CHILD'S "BEING DIFFERENT"
OWING TO ILLNESS AND TREATMENT SIDE EFFECTS

The strategies related to management of side effects of illness and treatment were mainly geared toward reducing the child's feelings of being different from his siblings or friends. Most mothers were aware of the child's feeling different from his peers and siblings.

Children felt different in regard to the way they looked and developed, their energy levels and physical compentencies and the reactions they got from their surroundings.

The strategies fall into four major areas: management of medical regimen, changes in body appearance and body functions, threats to performance of child's roles, and management of discipline. Most mothers were very innovative in initiating "normalizing tactics" to manage dietary restrictions, postural drainage, medications, hair loss, low energy levels, and keeping the child's roles.

Dietary Restrictions

There was little continuous battle about food management in families where mothers started to cook a fat-free diet for the whole family, or sent the cystic fibrosis cookbook to a cooking class at school and the whole class cooked and ate the appropriate food. When the child was invited to parties or eating out, the mothers baked a special cake and sent it along with the child. They also called the hostess in advance to notify her about dietary restrictions. Three mothers gave the children permission to regulate their enzyme pills in case they snacked on foods.

Postural Drainage

Complying with the postural drainage requirements was possible since all mothers were very careful to adapt the postural drainage time to the child's playtime. None of the mothers felt that it was "fair" to call the child in for exercises. One mother initiated at an early age doing the physical therapy in front of other neighborhood children: "Then they will all get on the floor and want me to do it to them to see what it feels like." In another family everyone would get on the floor and do the physical therapy as part of the family exercises.

Medications

In some families the child was responsible for taking his own medications. These mothers were confident that the child understood the importance of the pills and was mature enough to handle his medications. In two families siblings got their vitamin pills while the sick child got his medications, "so that no one would feel left out."

Hair Loss

Most families with older sick children thought that hair loss was one of the major traumas for the child and for them. Nevertheless, no child in these families stayed at home or secluded himself because of hair loss.

Many families prepared the children for possible hair loss. Most of them thought that a wig would be an acceptable solution. It was all of these parents' experience, however, that the child wore the wig only for a short time and then exchanged it for hats, scarves, or nothing. All parents emphasized to the children that hair loss was a temporary condition and assured them that hair would grow back.

Low Energy Levels
None of the mothers had set any special limits on how much time and in what activities the child should engage. It was usually the children who limited their activities when they felt tired or distressed. When mothers realized that the children did not have the energy to go out and play, some used to invite them to the house.

Keeping the Child's Roles
School: To reduce possible differences in academic achievements as a result of school absences and reduced energy levels, some mothers arranged for a home tutor, extra help from teachers and other students at school or helped the child themselves daily with schoolwork.

Sports: Parents encouraged children to be involved regularly in such sports as baseball, soccer, swimming, and scouting. At difficult periods they tried to find solutions without stopping the activity, like when a child "has been on the baseball team and didn't quite finish the season because his legs got so bad": following his father's suggestion, "the team made him just bat the ball and his friends all took turns running for him so he wouldn't have to run the bases."

Management of Discipline
Another area of great concern for all mothers was the management of discipline. At the time of the interview, all mothers were aware of their possible tendency to treat the child differently from his siblings due to the illness and its side effects. All mothers except one made a conscious attempt to treat the ill child in the same way they treated his siblings, or as if he were a healthy child. They discouraged siblings from making special allowances. They did not want the child "to be socially retarded in addition to his illness." Parents were also alert to the danger of the child's developing high dependency.

All mothers perceived medical personnel as firm in their belief of the need to continue with reasonable limit setting and discipline. It was very obvious that as long as these children were in remission, parents' great efforts to resume normalcy showed positive results. However, in time of crisis, normalizing measures, discipline, and strategies toward dealing with side effects of the illness and its treatments were no longer effective.

STRATEGIES RELATED TO MANAGEMENT OF THE CHILD'S DEATH ANXIETY
Several sources of possible death anxiety in the child were identified from interviews with the mothers. Death anxiety was generated from the child's inner perception of his physical condition, parents' and significant others' beliefs about the child's prognosis, the child's awareness of a death of another child with the same diagnosis, and the child's previous experience with death.

Although the prognosis of death was discussed with 10 children only, 17 children expressed their death anxiety in different ways. Some stated, "I don't want to die" or asked, "Am I going to die?" The most common answer to the child's question, "Am I going to die?" was "We are all going to die one day; I don't know when you are going to die." In an attempt to reduce the child's anxiety, some mothers tried to equalize his chances of dying with those of other family members.

Many mothers used their religious beliefs in trying to answer their child's questions. Some mothers tried to convey to the child that he was a special person if "God was ready to take him." "We have always said 'Jay, you are special, you know. God only gives things like this to special people that he knows can handle them.' And he said 'why do I have to be special? I don't want to be special any more. I want to be like anybody else. Why does God do this to me?'."

These mothers also believed in life after death and discussed with the child the image of heaven. One mother reported that her child said, " 'If I were to die, would I get to ride a merry-go-round and a horse?' And I said you can ride a horse forever and forever up in heaven' and he had a beautiful picture of heaven. Later, when he grew older, he didn't care how beautiful heaven was going to be. He didn't want to leave me. He always said 'When I die, will you promise to die at the same time?' So he won't be alone up in heaven. I told him that some day we will all be together again, but he wants to make sure we all die at the same time. He doesn't want to be alone up there or down here."

The nonreligious explanation that a few mothers adopted was, "When you are dead, it is only your body that dies. But your soul is leaving the body and can stay with us forever. We wouldn't be able to see you, or talk to you, but the soul would always be with us." Only one mother told the child that she didn't know what to expect after one dies. She further explained that there were different beliefs about it and that everyone has the right to believe in what seems right to them.

Death anxiety generated much anguish in parents and children. They constantly struggled to master the uncertainty and fear associated with death. This struggle was often failing, although the subject of death was dealt with very openly.

DISCUSSION

In addition to the mother's reports, I rated the overall loneliness of the ill children as higher or lower, based on the child's scores on the three study tools.

The children with chronic life-threatening diseases were somewhat lonelier than their healthy controls. Analysis of the loneliness of the ill group revealed that 11 children out of the 20 in the sample expressed higher levels of loneliness. These were children who suffered from visible side effects of illness and treatment and/or received detailed description of life after death.

How do these findings compare to previous research? There are no published studies on loneliness in children with chronic life-threatening disease. However,

Waechter (1968) and Spinetta (1973) are the only researchers who conducted a systematic study on areas related to loneliness in children with chronic life-threatening illness. I chose to compare the present study with Waechter's research only. Waechter's findings support the first hypothesis of this study that children with chronic life-threatening disease respond with more loneliness themes than do healthy children. As compared to the present study, Waechter documented on the one hand more death anxiety themes in the children with chronic life-threatening illness, and on the other hand no death anxiety themes in the healthy children. Three factors may account for these differences. The most important difference between the two studies lies in the historical time change between 1968 and 1977. The two study samples came from two "different generations."* Waechter's study was conducted at a time when survival rates for children with cancer and cystic fibrosis were lower than they are today. Very few children with cystic fibrosis survived beyond adolescence, and few children with cancer survived beyond 3 years from the time of diagnosis. These facts left hardly a doubt in the parents' minds as to the fatal outcome of the illness. It is likely that parents transferred their feelings of doom to their children. Imminent death, accompanied by death anxiety, were probably more central to these families' lives than they were in 1977 and definitely today when higher survival rates and possible cures instill hope.

Also, at the time of Waechter's study, discussion of death, especially with children, was taboo. Most parents and medical personnel used the protective approach in communications with the fatally ill child. Waechter claimed that the children's death anxiety resulted mainly from lack of open and honest communication about their diagnosis and prognosis. In contrast, parents and medical personnel in this study belong to a society where death and dying are discussed more openly. The medical personnel caring for this study population, who witnessed for years the ill effects of closed communication, themselves adopted and encouraged all parents to adopt the open approach in their communications to the child about his illness and possible death. The change in the communication approach may be partially responsible for the fewer death anxiety themes found in the ill children's stories in this sample.

A similar line of thought may explain why healthy children in this study did not differ from the ill children in the number of themes dealing with death anxiety, separation anxiety, and threats to body integrity. Mothers of both healthy and ill children reported on their children viewing frequent depiction of violence and death on television. Such exposure may raise the healthy child's awareness of death and his death anxiety levels, whereas the ill child, by virtue of his illness, was already aware of death and harbored death anxiety. I do not know how television viewing of death was dealt with by parents. The variance between healthy and ill children in this study, the fact that ill children seemed to receive more explanations about death, the fact that indiscriminate exposure to the idea of death may increase death anxiety in the healthy children, while open discussion geared to the

---

* This methodological issue is often discussed as a problem of cross-sectional research (Nunnally, 1973).

ill child may reduce some of his death anxiety, may explain the similarity in number of death anxiety themes in the stories of the two groups of this study.

Along with open discussion of death, both healthy and ill children were widely exposed to pictures and talk of crime, violence, separation, and divorce. In the children's stories the common themes of threat to body integrity depicted gunshots, theft, and robbery. Common separation themes for all children involved "a very sad woman, who was left by her husband who will never come back." It seems that in relation to anxieties of separation and body integrity the atmosphere in which all these children were living affected both ill and healthy children alike and thus blurred the differential impact of the illness upon the children's fantasies.

The third factor explaining the difference between the two studies is that Waechter's was conducted in a hospital setting, whereas this study was conducted in the child's home. Hospitalizations for children with chronic life-threatening disease are usually associated with crisis of diagnosis, exacerbation of illness, or approaching death. Crisis in these illnesses is highly related to increased death anxiety in both parents and children. Therefore, one can expect higher levels of death anxiety in hospitalized children than in those at home.

Increased survival rates, increase in open communication, and the use of the home setting explain the differences in findings between Waechter's and the present study.

All parents developed coping strategies for the problems of communications with the child and significant others in his social milieu, the "differentness" of the child, and the child's death anxiety. These strategies reflected the families' strength and resilience in dealing with on-going problems of living with chronic life-threatening illness. Many mothers were very innovative in their efforts to normalize the child's life. They thereby reduced the child's differentness and the amount of teasing and rejection he had to experience.

Anxiety about death may increase in children who are undergoing a crisis, as a result of messages both from within the body and from the environment. An increase in anxiety of death is likely to be followed by questions about death. If answers to these questions are loaded with anxiety, uncertainty, and descriptions of "aloneness in heaven," one should expect the child's loneliness to increase. Crises are also characterized by very low energy levels, mood swings, irritation, and restlessness due to the child's illness and heavy medication. During crisis, the child's differentness is most obvious to himself and others, and there is very little parents can do, besides providing warmth and understanding, to ease his pain. This is the time when many mothers become completely consumed with the care of the child, which ultimately results in the mothers' resentment of the child and the child's increasing loneliness. Loneliness seems to reach different levels throughout the illness trajectory, with peaks at times of crisis.

For the less lonely children, who were long into remission, the open approach to communication and active strategies to reduce differentness appear to be successful in alleviating their loneliness. The fact that the lonelier children had more visible side effects concurs with Goffman's theory of avoidance behavior related to visible stigma. These children were more often avoided and rejected by their peers and even by family members.

In conclusion, the children with chronic life-threatening illness in this study were lonelier than were the healthy comparison group. While open communication probably alleviated some loneliness related to illness and treatment in some children, indiscriminate open communication about death and life after death seemed to increase loneliness in other children. Children under crisis, and/or children with visible side effects of illness or treatment, and/or children who received detailed descriptions of life after death seem to be at higher risk of developing loneliness.

IMPLICATIONS FOR PRACTICE

The findings of this study suggest that two principles should guide the interventions of health professionals with the child who has chronic life-threatening disease and his family. First strategies should be geared toward strengthening the resources and coping abilities of the child, and second strategies should be aimed at altering the environment to accept and help the child with his special needs. The implications of the study fall therefore into four major categories: education of health care professionals; guidance of parents of children with chronic life-threatening disease; education of the general public, especially school teachers; and establishment of programs to aid the child in alleviating his loneliness. The first step toward helping the child is to make health care professionals fully aware of the occurrence of loneliness and its possible sources and manifestations. This knowledge will enable them to recognize the lonely child, assess the level of his loneliness, and identify its sources. When guiding parents in regard to the psychological and social impact of the illness upon the child, the medical team should share knowledge about loneliness and its sources (impaired communication with the child, the child's being different, the child's death anxiety). Only then can strategies for alleviating loneliness be developed.

Regarding strategies for alleviating loneliness, the findings of this study supported the recommendation of many clinicians for the use of open and honest communication with the child about his illness and prognosis. Adults, when communicating with the child about his possible death, must first come to terms with their own fears, uncertainties, and unresolved anxieties about illness and death. Children tend to become anxious whenever they sense anxiety in adults.

Special attention should be paid to discussions with the child regarding death and afterlife. Both health care professionals and parents must train themselves to listen carefully to the child's questions. Often, adults tend to give children detailed answers for which they did not ask. While explaining death and afterlife to children, parents should be alerted so as to avoid adding to the child's fear of separation and desertion in death by "comforting" stories about the child's being happy, but alone in heaven.

Parents should also be alerted to the increased probability of the child's developing loneliness in times of crisis.

Parents should be made aware of the existence of self-help groups of parents (e.g., the Candlelighters). Parents are able both to extend emotional support to other parents and to exchange valuable knowledge regarding the management of the child's differentness, fears, and concerns, as well their discipline of the child. The medical team should discuss with the parents the advantages of joining such a group as opposed to the possible disadvantages of experiencing additional pain and anxiety.

The general public should be better informed about the nature of chronic life-threatening illness and the problems the ill children are facing. Special attention should be given to informing the public that these illnesses are not contagious, so that people do not distance themselves from the ill child or instruct their children to do so out of fear of contagion.

When returning to school, the child is very vulnerable to developing loneliness as a result of teasing and possible rejection by his classmates. It is desirable for the medical team to contact the school teacher and school nurse to inform them about the child's illness. Several goals can be achieved by this contact:

1. The teacher will learn about the nature of the illness, treatments, side effects, and restrictions.
2. The teacher will receive the medical team's assessment of the child's emotional state and his special needs, so that she can be helpful to him.
3. With the parents' and the child's permission, the teacher can be encouraged to discuss with the class the nature of the child's illness and prepare them as to the possibility of visible side effects and (temporary) limitations.
4. Suggestions could be made to the teacher for class projects on subjects such as life, illness, and death. These projects would enable the ill child to join his peers in their efforts to understand and master these concepts without him being the focus of the discussion. Many of these tasks could effectively be handled by the school nurse.

As programs for the child with chronic life-threatening disease, therapeutic groups should be established. With the support of an experienced and warm professional using play, drawings, psychodrama, music, and so forth, these children would have an opportunity to work through some of their fears, concerns, and anxieties, which they may not be able to share in their healthy environment.

Often these children's loneliness results in or is accompanied by social isolation. Methods and principles for intervention with healthy social isolated children (Wanless and Prinz, 1982) should be assessed as to their possible relevance to the experience of children with chronic life-threatening illness. The suitable interventions could then be modified to intervene with lonely, socially isolated sick children.

Loneliness is a state most likely to develop in the child with chronic life-threatening illness, and even small success in alleviating its anguish increases the quality of life.

REFERENCES

Ablin AR, Binger CM, Stein RC, Kushner JH, Zoger S, Mikkelsen C: A conference with the family of a leukemic child. Am J Dis Child 122:362–365, 1971

American Cancer Society: 1975 Cancer Facts and Figures. New York, American Cancer Society, 1976

Benoliel JQ: Some thoughts on a concept of care. The case for the child with leukemia. Paper presented at a workshop, School of Nursing, University of Virginia, Charlottesville, 1972

Benoliel JQ: Anticipatory grief in physicians and nurses. In Schoenberg B, Carr AC, Kutcher AN, Peretz D, Goldberg I (eds): Anticipatory Grief. New York, Columbia University Press, 1974

Bluebond–Langner M: I know, do you? A study of awareness, communication and coping in terminally ill children. In Schoenberg B, Carr AC, Kutscher AH, Peretz D, Goldberg I (eds): Anticipatory Grief. New York, Columbia University Press, 1974

Bonney ME: Assessment of efforts to aid socially isolated elementary school pupils. J Educ Res 64:359–364, 1971

Boone DR, Hartman BH: The benevolent over-reaction. A well-intentioned but malignant influence on the handicapped child. Clin Pediatr 11:268–271, 1972

Burgert EO: Emotional impact of childhood acute leukemia. Mayo Clin Proc 47:273–277, 1972

Campbell JD: Peer relations in childhood. In Hoffman ML, Hoffman LW (eds): Rev Child Dev Res 3, 1964

Clancy H, McBride G: The isolation syndrome in childhood. Dev Med Child Neurol 17:198–219, 1975

Cowen EL, Pederson A, Babigan H, Izzo LD, Trost MA: Long term follow-up of early detected vulnerable children. J Consult Clin Psychol 41:438–446, 1973

Cytryn L, Moore PVP, Robinson ME: Psychological adjustment of children with cystic fibrosis. In Anthony EJ, Koupernik C (eds): The Child in His Family: The impact of disease and death, vol 2. New York, John Wiley & Sons, 1973

Deasy–Spinetta P: The school and the child with cancer. In Spinetta J, Deasy–Spinetta P (eds): Living with Childhood Cancer. St Louis, CV Mosby, 1981

Debusky M (ed): The Chronically Ill Child and His Family. Springfield, IL, Charles C Thomas, 1970

Denning CR, Gluckson MA, Mohr I: Phychological and social aspects of cystic fibrosis. In Mangos JA, Talamo RC (eds): Cystic fibrosis: Projections into the Future. New York, Stratton Intercontinental, 1976

Duke MP, Nowicki S: A new measure and social-learning model for interpersonal distance. J Exp Res Personality 6:119–132, 1972

Easson WM: The Dying Child. Springfield, Il, Charles C Thomas, 1970

Evans AE, Edin S: If a child must die. . . . N Engl J Med 278:138–141, 1968

Fromm–Reichmann F: Loneliness. Psychiatry 22:1–16, 1959

Futterman EH, Hoffman I: Crisis and adaptation in the families of fatally ill children. In Anthony EJ, Koupernik C (eds): The Child and His Family, pp 127–144. New York, John Wiley & Sons, 1973

Glaser BG, Strauss AL: Awareness of Dying. Chicago, Aldine, 1965

Hall ET: Silent assumptions in social communications. Am Anthropol 66:154–163, 1964

Horowitz FD: The relationship of anxiety, self concept, and sociometric status among fourth, fifth and sixth grade children. J Abnorm Soc Psychol 65:212–214, 1962

Hymel S, Asher SR: Assessment and Training of Isolated Children's Social Skills. Paper presented at the biennial meeting of the Society for Research in Child Development, New Orleans, Louisiana, March 1977

Johnson I: Interpersonal Distancing Responses of Black Versus White Females Paper presented at South Eastern Psychological Association Meetings, Atlanta, Georgia, 1972

Jung CG: Memories, Dreams, Reflections. New York, Vintage, 1963

Kaplan DM, Smith A, Grobstein R: School management of the seriously ill child. J School Health 44:250–254, 1974

Kastenbaum R: The child's understanding of death: How does it develop? In Grollman EA (ed): Explaining Death to Children. Boston, Beacon Press, 1967

Kerdinger FN: Foundations of Behavioural Research. New York, Holt, Rinehart & Winston, 1965

King MG: Interpersonal relations in preschool children and average approach distance. J Genet Psychol 109:109–116, 1966

Koocher GP: "Why isn't the gerbil moving anymore?" Discussing death in the classroom —and at home. Child Today 4:18–21, 36, 1975

Koocher GP, O'Malley IE: The Damocles Syndrome. New York, McGraw–Hill, 1981

Krulik T: Loneliness in School-Age Children Living with Life-Threatening Illness. Doctoral Dissertation, University of California, San Francisco, 1978. University Microfilms No. S.Z.N. 79-005548

Lascari AD: The family and the dying child: A compassionate approach. Med Times 97:207–215, 1969

Leiderman HP: Loneliness: A psychodynamic interpretation. Int Psychiatr Clin 6(2):155–174, 1969

Martin M: Parental and Interpersonal Determinants of Trust. Unpublished doctoral dissertation, Emory University, 1972

McAnarney ER, Pless IB, Satterwhite B, Friedman SB: Psychological problems of children with chronic juvenile arthritis. Pediatrics 53:523–528, 1974

Meisels M, Guardo CJ: Development of personal space schemata. Child Dev 40:1167–1178, 1969

Mijuskovic B: Loneliness: An interdisciplinary approach. Psychiatry 40:113–132, 1977

Moore JA: Relationship between loneliness and interpersonal relationships. Can Counsellor 8:84–89, 1974

Morrissey JR: Death anxiety in children with fatal illness. In Parad HJ (ed): Crisis Intervention: Selected Readings, pp. 324–338. New York, Family Service Association of America, 1965

Moustakas CE: Loneliness. Englewood Cliffs, NJ, Prentice Hall, 1961

Moustakas CE: Loneliness and Love. Englewood Cliffs, NJ, Prentice–Hall, 1972

Murray HA: Thematic Apperception Test. Cambridge, MA, Harvard University Press, 1943

Natterson JM, Knudson AG: Observations concerning fear of death in fatally ill children and their mothers. Psychosomat Med 22:456–465, 1960

Northrup FC: The dying child. Am J Nurs 74:1066–1068, 1974

Peplau HE: Loneliness and the Lower Socioeconomic Psychiatric Patient. Paper presented at the meeting of the Interdivisional Council of Psychiatric and Mental Health Nursing, New York, New York, May 1966

Peplau LA: Perlman D (eds): Loneliness. New York, John Wiley & Sons, 1982

Peters BM: Concepts of Hospitalized Children about Causality of Illness and Intent of Treatment. University of Pittsburgh; unpublished dissertation, 1975

Perlman D, Peplau A: Theoretical Approaches to Loneliness. In Peplau A, Perlman D (eds): Loneliness. New York, John Wiley & Sons, 1982

Reese HW: Relationships between self-acceptance and sociometric choices. J Abnorm Soc Psychol 62:472–474, 1961

Rotter JB, Chance JE, Phares EJ: Applications of a Social Learning Theory of Personality. New York, Holt, Rinehart & Winston, 1972

Rubin Z: Child without friends. In Peplau LA, Perlman D (eds): Loneliness. New York, John Wiley & Sons, 1982

Share L: Family communication in the crisis of a child's fatal illness. Omega 3:187–201, 1972

Shantz CU: The development of social cognition. In EM Hetherington (ed): Review of Child Development Research, Vol 5. Chicago, University of Chicago Press, 1975

Sigler A: The leukemic child and his family: An emotional challenge. In M Debuskey (ed): The Chronically Ill Child and His Family. Springfield, IL, Charles C Thomas, 1970

Singher LJ: The slowly dying child. Clin Pediatr 13:861–867, 1974

Sommer R: Studies in personal space. Sociometry 22:247–260, 1959

Spinetta JJ, Rigler D, Karon M: Personal Space as a measure of a dying child's sense of isolation. J Consult Clin Psychol 42(6):751–756, 1974

Spinetta JJ, Deasy–Spinetta P (eds): Living with Childhood Cancer. St Louis, CV Mosby, 1981

Stengel E: Suicide and Attempted Suicide. Middlesex: Penguin, 1971

Sullivan HS: The Interpersonal Theory of Psychiatry. New York, WW Norton, 1953

Tolor A, Donnon MS: Psychological distance as a function of length of hospitalization. Psychol Rep 25:851–855, 1969

Tropauer A, Franz MN, Dilgard VW: Psychological aspects of care of children with cystic fibrosis. Am J Dis Child 119:424–432, 1970

Vernick J: Meaningful communication with the fatally ill child. In Anthony EJ, Koupernik C (eds): The Child and His Family, pp 105–119. New York, John Wiley & Sons, 1973

Vernick J, Karon M: Who's afraid of death on a leukemic ward? Am J Dis Child 109:393–397, 1965

Waechter EH: Death Anxiety in Children with Fatal Illness. unpublished dissertation, Stanford University, 1968

Waechter EH, Phillips S, Holaday B: Nursing Care of Children, 10th ed. Philadelphia, JB Lippincott 1985

Wanlass RL, Prinz RY: Methodological issues in conceptualizing and treating childhood social isolation. Psychol Bull 92(1):39–55, 1982

Wayne P: The lonely school child. Am J Nurs 68:774–777, 1968

Weiss R: Loneliness: The Experience of Emotional and Social Isolation. Cambridge, MA, MIT Press, 1973

Wiener JM: What should the child know of death? Med Insight 5:25–33, 1973

Appendix 10-1

The WHO Scale

Code Number: _____

Birth Date: _____

Grade: _____

Siblings: 1. Age _____ Sex _____

2. Age _____ Sex _____

3. Age _____ Sex _____

Interview Date: _____

Dear Friend:

This is a game about who you share things with, things you do, see, or think about. There are 17 sentences describing things different kids like to share with different people. I shall read these sentences to you and ask you to pick your choice of "what would you like to share with whom?" All choices are right.

Thank you!

	Father	Mother	Only Me	Brother or Sister	Friend	Someone Else
1. You can invite anyone you wish to your birthday party; you would invite . . .	_____	_____	_____	_____	_____	_____

	Father	Mother	Only Me	Brother or Sister	Friend	Someone Else
2. If you were on a deserted island, who would you like to be with you?	____	____	____	____	____	____
3. You are worried about something. You would tell your worries to . . .	____	____	____	____	____	____
4. You organize a team. Who do you want to be on it?	____	____	____	____	____	____
5. You are in a boat on a lake. Who would you like to be with you?	____	____	____	____	____	____
6. You are afraid to go to the hospital. Who would you tell?	____	____	____	____	____	____
7. You are putting on a play. Who would you like to play the part of a true friend?	____	____	____	____	____	____
8. You are alone in a room. Who would you like to join you?	____	____	____	____	____	____
9. You were frightened the last time you had to get a shot. Who would you tell?	____	____	____	____	____	____
10. You take part in a big project. Who do you want to be your partner?	____	____	____	____	____	____
11. You are going to be a pilot of a rocket to the moon. Who would you take with you?	____	____	____	____	____	____
12. You feel lonely. Who do you tell?	____	____	____	____	____	____
13. You are in a party. Who would you like to sit next to you?	____	____	____	____	____	____
14. You are in the yard by yourself. Who would you like to join you?	____	____	____	____	____	____
15. You feel ashamed. Who do you tell?	____	____	____	____	____	____

	Father	Mother	Only Me	Brother or Sister	Friend	Someone Else
16. Something made you cry. Who do you tell?	___	___	___	___	___	___
17. You feel great. Who do you tell?	___	___	___	___	___	___
Total	___	___	___	___	___	___

Child known as:	Adult		Child	
very sociable, outgoing	AF =		CHF =	OM =
somewhat reserved				
lonely	AO =		CHO =	
Informant:	Group I	A =	CH =	OM =
	Group II	A =	CH =	OM =
	Group III	A =	CH =	OM =

11 · Consciousness of Dying and Projective Fantasy of Young Children With Malignant Disease

Margaret M. Malone

Abstract

Hypotheses regarding intrapsychic disruption, specific types of anxiety and fear, and defense structure in young children with potentially fatal illnesses were tested by administering two projective tests to 24 Irish children (ages 3–6) with malignancies and 24 matched controls with non–life-threatening orthopedic diseases. Responses of the children with malignancies showed more imagery related to, and descriptions of, negative futures, loneliness, bodily intrusion, and nonbeing. Possible explanations of these findings and their implications for the treatment of children with potentially fatal illnesses are discussed.

Contemporary studies of the dying process have been hampered by the superstitions of the general public and the psychological denial of health professionals, whose main emphasis is on the defeat of death. This denial is most marked in relationship to young children. Very young fatally ill children represent an indisputable failure on the part of the medical profession and thereby invite hostility, repudiation, and anxiety. With the exception of studies by Waechter[1] and Spinetta,[2] which refuted the belief that the ability to speak about death depended on the ability to understand its meaning, reports on 6- to 10-year-old terminally ill children suggest that a concept of death is based on cognition.[3–8] With viewpoints

Reprinted from J Dev Behav Pediatr 3:55–60, 1982.

more philosophically than empirically based, investigators have been unable to take any comprehensive and systematic positions on the thinking of very young children.

The psychological impact of specific experience-related events is considered a salient factor in the individual reaction to fatal illness. While age and intellectual ability may be important factors in the seriously ill child's perception of impending death, what seems more significant is the process by which changes in the child's psychosocial milieu impinge on his or her consciousness. Malignant neoplastic disease is especially distressing in young children under age 6 because of the intensive, repeated, and painful therapy. Serious illness in young children imposes a grave psychological threat at a time when adaptive functions are just beginning to operate. Young patients must learn to cope with altered emotional climates, long separations from parents, and devastating changes in self-image and self-concept.

The present study investigated the preconceptual awareness of the possibility of impending death among 3- to 6-year-old seriously ill children through recorded fantasy productions. A lack of direct expression of fear or awareness of death does not mean that these children are free from apprehensive thoughts about their fate. Young children rarely exhibit the reactions characteristic of dying adults. The fear of death internalized in the body may be denied, but it may also be exteriorized and displaced to fears of threat from without. Thus, the inner sphere may be changed to an outer sphere of threat.[9] Seriously ill children will then attempt to deal with their internal feelings by attaching them to a variety of objects or situations. Feelings about isolation, loneliness, and medical or surgical procedures may actually be expressions of a pervasive fear about survival. The three hypotheses of this study, based on this reasoning, were as follows:

1. Children with diagnosed malignant disease would present more intrapsychic disruption, reflected by more affective distress, less adequate defensive structure, and more threatening imagery in their stories on the Adapted Picture Test (APT), than children of the same age hospitalized for an orthopedic disorder.
2. Children with malignancies would express more stories relating anxiety about hospital and medical procedures on the APT and the Children's Apperceptive Test-Supplement (CAT-S) than the control group would express.
3. Children with malignancies would rely more extensively on fantasy, as evidenced by responses to the CAT-S, than would the controls.

METHOD

The study examined two populations: 1) 24 children with a diagnosis of malignant neoplastic disease who were inpatients at Our Lady's Hospital for Sick Children, Dublin, Ireland, and 2) 24 children from the same hospital with an orthopedic disorder not considered life-threatening by the medical staff. In maternal interviews conducted before the projective testing, it was ascertained that none of the seriously ill children had been directly informed as to the nature of their illness. The 48 children were paired on the basis of age, sex, socioeconomic status (based on occupation of primary wage earner), and long-term exposure to doctors and hospitals (defined as an illness lasting at least 4 months duration).

Tables 11-1 and 11-2 present diagnostic and demographic data on the two samples. Each group contained 12 boys and 12 girls; mean ages ('SD) were 57'9.73 months for the malignancy group and 58'12.98 months for controls.

PROCEDURE

To determine whether children with malignancies present more affective distress in story-telling and rely more extensively on fantasy, two projective instruments were used. The Adapted Picture Test (used through permission of the author, Dr. Eugenia Waechter) consists of four pictures originally designed for use with 6- to 10-year-old children. Because 85% of the children in the study were between 3 and 5 years old, it was necessary to adapt the original drawings. The kinds of responses expected involved a wide range of imagery related to different kinds of anxieties,

Table 11-1. Children with Malignancies

Patient	Age (Yr, Mo)	Sex	Diagnosis	IQ
1	5, 11	M	Leukemia	101
2	4, 11	F	Leukemia	73
3	3, 4	M	Leukemia	93
4	4, 0	F	Leukemia	108
5	5, 10	F	Wilms' tumor	114
6	5, 3	M	Leukemia	110
7	4, 3	M	Leukemia	100
8	4, 8	M	Leukemia	95
9	5, 0	M	Leukemia	107
10	3, 2	F	Lymphosarcoma	99
11	5, 0	F	Leukemia	95
12	5, 2	M	Hodgkins' disease	108
13	6, 5	F	Leukemia	109
14	4, 2	M	Leukemia	90
15	5, 2	F	Reticular cell sarcoma	106
16	4, 5	M	Leukemia	93
17	6, 10	F	Leukemia	126
18	5, 9	M	Leukemia	99
19	4, 4	F	Leukemia	89
20	3, 7	F	Leukemia	105
21	5, 3	F	Rhabdosarcoma	101
22	3, 3	M	Leukemia	110
23	4, 0	M	Leukemia	86
24	3, 0	F	Bilateral Wilms' tumor	96

Table 11-2. Children in Control Group

Patient	Age (Yr, Mo)	Sex	Diagnosis	IQ
1	5, 10	M	Fractured femur	90
2	4, 11	F	Fracture of axis vertebrae	74
3	3, 6	M	Interosseus inflammation of femur	96
4	4, 2	F	Osteomyelitis	116
5	5, 7	F	Fracture femur	98
6	5, 1	M	Dislocation of hip	103
7	4, 0	M	Osteoarthritis	96
8	4, 9	M	Gross displacement of hip	95
9	5, 4	M	Dysplastic right acetabulum	97
10	3, 4	F	Congenital type scoliosis	88
11	5, 0	F	Congenital bilateral hip displacement	104
12	5, 5	M	Congenital deformity of right shoulder	94
13	6, 5	F	Fractured femur	85
14	4, 6	M	Scoliosis	94
15	5, 5	F	Dislocated femur	107
16	4, 4	M	Compound fracture of midshaft right humerus	92
17	6, 7	F	Dislocation of hips	95
18	5, 11	M	Fractured femur	99
19	4, 2	F	Fractured femur	99
20	3, 5	F	Dislocated femur	96
21	5, 7	F	Aneurysmal bone cyst (causing hip dislocation)	108
22	3, 2	M	Osteoporosis of spine	90
23	4, 5	M	Fractured tibia	89
24	3, 4	F	Fractured pelvis	98

fears, and concerns of young children when they are ill. The Children's Apperception Test–Supplement,[10] a series of 10 achromatic drawings depicting animals in various social situations, was selected because of its relevance to the age group being investigated, usefulness as material for play techniques, and relationship of specific cards to somatic problems.

The APT and CAT–S were administered individually to the 48 children by the author. The APT instructions were as follows: "Tell me a story about this picture." "What are the children thinking?" "How does the story end?" "Make the story as interesting as you can." When the story ended, the child was asked, "What do you think will happen in the picture?" The four Adapted Pictures are shown in Appendix A following the final chapters in this text. Use of the puzzle form of the CAT–S enabled the children to manipulate all of the cards at once. Each child was told he or she would be shown a puzzle and then be asked to tell a story about the different pieces. The completed puzzle was shown first; the pieces were then emptied out of the frames, and the child was asked to "think of a story about each piece." A child who failed to tell a story was asked "What is happening?" "What are the animals doing?" and "What will happen next?"

DATA ANALYSIS

The 192 APT stories were examined separately for particular type of anxiety expressed. The Wilcoxon matched-pairs signed-ranks test was used to determine the independence of the samples and the significance of differences between groups. The scoring method was designed to determine the "total preoccupation with threat," and to provide comparative data on certain aspects of perceived patterns of adaptation to stress. On the scoring scales, the following types of expressed anxiety were assessed:

1. Negative affective scale: negative feelings, attitudes, or reactions to a threatened individual, external or internal threat, whether related to past or present events, or unhappy conclusion or ending.
2. Negative anticipatory state: fear or anxiety about not getting well as a definite possibility for the future.
3. Loneliness: fear of separation from significant figures or direct statement relating to loneliness.
4. Mutilation: statement or implication of body intrusion, e.g., injections, medical procedures, surgical techniques, bruising.
5. Death: any reference to or implication of nonbeing.

The 672 projective stories (192 from the APT and 480 from the CAT–S) were scored separately to determine the incidence of imagery reflecting anxiety about hospital and medical procedures (i.e., mention of a medical procedure, specific illness, pain, injury, operation, or hospitalization). This analysis determined the "degree of concern."

To determine the extent to which the CAT–S elicited apperceptive responses, each response was classified as enumerative, descriptive, or apperceptive.[11] Enumerative responses involved straight naming of one or two objects (e.g., . . . "four mice," "a slide"). Descriptive responses were limited to objective accounts of overt activities in the picture (e.g., . . . , "the foxes are running"). Apperceptive responses described feelings or mentioned activities not actually depicted (e.g., for Picture H, "he was lonely and had no one to play with"). For purposes of analysis, each of the 480 stories was placed in only one category to determine the "degree of fantasy."

Intellectual functioning was assessed by the Stanford Binet, administered the day before projective testing. No significant differences were found between the two groups of children (see Tables 11-1 and 11-2), and the total group had normal within-age variability. These results suggested that treatment for malignant disease was not associated with gross intellectual impairment in this sample. Analy-

Table 11-3. Psychological Criteria

Measure	Children with Malignancies		Controls	
	Mean	Range	Mean	Range
Degree of concern (CAT–S/APT)	3.8*	0.8	2.5	0.6
Degree of fantasy (CAT–S)	26.0†	16.30	20.5	10.30
Total preoccupation with threat (APT)	19.6*	6.38	13.2	1.28

* p < .05
† p < .01

sis of the IQ scores did yield two subgroups based on age (3–4 years and 5–6 years) within each group. This indicated that the pattern of IQ change over age was less homogeneous than the general IQ pattern among the two groups.

All scoring of psychological criteria was done by two independent judges (graduate students) who were unaware of the study's hypotheses and of the child's age, sex, IQ, and diagnosis. Inter-rater reliability (percentage agreements) for the projective stories was 94.6.

RESULTS

The two groups were significantly different on several variables (see Table 11-3). The data indicate that the children with malignancies presented more interpretation (i.e., more apperceptive versus enumerative or descriptive naming responses) than the control group (Table 11-4). The malignancy group showed greater dependence on the use of fantasy and presented more concept-dominated and imaginative themes than picture-dominated themes. The seriously ill children differed significantly from controls not only in the use of fantasy but also in the unrealistic treatment of events following the introduction of themes related to hospitaliza-

Table 11-4. Total Frequencies of Enumerative, Descriptive, and Apperceptive CAT–S Responses

Response	Children with Malignancies	Controls
Enumerative	23	53
Descriptive	142	210
Apperceptive	438	237

Table 11-5. Between-Group Analysis: Total Preoccupation with Threat*

Imagery	Children with Malignancies	Controls
Negative affective state	42	40
Negative anticipatory state	21	5
Loneliness	87	90
Mutilation	30	16
Death	7	0
Total	187	151

* Mean is derived from total score for five categories.

tion, pain, and injury. The introduction of such material in their stories appeared to arise "out-of-nowhere"; subsequent occurrences in the story, then, were determined more by the presence of such events than by the sequence of events with which these children began. The control group appeared more in command of fantasy material, and determined what happened in the story more as a personal involvement by using catastrophe to emphasize or "build" the type of outcome they had in mind.

Categorical examination of the APT revealed that the group with malignancies told significantly more stories that utilized negative affective and anticipatory state, loneliness, mutilation, and death imagery than did the control group (Table 11-5). On analysis of the total preoccupation with threat, the malignancy group achieved a total score of 187 versus 151 for controls; their scores ranged from 6 to 38, compared with a range of 1 to 28 for controls. Table 11-6 presents the data on subjects' use of categories. Almost half of the controls resorted to negative statements, but the seriously ill children did so more consistently. The second category, negative anticipatory state, was used by 9 seriously ill children but only 2 controls.

Table 11-6. Analysis of Subject Use of Categories

Category	Children with Malignancies		Controls	
	N	%	N	%
Negative affective state	14	58	11	46
Negative anticipatory state	9	38	2	8
Loneliness	21	88	12	50
Mutilation	8	33	5	21
Death	4	17	0	—

In the malignancy group, most children (N = 21) utilized aspects of loneliness in their stories, whereas only half of the controls showed this preoccupation. Thus, loneliness seems to be one of the most common feelings with which seriously ill children must cope. Mutilation imagery was used by 8 children in the malignancy group and 5 controls. None of the controls but 4 of the 24 seriously ill children expressed death imagery in their stories.

DISCUSSION

The findings of the present investigation suggest that 3- to 6-year-old children with malignancies have a vast range of feelings and highly developed fantasies regarding the threat of death. These seriously ill children were qualitatively and quantitatively different from the orthopedic control subjects in describing negative futures, loneliness, bodily intrusion, and images of nonbeing in protocols with a balance skewed on the side of negatively toned fantasy. Their stories included descriptions such as "This is a boy who is sick and not going to make it"; "He is going to die and he is 9 years old"; "She has no one to talk to." In terms of story content, the seriously ill children narrated more stressful situations regarding pain and injury than did the comparison group. In general, those who tended to blame others for their pain ("always giving me a needle") had more optimistic story outcomes ("The boy will take his medicine and go home") than those who internalized discomfort ("The little boy doesn't know why he got sick"), and provided less hopeful endings ("He'll be sick forever").

The 4- and 5-year-old seriously ill children who mentioned death fantasies were in relapse stages of the disease. These children always spoke of mutilation, but those who selected mutilation as a main theme continued with this theme and made no reference to death. The 3-year-old subjects, who expressed the most mutilation imagery, never spoke of nonbeing. These children may have been overwhelmed with environmental "cues" related to body deterioration and the toxic effects of their chemotherapy.[12] Mutilation concern has been described as a displacement of underlying concern regarding death. Jung[13] believed that the unconscious is very much concerned with how (painfully) one dies, whether the inner attitude of the consciousness understands death or not. Would it not be possible for even a 3-year-old to conjure up and draw upon fantastic possibilities when so mysterious and complicated a thing as his or her fate is involved?

Was the use of death imagery and preoccupation with threat themes an indication of these children's fate? It is possible that the death fantasies were less an awareness of a guarded prognosis than a way of trying to neutralize anxiety. Certain aspects of stories relating to death could be interpreted as compensatory or as efforts to master extremely distressing feelings. Symbolism could have brought the problem closer to an emotional understanding, particularly when the subject was something adults were unwilling or unable to speak about. By telling a story relating to death, these very young children with malignancies may have been able to accomplish in a simple medium what otherwise might have been far beyond their powers.

Such children may recognize that they may be dying in ways only thought to be possible in children over 10. The impact of malignant disease, feelings of loss, changes in self-concept, and the experience-related events of the illness appear to be significant variables in the awareness of the possibility of impending death. These children are at a developmental stage in which they are attempting to acquire control over the physical functioning of their bodies and, at the same time, to master ego controls. With the onset and duration of illness, they are "dispossessed" of their bodies, which become supervised objects for health professionals who exercise absolute rights, observe constantly, and directly influence responses. Similarly, adults who would normally support patients' rights to autonomy, individuation, and self-esteem often seem to change their attitudes in the face of potentially fatal illness, encouraging patients to become submissive, dependent, and passive.

Children may avoid asking questions about their medical condition because they realize that the topics of death and dying are difficult for parents and others concerned with their care. Displays of anger are also often avoided lest they lead to the children being left alone or deserted—a fate they may fear worse than death. Death appeared to loom most formidably as a threat of abandonment. To be separated from protective people is to be made vulnerable, and children with potentially fatal disease are vulnerable not only to dependency needs but to external threats. In relating to these children, it is important to create an environment that allows them to express thoughts and feelings about the terribly distressing circumstances in which they find themselves. One step that parents and health professionals can take early in the patient's treatment is to provide information regarding the feelings and emotions that are very likely to precede, accompany, and follow the onset of the disease. Such information may do much to reduce the level of distress for young children. There is great potential in understanding their need for support and also in recognizing and understanding parental feelings and behaviors toward the patient.

Seriously ill children's knowledge of what questions, reactions, and behaviors are acceptable, their past experiences, and their cognitive and affective perceptions of death all deeply influence their behavior. The process of dying is different in many ways in children compared to adults. The younger the patient, the less developed his or her ego functions, and the less right we have to "adultmorphize." The element of fear in dying seems largely to come about when fantasy mingles with facts and premonitions join hands with experience. It seems reasonable, then, that the symptoms and treatment of malignant disease are traumatic enough to be viewed as indicating the possibility of death by children as young as four years. An appreciation of death may come early to children undergoing extensive therapy, long before it does to their more fortunate peers.

REFERENCES

1. Waechter E: Death anxiety in children with fatal illness. University Microfilms International No. 69,310, 1968

2. Spinetta J: Death anxiety in leukemic children. University Microfilms International, No. 26,056, 1972
3. Morissey JR: A note on interviews with children facing imminent death. Soc Casework 44:343–345, 1963
4. Natterson J, Knudson A: Observations concerning the fear of death in fatally ill children and their mothers. Psychosom Med 22:456–465, 1960
5. Richmond JB, Waisman HA: Psychological aspects of management of children with malignant disease. Am J Dis Child 89:42, 1955
6. Solnit AJ, Green M: Pediatric management of the dying child. Part II. Child's reaction to the fear of dying. In Solnit A, Provence S (eds): Modern Perspectives in Child Development. New York, International Universities Press, 1963
7. Hoffman I, Futterman E: Coping with waiting: Psychiatric intervention and study in the waiting room of a pediatric oncology clinic. Compr Psychiatry 12:67–81, 1971
8. Borstein I, Klein A: Parents of fatally ill children in a parents' group. In Schoenberg B, Carr A, Peretz D, et al (eds): Anticipatory Grief. New York, Columbia University Press, 1974
9. Bahnson C: Emotional reactions to internally and externally derived threat of annihilation. In Grosser C, Wechsler N, Greenblatt M (eds): The Threat of Impending Disaster. Cambridge, MA, MIT Press, 1964
10. Bellak L: Thematic Apperception Test and Children's Apperception Test in Clinical Use. New York, Grune & Stratton, 1971
11. Byrd E, Witherspoon R: Responses of preschool children to the children's apperception test. Child Dev 25:35–44, 1954
12. Malone M: Body image and life-threatening disease: An appraisal on 3-to-6-year-old malignant children's perceptions. Transnational Mental Health Research Newsletter 23:5–8, 1980
13. Jung C: Relation Between the Ego and the Unconscious. Zurich, Rascher, 1928

12 · Concomitants of Death Imagery in Stories Told by Chronically Ill Children Undergoing Intrusive Procedures: A Comparison of Four Diagnostic Groups

Eugenia Waechter, Mary Crittenden,
Cynthia Mikkelsen, and Bonnie Holaday

INTRODUCTION

Advances in health care over the past two decades have dramatically changed the types of patients nurses serve and the ways they serve them. Children with formerly fatal illnesses, such as leukemia and end stage renal disease, now are maintained by intrusive procedures for long periods of time. Nurses who monitor those procedures have growing concerns about the quality of life and their own roles in supporting the well being of these children.

This study was funded by a University of California, San Francisco Academic Senate, grant and by a grant from the Murdock Boys Aid Memorial Fund, Department of Social Services, University of California, San Francisco. Special appreciation is extended to Mary Jane Allison, Director, Department of Social Services.

Reprinted from J Pediatr Nurs 1:2–11, 1986.

Research has shown that intensive procedures can trigger anxieties, including death anxieties or imagery in children (Gellert 1979; Petrillo and Langer, 1980; Rae, 1981). In the 1960's and early 1970's, studies explored subjective death anxieties in depth, giving attention to developmental changes, often using projective techniques (story telling, drawing, etc.) (Koocher, 1973; Natterson and Knudson, 1960; Spinetta, 1973; Waechter, 1971). Later studies focused more on objective behaviors including response to preparation for treatment, compliance with procedures, and later adjustment at home or in school, parental reactions to procedures, and parent–child communication. Thus in recent years fantasy life has been relatively ignored, even though concerns about the impact of new procedures on the total quality of life abound.

Nurses who administer procedures must understand the nature of anxieties associated with procedures and their correlates, in order to assess the child's reaction and provide appropriate interventions. Projective measures provide unique ways of assessing their feelings and fantasies. The current study was designed to probe the fantasy life of children who have different types of intrusive procedures, giving special attention to death imagery and its correlates, including intensity of treatment, parent attitudes and other characteristics of the stories. The specific questions for study were:

1. Do children in different diagnostic-treatment groups differ in the amount of death imagery they generate in stories?
2. Do parents of children in those groups differ in the openness of their communication about treatment and/or their attitudes to the treatment?
3. How does death imagery relate to parental attitudes about communications and to other characteristics of the stories within and among diagnostic groups? (See Box 12-1 for definitions.)

REVIEW OF LITERATURE

Perceptions of Procedure and Concepts of Illness

The literature on intrusive procedures, death imagery and parental communication sheds light on the issues. Clinical experiences and studies of children in medical settings show that children may perceive therapeutic procedures as hostile, unsupportive or punitive (Bergmann and Freud, 1965; Brewster, 1980; Oremland and Oremland, 1973; Skipper and Leonard, 1968). At different age levels, children show different types of anxieties: those age 5 years and younger are anxious about separation; those age 6–10 are concerned about potentially mutilating intrusions into their bodies (e.g., injections, IV's, surgeries); older ones are most anxious about permanent loss of body functions (Menke, 1981; Nagera, 1978; Peters, 1975; and Prugh, Staub, Sands, et al., 1953). Possibly the most damaging aspect is not the specific experience with procedures but the accompanying fantasies of being abandoned, punished, attacked or disfigured activated in children who are cognitively immature, still dependent on adult caretakers and

Box 12-1. Definitions

Death Imagery: Any association, description or reference to death or death related topics such as dying, going away forever, separation, funerals or terminal illness given in response to a projective type task. The responses are elicited by an ambiguous stimulus such that one would not expect comments about death. For example, one of the projective pictures used in this study was of a child holding her finger out to a female caretaker who is treating it in some way. The subject tells a story about a sick little girl. "She is getting a shot because she is real sick. They are scared that she will die. So she has to take the shot. She doesn't like it, but she does it."

Death Anxiety: Anxiety is a pervasive feeling of dread and apprehension. Death anxiety is a state in which anxiety over dying and fear of death are the salient behaviors.

unsure of their body integrity as they struggle to understand and cope with their experiences in treatment.

The developmental changes are congruent with Piaget's theory of cognitive development. Piaget (1960) demonstrated that pre-school children tend to think in terms of immediate, concrete personal experiences and do not fully understand causation. For example, the four year olds may associate the medical setting with pain because of previous experiences with injections, refuse to enter the room, and reject a potentially helpful procedure. From their egocentric perspective they may also think they did something to bring on the experience, such as disobey parents, as they begin to develop the concept of reversibility.

Events that are associated in time, place or content may also be regarded as causative. With increased maturity and opportunity to test experiences, older children develop a more mature concept of causation which takes into account factors outside themselves, such as disease or injury, and can understand cause and effect relationships.

The experiences that chronically ill children have with procedures may shape the ways they conceptualize their illness. There are no studies that compared concepts of illness in different diagnostic groups. However, there are indications that children perceive and cope differently with acute and chronic illness (Bergman and Freud 1965). Studies show that children with chronic diseases tend to view illness as a punishment for misbehavior (Brazelton, et al., 1953; Dubo, 1960; Schechter, 1961) or use the concept of self causation to explain it (Lynn 1962; Peters 1975).

THEORETICAL FRAMEWORK

Death Anxiety

For chronically ill children, frequent intrusive procedures constantly remind them of the chronicity and seriousness of their illness, and exacerbate death anxieties.

Although studies of death anxiety in chronically or fatally ill children are still sparse, there is evidence that age differences exist which are remarkably similar to developmental changes in anxieties generated by hospitalization and intrusive procedures. Under age 5, fatally ill children express separation anxieties, loneliness and fear of abandonment (Natterson and Knudson, 1960; Morrissey, 1963). In Malone's (1982) study, young children with malignant disease told significantly more stories that used negative affect, loneliness, mutilations, and death imagery than did the control group with acute orthopedic problems. She concluded that 3-to-6 year old children with malignancies have a vast range of feelings and highly developed fantasies regarding the threat of death. Between ages 6–10, chronically and fatally ill children realize the seriousness of their condition (Spinetta 1973, 1975; Waechter 1968, 1971). Death anxiety is overtly expressed as death themes and concern with threatening bodily intrusion or interference with normal body functions. Spinetta and Maloney (1975) found that terminally ill children expressed more death anxieties than did chronically ill counterparts. Spinetta (1973) also found that the children showed a high degree of general anxiety and concern about hospital staff and procedures. Waechter (1968) noted that terminally ill children did not express more concern about mutilations than controls. However, in none of these studies was the quality, type or duration of intrusive procedures differentiated or explored. Questions thus persist about the role of intrusive procedures in evoking death anxieties in chronically ill children who have different types of treatments.

These studies used a projective technique, the Thematic Apperception Test (e.g., telling stories about pictures) to assess death anxieties. Whether such projections are related to specific experiences or to repression of experiences is not clear. In the 1960's and early 1970's, health care providers and parents avoided discussing illness and treatments with children. Since children could not talk openly about concerns, presumably they were repressed and expressed indirectly through fantasy. Subsequent study showed that children adjusted better when parents communicated more openly (Binger, Blin, Feverstein, et al., 1969). In recent years, parents have been encouraged to discuss the illness and treatments with children; caretakers are urged to prepare children for procedures and involve them actively in the process. Whether open communication leads to reduced or increased expression of death anxieties is not clear. The relationship among death anxieties, intrusiveness of procedures and parental–child communications also remains obscure.

SAMPLE

Children were chosen for study who were between the ages of 4–10, had been treated for 3 months or more, were not experiencing medical or psychosocial crisis, and were followed on an outpatient basis. They were seen when the medical staff and parents gave consent and the children agreed. The subjects of this study were 52 Caucasian children, and their parents from middle class homes who volunteered to participate. The groups included: cystic fibrosis (CF), end stage renal disease (ESRD), juvenile onset diabetes (JOD) and leukemia (LK). Each of the four diagnostic groups selected for study had 13 children. The small sample pool prevented the use of a random sampling procedure.

Table 12-1 describes the distribution of ages and gender of the groups. The Duncan multiple range test showed that renal patients were significantly older than leukemia or cystic fibrosis patients, but not the diabetics; $(F = 3.42; p < .02)$; they also experienced the most intensive procedures $(F - 152.2; p < .001)$. The groups did not differ in gender, socioeconomic level or type of local community.

METHODOLOGY

Design

To explore these issues, this study used a comparative design to examine chronically ill children's apperceptions, giving special attention to the death imagery they generated in stories about pictures, and their parents' attitudes about communications and treatment experiences.

Instruments

The instruments used to collect data included a semi-structured parent interview and eight pictures developed by E. Waechter and C. Mikkelsen. The parent's interview assessed: 1) the amount of communication the parent reported having with the child about the diagnosis, treatments and prognosis (Disclosure Scale), 2) the amount of preparation they gave the child for specific procedures (Preparation Scale), 3) their attitudes toward the treatment regime (Treatment Scale), 4) their opinions about the child (Child Behavior Scale), and 5) their views about continuity of care over the past two years (Continuity Scale). The interview was designed to be as non-threatening to parents as possible, and to avoid eliciting "socially desirable" responses or implying medically desirable behaviors. The wording of questions and their order were controlled to provide comparable data. The interviews were pretested in a pilot study to ensure reliable, valid and relevant information.

Table 12-1. Characteristics of Subjects: Disease, Gender and Age Distribution

Category	Males	Females	Mean Age (Yrs)	Age Range (Yrs)
End stage renal disease	6	7	8.9	5.0–10.9
Leukemia	5	8	6.9	4.0–10.9
Juvenile onset diabetes	5	8	7.9	4.0–10.9
Cystic fibrosis	8	5	7.2	4.2–10.9
Total N =	24	28	7.9	4.0–10.9

To evaluate the children's responses to the intrusive procedures, a projective instrument was used, (see Box 12-2). This consisted of eight pictures. Four were developed for this study, to show children undergoing procedures, which included: a child walking to the treatment room, a child injecting a doll, an adult doing a finger prick procedure on a child, and a child in bed with an IV. Four pictures from the Thermatic Apperception Test (TAT) were also used. These included: a child seated on a door step, a man and older woman, a surgery mural, and a blank card. The children's pictures were pretested by giving them to 15 children, two or more

Box 12-2. Projective Techniques

The Thematic Apperception Test (TAT), developed by Morgan and Murray in 1935, is a projective technique which is sometimes used in clinical diagnosis and in research studies. A series of pictures with different degrees of reality or a fantasy content is shown to elicit stories. In evaluating the stories, attention is given to the heroes, their needs and drives, the impact of situational influences, the conflicts the heroes face, and the ways they deal with conflicts.

Alternative forms of the TAT have been developed for different age groups (Children's Apperception Test, Senior Apperception Test) and also for specific areas of interest (School Apperception Tests, Adapted Death Imagery Test). Waechter, Spinetta and Koocher have all developed versions to study death imagery.

Kagan (1961) defines apperception as "the integration of a percept with the individual's past experience and current psychological state." To understand apperceptions, the examiner must "listen with a third ear." That is, the examiner must be alert to subtle implications of the context (the stimuli presented, the format of presentation and the situation, including time, place and the role of the examiner), the process (how the story is told, in the terms of language used, feelings expressed and concept formations), and the content (what is described, omitted, added or distorted about the picture, how the hero and other characters behave and interact, what kinds of conflicts emerge and how they are resolved). In the case of children, developmental levels of language and concept formations require special attention, as does their background of experience both with the process of story telling and the content of the picture (Bellak, 1971).

The themes or images in the stories often do not correlate highly with overt behavior, but do reflect aspects of inner fantasy life that are crucial to understanding how the person thinks or feels, regardless of whether social circumstances permit direct expression of that behavior. For example, abused children may appear cheerful and compliant, yet their stories may reflect fears of assault, anger at self, or other destructive impulses. The same can be found in otherwise compliant pediatric patients.

Controversy exists whether responses to projctive tests, including TAT pictures which elicit death imagery, reflect concerns which may not be fully conscious and are repressed, allowed escape only through fantasy. Others maintain they represent a re-creation of a conscious experience or some combination of repression and re-creation, as the ego actively strives to understand and deal with inner and outer experiences. That issue is not readily resolved. Experience in using a standard series of pictures with a wide range of children, development of clear cut criteria for analyzing responses, and use of other information about the child's behavior and history can help clarify the issue for purposes of case studies and group research.

children at each age level, to determine if the pictures elicited appropriate stories which could be scored and analyzed.

The set of pictures was shown individually to each child. The instructions to each child were: "Tell me a story about this picture." Probes were used when needed to obtain the following information 1) Perception—what does the subject see in the picture; 2) Affect—how does the main character feel/think about the administrator and the treatment; how does the administrator feel/think about the main character and the treatments; 3) Motivation—what is the cause of the illness or problem, what is the purpose of treatment, why does the main character or administrator accept or reject the treatment; 4) Coping—what does the main character do about the situation; 5) Outcome—what does the main character expect will happen, what is the outcome of treatment, how does the story end; 6) Spontaneity—references to their own illness and experiences.

Procedures

After parent and child approval was obtained and consent forms signed, the child was seen by one author while another interviewed the parents on the day of the clinic visit or shortly after. The responses were tape recorded, with their permission. The procedures met the guidelines for protection of subjects outlined by the Committee on Human Experimentation at the University of California, San Francisco.

Data Analysis

The stories were rated on 5 point scales to assess: 1) the amount of death imagery, using the scoring system developed by Waechter (1968), which rated the number of references to actual and anticipated death, loneliness, and mutilation; 2) other characteristics of the stories adapted from the Cohn Weill Test of Emotional Development (1975), which included perception: Total number of stories, number of treatment stories and rejected cards (no stories given); affect, motivations and outcomes: Positive, neutral, mixed and negative; cause of illness: self, other and circumstance; coping: active cooperation, passive acceptance, passive avoidance and active resistance. For each variable, "don't know" or "no response" were also rated.

The criteria for coding of the parent attitudes and treatment intensity scales were established in advance. For each scale, subscales were established and rated on 5 point scales which were averaged to obtain the total score. The examiners made independent ratings of each interview which were later compared. When the ratings for a scale differed by one point, an average was taken; if they differed by two or more points, the responses were discussed, re-rated and the scores averaged. Agreement was high (Kendall coefficient, .86). For the independent ratings of the stories, the Kendall coefficient of concordance was again high (.92), most of the disagreements being minor (1 to 2 points on 5 point scales). When disagreements occurred, the scoring criteria were discussed and consensual ratings made.

Analysis of variance (*F* Test) was used to assess differences in the group as a whole, and the Duncan Multiple Range Test, to identify specific differences among the groups. Pearson Product Moment Correlations were used to assess the relationships among parent attitude scales, death imagery, and story ratings.

FINDINGS

Death Imagery and Other Story Content

Significant differences emerged in the amount of death imagery generated by the different groups (Table 12-2). On the Duncan test, at alpha level .05, the ESRD group had significantly more death imagery than any other group. However, the CF and LK had significantly more than the JOD group.

Few significant differences were found on the other story variables. Those that occurred were related more to what the children failed to say, rather than what they did say. Differences were noted in the number of rejected pictures, the leukemics rejecting more cards than any other group. Inability to attribute feelings (affect) to the main characters also differentiated the groups. Leukemics were least able to describe the hero's feelings. Diabetics tended to give more stories in which the patient felt negative toward the provider of treatment, but the difference was not significant ($F = 2.46$; $p < .07$).

In terms of motivations attributed, several differences emerged. Groups differed in the amount of self-blame for illness, the CF group giving the most self-blaming responses and the LK the least. Diabetics tended to attribute the cause to circumstances but the difference was not significant ($F = 2.35$; $p < .08$). ESRD and LK groups were somewhat inclined to report that the patient in the story did not know the administrator's motivation for treatment but that difference also was not significant. ($F = 2.45$; $p < .07$)

No differences were found in the coping strategies that the characters used. In general, the sample tended to use the passive acceptance or passive avoidance strategies.

Some differences did emerge in the outcomes. The ESRD and JOD groups, who were older, expected more negative outcomes of treatment. However, the LK and ESRD patients, who had the most intensive treatments, more often said they did

Table 12-2. Mean Differences in Death Imagery and Other Story Content

Story Content	F-ratio	Significance	ESRD	JOD	CF	LK
Death imagery	15.9	.0001	15.9	5.8	10.8	8.4
Perception: not given	2.76	.05	.15	.08	.15	1.38
Affect: not given	3.29	.03	2.85	3.31	1.23	5.46
Motivation: self-blame	3.04	.04	1.54	1.92	2.46	.85
Outcome:						
expected not known	3.13	.003	2.00	3.00	1.54	1.31
Final not known	5.09	.004	5.23	1.69	3.00	5.85

not know the final outcome of the story. No differences were found in the number of spontaneous references children made to their own experiences or illness.

Parent Interview Scales

Table 12-3 describes the results of the parent interview scales. On the five scales, significant differences occurred only on the disclosure scale. According to the Duncan test, the parents of ESRD patients reported the most disclosure about the disease and treatments, no differences being found in the other groups. No significant differences existed in parental attitudes to treatment, opinions of the child's behavior, the amount of preparation they gave the child for specific treatments or continuity of care. Most parents felt positive about the treatment, the child, and continuity of care, and provided preparation for specific treatments. (See Box 12-3 for a sample of a parent's interview.)

The continuity-of-care scale was dropped from the analysis, because parents varied widely in their definitions of continuity. Some viewed it as having the same doctor or nurse, some as having the same treatment, others as coming to the same place, while others felt it was not relevant, so long as the child was well cared for. Most children had multiple medical caretakers. The complexity of the treatment regimes in a tertiary care teaching facility and the severity of the child's illness required parents to be flexible in their definitions, several noted.

Relationship Between Death Imagery and Other Variables

With the story content, it correlated significantly with the total number and the number of treatment-related stories, indicating the power of the pictures to evoke death imagery. It also correlated with aspects of affect, motivation, coping strategies and outcome (Table 12-4).

However, within the diagnostic groups, the pattern of correlations differed in number and type. The LK group had a lower mean score for death imagery but the highest number of correlations between death imagery and story variables. The renal group which had the highest mean death imagery score had four significant correlations, the JOD had one, and the CF had none. The LK group thus contrib-

Table 12-3. Mean Differences in Four Diagnostic Groups on Maternal Scales

Variables	F-ratio	Significance	ESRD	JOD	CF	LK
MATERNAL SCALE						
Disclosure	6.8	.0007*	5.5*	4.1	3.4	3.5
Preparation	.16	.92	3.8	3.8	4.0	3.8
Treatment	.20	.90	4.0	4.3	4.1	4.2
Child behavior	1.32	.28	3.7	3.3	3.4	3.7
Intensity of RX	3.42	.02*	4.0	2.1	2.0	3.4

* Significant at $p < .05$ or better.

Box 12-3. Excerpts from Parents' Interviews

1. Disclosure, Preparation and Child Reaction

I want him to know as much as is right, but I don't know, it's hard. I can't tell him, I can't say what will happen, uh, the prognosis. I can't think about that. I mean . . . he knows the diagnosis. That was hard to tell at first. How, uh, what does that mean to an 8 year old? It's hard enough for us to get it. And you never know how teachers and family will react if he tells them. But he has to know. And the treatments—well, we try to prepare him as much as we can. If we know. Sometimes I don't really know what is going to happen, so how can I tell him? But I try. And the doctors and nurses are good. They help. If they have time, you know. Like what they will do, who will do it, how long and that it's to help him. He fussed a lot at first, but now he's good. He got used to it. So we want to help if it's something new. I know he'll get used to it if we can tell him first. I hate it if they don't have time to tell us. I really want to know first, so I can get him ready if I can.*

2. Continuity of Care

Well, it's important, but there are so many doctors. They keep changing. The doctor we talked to first isn't here. But . . . so long as they know what to do it is alright. I like it if it is the same nurse. She knows him and jokes with him, and makes him feel important. I guess that makes me feel important too! But all I care about is that he gets good care, and this is supposed to be the best place.

* From Crittenden, Waechter, and Mikklesen, 1977.

uted heavily to the correlations between death imagery and other story content. However, an intriguing pattern of similarities and differences emerged in the groups. In both the leukemic and renal disease groups, the hero tended generally to use active coping strategies and expect negative outcomes. The diagnostic groups differed in their attribution of motivation in a manner that suggested developmental shifts. In the younger LK group, death imagery was associated with self causation; a similar trend occurred in the CF group, but did not quite reach significance ($p < .058$). In the older ESRD group, causation was attributed to others. The hero in LK stories wanted treatment, while the hero in ESRD stories sought to avoid it, knowing it caused pain.

In the LK group, death imagery stories ended happily, while in the ESRD stories, they ended unhappily. The younger LK group also generated more references to their own experiences in their death imagery stories.

Death imagery correlated significantly with the intensity of treatment scales, but not the parent attitude scales (Table 12-5). The parent disclosure scale correlated significantly with only three other story variables: parents who disclosed more had children who gave fewer "don't know" responses, saw the hero and provider as liking each other, and the hero having ambivalent motivation for treatment (i.e., knew it was necessary but preferred to avoid it). Within the diagnostic groups, no distinctive pattern of correlations with story content emerged, as it did in the case of death imagery.

Table 12-4. Correlations Between Death Imagery and Other Story Content in the Total Group and Subgroups

		Diagnostic Group			
Variable	Total Group	ESRD	JOD	CF	LK
PERCEPTION					
No. of stories	.42*	.08	.07	.15	.85*
No. Rx stories	.52*	.51	.03	.29	.86*
No. card rejects	−.37*	.14	−.21	−.17	−.78*
AFFECT					
Hero dislikes Rx	.35*	.44	.14	.45	.79*
Hero likes provider	.25	−.15	−.26	.15	.75*
Provider likes hero	.33*	.18	−.46	.30	.69*
MOTIVATION					
Cause:					
self	.03	−.14	.16	−.23	.56*
other	.22	.56*	.12	.51	.39
circumstance	.39*	−.32	−.15	.54	.61*
Hero wants Rx	.09	−.26	−.30	−.22	.61*
Hero avoids pain	.33*	.58*	−.38	.42	.46
Hero has to	.16	−.25	−.20	.17	.71*
Provider helps	.35*	.23	−.60*	.10	.80*
COPING					
Active	.40*	.69*	.21	.14	.64*
OUTCOME					
Expects negative	.10	.09	.27	.17	.70*
Rx positive	.14	−.31	−.43	−.04	.58*
Story negative	.35	.74*	.50	.51	−.59*
SELF REFERENCE	.10	.48	.25	−.14	.55*

* Significant at *p* < .05 or better.

DISCUSSION

These children all had serious illnesses which required treatment in a tertiary care setting. The differences in age and intensity of treatments which we found highlight the range of individual differences in children with severe chronic illness. The differences pose a challenge for research with groups that are small in number but diverse in background characteristics.

In this sample, the diagnostic groups differed in the amount of death imagery they generated. ESRD patients who were the oldest and had the most intensive treatments produced the most. However, the contributions of age and intensity of treatment were less clear in the other diagnostic groups. The younger CF and LK groups produced more than the JOD who had less intense treatments. It would appear that intensity of treatments is a more salient feature than age in the production of death imagery. While previous research investigated the level and

Table 12-5. Correlations Between Death Imagery and Maternal Scales

Variables	Correlation	Significance
Disclosure scale	.23	.09
Intensity of treatment	.42	.002
Preparation for treatment	.18	.20
Parent view of treatment	.21	.14
Parent view of child	.09	.51

type of death imagery content, this study also looked at the way it was used in stories. The relationship between death imagery and other story content is clearly complex.

Not only did diagnostic groups differ in the amount of death imagery they generated, but also in the way they integrated it in the stories. In the CF and JOD group, death imagery was isolated from the other story content. The older JOD group, with the least intense treatments, had the least death imagery and it correlated only with a theme of assault (provider intended to hurt or harm). That finding supports Waechter's observation that those with less experience with intense treatments are likely to associate them with harm, while those with more experience may see them as helpful. The younger CF group with more intense treatments produced more death imagery but failed to integrate it with the plot, referring to it tangentially; their responses resemble those of a child who, in puppet play before surgery, mentions death, then drops the subject.

In the two groups which integrated death imagery with other content, developmental differences appeared, as might be expected. Though the younger LK group had the third lowest mean score in death imagery, when it surfaced, it saturated the content, that is, if a child produced any story with death imagery he repeatedly referred to death in that story. In the older ESRD group which generated the most death imagery, it impinged in selected ways. The older group gave more differentiated responses, were less egocentric in attributing motivation, were less inclined to refer spontaneously to their own experiences, and gave more realistic, logical outcomes to their stories. Therefore, both age and intensity of treatment merit further study.

One commonality emerged, however. Though passive acceptance tended to be the dominant coping strategy that chronically ill children in this sample used, when death imagery surfaced, passive acceptance declined and active coping strategies increased. Even on a fantasy level, these children apparently "do not go gentle into that good night," to use Dylan Thomas' words. Maintaining that will to live despite adversities is a crucial task for both the primary care nurse and the family.

In regard to other variables in the story content given by the total group, differences occurred more in what the child avoided saying, rather than what he actually said, with a few notable exceptions. Leukemics were more likely to reject pictures or give inconclusive outcomes. That could be due to their developmental stage, but Koocher (1973) noted a similar finding with another group of LK's, using the adapted Waechter TAT. Nurses need to be alert to what the child does not say, as well as what the child says. Both in research and clinical practice, the "don't know/no response" category needs to be assessed as scrupulously as the available content.

One might speculate that repression of death imagery is greater in children who cannot work it into the plot and share it with others in a meaningful, coherent way, than it is in children who do integrate it in the plot. If that proves true, then nurses need to be aware not only of the presence of death imagery, but also the context in which it is used and the way it is developed. Our findings suggest that research in death imagery needs to look at other variables in the story to fully understand its implications.

In these groups, parents differed in the amount of disclosure they reported giving to the children about their medical condition. Open disclosure was age-related, the older ESRD and JOD being given the most information. However, open disclosure did not correlate significantly with death imagery, and it correlated with only a few variables in the other content of the stories. Since parents who disclosed more tended to have children who gave fewer "don't know" responses, it may be that open disclosure frees the children to say more, but does not specifically affect what the child says. The intensity of the child's own treatments had more impact on the generation and use of death imagery. The children thus did not seem passive reflectors of their parents' attitudes but active responders to their own experiences.

Parents repeatedly admitted that the decision to tell the child about the diagnosis, treatment and prognosis was difficult and depended on multiple factors. Those included the child's maturity and temperament, the complexity of treatment, the need to involve the child in the process, the other stresses in their lives and the amount of support available to them. Many referred to help given by staff. That raises the issue of the social context of health care and its impact on parent and child. At the time of this study, ESRD and LK groups were served by nurse practitioners who helped coordinate an interdisciplinary team. Those children both generated death imagery and integrated it in the stories in developmentally appropriate ways. Whether availability of a coordinated team which provides consistent input and support allows the child to express and manage death imagery is another area for inquiry.

The parents did not differ on the other scales, suggesting commonalities in their style of coping with a chronically ill child, regardless of age, diagnosis or intensity of treatment. Most parents viewed their child and the treatments positively. They prepared them for specific procedures. Many noted that unexpected changes in routine distressed them, made them feel that the system of care delivery had betrayed their trust in the provider and their child's trust in them. Health care providers must therefore be alert to the parent's own need for open disclosure and consistency from staff.

Parents generally felt good about continuity of care. However, these parents had diverse definitions of continuity. In a tertiary care setting with multiple providers, that variable needs precise operational definition. To avoid erroneous assumptions and understand their needs, both providers and researchers must carefully assess the ways that family and patient view continuity.

IMPLICATIONS FOR NURSING

The results suggest that the intrusive procedures used to treat chronic illness are traumatic enough to produce death anxiety in children. Thus, one nursing intervention is to provide opportunities for fantasy play, such as drawing or story telling, without stressing or reinforcing death themes. Listen carefully to the content of the children's stories. What are the children letting me know about themselves and their lives? If death themes are present, do not assume that they represent repression or pathology. The stories are a part of the child's way of coping with actual or anticipated experiences. Learn to recognize the developmental progressions in death imagery. Our findings indicate that older children having intensive procedures will project more death imagery. In younger children, when death imagery surfaces it may saturate responses, due to the "all or nothing" responsivity and lack of boundaries seen in younger children.

Many parents will be upset by their child's use of death imagery. This is especially true of parents who have prepared their child for the treatments, because they feel that they have failed. The nurse needs to explain to the parents that use of death imagery in stories and pictures is a coping mechanism for the child.

The study of death imagery which Eugenia Waechter began in the late 1960's has declined in recent years. Since that time, medical advances offer new hope to children with formerly terminal illnesses and to those who care for them, but also create new threats to the quality of their life and well being. Further systemic study is needed not only into the level, types and developmental variations in death imagery. The ways it is used in stories, and the factors which may influence its manifestations offer intriguing possibilities to advance our knowledge of these children and their needs. We conclude with a quote from Dr. Eugenia Waechter's proposal (1973) for this study:

"Knowledge, therefore, of the manner in which children respond to procedures would provide a much sounder basis for the manner in which professional personnel could most profitably approach children, prepare them for procedures, support them during such experiences and later assist them in coping with the feelings aroused by bodily intrusion. Furthermore, should children with particular illnesses perceive and respond to these procedures differently than do other ill children, nursing and other professional intervention could be planned accordingly."

REFERENCES

Bellack L: The TAT and CAT in Clinical Use. New York, Grune & Stratton, 1971
Belmont HS: Hospitalization and its effect upon the total child. Clin Pediatr 22:590–600, 1970
Bergman T, Freud A: Children in the Hospital. New York, International University Press, 1965

Binger C, Ablin A, Feverstein R, Kushner J, Zoger S, Mikkelsen C: Childhood leukemia: Emotional impact on patient and family. N Engl J Med 280:414–418, 1969

Brazelton TB, Holder R, Talbot B: Emotional aspects of rheumatic fever in children. J Pediatr 43:339–358, 1953

Brewster A: The Relationship of Cognitive Development to the Child's Understanding of Illness. Unpublished doctoral dissertation, University of Michigan, 1980

Cohn H, Weil G: Tasks of Emotional Development Manual. Brookline: TED Associates, 1975

Crittenden MR, Waechter E, Mikklesen C: Taking it day by day: When children undergo hemodialysis and renal transplantation. Child Today 6(3):6–9, 1977

Dubo S: Psychiatric study of children with pulmonary tuberculosis. Am J Orthopsychiatry 20:520, 1960

Gellert E: Psychosocial Aspects of Pediatric Care. New York, Grune & Stratton, 1979

Kagan J, Lesser GS: Contemporary Issues in Thematic Apperceptive Methods. Springfield, Charles C Thomas, 1961

Koocher GP: Childhood, death, and cognitive development. Dev Psychol 9:369–375, 1973

Lynn DB, Glasser HH, Harrison GS: Concepts of illness in children with rheumatic fever. Am J Dis Child 103:42–50, 1962

Malone MM: Consciousness of dying and projective fantasy of young children with malignant disease. J Dev Behav Pediatr 3:55–60, 1982

Menke E: School-age children's perception of stress in the hospital, Child Health Care 9(3):80–86, 1981

Morgan CD, Murray HA: A method for investigating Fantasies: The Thematic Apperception Test. Arch Neurol Psychiatry 34:289–306, 1935

Morrissey SR: Children's adaptations to fatal illness. Soc Casework 8:81–88, 1963

Nagera H: Children's reactions to hospitalization and illness. Child Psychiatry Hum Dev 9(1):3–19, 1978

Natterson JM, Knudson AG: Observations concurring fear of death in fatally ill children and their mothers. Psychosom Med 22:456–465, 1960

Oremland EK, Oremland JD (eds): The Effects of Hospitalization on Children. Springfield, IL, Charles C Thomas, 1973

Peters BM: Concepts of Hospitalized Children about Causality of Illness and Intent of Treatment. Unpublished doctorial dissertation, University of Pittsburgh, 1975

Petrillo M, Langer S: Emotional Care of Hospitalized Children. Philadelphia, JB Lippincott, 1980

Piaget J: The Child's Conception of the World. Patterson, Littlefield, Adams, 1960

Prugh DG, Staub EM, Sands HH, Kirshbaum RM, Lenihan EA: A study of the emotional reactions of children and families to hospitalization and illness. Am J Orthopsychiatry 23:70:106, 1953

Rae WA: Hospitalized latency-age children: Implications for psychosocial care. Child Health Care 9(3):59–63, 1981

Skipper JK, Leonard RC: Children, stress and hospitalization: A field experiment. J Health Soc Behav 275–387, 1968

Schechter MD: The orthopedically handicapped child. AMA Arch Gen Psychiatry 4:247–253, 1961

Spinetta JJ, Rigler D, Karon M: Anxiety in the dying child. Pediatrics 52:841–845, 1973

Spinetta JJ, Maloney LJ: Death anxiety in the outpatient leukemic child. Pediatrics 56:1034–1037, 1975

Waechter EH: Death Anxiety in Children with Fatal Illness. Doctoral dissertation, Stanford University. University Microfilms, No. 72–26,056, 1968

Waechter EH: Chilren's awareness of fatal illness. Am J Nurs 71:1168–1172, 1971

Waechter EH: Perceptions of Children Toward Intrusive Procedures. Proposal approved by the Academic Senate, UCSF, 1973

13 · The Adolescent
With Life-Threatening
Chronic Illness

Eugenia H. Waechter

Many people living in the United States today have little contact with death. Our society has been characterized as one which denies death and avoids it in ways which are sometimes unreasonable, illogical, or bordering on fantasy wish fulfillment. Although there is now more open discussion of death and more concern about the philosophical, ethical, and moral issues surrounding life and death, anxieties and fears about death still seem to have increased in the past decade.

Attitudes toward death were different several generations ago when the death of a young person was not a rare occurrence. Parents accepted the possibility that not all of their children would survive into adulthood. They also had greater experience with death, since many older family members were cared for and died in the home, surrounded by those they loved. Because of closer acquaintance, death was not considered an uncomfortable topic of conversation, and adults, in acknowledging death as a natural part of existence, formed personal philosophies of living and dying.

Although the death of the elderly, disabled, or infirm in our society is often considered a "blessing," the death of children or adolescents is seen as the ultimate tragedy. Inasmuch as they have just begun to live, and because of our youth-oriented society, the young are highly valued in themselves as well as for their future potential. Adolescents on the brink of living fully are seen as having everything to live for. Yet, adult society also views adolescents with ambivalence. Whereas the death of a young college student is greatly mourned, far less compassion may be shown for adolescents who have fatal accidents while speeding in

Reprinted from Mercer RP: Perspectives on Adolescent Health Care. Philadelphia, JB Lippincott, 1979.

automobiles or who become fatally ill while addicted to drugs, alcohol, or a way of life that is opposed to society's standards. These adolescents are often written off as "no great loss" and receive little sympathy from society or even from their parents and relatives.

Professional caretakers, as products of their society, may have difficulties in caring for adolescents, particularly those who are facing imminent death. Yet ill and dying adolescents are perhaps more in need of understanding and of knowledgeable, empathetic, and concerned care than are individuals in any other developmental phase of life. In order to give such care, health professionals of every discipline must examine their own attitudes toward life and death, have a sincere interest in and respect for all adolescents as individuals of worth and dignity, and become knowledgeable about the ways in which adolescents view death, the possible responses to incurable illness, and techniques of communicating with them when they are anxious and afraid.

THE ADOLESCENT'S CONCEPT OF DEATH

A mature concept of death is built slowly throughout childhood, both as a result of experiences with death and as a function of expanding intellectual awareness that encompasses aspects of time perspective, logic, and reasoning ability. In Western society, adults often "protect" children from what they feel are the harsh facts of life and death, and this practice can lead to a sense of unreality and distortion of the concept of death. Such misconceptions are further reinforced through the influence of television programs, since an actor may appear to die in a given play and yet reappear alive and happy on subsequent days.

Studies of child development by Inhelder and Piaget (1958) in Switzerland, Nagy (1948) in Hungary, Gesell and Ilg (1946) in America, and Anthony (1972) in England all agree that up to the age of about three years, children have little or no mental picture of death. To them separation and death are synonymous. They have not yet learned to ask the question, "Why?" which signals the awareness of function. They are at first puzzled by death; death is inexplicable and is a mysterious phenomenon, since in their experience anything that happens is wished so, or controlled, by themselves or by their parents.

Children's first experiences with death (usually of an insect, bird, or animal) lead them to equate death with separation, sleep, or going into a grave, coffin, earth, or water. Children under the age of five also have a sense of reversibility or lack of finality in death, since individuals who "go away" do return and characters on television appear and disappear inexplicably.

During the early school years, children are aware of the reality of death but may conceptualize it as gradual or temporary. Because of early experiences with the death of animals, they often view death as the end result of violence or aggression. They may also personify death as someone (a "death man" or a skeleton) who comes to carry people away (Nagy, 1948) and they elaborate the concept of death with many religious and cultural meanings. In fact, many six-, seven-, and eight-year-olds may be intensely interested in the rituals surrounding death and spend considerable time in enacting burial scenes. Children of this age are often much more preoccupied with death than many adults are willing to admit. Though one reason for this activity is to gain intellectual mastery over a mystery, such preoccupation is also partly due to a growing suspicion that they also are mortal.

From the age of nine until adolescence, children usually accept death realistically and are aware that death is the common lot of humanity; many are interested in what happens after death. However, many also are secretly in great fear and terror of nonexistence. They often invent rituals to lessen their anxiety, behave recklessly and take chances to prove themselves invulnerable, or cover their fear by jokes and tough attitudes. They may also deride death by mutilating or killing insects and small animals. Such cruelty may serve the purpose of giving them a sense of control over death at a time when they are feeling very helpless in averting death for themselves or their loved ones.

There is still much room for research regarding the concept of death during adolescence. Most developmentalists and health professionals assume that by early adolescence most individuals have reached a level of cognitive growth at which the finality and inevitability of death are comprehensible, though it may not yet be accepted emotionally. It is also assumed that the adolescent's aptitude for hypothetical–deductive reasoning allows him to dream about the future, to anticipate and to concern himself with philosophical issues of life, death, and reality.

This is true for many adolescents, particularly for those in the middle and late stages of the developmental period. However, it is not true for all. Many individuals have not and may never reach the level of formal thought described by Piaget (1958). Others may have had previous experiences with death which have led to a distortion of the concept. For some, death may still be seen either as a redeemer or as an avenger that punishes for sins committed (Reigh and Feinberg, 1974). For many adolescents, who already have a tendency to feel guilty as they attempt to separate from parents, death may be seen as a confirmation of essential badness. This is reinforced by the inevitable breaking of many family and cultural rules as they test their independence.

In a small research study in Canada, Olsiak (1976) asked 14- to 19-year-old healthy adolescents about their concepts of death. She found that young adolescents often had vague, strange, frightening, and mysterious concepts of death, whereas older adolescents tend to have more definite conceptions of an afterlife. Philosophical convictions grew stronger with age, as did definite concern for others, should they learn of their own fatal illness.

The adolescent who is under personal sentence of death is even more deeply convinced that his dying is a dreadful retribution for his offenses. Many adolescents do indeed die as a result of breaking the rules of society in regard to alcohol, drugs, and speeding automobiles. Many accidental traumas are a result of testing and exploration. To some it seems that a punishment as severe as death can only be due to essential badness.

In addition to guilt and depression, however, the adolescent with a life-threatening condition or illness is also bitter, angry, and bewildered. He may know that he has broken many rules, but he is deeply shocked at the magnitude of the punishment, which also implies rejection by parents, by society, and by God (Easson, 1970). Because he is resentful toward those people whom he still depends on and cares for deeply, his quiet depression and helplessness deepen. Many dying teenagers feel that no one can understand them, and they face death lonely and alone.

RESPONSES OF THE ADOLESCENT TO LIFE-THREATENING ILLNESS

Such a sense of isolation is also a result of separation from the peer group, which has become all-important as the ties to parents and family loosen. This is particularly difficult for those adolescents who have disrupted family bonds abruptly or drastically. Teenagers who have felt deprived or rejected by parents during childhood and those who have been very close to parents and siblings may, of necessity, become extremely dependent on peers for direction, for support, and for the comfort of companionship. These teenagers are extremely vulnerable when faced with life-threatening illness, for the group may be of little help.

Younger adolescents are struggling to establish their own independence, self-sufficiency, and plans for the future. The serious illness and possible death of a friend is threatening to them, in that it points up their own vulnerability and frailty. At a time when strength, beauty, and body image are of utmost concern, they are uncomfortable with illness, mutilation, or disfigurement. In order to cope with feelings they may not have had to face before, they must withdraw from former close relationships.

Dying adolescents also contribute to the loosening of such ties. In defending themselves against the threat of abandonment by friends, they often deny their need for them by emphasizing their own self-sufficiency and independence. Fearing rejection by friends, they may repulse friendly overtures. Feeling very different, they set themselves apart to prevent exclusion and to avoid pity they do not want.

Alienation from former friends intensifies conflicts with parents, conflicts that may previously have been partially solved. If the teenager turns to his parents in his loneliness and need for understanding, he may feel that he is surrendering and returning to a former, outgrown, childlike state. As he becomes increasingly dependent on them, he resents his overdependence. Longing to be cared for and protected, he may violently reject his parents and the caring and concern they offer. Admitting such feelings to himself is infinitely threatening to his sense of control over himself. Wanting attention desperately, but proud, he may cut himself off from all warmth. When marital discord and financial strain affect his parents, the adolescent is further burdened with the knowledge that he is the cause of the strain. Often communication between the teenager and his parents deteriorates to stoical role playing—the teenager misinterprets his parents' protectiveness as sympathy and the parents feel rejected and helpless.

Young teenagers are also very aware of their bodies. They are extremely sensitive to the feelings they are experiencing and most perceptive of the world around them. They feel and live intensely, experience deeply, and live completely. They perceive acutely the beauty of a sunset, the beat of music, the sensation of walking barefoot through the grass.

The young adolescent wants to live. Acutely aware of his body, he senses its deterioration, whether or not his diagnosis and prognosis have been shared with him. At a time when the whole world is opening up, he is led to the mountain like Moses and shown the promised land and adulthood—but learns that it is not for him (Aune, 1974).

Understandably, the young adolescent is bitter and resentful and asks, "Why me?" "To whom can I assign blame?" Deeply living life, he can appreciate losing everything in dying. He has just come to realize what life can hold when the visions and dreams are snatched away. Not knowing where to direct his anger and bitterness, he often struggles on alone.

Although he may previously have loudly disclaimed agreements with the established social system and his parents' standards and religious principles, contemplation of his own prognosis may force him to consider some aspects of religion. He asks himself, "Is there a life after death? If so, will the sins I have committed in anger and rebellion against God and parents prevent me from getting there?" Unsure and ambivalent, he attempts to find answers to profound questions and meaning for his sufferings. If discouraged from asking such questions, his emotional isolation deepens.

Teenagers in midadolescence have developed more self-confidence, self-control, and pride in themselves as individuals. They take great interest in their appearance and are more comfortable with a consolidating body image. Self-esteem is high as they see themselves as individuals in their own right for the first time and contemplate a future which may now hold more concrete plans for college, career, or the work world.

Death can only mean defeat for the adolescent on the threshold of mastery. The 16-year-old youth is well aware that death will take away all of his physical and mental powers, will strip him of his competency and of his future. The 16-year-old young woman often, in addition, faces the destruction of her physical attractiveness through deterioration, deformity, or disfigurement. It is not surprising that young people who are undergoing such major alterations of body image and destruction of hopes have self-doubts and low self-esteem, or that they withdraw from contacts with the opposite sex and reject the advances of others. This is a cruel reality, and the adolescent will reasonably react with anger, bitterness, and hopeless rage at the futility of life—rage at the waste; rage at his powerlessness to change his fate (Aune, 1974). Because the adolescent at this age has tasted mastery and self-achievement, the deprivation is the greater.

Those adolescents, however, who have become more secure in their own individuality may not need to reject their parents as violently as does the young teenager. With greater self-confidence, they no longer need to defend themselves as strenuously against love and comfort lest they become children again. Even though they feel bitterness and rage, the need is less intense to direct such feelings toward parents, particularly when communication lines have been maintained and concerns can be discussed openly. When such communication lines are closed, however, the young person is not allowed to disclose feelings, bitter episodes of fighting between the adolescent and parents may occur until the adolescent finally becomes severely depressed and withdrawn. Neither side knows how to break the silence, which may last to the end.

When communication is open, the adolescent's rage may periodically erupt against his family, but usually the older teenager will attempt to control and direct these feelings elsewhere. Explosions are usually triggered by changes in treatment procedures, lack of proper explanations, or threats to the adolescent's sense of independence—for example, not allowing him to have a voice in decisions that concern him. When the adolescent is the last to know about a new therapy which is being considered, he rightly explodes and considers it unfair, for, after all, it is his body "they're doing it to." Though angry and hurt, he may continue to smile at hospital personnel for fear of being further excluded from decision-making processes in the future.

When the older adolescent, on the threshold of maturity, is faced with death, his worries and concerns also encompass lost relationships. These relationships may be infinitely dear and important, since they may involve present or future marital partners and hopes for the security of family life. Peer relationships now are also more mutually rewarding and constant. The older adolescent grieves for the loss of all of these close, rich, and meaningful emotional bonds. This mourning is all the more intense because the dying late adolescent cannot reinvest emotionally as can those he will leave behind.

The late adolescent has just arrived at the door of adulthood. Concrete plans must now be relinquished. If the young man or woman is married, he or she may make efforts to have a child, even though it is medically ill-advised, so that something of themselves will live after them. This investment in the future is assurance that their fading existence will not be completely erased.

Reigh and Feinberg (1974) have delineated three distinct phases which adolescents go through as they progress toward death. The first phase is characterized by anxiety, depression, and a gradual withdrawal from the environment. The second phase is one of motor activity, which represents a return to earlier developmental patterns when tension and anxiety were relieved through motor discharge. The third phase is a regression to an even earlier developmental period when touch and closeness brought relief from anxiety.

In coping with the intense threat of premature death, adolescents use much denial, which often permits them to live with their illness. As time progresses, both the adolescent and his family may begin to grieve in anticipation of death (Lowenberg, 1970). This "grief work" often allows the adolescent to accept, at last, the inevitability of his own death. As death approaches, the world of the adolescent narrows to his bed and to a few loved members of his family. Even the young adolescent is able to accept the caring of warm and loving relatives. He can allow himself to be babied, as death grows nearer, as long as he is not treated disrespectfully.

FAMILY RESPONSES TO LIFE-THREATENING ILLNESS

When an adolescent becomes seriously ill, it is natural for parents to ask "Why?" "Did this happen because of something I have done?" "If I had noticed the symptoms earlier; if I had brought him to the hospital or doctor earlier, would he have gotten so sick?"

Such feelings of guilt are almost universal. Despite the fact that most parents know intellectually that illness is not divine retribution for sin, guilt is still felt on a deeper emotional level. The question is still there. "How could Got let this happen? Has He stopped listening to us? Has He deserted us?"

Guilt is the feeling experienced most intensely by parents—along with disbelief or shock. The parents are concerned that they may have been neglectful in not watching their son or daughter closely enough, and their self-chastisement extends to every level of the relationship. They worry that they have not loved enough, have not gotten to know their child well enough, have not given enough attention. Each parent has different feelings about how he or she has failed, and the desolation of each is very real. This is particularly true during the time of adolescence, when family quarrels, misunderstandings, and miscommunication may be a way of life.

Such guilt must be affirmed as normal. It does no good to tell parents, "You shouldn't feel guilty." In fact this only leads them to suppress their real feelings, to feel that they are abnormal—or even losing their minds. It is much better to say, "I can see why you would say that. Most parents feel that way." Then parents must be helped to see that they now have a choice: to be overwhelmed and engulfed by their natural feeling of guilt, or to admit them, accept them, let them subside gradually, and go on with attending to their son or daughter now. They can share now and appreciate him or her and bring the family closer together.

Just as guilt is a normal part of grief, so is anger. Parents are understandably angry at this total disruption of their lives, because of the threat to the future and to all of the plans they had for their adolescent who is now on the threshold of justifying them as parents. Most of all, however, they are angry because of the sense of helplessness they feel. They usually do not know what caused the illness, what to expect now and in the future, what they may be called upon to bear, and what their responsibilities might be. Because of this sense of helplessness to alter events, they are also afraid.

Because of these feelings of guilt, anger, fear, and because they do not know where to direct such feelings, they frequently direct hostility toward the staff as an alternative to directing it inward or toward God. Though it is often difficult for the staff, such hostility is actually an indication that the parents have moved beyond the phase of denial in the grieving process.

Other parents may avoid the threat of death for a considerable period of time in order to protect themselves from overwhelming anxiety. They may be unable to function if these avoidance mechanisms are taken away early in the course of the disease. Denial can be considered adaptive behavior when nothing can be done to alter the threat. It has also been noted that such behavior is usually abandoned as the illness and deterioration progresses.

On the other hand, if denial is perpetuated through the illness, communication with the adolescent—who is always aware of what is happening—may break down. Further isolation of both adolescent and parents is the inevitable result. Anticipatory grief is also impeded, and, as a result, the terminal phase of the illness is a greater shock, because they have not had time to prepare and much may have been left unsaid and undone.

Not all parents are able to support their dying adolescent. For some, the relationship with their son or daughter was so stormy prior to the illness that they are unable to reestablish a meaningful relationship at a time when the adolescent is also feeling guilty and irritable, and perhaps projecting blame towards them. Other parents need to intellectualize; they may spend much time in learning all of the medical details of the illness yet may avoid seriously discussing the illness with their adolescent child. Some parents find the stress and guilt so painful that they are unable to visit their adolescent when he is hospitalized or to function effectively when they do visit without concerted staff support.

During the time when the adolescent is acutely ill and hospitalized, families live "one day at a time." The former smooth operation of the family is disrupted and life revolves around the ill teenager. When the illness is chronic, the disruption is also a long-term problem. In many instances, the pattern of family life will be changed from the initial period of diagnosis until some time after the adolescent's death, when a reorganization of family roles takes place. In some cases, the family may be completely and permanently disrupted through divorce or separation of the parents.

Long-term illness is usually also accompanied by remissions and exacerbations. Because of this, the family must adjust and readjust constantly in an effort to retain equilibrium. Further, as the disease progresses, and as the family grows and changes, the home situation may also be constantly changing. The needs of family members and the interactions between them change, as siblings mature and develop and as parental needs vary. Therefore, the family must always learn to cope anew.

Parents of adolescents with life-threatening illness tend to be less sociable and more withdrawn than other parents. This is partly because the community of "normal" families does not understand the changes which must occur in a family that is supporting a seriously ill member. It is also partly because of the fact that "differentness" and the words "cancer" and "leukemia" still carry stigmas in our society. Chronic illness may also cause families to adopt a pattern of illness behavior as an integral part of their lives. For example, families with an adolescent who has cystic fibrosis are confronted with seemingly unending responsibilities related to treatment regimens and diet restrictions. They can never forget for a moment that their adolescent has a serious illness and that the state of his health is their constant responsibility.

Financial troubles are a chronic problem for many families with high medical expenses. Income may be reduced and expenses are generally greatly increased. Frequently, additional employment is needed, and this further reduces the time that parents can spend together. The inaccessibility or unavailability of community resources enhances the vulnerability of the family to other problems.

Many families are not informed about resources which are available to help financially and in other supportive ways. Other families are fearful and therefore unable to use the resources; or they may be unsophisticated about finding their way through our often fragmented maze of medical and supportive services.

Siblings also have many problems when an adolescent member of the family becomes seriously ill. Young children are often thrust very much into the background of the medical crisis. They are often left with various members of the extended family and may suffer greatly when deprived of parental care. When young children are at home, living conditions may have deteriorated severely, especially because of the inevitable disruption of routines necessary to their security. As their insecurity increases, their demands for attention increase. However, where previously parents responded to demands, they may now see them as unreasonable. In addition, siblings may take responsibility for the illness and feel generally guilty, "bad" and unlovable.

Older children also have many problems. Although they are intellectually better able to understand the situation and no longer ascribe guilt to themselves through magical thinking, they still react on a deep emotional level. They still resent deeply the decreased attention to their needs and the disruption in their lives. Many are asked to take on new responsibilities in the household. Though they may appear to pitch in willingly or even enthusiastically, in reality they may deeply resent their new responsibilities. Because of their cheerful outward manner, parents may become comfortable and now look deeply into the true feelings below the surface.

Many children are also afraid that their siblings' disease may strike them at any moment. Not wishing to ask the fearful question, they may withdraw from friends and involvement with others, wishing only to be left alone.

Because of decreased personal attention from their parents, older children also often feel less loved and therefore less lovable. Lack of finances and increased responsibilities prevent them from enjoying many things that their peers have and do and limit interaction with them. Often older girls resent the premature role of mother and choose never to accept it again. Others eventually become hostile to their parents and never again have the same warm and loving relationship with them.

Some recent studies (Madison and Raphael, 1971) indicate that neglect of siblings results in hostile and aggressive responses to the affected child or adolescent. They also document the fact that siblings have a higher incidence of school problems, emotional problems, obesity, and school failure.

It has also been noted that when a child or adolescent in the family dies, siblings may again accept blame, which can result in a sense of hopelessness, anxiety, and pervasive feelings of personal "badness" and unlovableness. They may also fear that other members of their family may die and they may therefore experience other separations with deep distrust and anxiety—perhaps for a lifetime.

FURTHER ASPECTS OF NURSING SUPPORT AND INTERVENTION

The care of fatally ill adolescents has frequently been referred to as one of the most difficult tasks faced by nurses. Students of nursing are frequently close in age to the dying adolescent and can therefore identify with him or her intensely. This close association makes it difficult for them to handle the situation from a professional standpoint rather than from a personal point of view. They fear that they will be unable to talk to the adolescent or listen to his or her fears and concerns without revealing their own personal responses. Some may never have had an experience with death or may not have formed a personal philosophy of life and death. For these reasons they also need support when dealing with a dying adolescent and his family.

Nurses who work with adolescents who are facing death need to understand that outbursts of hostility and rage are usually not meant for them personally, but are a result of the situation in which the teenager finds him- or herself. Teenagers cannot be expected to handle their emotions as adults do. On the other hand, nurses can convey the expectation that with help and support the adolescent will be able to handle feelings more appropriately. Providing activities into which he or she can channel furious rage will help to work out some of the bitterness, support self-esteem and a sense of self-control, and prevent disruption of the treatment regimen. Parents can also be helped to understand the reasons behind their adolescent's anger and bitterness. If they can continue to show by their actions that they still support and love him or her, despite behavior, the adolescent may be better able to accept comfort without losing face. Attention from relatives expressed in cards, letters, and visits also helps the adolescent to appreciate that he or she is not really alone, despite the feelings of desolation that are always present. Though unable to express gratitude before such attention, the loneliness and bitterness may become less acute.

Though the teenager may have become isolated from former friendships, much can be done to promote friendships with other adolescents who have similar interests and problems. Together, they may be able to share their fears and frustrations, discuss their relationships with family, and consider their thoughts of philosophies about life and death.

Nurses can also promote adolescents' sense of independence and control over their situation as far as possible. They can be advocates for them to ensure that they have a voice in decisions and play a role in their own care. Answering all questions honestly, avoiding condescending treatment or attitudes, and keeping restrictions to a necessary minimum will protect the personal dignity of adolescents.

Dying adolescents, above all, need nurses who will listen to them when they are able to share concerns, fears, and frustrations. They will usually indicate by their questions the kind of information they wish. If the teenager initially needs to deny absolutely, he should not be obliged to face unpleasant and unbearable realities that he cannot yet tolerate. When he is strong enough to face reality more directly, he will usually indicate by his questions that he now wants to discuss his situation more fully. At no time do adolescents appreciate false cheerfulness, to which they are very sensitive. Hope, however, can realistically be offered for shorter-term goals as the disease progresses. Most of all, dying adolescents appreciate adults who can sit with them and be comfortable in an atmosphere of silence.

In the terminal phase, adolescents usually select one or two adults to share their thoughts and feelings. Knowing that they cannot get well, they are often ready for death to come and are resigned to the inevitable. Some younger adolescents may resist to the end, lonely and proud, but this is relatively rare. In many cases, as death nears, adolescents show amazing strength, comforting their parents who are in pain and providing meaning to this tragedy by teaching parents and nurses the value and ideals of living.

REFERENCES

Anthony S: The Discovery of Death in Childhood and After. New York, Basic Books, 1972
Aune R: Adolescence and Death. Unpublished manuscript, 1974
Brown A, Bjelic J: Coping strategies of two adolescents with malignancy. Matern Child Nurs J 6(2):77–85, 1977
Easson W: The Dying Child. Springfield, IL, Charles C Thomas, 1970
Gesell A, Ilg F: The Child from Five to Ten. New York, Harper & Brothers, 1946
Gyulay J: The Dying Child. New York, McGraw-Hill, 1978
Hermann N: Go Out in Joy. New York, Simon & Schuster, 1977
Kikuchi J: A leukemic adolescent's verbalizations about dying. Matern Child Nurs J 1(3):259–264, 1972
Kikuchi J: An adolescent boy's adjustment to leukemia. Matern Child Nurs J 6(1):37–49, 1977
Lacasse C: A dying adolescent. Am J Nurs 75:433, 1975
Lowenberg JS: The coping behaviors of fatally ill adolescents and their parents. Nurs Forum 9(3):269–287, 1970
Madison D, Raphael B: Social and psychological consequences of chronic disease in childhood. Med J 2:1265, 1971
Mitchel M: The Child's Attitude to Death. New York, Schocken Books, 1967
Nagy MH: The child's theories concerning death. J Genet Psychol 3:73, 1948
Olsiak M: Adolescence and impending death." Can J Pub Health 67:65, January/February 1976
Reigh R, Feinberg H: The fatally ill adolescent. In Feinstein S, Giovacchini P (eds): Adolescent Psychiatry, vol. 3. New York, Basic Books, 1974
Schneidman E: Death and the College Student. New York, Behavioral Publications, 1972
Schowalter J, Ferholt J, Mann N: The adolescent patient's decision to die. Pediatrics 51:97–103, 1973

Commentary

Contributions to Research

Mary R. Crittenden

OVERVIEW OF CONTRIBUTIONS

Just as Sigmund Freud removed the taboo on the mention of sexuality and as Kubler–Ross did for death in adulthood, so Eugenia Waechter did for childhood death. In an era when fatally ill children were told little if anything about their condition, that was a revolutionary step; at that time, children presumably were unable to understand the concept of death even if they were told, a view that neatly absolved health professionals of responsibility. Dr. Waechter saw that view as more the problem of the adult than of the child. She believed that the child was not the passive recipient of knowledge, but an active seeker, one who knew more than we realized.

Her primary personal interest was the quality of life, not death alone. With amused amazement, she once recalled that a stranger sought her out to ask if she was "the death lady." Her response was quick. She told the inquirer she studied death for what it taught us about the ways children lived and what they needed from parents and health professionals to live fully, freely, and actively, regardless of their medical states.

Her consistent professional goal was the advancement of nursing. She held a Ph.D. in child development from Stanford University where she worked with, and was respected by, eminent psychologists, but she remained first and foremost a nurse. I knew her as a professional who had the unique ability to work collaboratively with other disciplines, while maintaining her own strong sense of the dignity of her own profession and its ability to give and take with others on an equal footing. She helped move nursing into another era, beyond providing direct patient services, beyond administrating them, into research and teaching of core issues.

In an era when few nurses did definitive research, she worked for the systematic development of scientifically based knowledge. Unafraid to question existing beliefs, she insisted the clinical assumptions had to be tested against empirical realities.

She wanted health care providers to understand the complexities of the child's life. In a time when interest in projective techniques had waned, she had the vision to view that method as a unique means to probe children's reactions to disease. Up to that point, interviews and questionnaires given to adult caretakers, sometimes supplemented by child observations, were the major methods of study. To ask the child directly about concerns of death was unthinkable in the late 1960s. Storytelling methods, she felt, yielded unique data about their ideas, feelings, and fantasies that should not be ignored—"one piece of the puzzle," she said, "but an important piece." Even though the theory and methodology of projective assessment had been, and still is, widely criticized, she accepted the onerous task of applying that method in a scientifically rigorous fashion. In terms of the topic, sample, and methodology, her dissertation was far from easy to defend. Are projections the product of unconscious processes, or the conscious reproduction of past experiences, or an effort to cope, or some combination of the above; are the methods psychometrically reliable or valid; are they as efficient and clinically useful as more direct methods? Rather than wallow in debate or abandon the challenge, Gene accepted full responsibility.

To implement her study, she developed her own instrument, the adapted thematic apperception test (TAT), with its own scoring system that was sufficiently objective to be replicated in other studies. To create a tool that allows us to measure experiences in a new way is truly revolutionary.

Her position that projective methods do yield provocative data was confirmed, ironically enough, by a criticism of her study. A committee reviewing the proposal was concerned that the children might be upset about the "autopsy picture" (TAT card 8BM, commonly called the surgery mural, which Gene described as "boy in front of mural depicting an operation"). She was delighted to inform the critics that the card often elicits stories of achievement or desire to serve others (e.g., a boy dreaming of becoming a doctor).

Gene wrote one of the few dissertations that led to further studies. Her adapted TAT cards led other investigators to probe the responses of fatally and chronically ill children (Spinetta, 1973, 1975; Malone, 1982; Koocher, 1982). She also wanted to explore parental communications and other components of the child's stories, both within and among specific diagnostic groups, hence our study. Slowly, a body of knowledge emerged that perhaps did not give us better answers, but did let us ask more specific questions. To encourage further study of the issue that intrigued her, I will touch on two topics, the components and correlates of death imagery.

COMPONENTS OF DEATH IMAGERY

The problems of operational definitions of terms and their categories are manifold and complex, as Gene well knew. The task of analyzing and specifying them is far from over. Our underlying assumptions need to be constantly critiqued. That is the inheritance Gene left us.

Waechter (1971) put her own assumption on the line: "the rationale of the present study assumes that concern with non-being may be displaced to concern with threat from without and the concern with loneliness may be an expression of concern with the ultimate separation of death. Moreover, fears of separation, intrusive procedures, and pain may substitute for an underlying general apprehensiveness about survival" (p 161).

In the various articles reviewed here, the global concept under study has several names: death imagery, anxiety, fear, threat, and so forth. Are these concepts synonymous, partially similar, or unique? Spinetta (1973) pointed out, "whether or not one wishes to call this non-conceptual anxiety about the child's own fatal illness 'death anxiety' seems to be a problem of semantics rather than fact. To equate awareness of death with the ability to conceptualize it and express the concept in an adult manner denies the possibility of an awareness of death at a less cognitive level" (p 844). That position is certainly valid in the early stages of study of a new topic. However, to advance the study further, operational definitions must be spelled out.

The components of loneliness, separation, and abandonment, which we tend to group, and those of mutilation, body intrusion, and assault on body integrity, which also group, need to be specified so that we can tease out the ways they combine in a global rating for different subgroups. Spinetta saw a link between loneliness and body intrusion in the fatally ill group; the concept of loneliness also often surfaces in the preschool group as well. The relationship between loneliness, a feeling or affective component, and abandonment by others or separation from them, an action or behavioral component certainly bears further scrutiny. In that regard, the literature from other areas needs attention. For example, Marcoen and Brumage (1985) studied loneliness in healthy children and youths and found some sex differences, variations in peer- and parent-related loneliness, and relationships to social sensitivity. Conceivably, these attributes might be useful to assess in stories generated by children with serious illnesses.

Standards for scoring the currently used components are sufficiently clear to permit reasonably reliable interrater agreement. However, I vividly recall the many battles about the proper classification of a child's response, "Did the doctor *mean* to kill the boy or was it just an accident"; "did the dolly *know* she was going to die?" Whether brief indirect reference to death merits the same weight as persistent and/or direct mention also is an issue. Such debates are the joy of research and its frustration, and Dr. Waechter knew both well. The emerging literature on children's ability to use emotionally descriptive language (Ridgeway, Waters, and Kuczaj, 1985) may help us probe children's verbal projections more precisely.

CORRELATES OF DEATH IMAGERY

The several studies probed relationships among death anxieties and other attributes, including those related to the child's illness, background, and social context, as well as other characteristics of the stories. On-going analysis will help us understand the implications of death imagery, the issues needing further study, and their implications for clinical practice.

In regard to factors related to illness, Dr. Waechter looked at severity in four groups ranging from fatally ill to well, and later explored the type of diagnosis. The chronicity or duration of illness also received attention, and the implications of repeated complications versus chronic stability were touched upon in the articles. The evidence is strong that fatally ill children generally express more death anxiety than the less seriously ill, though types of disease (e.g., cystic fibrosis) may account for some variation. Spinetta also draws attention to the effects of age, severity, and duration of illness on anxieties, noting that the anxieties of the younger chronically ill ebb in time, while the reverse was obtained for the leukemics. The impact of the age at onset of illness, the types of treatments, and the other medical complications remain to be explored.

In regard to the child, demographic, cognitive, and affective components have been studied. The demographics of age and sex have been more widely studied than those of socioeconomic status or ethnic group. Malone's (1982) study of Irish children, which extended the inquiry into the preschool group, did indicate the commonality of findings in diverse groups, if not the universality.

To check for cognitive factors, Spinetta (1975) used a ratio measure to control for effects of verbosity and age. Malone (1982) included an IQ test, the Stanford Binet. She noted that "the treatment for malignant disease was not associated with gross intellectual impairment in this sample." On the surface, that finding disagrees with neuropsychological studies in this country, which have shown impairment. However, the impairment may not show in global scores on tests like the Binet. Moreover, the average mean score on one test cannot reflect longitudinal changes in function of individuals or the group. In addition, "average" functioning for formerly bright children does represent presence of impairment, as other studies have shown (Meadows, 1980). I stress the issue because assessment of cognitive components of death imagery need to take into account the findings of recent neuropsychological studies, which suggest cognitive problems may occur that need to be taken into account.

Among the affective components studied are general anxiety (Waechter), situation specific anxiety, and interpersonal distance (Spinetta). Their relationship to death anxieties points to the need to look at the social context of the study, the inpatient setting vs. the outpatient (Spinetta), differences in clinic settings (Spinetta, Waechter) or staffing patterns (Waechter), and family background, including communication, warmth, past experience with death, and religion (Waechter). In regard to openness of communications, it is noteworthy that parents in Malone's Irish study (1982) were as guarded as those studied here in the late 1960s and 1970s. Even though Waechter and others have been persuasive advocates of freer communication, we cannot assume that the message has been widely received or accepted in our own era.

Other characteristics of the stories have also been assessed. Dr. Waechter's pioneering study in 1968 looked at cause, affect, outcome, and so forth; her follow-up study used categories from the Cohen and Weil (1971) Test of Emotional Development to probe further. Malone outlined the operational definitions of her variables, and further classified the stories as enumerative, descriptive, or apperceptive, finding that young fatally ill children do indeed give more apperceptive responses, which reaffirms Gene's hunch of 14 years ago.

PROBLEMS AND PROJECTS

The use of projective measures is not without danger, either in research or clinical practice, but Dr. Waechter recognized that the advancement of knowledge required judicious risk taking. She fully recognized that problems compound when studies of low-incidence problems must be done in high-risk populations, using minimally standardized measures whose reliability, validity, and even practicality are questionable.

Clearly there is work to be done to advance theory, research, and practice. The terms we bandy about require sharper operational definitions; the components of global death anxiety ratings need to be teased out and their relationship specified; the correlates need to be cross-checked and extended.

The need to accumulate enough subjects within a reasonable time span has led us to study "mixed bag" groups of subjects and controls. The comparability of the findings and amenability to generalization thus is suspect. The complexities of locating appropriate groups may well lead investigators to develop computerized data banks, clearly coded to specify salient variables for study, using increasingly sophisticated methods of data analysis.

Dr. Waechter's chapter in Wass and Corr (1983), published posthumously, described her view of the state of the art at that time. It was clear that the work she began in 1968 had borne fruit. The conspiracy of silence had been broken. In some areas, at least, parents and staff talked more openly, and that raised new questions. Can too much openness be as bad as too little? The data from our subjects suggested it might be, but the numbers were few. That chapter described in detail the findings from our leukemic patients. She had intended to develop those results in another publication, as a companion piece to our other publications, geared for parents, but that chapter now stands as her own memorial.

She recognized that advances in pediatrics had created a new cohort. Oncefatal illnesses now had more optimistic, though less certain, prognoses. In effect, we can do more to keep them alive, with fewer resources to ensure an acceptable quality of life. Gene urged continued scrutiny of our assumptions and clinical findings as we faced new challenges. The literature on the ways that children cope with illness and death has begun to bloom (Eiser, 1985; Wass and Corr, 1983; Koocher, 1982; Lonetti, 1980). In those and other writings, Gene's work repeatedly is cited as seminal. A body of knowledge emerges that cries to be integrated with other observations of the ways children cope with stresses (e.g., Murphy's and Gamezy's articles in the 40th Commemoration of H. Murphy's opus, edited by Rabin et al, 1981), since coping with death is crucial to coping with life, as Gene reminded us.

Eugenia Waechter has left a legacy. Krahn (1985), in describing use of projective methods in pediatric settings, questioned the children's apperception test and the test of emotional development, but concluded that "it appears that the Waechter pictures can be very helpful in assessing fears and providing a stimulus for acknowledging and discussing children's fears about their illnesses." Dana (1984), also discussing the practice and teaching of personality assessment, gave special attention to projective TAT methods, indicating that the method is far from dead. It may be that we are about to experience another rebirth of this psychological phoenix, as we realize the limitations of objective measures for understanding the complexities of our reactions to illness and other stress.

Though the task is formidable, Waechter's studies and those that follow provide a base for more rigorous inquiry and more effective clinical practice. The work we do for the child we serve is its own tribute to her contributions, not the words we say about her.

REFERENCES

Cohen H, Weil R: Tasks of Emotional Development: Manual. Lexington, Heath, 1971

Dana R: Personality assessment: Practice and teaching for the next decade. J Personal Assess 48:46–54, 1984

Eiser C: The Psychology of Childhood Illness. New York, Springer-Verlag, 1985

Koocher G: The Damocles Syndrome. New York, McGraw–Hill, 1982

Krahn G: The use of projective assessment techniques in pediatric settings. J Pediatr Psychol 19:179–193, 1985

Lonetto R: Children's Conception of Death. New York, Springer-Verlag, 1980

Malone MM: Consciousness of dying and projective fantasy of young children with malignant disease. J Devel Behav Pediatr 3:55–60, 1982

Marcoen A, Brumage M: Loneliness among children and young adolescents. Devel Psychol 21:1025–1031, 1985

Murphy LB: Exploration in child personality. In Rabin A et al: Further Explorations in Personality. New York, John Wiley & Sons, 1981

Ridgeway D, Waters E, Kuczaj K: Acquisition of emotion descriptive language. Develop Psychol 21:901–908, 1985

Spinetta J, Rigler D, Karon M: Anxiety in the dying child. Pediatrics 52:841–845, 1973

Spinetta J, Maloney LJ: Death anxiety in the outpatient leukemic child. Pediatrics 56:1034–1037, 1975

Waechter E: Children's awareness of fatal illness. Am J Nurs 71:1168–1172, 1971

Wass H, Corr C: Childhood and Death. New York, Hemisphere, 1983

Commentary

Life-Threatening Illness in Children: A Tribute to Eugenia Waechter

John J. Spinetta

When I first met Eugenia Waechter in 1969, I had just entered the doctoral program in clinical psychology at the University of Southern California. As an older student with a prior master's degree, I was able to free up some class time to spend extra hours at Children's Hospital of Los Angeles. During my first year at the hospital, my future mentor and dissertation director, Dr. David Rigler, introduced me to his many areas of research and clinical interest, primary among which was his interest in children with cancer. As we began to formulate ideas on how to go about talking to and interacting with the younger children in ways that would yield us hard data on how the children were coping and how we could best intervene to help them cope more adequately, Dave invited Eugenia Waechter to Children's Hospital to talk to us about her own just-completed dissertation on anxiety in fatally ill children. That's how I met this great lady.

My first impression of Eugenia was that of a powerful yet kind woman whose love for the children was obvious and sincere. I liked her from the start.

As we spoke after her formal presentation and during dinner later that evening, we discussed common research interests. Over the year that followed, I corresponded with Eugenia about my own dissertation interests and ways in which I could build on what she had pioneered. Although more than a dozen years and many publications had preceded her work, there was very little regarding children's awareness and understanding of their own illness prior to her work that could be judged as hard-nosed or firmly planted in good research method. Eugenia broke new ground in her storytelling method of obtaining from the children expressions of their own understanding of what was happening to them. With her carefully drawn pictures, four of which were developed specifically for the study and four chosen from a larger standardized measure, Eugenia was able to pinpoint in the children with cancer an awareness of death and body intrusion that far surpassed what prior researchers thought children knew about their illness. She was able to demonstrate that children with cancer, under 10 years of age, were not only anxious about their illness and understood, at their own developmental level, some of the implications of the illness, but were able to talk about it, albeit indirectly. Dr. Waechter's work began what was to become a new era in the study of children's awareness of their own fatal illness.

Through the help of my own advisor, Dr. Rigler, and with frequent consultation with Eugenia Waechter, I developed a dissertation study that built on Eugenia's pioneering work. With her full cooperation I used the four pictures of hospital scenes she developed as part of my own study, adding to her efforts a three-dimensional replica of a hospital room, which allowed me to tap further into the children's level of awareness and understanding. Our study at Children's Hospital of Los Angeles was able to demonstrate that at some level, often preceding their ability to fully conceptualize and to verbalize it, the children with cancer were aware that theirs was no ordinary illness. We were able to demonstrate that the greater anxiety and preoccupation with threat to body integrity and functioning of the fatally ill child, when compared to a matched chronically ill counterpart, despite efforts to keep the child from becoming aware of his prognosis, indicates that the child somehow picks up a sense that his illness is very serious and very threatening. The fatally ill child is aware that his is no ordinary illness.

It became clear, both from my follow-up study and from Eugenia Waechter's earlier work, that even though the concerns of the 6- to 10-year-old leukemic child might not take the form of overt expression about death, the more subtle fears and anxieties were nonetheless real, painful, and very much related to the seriousness of the illness. Whether one wished to call this nonconceptual anxiety about the child's own fatal illness "death anxiety" seemed more a problem of semantics than of fact. To equate awareness of death with the ability to conceptualize it and express the concept in an adult manner denied the possibility of an awareness of death at a less cognitive level. If it is true that the perception of death could be engraved at some level that precedes the child's ability to talk about it, then a child might well understand that he is going to die long before he can say so.

It became clear as well, from my own study of interpersonal distance behavior, that the placement of significant adult figures by the dying children was reflective of a growing sense of psychological separation of the dying child from the hospital, both people and circumstances, for reasons specific to each child's prior reinforcement history. Not only did the fatally ill child feel this separation from the very first hospitalization and sense its increase with subsequent admissions to the hospital, but, for whatever reason, the child would not or could not protest this separation.

What Eugenia had begun was a series of sensitively based research projects into what young children with cancer were feeling and thinking, a series of research projects that led, during the next decade, to more open and child-centered approaches to the psychosocial treatment of pediatric cancer.

During the course of the years that followed Eugenia's original work, medical advances changed childhood cancer from an almost universally fatal illness to a chronic illness in which over half of the children are now able to live into adulthood. Along with the changes have come concerns for and research into the sequelae of medical treatment, and the concerns that the children express and experience as they grow through school and into adulthood, concerns centering increasingly on issues of learning deficiencies, employability, insurability, and living with physical effects of medical treatment. It was Eugenia's pioneering work in the late 1960s that set the tone for the current atmosphere in the field of pediatric cancer, one in which the psychosocial, educational, and vocational concerns of the child are treated with as much seriousness and attention as are the medical concerns.

Eugenia's work during the 1970s extended far beyond the field of childhood cancer into other equally important areas of concern in the field of child and maternal health, and in psychosocial repercussions on family members as well of having a child in the family who is suffering from an illness. This book attests to the many fields of interest that Eugenia's work touched. However, from my own personal and professional perspective, Eugenia lives on in my memory as the pioneer in the area of children's understanding of their own fatal illness, a pioneer who gave my own career both a personal support and a professional underpinning. Eugenia Waechter was a great woman, both in her career and in her person. I will always remember her.

Interventions With the Child and Family

14 · Nursing and the Dying Patient

Eugenia H. Waechter

The inescapable fact of universal physical extinction has deeply concerned humanity down through the ages. It is a bewildering and mystifying phenomenon and a fact of life which cannot be altered, despite scientific and medical advances. The "taboo" surrounding death in 20th century American culture and society has been well documented. Americans attempt to deny death by avoiding it, protecting children from contact with it, and by disguising its reality.

Nurses and physicians have also learned to avoid confronting death. Nurses encounter multiple difficulties because they are not educated or trained to deal with death. It cannot be disputed that the performance and behavior of nurses are often highly irrational and emotional when contemplating an approaching death. Death and dying negate both the social and professional emphasis on youth, alertness, independence, accomplishment, self-sufficiency and self-fulfillment. The purposeful and unconscious efforts of nurses to avoid prolonged contact with the terminally ill compound the difficulties of patients who are dying in a modern hospital.

Nurses, along with other professionals and the general public, are now becoming more interested and aware of the many issues surrounding life and death. With organ transplants, methods of population control, and life support systems, there are questions of "Who shall live?" "When does death occur?" "Who has the responsibility for making these decisions?" The right of the individual to determine the way he lives and dies is now being openly discussed in both public and professional circles.

Nurses must be intimately involved with these issues. They must be physically present and responsible when questions of life and death arise. Also, they must

From Davis R, Neiswender M: Dealing with Death. Los Angeles, University of Southern California, Ethel Percy Andus Gerontology Center, 1973.

come to terms with their own concerns about death before they can help the dying patient. Through educational experiences, by attending meetings, and by planning ongoing ward conferences, nurses are beginning to deal with death.

This concern is important, since nurses can influence the way individuals under their care face death. A nurse is often the closest person to the patient because of her care giving activities and because of the hierarchical nature of our institutions. Nurses who observe the terminally ill constantly often know them best. These nurses can lessen the loneliness which our present system imposes. Nurses can also balance the alternating emotions of denial, anxiety, anger, guilt, depression, bargaining, and hope in the terminally ill person. Although pain and grieving are inevitable, much of the dying experience can be influenced by caring professionals and by meaningful relationships. Of course, no one can completely understand how the dying person feels. But nurses can provide an atmosphere of caring and can help the patient die in dignity. I would like to share some of the concerns expressed by terminally ill persons and discuss some of their implications for nursing care.

CONTROL

Patients in today's hospitals sense a sudden and complete loss of control over their lives. They lose control in the major aspects of life and death, and also in the small but important areas of daily living. They no longer have control over when they will get out of bed, what they will wear, or even when they will brush their teeth.

We have all learned that children are dependent and that adults must be independent. Adults who pride themselves on independence and self-control often find hospitalization very frustrating. Patients strenuously resist being dependent. The feeling of a loss of control is even more characteristic of the person with a poor prognosis. The inevitability of his death is a constant reminder of his ultimate powerlessness in the universe.

Nurses can help the dying person feel in control of his life. By respecting the individual and his remaining freedom, nurses can reaffirm the patient's value as a person. Nurses should respect the patient's likes and dislikes, his thoughts and preferences. Support, rather than permissiveness, encourages the patient's personal dignity and self-respect.

The aged are often characterized as childlike and helpless. They have lost much of their former power over life. The aged need particular evidence of respect. The aged need to maintain a sense of self-esteem, to be able to influence their environment, and to feel that their wishes matter to the people around them. Nurses have the opportunity to encourage patient decision-making and independence. The gradual yielding of choice and control to others is inevitable as the patient's physical condition deteriorates. However, perhaps the patient himself can best sense when he must relinquish control.

ANGER AND DEPRESSION

Anger and depression are often seen in the dying person. They are responses to loss of a past life and experiences in the present. Every dying person has the right to grieve his own dying. Grief can be a consequence of isolation, powerlessness, loneliness, or abandonment. Grief is also present when dying is associated with punishment for past or current offenses. Understandably, the dying person often resents a hostile fate. Since it is difficult to resent an abstraction, the patient's anger may be turned onto his family and friends. Or, more usually, the anger is directed at the caretaking agents.

It is difficult for the nurse, as for anyone, to receive anger without responding or retaliating. Criticisms of hospital procedures or nursing actions strike at a nurse's professional and personal sense of worth. Complaining and demanding patients make nurses angry, which only makes it harder for them to communicate with the dying person.

Discussion on the ward could help nurses understand the patient's anger. By understanding the displaced anger, grief, and "demandingness," nurses might be less inclined to withdraw from the dying patient. If patients feel supported, perhaps they will be less angry.

DENIAL AND HOPE

Denial seems to be a necessary mechanism which protects the dying individual from the anxiety and pain. We seldom think of the dying person as "accepting" his fate. Unfortunately, too often we say the dying patient denies his condition without considering questions such as: "What is the threat being avoided?", "What are the fluctuations of this response?", "To whom is the denial directed?" It is rare for a person to deny completely a progressive illness. Some professional personnel are exposed to more of this denial than others, probably because they expect to see denial in the dying patient. We may even encourage denial because it can be more comfortable for us.

Patients who choose to deny death should be allowed to do so. Yet some individuals may face death willingly even though they do not actively wish for it. Nurses may erroneously infer that the threat causing denial is that of death itself. Actually, the threat the patient is reacting to may be more related to disruptions in meaningful relationships, to changes in his self-esteem and self-worth, and to fears about pain and suffering. Concerns about family integrity may also be threatening. Although nurses do not have the power to remove the threat of death, they can encourage hope by relieving physical problems and pain, by supporting the patient's sense of self-esteem, by encouraging patient–family contacts, and by actively showing their caring for and interest in the patient.

RELIEF FROM PAIN

Hopelessness is a reaction to endless suffering and pain. When pain is constantly present and expected, individuals naturally try to withdraw from the hurting environment and people. Physicians can prescribe medication to relieve the suffering. Nurses can also help minimize pain. Nurses can help by listening and hearing what the patient communicates about his pain, by observing the effects of medication, and by sharing this information with the physician. Nurses can provide small but important services to increase the patient's comfort. Nurses can encourage medication to be given so that the dying person does not have to ask constantly for relief or have to live in anticipation of pain.

BODY IMAGE

Patients can become very distressed over changes in their body image, whether these are due to progressive destruction, wasting, or to therapeutic efforts. Indelible marks on the body to guide the radiotherapist, voice changes, loss of hair due to steroid therapy, or disfigurement in other ways can make patients feel humiliated and can lower their self-respect. Accustomed to such body changes, the staff becomes insensitive to them. Nurses can reinforce the patient's self-image and self-respect by being careful, respectful, and tender in caring for the patient and by helping patients groom and dress themselves. This can help the patient feel he is still the same person. The patient's identity can be further reinforced if he is allowed to keep his personal belongings with him.

COMMUNICATING WITH THE DYING

Communication with the dying person is perhaps the most difficult aspect of nursing care. The questions: "What do I tell?", "What do I say?", and "What do I hide?" are constantly asked in ward conferences or in private discussions among nurses. Nurses know that most dying patients realize they are dying. Patients generally will talk about their condition if they are allowed to. The dying patient, however, learns to be silent because he learns that no one wants to talk about death with him. A barrier develops between patient and staff, which increases the patient's isolation, alienation, and suffering.

Nurses do not need to be terribly concerned about what they say to dying patients. Probably, the dying person has no more than a simple need to communicate and to feel "in contact" with others. He needs reassurance about such matters as, "Will I get relief from pain?", "Will I be alone?", or "Will I be cared for?" Nurses can give easy answers to these questions. The patient's comfort relates directly to their care taking activities. Sitting with the patient, even silently, tells him that the nurse is not too hurried or harrassed to listen to him. He is reassured that what he has to say is important, and that someone cares. Also, sitting beside the patient lets the two people communicate with each other on "the same level." Although nurses are often uncomfortable when they are not actively "doing," sitting and talking can be a most important aspect of nursing care. This is a way for nurses to get information for more appropriate and individualized care of the patient.

The Unconscious Patient

Communication with the "unconscious" patient is often overlooked. This is terrible because even if the signs of consciousness are minimal or nonexistent, the patient may still hear and retain some awareness of his environment.

I recently interviewed a critically injured young woman who had been hospitalized for some weeks as a result of a car accident. Unable to respond either physically or verbally, she was still able to hear the conversations around her. What she heard terrified her. The impersonal and undignified way her body was treated was painful but she couldn't communicate her pain or anger. She used up her energy worrying about dying. Even the postures and movements of visitors in her room told her she was not doing well. She commented, "No one came close to me. They stood around like they were at a funeral."

This woman has asked me to tell you the things that comforted her. Her mother visited frequently. She was the only person who continued to call her by name, to talk to her, and to hold her hand. This reassured the woman that everyone had not given up and that someone still cared. She liked being told the time and the day and being told about her condition. The patient said that the nurses talked to each other while they were caring for her. They were not only impersonal, but sometimes critical of her. They never talked directly to her until she was actively alert. I think her experience has a great deal to say about us as nurses.

PREPARATION FOR DYING

As death approaches, small things matter a great deal to the patient. Moments alone with family and friends, "goodbyes," and parting letters or gifts can all be comforting. Nurses can best assure that each person under their care dies as they wish to. Nurses can help the patient to finish the things he wants to finish, and to do the things he has left to do. Nurses can assure the patient he will be kept as comfortable as possible, and that he will not be left alone.

THE FAMILY OF THE DYING PERSON

Dying certainly affects the family of the terminally ill person. Many feelings are expressed: grief, guilt, hostility, resentment, deprivation, anxiety. The family or friends of the dying person may urgently feel the need to compensate for their past inadequacies in the relationship. They may feel guilty for having been unable to prevent this calamity. They may "need to be needed" by the dying individual, sometimes inappropriate to the importance of the past relationship. These feelings that are normal during grieving may be expressed toward the professional personnel since it is generally unacceptable to express them to the dying individual. For example, anxious and worried family members may constantly argue and complain to the staff. Nurses, busy with their professional duties, often find these situations extremely uncomfortable.

The total nursing care of a dying individual must also include plans for the "care" of family members. Nurses can help family members grieve by taking time to listen to them. A "listener" who is not a member of the family is often in the best position to lessen the anxiety associated with anger and guilt. Feeling understood, the family may cease being a "nuisance." As their anxiety decreases, they will be able to communicate more easily with the dying person. Maintaining good communication between the patient and his family is an important part of nursing care.

DEATH IN CHILDHOOD

The death of a child is particularly sad. It implies social loss, undeveloped potential, and unfulfilled hope. Children, even more than adults, may find themselves largely alone with their fears, anxieties, and uncertainties. Yet, this is a time when comfort, nearness, and sympathetic understanding are most important. Fantasy can be more frightening to a child than physical death. The loss of human contact and comfort may accompany and exaggerate the fear and physical discomfort.

How and what do children with a fatal disease tell us about their fears and anxieties? A child's response to a fatal illness is different from that of an adult. They are most closely protected from knowing about their diagnosis, prognosis, or treatment. Also, their cognitive processes and emotional development are not yet mature. They may be more dependent on the hospital people than adults are.

Because of the lack of systematic research, there is little known about how children feel about dying or about the impact of a child's death on the family. Available research indicates that children under the age of ten are not fearful of dying. Most of these studies, unfortunately, are based on interviewing and observing of the parents. There are only incidental clinical observations of the child's behavior.

I feel we need more informed data so we can develop a nursing care program for the dying child. I have conducted several research projects in this area. It is my feeling that in spite of our efforts to protect the dying child, meaningful adults communicate their anxieties and fears to the child. This happens when emotional "climates" change in their homes and when their family becomes evasive or falsely cheerful.

In a study I hypothesized that six to ten year old children with a fatal illness would indicate more anxiety related to death than would children with chronic or brief illness, or than would well children. I further hypothesized that the amount of anxiety would be related to the warmth of the mother–child relationship and to the opportunities the child had to discuss his illness with his parents or other meaningful adults. Each of the children was shown a set of eight pictures to elicit fantasies about their present and future body integrity and functioning. A general anxiety scale was also administered to each child. Finally, the parents of each child participated in a tape-recorded interview session. The analysis of the general anxiety scale indicated that the mean score of the subjects with a fatal illness was nearly double the score for the hospitalized children and three times the score for the healthy children. These findings support the hypothesis that in spite of our efforts to protect dying children from being anxious about death, they are still very anxious about it. At least they express more generalized anxiety than do healthy or moderately ill children. The stories told by the fatally ill children relate to specific themes of death, mutilation, or loneliness much more often than do the stories of children with a more positive prognosis. These dying children also had more depressive feelings and they used wish-fulfillment more often to relieve threat. Also their stories contained more themes relating to sadness, worry, and fear.*

The maternal interview was used to estimate the opportunities the child had to discuss his illness with his parents or with the professional personnel. Parents did feel very strongly about this question of awareness. Some felt that their child should know as much as possible about his illness. Others went to great lengths to insure that the diagnosis would not be mentioned to the child. Many parents felt unable to cope with the feelings involved in a frank discussion with their child about death. Only two dying children had discussed their deaths with their parents; six had received very little realistic information regarding their illness; and the others had been informed that their illnesses were temporary and trivial.

Which was the best procedure to follow in this respect? Many of the parents were deeply troubled by this issue. Would it be in the best interest of their child to keep the diagnosis a secret? Or would it be more helpful to him to discuss his questions frankly and completely? Parents of children with leukemia or other malignant conditions were reluctant for the child to hear the words "leukemia" or "cancer." They felt that these words were negative, fearful, and implied certain death. Several parents were afraid that their child would be avoided by his friends if they knew the diagnosis. Many parents wanted to know the best way to help their child, others strongly felt that discussing death would be impossible for them.

The differences were often striking between the child's awareness about death (as inferred from his imaginative stories) and the parent's feelings about the child's awareness. Although most of the subjects in the fatal group had not discussed death with their parents, the percentage of death imagery in their stories was sixty-three percent. Thus, many of the children who had not been told their diagnosis nevertheless indicated their awareness of it in their imaginative stories. Often the characters in the story were given the subject's personal diagnosis and symptoms. The data suggests that dying children who are able to discuss their fears and concerns about death express less specific death anxiety, as measured by the projective test.

Some illustrations from the children's stories may highlight their awareness and fears about their future death. One six year old boy was in the terminal stages of leukemia. He had discussed his illness with his parents in terms of "tired blood." He told the following story after viewing a picture depicting a woman entering a room with her face in her hands:

This is about a woman. She's somebody's mother. She's crying because her son was in the hospital and died. He had leukemia. He finally had a heart attack. It just happened . . . he died. Then they took him away to a cemetery to bury him, and his soul went up to heaven.

The woman is crying. But she forgets about it when she goes to bed. Because she relaxes and her brain relaxes. She's very sad. But she sees her little boy again when she goes up to heaven. She's looking forward to that. She won't find anybody else in heaven—just her little boy that she knows.

---

* EDITOR'S NOTE: See Chapter 12 and Appendices A and B.

The story illustrates this boy's awareness of his present and probable future, the influence of religious instruction on his fantasy, and the loneliness he felt. He feels helpless, but certain about the inevitable future.

An eight year old girl with cystic fibrosis told the following story about a picture of a small child in bed with a nurse standing nearby:

One girl was reading a book in the hospital. The nurse was over by the bed. The girl's name is Becky. She had the bad coughing. She had trouble with her lungs. She had lung congestion. The nurse is looking at her chart. Becky is thinking they're going to do an operation. Becky is only eight years old. She thinks they are going to hurt her and she doesn't want it. And they did give the operation. They gave her a sleeping shot. She didn't like shots. The same nurse always gave it, because she knew what to do. Becky died. Then her mother came to see her and they told her she died. But the mother didn't like to hear that.

This story illustrates the child's acute awareness of her condition. In many other instances, the children seemed to attribute their own diagnosis and symptoms, concerns and fears to the characters in their stories. The helplessness of the child is again apparent in this story. She expressed her inability to alter events, her fears of mutilation and pain, her certainty about an inevitable future, and her sadness.

Some of the stories not only indicate the helplessness the child may feel, but also suggest that the environment is nonsupportive and even actively hostile. A seven year old boy with cystic fibrosis comments in one of his stories: "The little boy had to stay in the hospital because the doctor wanted it. He got a shot in the back; a big needle. He was scared of shots, and didn't want it. And the doctor did it hard. His lungs are gone—he can't breathe. His lungs got worse and he didn't get well. He died, and he was buried with a big shovel." One boy with leukemia told the following story to a picture depicting an intravenous infusion: "This boy had a blood problem. It's a very bad thing, and he's not feeling good. The doctor put the tube in. To drain out his blood. He took a whole lot of blood. The boy dies, he gets buried. He feels unhappy because he did not want to die. He is mad at the doctor. He don't know why the doctor did that to him—cause he wanted his blood to test. . . ." In other stories children made such statements as: "They (the hospital personnel) put a tent on him and freeze him too." "The nurse turned off the lights and the door was closed, and he was lonesome and scared." "The little boy is very sick—he's mad too, because he wanted to go home." These stories illustrate children's perception of the treatment procedures and of the unsupporting environment. They may not appreciate the therapeutic intent of hospital personnel, and may be preoccupied with feelings of fear, anger, and loneliness.

The child's loneliness is accentuated because time stretches interminably for him between parental visits. As one six year old girl said, "She has to be in the hospital for long days and never gets to see her Mommy and Daddy. She's very lonesome." This same little girl also stated that the child "got sick" by "not coughing up the mucus." Young children seem to blame themselves for being sick and may feel guilty as a result. A child's sense of causality is different from an adult's. One little girl said: "That's a little boy just sitting there. Somebody killed a bird. He's thinking about the dead bird. The bird got killed because the bird was bad. The boy is a bad boy too—so something is going to happen to him." Children think that if they are punished, it is because they have been very bad. Nothing could seem more punishing to the young child than separation from his parents and the treatment he often receives in the hospital.

IMPLICATIONS FOR NURSING

The findings of this research suggest that in spite of efforts to protect children from knowledge of their prognoses, they are considerably preoccupied with death. They express feelings of loneliness and isolation; they sense a lack of control over the forces impinging on them. There is a dichotomy between the parents' perception of the child's awareness and the expression of awareness by the child. The evidence suggests that the child is quite aware of his dying. It seems possible that he becomes aware through the altered affect in his total environment and from parental anxiety communicated in non-verbal ways. It also suggests that adults may be blinded to the child's anxiety because of their own personal fears and concerns and their own sense of helplessness. Professional personnel attending seriously ill children may also be unaware of the child's awareness and anxiety. They may have their own personal defenses about death and sense their own professional helplessness to alter the course of events.

Research indicates the therapeutic effectiveness of communication about death between dying patients and their families. A sympathetic and professional person who has faced his own anxiety about death could well assist dying adults or children and their families. To help effectively, nurses must develop a sense of capability and security in working closely with dying adults and children. This sense of competency and empathy can be developed through educational experiences and by discussion and support following encounters with death on hospital wards. Students, sharing their experiences with supervisors and other professional personnel, can gain an understanding of death. If the nurse is able to give of herself in the face of death and if she is supported in her efforts, she will grow both personally and professionally. Also she will gain a sense of security, empathy, and competency to help meet future experiences with greater equanimity. Keeping dying children in contact with their peers on the ward is a good idea. Do this as long as the child has the energy to profit from the companionship and the comfort of these friendships. Placing the child on the ward can help decrease the child's feelings of isolation. Also these efforts to relieve loneliness in dying children may reduce some of the anger they feel. If their anger becomes internalized, it can increase the child's sense of hopelessness and depression. If the nurse can accept the child's expression of anger and hostility, it may prevent this anger from being internalized. On the other hand, being too permissive of a child's behavior may make the child feel even more helpless and angry.

Whether or not to tell a child he has a fatal illness appears to be a meaningless question. Rather, it seems clear that the questions and concerns which these children apparently have should be dealt with. Children must be prevented from feeling isolated and alienated from their parents and other meaningful adults. The "protection" of the child, the "aura" of secrecy, can make him lonely and even hostile. Protecting the child increases *his* burden. The nurse, who is willing to discuss the child's concern, has the opportunity to understand and clarify some of the child's misconceptions about death. Young children's concepts of death are not complete. Their sense of causality and reasoning are not mature. They may come to feel guilty for past misdeeds. These anxiety-producing and fearful convictions consume the child's energy that is necessary for maintaining important relationships.

Working with Parents

Assisting parents who are facing the loss of their child is another difficult challenge for the nurse. The threatened or actual loss of a child is one of the most shattering and tragic of experiences. How this challenge is met depends upon the circumstances of the child's illness and the resources of the parents, both personal and environmental. The parents' personalities and the closeness of the family circle become important factors in dealing with this severe emotional crisis.

The way the diagnosis is told to the parents is vitally important in determining their later attitudes to the hospital staff. If they are informed in an abrupt manner or in a way which eliminates any hope, the parents may become hostile. No matter how gently this news is imparted, however, some anger can be expected.

The initial hospitalization of the child can initiate severe separation anxiety in the parents. It relates to the threat of permanent separation. During this time, the mother needs to be as physically close to her child as possible. This will help her begin to cope with her anxieties of separation and with the guilt she may feel for failing to recognize the early symptoms of the disease. She may also feel she failed to protect the child, that she did something wrong, or that she failed to appreciate the child to a greater extent before his illness. The mother may feel hostile toward nurses who assume maternal functions during hospitalization and who interrupt her need to give of herself to her child. Anticipatory grief is almost universal. It has the function of beginning the emotional separation which is necessary to bear the pain. Although intellectually parents may no longer expect a cure to be found in time, they need to continue to hope. They are eager for new treatments and efforts designed to prolong life. As they see the disease progressing, most parents experience an increase in anticipatory grief, including a preoccupation with thoughts of the ill child, depressions, weeping, and somatic symptoms such as apathy and weakness.

This "grief work" is necessary for parents. It prepares them for the final separation. Most parents need to search for an acceptable meaning in this tragic occurrence. Also during this time many parents wish to become involved in the care of other ill children. The parental response to the ultimate death of the child is dependent on the available support and the length of time since the diagnosis was made.

The nurse can be of great assistance to the parents through this tragic period. She can encourage the mother's presence at her child's bedside. The mother and child should not be separated from each other more than is necessary when permanent separation is soon to take place. The nurse can also avoid assuming details of the child's care which the mother can perform. This can help parents to feel valuable in face of their helplessness. Parents also need to have as much daily information about their child's progress as possible. They need to know the activities on the ward while they are absent. These details can be of tremendous significance to parents anticipating the death of their child.

Many parents may feel a great need to talk about their child. They may feel heightened anxiety when they are alone. Taking time to listen to parents is an important aspect of nursing care. It tells the parents that the child is appreciated and understood and that the nurse is aware of how special he is to his parents. These discussions give the nurse clues to increase her understanding of her patient and his behavior. In this way, she can maximize her effectiveness as a nurse. In discussion with parents, as with the families of adult patients, the nurse may need to accept their hostility. She must not retaliate and must try to understand the source of the parents' anger, which may not be conscious.

At the time of actual bereavement all parents need consideration, empathy, and emotional support. This is also a time which is very difficult for the nurse who has come to feel for and with her patient. It is natural for the nurse to feel grief at this time. It is not "unprofessional" to allow families to see feelings of loss. Yet, in order to support them, nurses must not withdraw into their own grief. Much of the helping person's strength is in his ability to experience the pain of the tragic situation without being overcome by it.

The parents of a dying child will need privacy and the opportunity to express emotion in their own way. Parents need to grieve and to weep. If their grieving is delayed by their felt need to "maintain," this grief may reappear later. The nurse can be helpful by her permissiveness and acceptance.

The tragic circumstances this paper deals with are at once challenging and painful for nurses. Yet, despite the pain of involvement, nurses who can meet the challenge with understanding and empathy may be able to experience a sense of personal loss without a sense of depression.

BIBLIOGRAPHY

Abrams S (ed): Psychological Aspects of Stress. Springfield, IL, Charles C Thomas, 1970
Achte KA, Vauhkonen ML: Cancer and the psyche. Omega 2(1):46–56, February 1971
Alexander IE, Adlerstein MM: Studies in the psychology of death. Perspective in Personality Research. New York, Springer-Verlag, 1960
Aschaffenburg H: Pain in retrospect. Voices: The Art and Science of Psychotherapy 5(1):24–26, Spring/Summer 1969
Aspy DN: The end of hold back. Voices: The Art and Science of Psychotherapy 5(1):48–51, Spring/Summer 1969
Bachmann C: Ministering to the Grief Sufferer. Englewood Cliffs, NJ, Prentice Hall, 1964
Baker JM, Sorensen KC: A patient's concern with death. Am J Nurs 63:90–92, 1963
Baker A, Golde J: Conjugal bereavement: A strategic area of research in preventive psychiatry. Working Papers in Community Mental Health. Cambridge, MA, Harvard University Press
Barnouw V: Chippewa Social Atomism: 'Feast of the Dead.' Am Anthropol 63(5):1006–1013, 1961

Beach HD, Lucas RA (eds): Individual and group behavior in a coal mine disaster. In Disaster Study No 13. Washington, DC, National Academy of Sciences, National Research Council, 1960

Beaty NL: The Craft of Dying: A Study in the Tradition of the Ars Moriendi in England. Doctoral dissertation, Yale University, 1956

Becker E: The Meaning of Birth and Death. New York, Free Press, 1962

Becker H: The Sorrow of Bereavement. J Abnorm Soc Psychol 27:391–410, 1933

Bendann D: Death Customs: An Analytical Study of Burial Rites. New York, Alfred A Knopf, 1930

Bishop RK: The Theme of Death in French Literature from Villon's "Grand Testament" to the Middle of the 16th Century. Doctoral dissertation, Princeton University, 1943

Blackwook A: The Funeral. Philadelphia, Westminster Press, 1942

Blauner R: Death and Social Structure. In Neugarten BL: Middle Age and Aging. Chicago, University of Chicago Press, 1968

Bowers M et al: Counseling the Dying. New York, Thomas Nelson, 1964

Bowman L: The American Funeral: A Way of Death. New York, Paperback Library, 1964

Boyar JI: The Construction and Partial Validation of a Scale for the Measurement of the Fear of Death. Dissertation Abstracts 25:2041, 1964

15 · Why Nurses Choose to Work With Dying Patients

Delphine Eschbach

"The provision of terminal care is relatively simple if the time for dying is short. . . . terminal care becomes complicated and often difficult when the course of dying is prolonged, when pain is difficult to manage, when the staff becomes personally involved with the patient or family, when the use of life-prolonged activities continues indefinitely or indiscriminately" (Benoliel, 1971). In the past, communicable diseases, with a relatively short dying trajectory, were responsible for a high percentage of the deaths of children in this country. Today, communicable diseases are relatively rare as a cause of death. Instead, disease with long-term dying trajectories, such as cancer, present problems for those who care for the afflicted children.

Many of these children with long-term, life-threatening illnesses will require hospitalization, either on an episodic or on a long-term basis. During these periods of hospitalization, nurses are involved in providing care for these patients. As the number of persons dying over an extended period of time increases, so will the need for nurses to care for them. A number of studies show, however, that many nurses avoid dying patients. Some nurses do elect to work in settings where a relatively high percentage of their patients have a lingering dying trajectory (Glaser and Strauss, 1968).

In an attempt to better understand why some nurses elect to accept and retain employment in these settings, a study was done on 46 registered nurses employed in lingering dying trajectory settings in three hospitals (a 493-bed teaching hospital owned and managed by a large state university, a 363-bed general hospital owned and managed by a Catholic religious order, a 212-bed research hospital devoted to the care of patients with catastrophic illnesses and supported by charitable donations and grants in the Los Angeles–Orange County area of California) (Eschbach, 1980). Patients in these hospitals included some children, but were mainly adults. The subjects in the study were divided into two categories: (1) those who had worked in lingering dying trajectory settings for 5 years or longer and (2) those who had worked in those settings for less than 1 year.

DATA COLLECTION

The data collected consisted of responses to a two-part questionnaire and to a follow-up interview. The questionnaire, developed by the investigator, was a self-administered, paper and pencil instrument. Part 1 was concerned with demographic data. Part 2 was concerned with the reasons why the subject had accepted and/or retained employment. The subjects were asked to select from a list of 15 items the 5 most important reasons influencing their decision to accept employment and to rank those 5 reasons in order of importance. Those employed more than 5 years were asked to select from the list and rank the 5 reasons for remaining employed. In the interview nurses were asked the most positive and most negative things about their jobs and to describe the most satisfying and most dissatisfying experience they had had on their job. They were also asked what changes in their job would make it more satisfying to them.

In the mid 1950s Herzberg and his associates advanced the motivation–hygiene theory, which focused on the nature of the job and included both the nurse's individual needs and the work environment as factors determining motivation to work (Herzberg, 1959). In an attempt to answer the question, "what do people want from their job?" he interviewed engineers and accountants, asking them to describe a time they felt exceptionally good and a time they felt exceptionally bad about their jobs and asked for details about the events and their accompanying feelings and responses. From analysis of the content from these interviews Herzberg developed a theory that the primary determinants of job satisfaction (motivation) are found within the job itself (achievement, recognition, responsibility, etc.) and the primary determinants of job dissatisfaction (hygiene) are found in conditions surrounding the job (salary, working conditions, etc.). This theory was used as the basis for this study. Questionnaire and interview items were classified as either motivation or hygiene factors. For example, responses to the question "When you first accepted employment in a lingering dying trajectory setting, what were your reasons for taking the job?" classified as motivation factors included such responses as "saw this as a way to grow as a nurse," "believed I could contribute to the welfare of the patients," and "was a challenge to my nursing skills." Responses classified as hygiene factors included items such as "close to where I live," "best paying job available," and "only job available at the time."

RESULTS

The majority of respondents cited motivation factors as their reasons for accepting a job (total sample 70.6%; group employed more than 5 years, 58%; group employed less than 1 year, 81.7%). The specific reasons most frequently given were

1. Believed I could contribute to the welfare of the patients there
2. Believed the institution had a philosophy of patient care similar to my own

3. The job was a challenge to my nursing skills
4. Saw this as a way to grow as a nurse
5. Saw this as a way to grow as a person.

Motivation factors were also found to be more important than hygiene factors in inducing nurses to retain employment for 5 years or longer (69.3% motivation factors). Specific reasons most frequently cited were

1. Believe I contribute to the welfare of the patients here
2. Work is a challenge to my nursing skills
3. Like the kind of people who work in this type of setting (a hygiene factor)
4. Working with this type of patient helps me grow as a person.

Responses to the interview question about most satisfying job experience were even more heavily weighted toward motivation factors (96% of total sample). In relating satisfying experiences 61% of the total sample told of an event wherein they helped a patient and/or the patient's family. Specific responses included items such as "helped a patient face death," "able to talk to patient and help face illness," "helped patient stand up for her rights." A plurality of the responses to the interview question about most dissatisfying job experience comprised hygiene factors (48% of total sample). The dissatisfying experiences responses most frequently given dealt with being short of time and/or staff, leading to poor patient care.

A significant number of the responses (26% of the total sample, 12% of group employed less than 1 year, 42% of group employed more than 5 years) fell into neither the motivation nor the hygiene category. These "other" responses were of two general types: ethical questions about dying (why this particular patient had to die, the right to die, etc.) or "can't think of any."

DISCUSSION

Responses to the questions about satisfying and dissatisfying experiences supported Herzberg's theory that job satisfaction results from motivation factors and job dissatisfaction results from hygiene factors. If this is so, one might expect that the question, "What could be done to make this job more satisfying?" would elicit motivation factor responses. The findings of this study did not meet that expectation. For the total sample of nurses, 74% of the responses to this question were in the hygiene category with "more or adequate staff" and "more time to care for patients" being the two answers most frequently given.

Although it appears that this finding contradicts Herzberg's theory that job satisfaction is the result of motivation factors, it may not be so. Herzberg states, "When there are deleterious factors in the context of the job, they serve to bring about poor job attitudes. Improvement in these factors of hygiene will serve to remove the impediments to positive job attitudes" (Herzberg, 1959). The hygiene factors responses in this study may reflect this premise. Removal of impediments cited may allow the respondent to experience more frequently the satisfying experiences of helping patients and their families and the feeling of doing a good job.

According to the National Association of Nurse Recruiters, the national average annual turnover for registered nurses is 32%, while the American Nurses Association cites a turnover rate of 40% (Wolf, 1981). This means that 3 to 4 of every 10 nurses quit their jobs every year. Another study reported that in 1981 the average turnover rate for hospital nurses was 50% (Price and Mueller, 1981). One survey showed that in some metropolitan areas registered nurse turnover is as high as 200% (Hospitals, 1980). Kramer (1974) quotes statistics from one study showing that 28.9% of new B.S.N. graduates left nursing during a 2-year period because of job dissatisfaction. One need only look at statistics like these or talk to directors of nursing services in hospitals to realize that nursing turnover is a major problem. Although the Lyons (1974) and Gulack (1983) studies showed reasons other than job dissatisfaction (illness, retirement, transfer of spouse), other studies such as Gellerman (1968), McClosky (1974), Hallas (1980), Wandelt, Pierce, and Widdowson (1981), and Deets and Froebe (1984) show that nurses leave jobs because of job dissatisfaction. If hospitals wish to have their nurse employees remain employed, therefore, it is important that they work toward providing job satisfaction for these nurses. The findings of this study indicate the need for hospitals to provide opportunities for nurses to obtain internal rewards and self-actualization in their work. The emphasis placed by nurses participating in this study on contact or relationships with patients and the satisfaction they receive in feeling they have helped a patient and/or family, combined with their concern over lack of time and/or staff, clearly indicates a need for hospitals to arrange work situations that will meet these needs.

Hospitals are presently faced with increased pressure toward cost containment. It appears to many hospital administrators that the easiest method by which to effect savings is to assign heavier work loads to nurses and thus cut back on the number of nurses needed. On the surface this solution may appear reasonable. In practice it is not. Rather than providing the increased time and staff that would allow nurses to have more contact and relationships with patients, it does just the opposite. With the resulting decrease in job satisfaction nurses leave their jobs. Hospitals must then expend time and money to recruit new nurses. The money spent for advertising, for employing nurse recruiters, and for breaking in new employees might be more wisely expended in providing opportunities for job satisfaction for currently employed nurses so that they will remain in their jobs.

The expressed desire for contact and relationships with patients and for the feelings associated with helping patients and/or their families might best be met by changing patterns of nursing care. A move toward primary care nursing would allow nurses the opportunity to gain job satisfaction by giving direct bedside care. It is evident from this study that nurses want to nurse. They want the freedom to use their nursing judgment and skills to provide the highest level of patient care of which they are capable. Hospitals would do well to look at their policies and rules regarding nursing function and practice. Nurses responding to this study stated that many such rules and policies are outmoded, unnecessary, and, to quote one nurse, "downright ridiculous." Schools of nursing are producing graduates educated and eager to provide a high level of patient care. When these nurses find that the organization of the hospital does not allow them to practice effectively and precludes them from obtaining job satisfaction, many of them leave their jobs.

The expressed lack of confidence in their own nursing skills and the concern about feeling they are doing a good job on the part of newly employed nurses have implications for the hospitals employing them. It is important to provide opportunities for these newly employed nurses to improve and perfect their nursing skills by offering inservice classes, by assigning them to work with more experienced and skilled nurses, and by providing access to help and guidance from supervisors. At the same time opportunities to improve skills are being offered, it would appear important to provide support and encouragement for these newly employed nurses. Their concern for doing a good job would suggest that employers should give frequent, positive feedback on performance and attempt to provide work situations that will lead to successful performance on the part of the nurses.

The finding that so many nurses in this study considered it important that the hospital's philosophy of patient care match their own demonstrates a need for hospitals to pay more attention to this aspect. Most hospitals make statements that they do not discriminate, provide a high level of care to everyone, and are patient centered. It appears that many of them have not developed a philosophy of care much beyond such generalities or if they do have something more in-depth it remains only on paper and is not used in regulating daily patient care. It would appear that nurses want their employing hospitals to have a well-developed philosophy that is actually reflected in their day-to-day policies. It also points out the need for a nurse considering employment in a given facility to review its philosophy and give careful thought to whether it is congruent with her/his own personal philosophy.

Although much has been written about the need to nurse the whole patient and great emphasis is placed on this in most schools of nursing, it appears that the actual practice of employers (hospitals) has not changed greatly in this respect. To a great extent, the emphasis is still on the nurse's "doing up" a certain number of patients. The nurse who produces in the shortest amount of time the greatest number of bathed, bandaged, and medicated patients in beds with square corners is praised and rewarded as being a "good nurse." Many nurses stated that they believe good patient care encompasses the whole patient, including the psychological, social, and spiritual as well as the physical or physiological aspects. They wanted to work in hospitals that not only professed such a philosophy on paper, but also demonstrated it in practice by supporting and commending nurses who spend time talking to patients, interacting with families, and other activities beyond the mere provision of basic physical care.

The findings of this study indicate support of hospices. The hospice concept has a strong, well-developed philosophy of care that focuses on provision of psychological and spiritual support to dying patients and their families. Nurses who have a similar philosophy and who want the opportunity of close contact and relationships with patients and their families may well find more job satisfaction in a hospice than in an acute care setting. Hospitals might look at the possibility of either setting up hospices as part of their facility or of sending lingering dying trajectory patients to a hospice rather than providing care for them in the hospital. Providing care for dying patients and "cure" for acute patients in the same setting does not appear to be the most effective system.

The high percentage of responses relevant to philosophical/ethical aspects of death and dying indicates a need for increased education and discussion in this area. Course work in their basic nursing program related to the psychosocial aspects of dying were reported by a majority (63%) of the respondents in this study. A large number of these respondents amplified their responses with statements such as, "we had some, but not nearly enough." It appears that there is a real need for more emphasis on death and dying in schools of nursing and on the realities of nursing practice. The production by schools of nursing of graduates who have theoretical knowledge of death and dying and who had the opportunity to explore, and perhaps to resolve, some of their own concerns and feelings, should lead to an increase in the number of nurses capable of and willing to work in lingering dying trajectory settings.

Regardless of the amount of preparation in this subject given to students in schools of nursing, the nurses practicing in lingering dying trajectory settings demonstrate their need for education on an ongoing basis. Hospitals should make such education available to their nurses and encourage attendance through time released from work, payment of tuition, or similar methods.

Nurses working in lingering dying trajectory settings also mentioned the need for personal support. They described the stress involved in caring for dying patients and their need for communication and support from their fellow nurses and supervisors. Nurses from one facility described the availability of support services such as group sessions or regular meetings between psychiatrists or psychologists and nurses to discuss feelings and concerns as being of great help to them. Provision of such support by hospitals should lead to increased job satisfaction on the part of their nurses.

In the provision of optimal nursing care to long-term dying trajectory patients, whether they be adults or children, four groups need to be considered—the dying person, their families, the nurses providing care, and the hospitals employing those nurses. Employers (hospitals), employees (nurses), and the patient and/or family all share responsibility for maintaining and improving good nursing care. Nurses need to give serious thought to and assertively publicize their needs; employers need to listen and to make changes that will enable those needs to be met. Patients/families can influence this process by giving feedback to both nurses and employers—supporting the positive nursing actions and pressing for elimination of negative factors. Nurses who achieve a high level of job satisfaction are more likely to provide good nursing care; nurses who are allowed to give good nursing care are more likely to achieve a high level of job satisfaction. In such situations everyone involved reaps the benefits.

REFERENCES

Benoliel JQ: Nurses and the human experience of dying. In Fiefel R (ed): New Meanings of Death. New York, McGraw-Hill, 1971

Deets C, Froebe D: Incentives for nurse employment. Nurs Res, pp 242–246, July/August 1984

Eschbach D: An investigation of the reasons why nurses accept and continue employment in positions in lingering dying trajectory settings. Doctoral dissertation, University of California, San Francisco, 1980

Gellerman S: Management by Motivation. New York, American Management Association, 1968

Glaser B, Strauss A: Time for Dying. Chicago, Aldine, 1968

Gulack R: Why nurses leave nursing. RN, pp 32–37, December 1983

Hallas G: Why nurses are leaving nursing. RN, pp 17–21, July 1980

Herzberg F, Mausner B, Snyderman B: The Motivation to Work. New York, John Wiley & Sons, 1959

Hospitals: Nursing Shortage Linked to Hospital Environment. Hospitals, pp 18–19, January 1, 1980

Kramer M: Reality Shock. St Louis, CV Mosby, 1974

Lyons R: Reducing nursing turnover. Hospitals 44, 74–78, May/June 1974

McClosky J: Influence of rewards and incentives on staff nurse turnover rate. Nurs Res 22:239–247, May/June 1974

Price JL, Mueller CW: Professional Turnover: The Case of Nurses. New York, Spectrum, 1981

Wandelt M, Pierce P, Widdowson R: Why nurses leave nursing and what can be done about it. Am J Nurs, pp 72–77, January 1981

Wolf G: Nursing turnover: Some causes and solutions. Nurs Outlook, pp 233–236, April 1981

16 · Outcomes of Care

Eugenia H. Waechter

The issue of outcomes of care is one that is basic to professionals working with families under any circumstance, but particularly when a child's life is threatened. Until we are certain of the goals to be reached, we are unsure in planning a course of action and indecisive about the relevancy of professional interventions or the possible outcomes to be expected.

In consideration of this larger issue, many underlying questions come to mind:

1. Who determines the goals of care to be achieved?
2. Do professionals of different disciplines have varied goals for care?
3. If so, can these varied goals be integrated into a combined effort that is complementary rather than fragmented?

Another question to be considered involves time dimensions. Do not our goals change in tune with the trajectory the child and the family traverse from diagnosis to possible death? How can we best remain flexible to alterations in the family's conditions and needs?

A further consideration is that of the objects of our concern. Our goals for care cannot be unilaterally directed, or the general outcomes of care may be abortive. Professional concern must encompass a number of facets: concern for the child, concern for the parents, concern for the siblings, and concern, often overlooked, for the professional personnel themselves.

A large issue, now under investigation in several large medical centers, is that of prediction. With shortages of highly trained personnel, are there ways of predicting families who are "at risk" or vulnerable and thus in greater need of intensive professional concern to prevent major disruptions in living? If such prediction is possible, valuable professional expertise may be conserved and better utilized.

Speech given at St. Louis University, St. Louis, Missouri, May 14, 1976.

A last question that must be asked is that of determination of outcome. How can we best measure what professional interventions have achieved. Are there universal yardsticks, or must we individualize both goals and measurements of progress toward those goals?

DESIRABLE OUTCOMES

Determination of the goals to be achieved must certainly be a function of the medical team, arrived at in concert and in a cooperative rather than competitive spirit. Cooperative team function is essential in any worthy professional endeavor, but never more so than with life-threatening illness. Each member of that team, physicians, nurses, social workers, pharmacists, occupational and physical therapists, and others must see themselves as professional colleagues, and each must contribute their professional knowledge and expertise to determine the needs of the entire family and thus to plan goals to be achieved. Without such joint planning from the very outset, individual professional goals may be in conflict and may cancel out possibilities and endanger the overriding desirable outcome.

Certainly, professionals from different disciplines may vary in the manner in which they view the crisis within the family and the relative importance of the various components of the overall problem and, therefore, the desirability of certain outcomes. Such variations stem from different guidelines derived from educational backgrounds and subsequent experiences. Some professionals may be content with preventing gross damage to the child and his family and maintaining equilibrium. Others may be more deeply concerned with controlling disease and maintaining the life of the child. Some may consider that the provision of the best technical care possible is sufficient, whereas others are concerned with supporting the family through a most stressful period—assisting them to live with day-to-day problems in order that the family may emerge from the experience with a sense of self-esteem in having done their best under difficulty.

My personal hope is that the medical team will find all of these goals important and none of them sufficient in itself. I feel that the most positive outcomes to be envisioned for each individual involved in this long-term stress are to cope successfully, to master and to integrate experience, and thereby to grow in emotional, social, and intellectual capacity. The single overriding goal of professional intervention, then, which subsumes individual aims, would be to support and extend the growth potentials of the child, the child's family, and the professional staff.

The Children

The medical team must make a commitment to children while they are here. They must always be considered as living children, though they may be dying. The danger inherent in seeing children as dying is that of freedom for abandonment before their actual death. Their continued development is tremendously important until their last breath, and they must be supported—allowed and encouraged to experience the full range of human emotion, actively engaged in the business of life and kept in contact with other significant people in their world.

It may seem to some that to support the goals of continued growth and life in the midst of disease and death is a paradox. It *is* a fascinating paradox; yet no professional can function adequately and successfully with children or their families if those children are viewed continuously within the context of death. It is an extremely difficult challenge to remain constantly available to the child and yet to let go when the timing is appropriate.

All children deserve and need the support of the professional team to live in dignity; to master difficult situations at the level of which they are capable; to find whatever pleasure is possible in their circumstances; to draw closer to others with the freedom to discuss both life and death; to reach their potentials for living, loving, and sharing of their experiences; and to die with dignity.

The Parents

Despite the overwhelming nature of the death and dying experience, most parents also have the potential to grow; to become more capable of giving, supporting, and sharing; and to develop greater capacities for meeting future crises through this experience. Although we cannot, nor should we, protect or prevent parents from suffering, we can assure them that we will walk with them along the way to lend strength as they find it helpful and needful and to prevent the sense of depersonalization that often accompanies encounters with our system of health care.

Though parents may not be able to "accept" the death of their child, many are able to find some meaning in the experience, which is acceptable to themselves; to integrate this loss within and between themselves; to reformulate family life; and to face life and the future courageously once again.

Siblings

The possible eventual negative outcome of care for young siblings of the ill child may have far-reaching effects unless their needs are also considered in arriving at the goals for care. The death of a sibling often confronts children with an intense emotional crisis for which they are often unprepared and frequently insufficiently supported. Many children have been sheltered from the reality and inevitability of death, and when suddenly confronted with the possible permanent loss of someone central in their lives, they may experience a threat to their very survival.

In evaluating the possible outcome that death of a sibling has upon the individual child's attempts to cope with such a catastrophic experience, a number of factors must be considered: 1. The child's intellectual and emotional developmental level, including the adequacy of ego development at the time of the loss; 2. The quality of the prior relationship with the deceased sibling and with the remaining siblings; 3. The quality and quantity of the environmental supports available; 4. All other concurrent additional stressors, such as reality-based deprivations in the home surroundings.

Since young children have not yet developed an extensive system of defenses to deal with the shock entailed in loss of a sibling, their immediate response may be a pervasive denial—through leaving the scene in a psychological sense. If they do not have support during the illness of their brother or sister and immediately after death, they may be unsuccessful in absorbing or integrating the loss.

Young children often have great difficulty comprehending the nature of death due to immaturity of intellectual functioning. During the toddler period, children's thinking assumes a magical quality, in that they believe that their wishes or feelings influence outside events and that they have the power to make their desires "come true." At this time they love completely, hate intensely, and are unable to reconcile the two emotions. When they feel rivalrous with their sibling for their parents' love, they may wish the sibling to "go away." When this actually occurs, toddlers may well feel that their wishes were responsible.

During the preschool period, siblings may have misapprehensions and uncertainties about whether the dead child will return as well as concerns about the reason for the separation. Their previous experience has taught them that "lost objects" may eventually return, and they are unable to conceive the meaning of the word "forever." In their immature reasoning, the departed loved one exists "somewhere" and retains the power to make decisions. Since the loved sibling does not return with the passage of time, the children may reason that the loved one does not wish to be with them any longer or that the sibling does not care for them. The accompanying feelings of worthlessness may complicate children's loss and sense of abandonment.

From a child's point of view, all events are purposive, resulting from the direct wishes of human beings or by direct divine intervention. Therefore, children are concerned mainly with "who" is to blame for the separation, rather than with "what" is to blame. In addition to examining their own responsibility, children may also assign blame to the surviving parents or become angry with God for personal involvement in their loss.

Young children's sense of culpability in the death of a sibling often results in a sense of hopelessness, anxiety, and pervasive feelings of personal "badness" and unlovableness. In the minds of children, purposive abandonment is proof that they are unworthy of love and care, and they may desire or actively seek punishment in an attempt at atonement. Former initiative may be replaced by apathy and former security with a deep-seated distrust of the world and its unpredictability. Children may fear that they or other members of their family may also die, and they may, thereafter, experience other necessary and temporary separations with deep distrust and anxiety. Such early losses may leave deep scars on the growing personality, to the extent that whenever a loss occurs in later life, there may be a regression to early modes of thinking and emotion. Memories of this early childhood separation, with the accompanying bewilderment, confusion, and anxiety, as well as aggressive impulses, may again rise to consciousness.

When the siblings are older than the child who has been ill and family unity is extensively disrupted by the loss of the child, the remaining siblings may redefine their identity or attempt to assume a new role within the family. This role may be difficult or impossible for the child to fulfill, thus causing further degeneration of self-esteem.

One of the major goals of care, often frequently overlooked yet directly related to preventive mental health, is the support of the growth potentials of other children within the family. This can be accomplished through (1) direct intervention with siblings whenever indicated, such as inviting them to join their parents as an integral part of the medical team or to take part in private discussions related to their particular questions, fears, and concerns and (2) indirect intervention through supporting the parents in all ways previously discussed. With a lessening of personal anxiety, parents will have more energy to expend on their other children, and with professional assistance, parents are more able to deal openly with their needs and concerns.

RETAINING FLEXIBILITY

Almost any long-term illness comprises several stages from the time of diagnosis to death. The period of diagnosis is usually one of acute crisis, but this phase may be followed by periods of remission and relapse before death actually occurs. Each phase involves different and perhaps opposing orientations for both child and family with respect to time dimensions, on-going family activities and setting of priorities for the needs of individual family members and the needs of the family as a unit.

In setting goals for care, the medical team must anticipate such changes and constantly keep in mind the forces that operate upon and within the family, retaining sufficient objectivity to remain alert when evaluating priorities for care and family needs during each successive phase. Early planning for positive outcomes must also incorporate subsidiary goals for immediate, intermediate, and long-term goals. For example, priority goals during hospitalization may be assisting parents to deal with the immediate pain, retaining close physical proximity to the child when he is in greatest need of support, and finding pleasure in small transactions. Intermediate goals may involve supporting parents to encourage the child's relinquishment of the nurtured role and gathering strength to meet future crises. Long-term goals may be assisting the child to die with the least possible anxiety and dread while helping parents to maintain their relationship to the child until the time of death.

Such goal setting involves consistent review and evaluation of short-term outcomes and possible redefinition of direction for professional intervention in the light of additional knowledge about the family members and their individual and collective needs. It also requires the ability to pull back for a time from the intensity of the experience to allow for a clearer perspective of the total situation.

MEASUREMENT OF OUTCOMES

Measuring outcomes of care or evaluating intervention has continued to be both necessary and problematic. It is necessary since future planning depends on responses to past care. It is a problem because evaluation is greatly dependent on the precise articulation of goals and the personal stance and biases of the evaluator. Progress in medical, social, and emotional areas must be evaluated, yet these areas are usually greatly interdependent.

Medical response to treatment can usually be measured fairly accurately; however, progress in social, intellectual, and emotional development of the ill child and of the family may need to be inferred from behavior. Although these aspects of response to intervention are more vague and subject to personal interpretation, they are certainly not less important.

Careful and precise observation, empathetic listening, pooling of information, and objectivity are required in order to draw conclusions about the further need for professional intervention at every stage of the child's illness. The measurement of eventual outcome of family reintegration after the child's death requires continued contact with the family over a period of time that may vary according to the family's internal and external resources.

PREDICTION

In talking with many parents during the past 10 years, I have asked them whom and what they have found most helpful in making this long-term stress bearable. They have given various answers, but among the people usually mentioned are the spouse, other immediate and extended family members, friends, individuals on the health care team (along with trust in the medical regimen), and religious figures. Some families find great comfort in their religious beliefs and the prayers of concerned friends and neighbors. Others find release meeting with parents of other children that have the same illness, but find it difficult to talk with former friends whom they feel are avoiding the family or are unable to understand what the family is experiencing.

No one source of help and comfort is consistently mentioned. However, a pattern has emerged from the interviews that helps to predict which families may be in need of greater support from the medical team when confronted with life-threatening illness:

1. The state of the marriage itself. If the marriage is stable at the time of diagnosis, each partner mentions the other as a prime supporter and communication is open and shared; the basis for withstanding crisis is strong and viable. If on the other hand, either parent fails to mention the other, negates the other's contribution to family management, or rescinds previous statements about the partner's support, the medical team must be alert to possibilities of additional strains on family life that may eventually result in family breakdown or disruption.
2. The accessibility and emotional closeness of extended family members and friends. When such environmental supports are numerous, available, and emphatic, they can provide both material and emotional assistance of great significance.

3. The number and severity of other stresses impinging on the family. When other health problems, financial strains, or family difficulties drain parental energy, the family will require professional care to relieve these additional stressors in order to better cope with the situation.
4. The ability of parents to acknowledge, to reach out to others, and to utilize available environmental supports. When such ability is lacking, each or both may feel isolated in their stress despite the deepest wishes of others to assist them. Such inability may be due to deep-seated personality factors, an unwillingness to allow others to see their distress, fears of rejection or of being observed as "falling apart at the seams."

The final outcome for each family member involves a fine balance between the amount of stress and the available internal and external support systems. When preliminary investigations indicate additional stresses and/or insufficient resources, the family must be considered vulnerable and given priority in professional planning and intervention.

SUPPORT FOR THE HEALTH CARE TEAM

Functioning as a member of the health care team that is concerned with families of children who have life-threatening illnesses is difficult, challenging, and consumes large amounts of energy. It also requires commitment to the team effort, to the family and child, and to the philosophy of care. Health care professionals commonly feel thwarted in resolving the on-going sense of dependency, uncertainty, and helplessness experienced by families of terminally ill children.

A constant danger for health care professionals is that they set unrealistically high goals for outcomes of care both for the families and for themselves. When unrealistic goals for families prove impossible to meet because of limitations in personal or environmental resources, the resulting sense of failure for both family and professionals may be damaging to self-esteem.

Members of the professional team must also recognize and accept their own humanity and limitations. "Being all things to all people" is an impossible goal to maintain for any length of time. Despite our wishes to give of ourselves to others in unlimited quantity, attempting to do so is unrealistic and may actually limit professional growth.

Recognition, knowledge, and acceptance of personal strengths and limitations enhances both the team interaction and the potential for personal and professional growth of each team member. Greater understanding of self and other enables team members to work through each experience together, rather than separately with a sense of loneliness and isolation. Mutual care-giving allows team members to grow in their capacities to give.

17 · How Families Cope: Assessing and Intervening

Eugenia H. Waechter

How parents cope with long-term and possibly life-threatening illness depends upon many factors: whether the defect or illness was present at birth or acquired, the demands placed upon parents, and the resources available within parents and in their environment. This paper will review all these factors. Let us consider first how parents respond to the birth of a child with a defect or long-term illness.

During pregnancy, every woman wishes for and fantasizes about having a perfect child and fears the birth of one who is in some way damaged. When the baby is born with a physical defect, the discrepancy between the fantasy and the reality precipitates a tremendous sense of loss—loss of a desired goal, of the expected perfect child, of important elements of self-esteem, and of satisfaction in the birth process. An overwhelming sense of failure is substituted for expected pride in the child, which may have been hoped and wished for for years. Profound grief is the normal response to such loss—grief characterized by preoccupation with each part of the loss and the special meaning it has to parents. The more serious the condition, the more powerful is the impact of the experience.

In a recent study, I interviewed many parents of children born with long-term handicaps or illness. All reported initial feelings of shock, grief, anger, shame, and disbelief—which varied in intensity and duration. These parents are grieving for their lost perfect child. Anger, a normal element of grief, may be directed outward at anyone in the environment (although rarely to the infant), or it may be directed at the self in deepening depression. When parents frequently ask, "Why did this have to happen?", they are searching themselves for former sins or some biological inadequacy. For the mother, her failure to produce a perfect child may be a threat to her sense of adequacy and individual worth. This is understandable, for

Speech given at the Children's Health Center, University of Minnesota, Minneapolis, Minnesota, March 29, 1978.

the child just born is still an extension of herself, and a defect in the child is, therefore, a defect in her.

INITIAL COPING

Feelings of shame and embarrassment generally accompany feelings of inadequacy. These feelings may be heightened by the reserve that parents encounter from their families and sometimes from professional people. Disbelief and withdrawal is the method commonly used to escape, at least temporarily, from an intolerable position.

Following the immediate shock and withdrawal, which may last from a few hours to several weeks, parents are beset with fears of many kinds as they gradually become aware of the enormity of the problem. They fear the social stigma of "differentness," the response of family and friends, their future responsibilities, and doubts about their ability to cope. Feelings of loss of self-esteem may prompt them to frantically seek a "scapegoat" in order to defend their own psychological functioning and handle their own feelings.

Other parents may continue to appear confused and bewildered, despite the efforts of professionals. Until they have come to some partial resolution about the loss of their perfect child, and about their own dilemma, they cannot see their real baby's needs or become attached to him.

FACTORS INVOLVED IN PARENTAL COPING
IN RELATION TO THE CHILD

A number of factors have been found that affect how parents cope with the birth of a child that has a life-threatening illness or congenital defect. Among these is the *appearance of the child*. All parents feel deeply about how their child looks. Our society sets rigid standards regarding appearance. Parents of facially disfigured children respond most profoundly. Clefts of the lip and palate are particularly difficult for parents. Most are reluctant to have their baby seen, and most are also eager for immediate repair. A gross facial deformity seems to violate the sense of body intactness. These parents feel that when wholeness is restored, problems will be minimized.

The feeding experience can be very frustrating for mothers. Breast feeding may be impossible, with implications of inadequacy in the maternal role. Bottle feeding can also be threatening. One mother reported, "The main thing I was afraid of was her feeding. She had to have a bigger hole in her nipple than usual, you know, and I was constantly afraid that she would choke . . . in fact, I had dreams about it. Mom stayed with me, and I'd yell out in my sleep that Lisa was choking again."

Other gross deviations such as absence of a limb or multiple malformations also evoke profound responses. However, this is not always true. Occasionally, what seemed to be a minor imperfection, such as a birthmark on a portion of the body that would not be exposed, evoked intense parental reaction. It seems clear that parents cannot take lightly any visible deviation from the perfect child they had expected so long.

Parents of children with chronic or life-threatening illness look into a future that is suddenly bleak. When the infant's condition at birth is so poor as to necessitate continued hospitalization, anticipatory grief is intensified and it is most difficult to deny the reality of the tragic situation. Frequently, all semblance of former family life is suspended while the outcome of the fight for the child's life is in doubt, and parents "live one day at a time." The obstacles to maternal–infant bonding are often almost insurmountable due to physical separation, the child's illness, and the distinct possibility of total and lasting separation. Many parents are unwilling to invest in a child whose potential for immediate survival is slim. Such reluctance is often reinforced by attending caretakers who feel that parents, if they become attached to the infant, would have greater emotional pain when the child dies.

On the other hand, when the child's condition at birth is sufficiently satisfactory to allow mother and infant to be discharged from the hospital, family life may resume a more normal tempo except for the special requirements of the infant. Future orientation may be reactivated and overt grief responses can be submerged in the realities of day-to-day living. Parents are usually concerned about maintaining a "living" relationship with their child and thus cannot allow themselves to look too far into the possible future. It may be easy to believe that perhaps the diagnosis was a mistake when the child looks and behaves so well. When the child must be rehospitalized, however, the reality is reconfirmed, parental grief is reactivated, and the situation with all its complexities must be confronted anew and reexamined in all of its facets.

TASKS NECESSARY TO SUCCESSFUL COPING

A number of "psychological tasks" must be accomplished by the parents of a child with a chronic or life-threatening illness, whether the illness was present at birth or acquired later. These tasks will also facilitate the self-acceptance that is so necessary in order for parents to deal realistically with their child.

Cognitive confrontation involves the difficult task of acknowledging that the child is ill or defective. It also involves searching for realistic information as to the cause and symptoms of the illness or condition. Conscious awareness and acceptance of negative feelings are a result of this experience. These negative feelings (disappointment, shame, frustration, anger) must be allowed free expression so that communication between parents can be encouraged and maintained. When this is suppressed, parents will be less able to resolve their grief or deal realistically with their feelings in the future.

Parental openness to others is the ability of the parents to reach outward to others for support and planning for the future ("I am not alone"). With this step, the parents begin to develop both a formal and informal support system.

DEVELOPMENTAL CONSEQUENCES OF CHRONIC ILLNESS

We are concerned about the manner in which parents originally cope with the illness because it will also have long-lasting effects on the development of the child. Unless parents are helped with their feelings of anger, guilt, self-accusation, and grief, the child will also suffer. Mattsson (1972) has indicated that many children with chronic illness fall into three main patterns:

1. The child is fearful, inactive, markedly dependent on his family, (especially his mother), and lacks outside activities. The child is passively dependent; the mother is overprotective.
2. The child is overly independent, often daring, and engages in prohibited and risk-taking activities. The child uses strong denial of realistic dangers; the mother is oversolicitous and guilt ridden.
3. Less commonly, the child is shy, lonely, and resentful—directing hostility toward normal people. The family usually emphasized his defect and tends to hide and isolate him. The child develops the self-image of a defective outsider.

The response most frequently seen is a vicious cycle of overprotection and over-permissiveness from the mother, leading to a dependent, demanding child. The child then elicits the resentment of his parents. This is usually suppressed, but can lead to periodic outbursts of anger. These outbursts lead to greater parental guilt.

Balancing demands against resources, many parents are able to accept their child's limitations with equanimity, are able to deal realistically with problems, and can impose restrictions and limitations on the child without feeling guilt. They are able to encourage independence and interactions with peers and support their child's development. At the same time, they are able to continue their own lives without great feelings of deprivation.

What differentiates these parents from those who cannot accomplish these goals? I believe it is a matter of balancing the demands placed upon the family with the resources available to them.

The demands placed upon families with chronically ill children are often very high. They vary, of course, with the type and severity of the illness, the amount of treatment that must be carried out in the home, the necessity and frequency of medical care visits, the age of the ill child, the costs of medical treatment and associated expenses, and the threat of death.

Families may become limited in mobility, because fathers may be afraid of changing jobs for fear of losing insurance benefits. Mobility may also be limited because the family must remain near medical care facilities. Vacations for the family may be limited because of the cost and because parents may be fearful of taking the child from the medical care they trust. Often equipment that must be transported requires electricity.

Often parents must cope with the affected child's rebellion against the daily therapy, medication, diet, and so on. Yet parents must continue to insist on all daily treatment measures because they know that these are necessary to keep the child relatively well.

Children with chronic illness also become angry and resentful about their disease and its effect on their daily life. Both the disease and its treatment profoundly affect their concept of self, body image, self-esteem, peer relationships, and emotional development. When they become old enough, they may question the cause of the illness and assign blame for their predicament. The mother of one youngster with cystic fibrosis told me, "He wants to know whose fault it is. He's very firm about it's either God's fault or it's mine and his dad's. Especially if he's feeling bad. He has his low days. Like if he wants to play with the boys and he's having a lot of trouble and he can't go out and he just plain doesn't feel good, he'll say, "How come I have CF and whose fault is this and how come the Heavenly Father gave me CF? If he didn't, then how come I have it?"

Family life often revolves around the necessity for at least one parent to spend many hours weekly in the hospital. When parents must travel some distance to the care setting, the problem is accentuated. There is often little time and energy left for family activities, and all members of the family must be involved in planning for and accomplishing routine tasks of daily living. Parents often feel dispirited, tired, and anxious. These problems are certainly magnified if there are other concurrent problems to face. These can be as many and varied as life itself. For example, difficulties in the marriage (whether or not caused by the present situation), problems of any nature with other immediate or extended family members, problems at work, etc.

COPING RESOURCES

What then do mothers and fathers use as resources when multiple stresses deplete their energies? In my recent study, most of the parents found strengths in family members—husbands, siblings, and relatives. Many relied on the medical and nursing staff, especially in moments of crisis. Some turned to friends, religion, or the church. A few mothers found relief in hobbies or in reading. All ultimately found strength in themselves, in their capacity to take it day by day, drawing on whatever resources they could find. By electing treatment, parents ally themselves with the medical world against the threat of death, and they learn to accept it as a part of their way of life.

Other vital resources that exist within the family include their ability to think, reflect, and perceive; their ability to communicate; their ideals and values; their capacity to love; and their capacity to work.

Many parents have rich resources within themselves to call upon in time of trouble. If they have had childhood experiences that allowed them to grow into an emotionally healthy maturity, they have much more ego strength to face problems and stress. This may be related to age, but is not entirely so.

All of their life experiences, and the support they had in mastering previous stress will come into play as they face the present and the future. If they have met previous developmental problems successfully—mastered previous stress—they will have more strength and optimism. If they have had previous experiences they were unable to cope with, current problems may become too much for them to handle.

The strength of the marriage itself is a vital factor. The number of years married plays a part, though this is partially a factor of the developmental and emotional maturity of the parents. But if the ties between the parents are strong, and communication between them is good, they can draw much strength from each other in adversity. If this is not true, the marriage itself may founder on the shoals of this chronic stress.

The closeness and presence of relatives also makes a difference. This may be emotional support for the parents, or in support services that give the parents some relief. At times relatives can take over some of the household responsibilities, stay with the other children while the parents have to take the ill child to medical care, etc. Any of these services can make a tremendous difference in the coping capacities of parents.

Educational level seems to play a part in parental coping capacities. Perhaps because educated parents are more sophisticated managers of medical problems, because educational level and emotional maturity are somewhat correlated, or because educational level is also equated with higher income levels.

Many parents get much comfort from religious beliefs, whether or not they are active in any particular church. Despite their frequent anger toward God, they also derive some comfort from the prayers of others, the involvement of the religious community in their problems, and the fact that belief in God provides them with a *meaning* for what is happening.

The amount of community understanding is certainly important. Unfortunately, this often varies with the type of illness, disability, or disease. Society is more understanding and tolerant of some conditions than they are of others. The words *cancer* or *leukemia* still incite fright in many people. One mother told me,

Parents should also be told that they might just get some pretty funny reactions from other people that they have to tell. And that sometimes shakes you up more. It's kind of shocking to have somebody react that way. It's a word that people don't even mention to a large degree and some people are unable to give support except those who have faced death to some extent themselves. For someone who has never faced it . . . my neighbor, I think, has managed to convince herself that Angela has a form of anemia and that she's going to get all better. For a while, she avoided me like the plague. You say, "leukemia" and people run.

Certainly the experiences the parents have previously had with the medical world and their experiences with chronic illness are most important. If they have had experiences that have provoked very negative feelings in themselves, they will have much greater difficulty dealing with their feelings and dealing with their child.

A most important resource, of course, and one that is most significant to us, is the amount of professional support received and the quality of that support. In a recent study, Mattsson (1972) found that over 45% of families with chronically ill children were not receiving active, continuous medical care, visiting doctors only during acute episodes. Certainly only through continuous care can preventive medicine be practiced and families receive support and guidance.

NURSING INTERVENTION

In making the assessment, the nurse must consider all of these factors. In addition, the nurse must consider a host of interactional patterns within the family. The nurse must take into consideration the division of responsibilities within the home, the values of the family, the patterns of growth, and independence in the family.

Much of this can be done by observation and by listening. Parents can be our teachers and our students, both inside the hospital and in their home and community. Observation of the parent's interaction and observation of the parent–child interaction will often tell us the roles each person plays in the family. How do the parents discipline their child? How do they show affection? Talking to the parents (and to the child), observing, and listening are the tools for making an assessment about the family as to vulnerability to stress or their potential for making a healthy adjustment.

Planning for care must, in all instances, remain a joint venture between the family and the health care team, taking into consideration the needs of the entire family. In addition to all the points mentioned, nurses have many opportunities to be of help. They can foster family involvement in the child's care and encourage healthy parent–child interaction. They can help parents express their feelings in order to live with the burden of their child's chronic illness. Parents need to know that there are no perfect parents and that everyone makes mistakes. They need to learn that on occasion many parents may forget a treatment, get angry, or feel resentful. Above all, they need help to realize that their own lives must continue.

REFERENCE

Mattsson A: Long term physical illness in childhood: A challenge to psychosocial adaptation. Pediatrics 50:801–811, 1972

18 · Working With Parents of Children With Life-Threatening Illness

Eugenia H. Waechter

I have often felt, as parents do, that when a child is dying the world should stop—at least for a little while. I have also felt angry with the outside world when it carries on with business as usual. Many parents have shared their experiences and feelings with me over the past 10 years and now I'd like to share with you what I have learned about their hopes and sorrows, their fears and concerns.

The importance of understanding and assisting parents and families in such a circumstance can hardly be overestimated. We are not only interested in the family as a unit and the welfare of the individuals within that family as a worthy goal for professional concern in itself, but also interested because of the immaturity of the ill child—he is very vulnerable and his family unit is his primary support. Only by assisting the family can we give comprehensive and supportive care to the child who has a life-threatening illness.

However, assisting parents who are faced with the possible loss of their child is also a difficult challenge for the nurse because the threatened or actual loss of a child is one of the most shattering and tragic of experiences. It is only through meeting such a challenge, nonetheless, that nurses can learn that assisting and supporting parents and families through such a period of crisis can lead to both professional and personal growth rather than to a sense of depression or failure.

Paper presented May 14, 1976 at a conference entitled "Children and Death: A Developmental Approach," St. Louis University.

246 ·

PARENTAL RESPONSES TO LIFE-THREATENING ILLNESS

At the time that their child is diagnosed as having a long-term illness with a poor or doubtful prognosis, parents are plunged into anticipatory grief. Anticipatory grief precedes actual loss and usually encompass all of the stages described by well-known theorists, including denial, anger, bargaining, depression, and acceptance. These states of feeling do not usually follow in order and discrete stages, however, but all elements may exist together in one person at any one time, or states may depend on changing realities, including the medical condition of the child. The danger inherent in delineating discrete stages lies in the possibility of remaining content with labeling rather than dealing with the real emotions and feelings that the labels describe.

Anticipatory grief encompasses the entire family while the dying child remains as an integral part of that family. This presents unique problems in that parents must balance the constant threat of loss of their child while maintaining a relationship with that child. This process may require that, to a certain extent, parents shut out their grief from consciousness at times in order to allow the relationship to continue, while also maintaining the capacity to mobilize their grief when circumstances warrant. When parents become completely immersed and preoccupied in their own grief, their ability to maintain a supportive relationship with their child may be limited since their energies are consumed in dealing with their own feelings. As a result, they may attempt to "protect" their child from knowledge of the diagnosis or prognosis, since recognition of their child's needs, fears, and concerns may pose an additional threat to their coping capacities.

One difference between anticipatory grief and conventional grief often mentioned is that anticipatory grief accelerates over time as the child comes closer to death, whereas conventional grief decelerates with the passage of time. In my experience, this is not always true. If the period from diagnosis to death is a lengthy one, grief may accelerate and then wane as the grief work accomplishes its purpose of loosening the bonds to the child prior to death. In rare instances, the bonds may be unduly loosened, resulting in premature detachment from the child before the child actually dies. This may add to the loneliness and sense of isolation that the child is experiencing and constitutes a circumstance for professional concern.

Conventional grief and anticipatory grief also have similarities, particularly in the coping strategies or defenses used. Feelings may be denied, diverted, projected, repressed, or displaced. Each of these mechanisms must be understood by the professional working with parents who are attempting desperately to find some meaning acceptable to themselves for their experiences and the threatened loss of their child.

Diagnosis

The diagnosis of life-threatening illness in their child is a tremendous shock, and years later parents remember all of the circumstances surrounding the imparting of this news as though it were indelibly imprinted on their minds. Almost all parents report feeling shocked and stunned, and they respond to the news as to a personal and physical blow. Some parents state that the diagnosis was a "blow in the face"; others feel as though they were "hit on the head," even though they may have suspected the diagnosis previously from the child's symptoms, the diagnostic tests ordered, or because of the behavior of the professional staff.

Many parents feel "numb" after hearing the words cancer or leukemia and they have difficulty concentrating on any further explanations at that time. Immediately others want much more information relating to their child's chances for life or to projections about the length of time they might still have with their child.

All parents are under great stress, and most behave in a disbelieving manner as though they are unable to assimilate the news. This is a period of crisis and great anxiety. Perceptions may be distorted, and parents are extremely vulnerable and sensitive to the behavioral nuances (facial expression, etc.) of the people around them.

The manner in which the diagnosis is imparted is of vital importance to parents and may determine their later attitudes toward hospital personnel. If they are informed in an abrupt manner, or in a way that eliminates all hope, parents are plunged into depression and anger that later may be reactivated on any pretext, either realistic or distorted.

Parents wish to be told the diagnosis in privacy, with dignity and human compassion. They understandably respond strongly if the news is imparted in a hospital corridor, laboratory reports read to them over the phone, or if the physician has not time to spend with them after giving them the news. Unfortunately for parents, in my experience, the diagnosis is often imparted in this manner. Informing parents of life-threatening illness in their child is most difficult, and professional personnel may feel the need to escape. Unfortunately, when they act in response to their own needs, parents are left to cope alone during this period of crisis.

In addition to privacy, dignity, and empathy, parents also ask for honesty at the time of diagnosis. Such honesty sets the stage for subsequent transactions between the family and the professional staff. However, the degree of openness and the amount of information given initially must vary with the capacities of the individuals concerned to deal with such information. The amount of information given should match parental capacities for absorbing such information. Individual differences in parental needs may pose a dilemma for the medical team, demanding flexibility in approach and sensitivity to the cues that the parents give.

At this time parents also need to be assured of continuous support from the medical team in the future; the need to know that they not only will not be alone in the struggles ahead but they also will be integral team members who "are doing this together." During this initial visit, parents may, in fact, already have chosen the member of the team to whom they can relate most closely.

In the midst of the immediate crisis surrounding the diagnosis, parents are also faced with a great many tasks and decisions. For instance, in the treatment of leukemia today, parents may be asked to assist in making decisions about treatment programs to be followed in the months ahead. In addition, parents must decide how to maintain or modify their usual parental functioning as they adjust the family to the new reality. There are also innumerable decisions that must be made regarding the child's understanding and anxiety about his illness and the necessary medical procedures for diagnosis and treatment.

Most parents are eager to hospitalize their child immediately in a frantic effort to reverse the diagnosis or to initiate treatment that may save the child. During this time, both mother and child experience acute separation anxiety which is related to the threat of permanent separation. The mother may behave as though her child is going to die immediately, and she may have a tremendous need to stay with her child. At this time the health care professional must assist parents in every way possible to remain close to their child so that they relieve some of their acute anxiety and at the same time maintain the child's "life line."

Initially, most parents need to deny the implications of a threatening diagnosis, either by screening it from their awareness or by making extreme efforts to reverse it. This denial usually does not include the fact of the child's illness and many parents feel they need additional consultations and diagnostic procedures from other physicians of their acquaintance. When the diagnosis is verified both hostility and continued denial, along with a lack of affect, are intensified.

Feelings of Guilt

After treatment is instituted and the reality of life-threatening illness is acknowledged, most parents feel guilt and express it through such questions as, "Why me?", "What could have caused it?", or "Why did this have to happen?" They often blame themselves for not having recognized early symptoms of the disease, for not appreciating the child more before his illness, for failing in some way to protect the child, or for some previous wrongdoing or omission on their part. Some may express the feeling that they are being punished by divine providence for former sins and they may become angry at God, angry at themselves, and even angry at their child because of the threat of the child leaving them. This can be illustrated by the following comment made by the separated mother of a 5-year-old leukemic boy during a tape-recorded interview:

I'm so upset about everything. You know, I think John's the only thing I've got. My parents aren't going to live forever. I doubt if I'll ever be able to get pregnant again because they had to operate on me to get pregnant and then the ovarian cyst grew back on me—and I don't get my periods anymore and I doubt if I'll ever have another child. I don't have a husband or anything. I think of grandkids later, things that you think of, you know, that you want. I'm just so upset and I really get angry. I get angry at the doctors, I've been angry with John, I get angry at myself. I wonder why he's going to have to die. I get angry with God. I get really mad at God. I say why did he have to pick John? Why didn't he pick some kid that the parent didn't give a damn about their child. John and I are really close. When I said I get angry with John, what I mean by that is that he's going to leave me, he's going to die some time and leave me and I don't want him to. Do you understand what I mean? I know I shouldn't get angry with the doctors, it's not their fault. I don't really get angry with them. I just get terribly upset. I just get upset with everyone, you know? I don't know who to blame it on, I guess that's it. I keep blaming it on myself. I think, what have I done? What have I done to get this? I believe your hell is right here on earth. I don't mean to get religious because I'm not really religious, but, what I mean is, I believe your hell is right here on earth, and I feel like I'm going through hell right now, you know. What have I done?

This comment illustrates the intense agony many parents experience when the diagnosis can no longer be denied. In this particular instance, anxiety was greater for lack of internal and external environmental supports.

Needs to Communicate

At this time most parents feel an intense need to talk to an empathetic listener about what is occurring. Talking about their feelings helps parents to come to terms with such feelings, and talking about their child helps parents to begin the anticipatory grief necessary for the final separation. One mother of a 5-year-old girl with leukemia commented: "I think we could have used anybody to talk to right then. Yeah. You feel like you've been hit over the head and just walk around sort of stunned for a month—a month and a half at least. It's listening to thoughts out loud . . . I think particularly that most people probably could use someone to talk to."

Needs for Information

After the period of diagnosis, most parents also feel the need to know as much as possible about the illness. This is particularly true for fathers. Parents feel comfortable with professional personnel who answer their questions fully, completely, and truthfully to give them a sense of regaining some measure of control over a situation in which they feel very helpless. It also helps parents to cope when "they know what to expect." Truthful answers given in an empathetic manner also strengthens trust in those to whom they must entrust their child's life. In this respect, the same mother commented: "Mostly we needed more information just on this particular thing. One of the residents, Dr. Frank, who was here at the time, was very willing to come and listen to us, which was a great help. He talked to us and could answer our questions about it as we thought of them. And that was quite a bit of help. For us it was more helpful to talk to someone who could give us information about the disease."

Nurses also have a great responsibility in that parents need to have as much daily information about their child's progress as is possible for them to understand and assimilate. Although reports of physical progress are in the realm of the physician, nurses can help to keep parents in touch with their physician. Nurses can also discuss with parents the details of the child's day and the activities on the ward while they are absent. Such details can be of tremendous significance to parents of children whose lives are threatened.

Most parents feel a great need to talk about their child during the first hospitalization and feel heightened anxiety when alone. Taking time to listen to parents is an important aspect of nursing care. It further conveys to parents that their child is appreciated and understood as an individual—that the nurses who are involved in important and intimate physical and emotional care of their child are aware of the child's uniqueness as a valued individual of great importance to the parents. Such discussions can also provide clues to enhance the nurses' understanding of their patient and of his behavior, which contributes to the effectiveness of nursing intervention.

In such discussions with parents, nurses must understand and accept hostility without retaliating when it is directed toward themselves, the hospital, or other medical personnel. In most instances, the anger is not directed toward the nurse personally, but results from totally overwhelming circumstances, displacement of anger, or projections of guilt that the parents may not be conscious of. It is often easier to blame someone else for such a tragedy. In other circumstances the parents' anger may be justified; this can give nurses valuable clues about how to assist the parents individually and in their relationship with their child. Although it may seem initially comforting to nurses, they must also avoid giving reassurances about the survival of the child or premature reassurances about parental feelings of guilt about the illness. Giving such reassurances without listening carefully to the parents only conveys to them the sense that they are not being understood, which may thereby intensify their feelings of hostility.

Congenital vs. Acquired Illness

When the illness is congenital (such as cystic fibrosis) that is diagnosed early in life, parents are often undergoing a dual grief process. At the same time that they are grieving over the diagnosis and the probable future loss of their child (and of future children), they are also grieving for the perfect child that they had anticipated for the past 9 months. If any of their previous children have the disease or they have already lost a child, this dual grief may be more intense.

In addition to grieving for the child, parents are also experiencing a tremendous blow to their self-esteem. They may feel embarrassment, shame, and ask themselves, "What is wrong with us as progenitors of children?" Guilt is also intensified since there is some reality in the question, "What have we done to our child?"

These parents are in great pain and regarding their personal feelings, they will be unable to see the needs of their child until they receive support and help. Such inability to relate to their child's needs must be understood and professional efforts directed to supporting the parents in order to promote a future constructive parent–child relationship.

Although many children with cystic fibrosis now live much longer than they did some years ago, explanations about their child's potential life span may not be reassuring to the parents. As one mother stated: "Well, I tried a couple of times to get a more definite answer as to how long he would live. I was really after a definite answer and I didn't get one. The doctor said, 'I have a young man in his twenties who is still doing well, whom I've treated over the years—the philosophy is he'll still have a long, full life and he'll be ale to accomplish a lot.' I still feel cheated. He's my son and he should be able to be an old man."

Although we as professionals have a need to comfort parents and to say, "Everything is going to be all right," such false reassurance may merely convey to parents that we do not understand their feelings and emotions.

At the time of diagnosis of illnesses such as cystic fibrosis, parents must also assume tremendous responsibility. The message is often conveyed that the length of time the child has to live depends on the parents care. There is truth in this, inasmuch as most of the on-going treatment for cystic fibrosis is carried out in the home. Nevertheless, such a message of responsibility must be tempered with other realities in order to prevent parental feelings of failure and guilt. Unless this is done, whenever the child must be hospitalized parents may rightly feel, "We've done everything we can and yet are unable to adequately protect our child."

Periods of Remission

During periods when the child is physically well, the threat of imminent death is suspended. During this time the focus of the family returns to life maintenance, and a future orientation can be remobilized. Family life may readjust to a more normal tempo and previous parental activities are resumed. Overt grief responses are usually submerged in the realities of day-to-day living.

During this time, parents are concerned about maintaining a "living" relationship with their child and thus cannot allow themselves to look too far into a possible future. Parents, however, need to be assured that professional personnel are continuing their concern and involvement by maintaining contact between hospitalizations, responding to crises, or merely sitting down to talk with them at clinic when there is nothing pressing. Such conversations are usually focused on day-to-day problems, not on the child's death because parents are now focused on life with their child.

Relapse

When the child must again be hospitalized, anticipatory grief is remobilized and intensified. During remission it was easy to believe that perhaps the diagnosis was a mistake since the child looked and behaved so well. On relapse, however, the reality is reaffirmed and the probable eventual outcome is underlined. All rules of family life are again suspended and time stands still. Parents live "one day at a time," while again searching for the meaning of this experience.

During the child's hospitalization, the parents (and particularly the mother) must be physically close to the child as much as possible in order to cope with renewed separation anxiety and with guilt about the diagnosis. In addition, the mother must feel that she is doing everything possible for her child and that she is still a good mother despite the child's prognosis and her feelings of helplessness. The continuation of "mothering" is also very necessary to the child's sense of continuity as an important member of the family. To illustrate this, one mother commented:

I enjoy taking care of Jeff. I think he enjoys his mother fussing over him just like he always did. I think it is helpful to feel that I am still helpful to Jeff. Yes. Definitely. Even if I'm just helping in a small way. And it helps to take up all that time too—when you can only think. And I think a mother putters and when I come to the hospital I immediately want to putter—to straighten the bed, organize his belongings—and immediately start taking care of him. His bed is home to me and it is as if he was home, while he's in the hospital. I still feel like his mother.

Another mother stated: "While I'm here, I want to take care of him with the things I can do. Of course, I know that there are some things the nurses can do better and some things only they can do. But little mothering things like giving him the urinal or something gives me the feeling that I can still take care of Danny while he's in the hospital. I still feel like his mother."

Nurses need to be aware that any mother may feel anger when her maternal functions are usurped, but this is particularly true for the mother of a child with a life-threatening illness, for she has a great need to give of herself to her child. It is also necessary for parents to feel that the nurse is understanding and supportive of this need in order to avoid a sense of rivalry with the nurse that can only add stress and discomfort. Nurses who assist parents to feel confortable and "at home" in the hospital are contributing greatly to the emotional support of the child. On the other hand, parents must not feel that they are being left alone with a seriously ill child. They must feel that they are cooperating with professional staff and not competing with them.

Parents also need to feel that when they must leave their child, they can trust the nurses to "take over" these mothering functions, in addition to the general vigilance and professional interventions only they are equipped to give. In this respect, one mother commented: "Well, I am worried at night when I go home. The nurses showed me that the transfusion was all right before I left last night, but I was so worried. Sometimes they have trouble with it stopping. And when I'm there I can watch it. And I was afraid of—well, they have to irrigate it when it stops. And it's painful. I hate to see him have to go through that. I was kind of worried last night and doing those little things for Dean. I kinda wanted to stay there and watch the transfusion and Dean myself."

Parents also need to feel that they will be informed immediately about any changes or alterations in the routine or treatment of their child, no matter how minor. Failure to do this may cause unnecessary anxiety and undermine the confidence that parents must feel in the nurse and the physician. In respect to this point, one mother stated: "Last Friday I saw this slip on Billy's record that said, 'New Orders.' And it worried me and it worried me, and I didn't ask and I couldn't sleep all night. The way it turned out, I'll never do that again. But I wish someone had just told me. Because it really was nothing, it was just a routine on Fridays that they have to do."

Even though parents may no longer expect a cure for the diseases to be found in time to save their child, they nevertheless need to continue to hope and to most eagerly accept new treatments and any effort that may prolong life. Hope is indispensable to continued functioning although the nature of hope may change from hope for a cure to hope for additional time—months, weeks, or even days—that they have to spend with their child.

Fathers

Much more attention has been given to mothers of children with life-threatening illness than has been directed to fathers. This is mainly because mothers more often stay with their ill children and more often are involved in treatment aspects of the disease.

Fathers may have a particularly difficult time when their child becomes ill. They do not have a prescribed role when the child is hospitalized as mothers do. Also, to a greater extent than for mothers, our society limits the father's expression of grief. Whereas mothers are able to work through some of their grief in day-by-day interactions with their child and receive professional support, fathers are often given less opportunity for this because of financial and other responsibilities and pressures. The parental role of family protector may also be threatened, resulting in a greater sense of helplessness. As one father stated, "I can fix almost anything around the house. I can fix all kinds of things, but I can't fix this."

One method fathers often use in coping with this experience is to learn all they can about the disease itself through questioning physicians and others and through reading whatever they can find specific to the illness. Though they may feel helpless regarding the diagnosis, such information assists them in regaining some sense of control in a most ambiguous situation. Knowledge of "what to expect" also assists them in mobilizing their energies toward the future.

In some instances, the mother may become preoccupied with her ill child, increasingly excluding the father and others in the family from participation in her grieving process. In building resentment at what may be interpreted as neglect and exclusion, the father may escape and absent himself by burying himself in his work and other pursuits. As the mother proceeds through the anticipatory grief process, the father may not keep pace, so that communication between them may become more difficult and strained. In those instances where the father has been minimally involved during the child's illness, he may have a severe grief reaction at the time of the child's death.

Siblings

When there are other children in the family, parents may have great difficulty dealing with the children's questions about the illness and maintaining previous patterns of family interaction. Though most parents wish to treat the ill child in as "normal" a manner as is possible, this is often very hard for them to accomplish. Normal rules of discipline may be suspended, which often conveys to siblings that the ill child is more important to the parents than they themselves are. With a sense of loss of love, they may increase their demands for parental attention, thus placing further pressures on the family.

Many parents recognize the real deprivations their other children may undergo with the parent's frequent absences, financial burdens, and lack of energy to maintain familiar family routines. With professional support, they also often recognize that complete removal of former disciplinary rules is also disorganizing for the child who is ill, since it withdraws former lines of security. One mother described her experiences with her 5-year-old leukemic daughter in these words:

Oh, yes, we had great difficulty with discipline . . . like, when there was a crisis, I'd take care of her first. Gina used to push down her brothers and walk on them if they were in her way. She would push them down and it got to be okay because I never punished her for it. As soon as I got some of that stuff straight with Dr. Fisher, she was going to her room more . . . being punished and she gained a lot. She became more secure . . . that we loved her and what her place was in our family. I think she really thought to herself, "I must be pretty sick if I can get away with this kind of behavior." As soon as we stopped letting her, she started talking. Dr. Fisher helped me to see that kids don't want to go to Disneyland every month. They just want to live normal lives. You have an urge to do everything you possibly can right now and the heck with anyone else; but as soon as you see the changes aren't good . . . the child being sick works for the child . . . Bah! She was horrible.

Certainly, parents need much support in finding the courage and the words to communicate openly with their other children, to allow them to participate in the grieving process while maintaining as normal a home life for the entire family as is possible in the circumstances. This is not easy task to accomplish when stress is high and energy is low. Some parents can find comfort in the fact that they will still have a child or children remaining after the death of the ill child, and they may draw closer to them. Many parents, on the other hand, are resentful if professional personnel attempt to comfort them by pointing out that there are other children in the home, because their love, concern, and anxiety is directed toward the ill child. They rightly feel that no matter how many children they may have, they cannot spare this child.

Further Hospitalizations

As the length of time since diagnosis increases and the disease is seen to progress, most parents experience an increase of anticipatory grief, including a preoccupation with thoughts of the child, depression, weeping, and somatic symptoms, including apathy and weakness. This "grief work" is necessary for parents in order to prepare them for final separation.

With succeeding hospitalizations many parents may wish to become involved in the care of other ill children on the unit, and the intense clinging to their own child may be somewhat lessened. Nurses can make these efforts possible for them, thus supporting parents in their desire to be of assistance to all children. Nurses may also need to understand such changes in parental behavior and to avoid judging the parents' behavior as being less devoted toward their own fatally ill child. On the other hand, they must also maintain and support the parent–child relationship whenever possible in order to protect the child's need for parents.

Throughout this period of time parents require whatever environmental supports are available to them. The relationship that can be of greatest support is the marriage itself. The degree to which the partners derive strength and emotional comfort from each other depends on the length and stability of the marriage and the ego capacities of the individuals concerned. Such a shared tragic situation can draw the parents closer together, but as previously mentioned, this is not always true.

Many parents may find great emotional support in religious beliefs from which they derive courage, meaning, and faith in the "rightness" of future events, whether for positive or negative outcome. Religious observances, the ministrations of priest, rabbi, or minister, and the prayers of others can convey to parents the sense of their sorrow is shared and that others also care and have faith in their ability to bear their pain.

Nurses can be supportive to parents by helping them to keep in touch with hospital chaplains, their personal priests or ministers, parents of other children ill with the same disease, or other professional personnel such as social workers or counselors who can assist them in coping with this experience. In doing so, however, nurses should continue the support that only they can give throughout the child's hospitalization.

Death

The parental response to the ultimate death of the child depends on the available support and the length of time since the diagnosis was made. If this is an extended period, the actual death of the child may well be experienced as an anticipated loss at the end of a long sequence of events. The parental response is also related to the psychological significance the child held for the parents; the child's age, sex, and place in the family circle; and the physical energy available to parents.

When the child is dying, some mothers may not feel able to remain in the child's room, and she may feel a need to escape from great distress. A nonjudgmental attitude and understanding on the part of the nurse if the mother does "run away" can give the additional needed support for her to approach the child physically and emotionally. In this instance the nurse may also need to help the child to cope with the absence of the parents and to provide substitute comfort.

At this time of actual bereavement, all parents need consideration, empathy, and emotional support. This is also a very difficult time for nurses who have come to feel for and with their patients. It is natural for nurses to feel grief at the death of a valued patient, and it is not "unprofessional" to allow the parents to see that they also feel the loss of the relationship. It is to be expected that nurses will also welcome the emotional support that can be given by co-workers and others. Yet in order to be supportive to parents, nurses must not withdraw into their own grief, for this is a time when parents greatly need the strength and empathy that nurses can offer them. Much of the helping person's strength is the ability to experience some of the pain of the tragic situation without being overcome by it.

At this time, the parents need privacy and the opportunity to express emotion in their own way. Nurses will need to accept the expressions of sorrow, the sense of loss, and the expressions of guilt that may be reactivated at this time. Nurses may also need to accept expressions of disbelief and anger as well as indicate a respect for the cultural, religious, and social customs of grieving.

Nurses must realize that the parents' need to grieve and weep is important and constructive in assisting them to assimilate the loss that they have sustained. If this is delayed by the need to maintain the morale of others, grief may reappear later with a new loss of any nature. Nurses can be helpful by their manner of permissiveness and acceptance, by their own support, and through facilitating the presence of others who have had a helping relationship with the parents.

In the long run, however, much as we can help parents, death is very personal to each of us. As one mother stated, "Prayers, family, husband, doctors, and nurses are a source of comfort. But, you know, in a situation like this—you do feel alone. You can't help it, you know."

19 · Living With Childhood Cancer: Impact on the Healthy Siblings

Robin Fireman Kramer

Abstract

The purpose of this study was to determine healthy children's perceptions of what it is like to live with a brother or sister who has cancer. The research project, exploratory and descriptive in design, was based on interviews with 11 healthy siblings of leukemic children. The well children's responses, which were analyzed according to the qualitative method of content analysis, indicated that they experienced three major sources of stress: emotional realignment within the family, separation from family members, and family disruptions and changes brought on by the ill child's therapeutic regimen. The illness experience also resulted in positive consequences for the healthy siblings. Their comments indicated an increased sensitivity and empathy for the ill child, enhanced personal maturation, and greater family cohesion. Overall, the leukemic child's illness had a profound impact on the well sibling's life. The findings demonstrate that healthy siblings of pediatric patients have unique concerns and feelings that should be taken into consideration when planning family-centered care.

When a child is diagnosed with cancer, it is really a family experience. No member is spared the stress that accompanies the illness. One sibling summarized the impact of his sister's illness on his life by saying, ''I felt kind of mad that she was getting this disease . . . it was wrecking my life, like taking it away. But now she's

(Reprinted from Oncol Nurs Forum 11(1):44–51, January/February 1984).

getting better, and we are starting over again. It's like we have a new life." (A.T. age 10)

This child's words also allude to the new challenge that families face as a result of the improved outlook for the most pediatric cancers. Since children with cancer can now expect to live free of disease or in remission for several years, families must learn to integrate the illness and treatment regimen into their daily routines, trying to return to a quasi-normal way of life.

However, it is still stressful to live with the uncertainty of the prognosis and the ups and downs of therapy. The majority of psychosocial research in this area tends to focus on the reactions and needs of the sick child and parents. Recent studies[1-6] and the author's personal clinical experience have suggested that well children in the family are affected in a unique way by a sibling's cancer illness. For example, two studies have described the healthy children as experiencing stress (feelings of isolation, anxiety, and depression) similar to that of the ill child, and in many instances it is of equal or greater intensity.[1,2] Unfortunately, their special needs and concerns often are unrecognized or inadvertently neglected. This study was therefore designed to describe how a pediatric cancer illness affects the well children in the family.

BACKGROUND

It has been only within the last five or six years that researchers have begun to explore how a pediatric cancer illness affects the well children in the family. In one of the earliest studies, Gogan et al.[3] found that the healthy siblings of long term childhood cancer survivors did not remember the illness associated experiences as particularly traumatic. The number of intervening years between the diagnosis and the interview, the young age of the well children at the time of the ill child's diagnosis and treatment, suppressed feelings, and a lack of family openness in discussing the illness were acknowledged as possible variables influencing this lapse in memory. The only long-term effects reported were lingering feelings of sibling rivalry and guilt.

In contrast, Peck[2] found that parents assessed the long-term sibling impact to be profound, attributing adjustment difficulties to overindulgence of the sick child and frequent separation. Sibling reactions included behavorial problems, psycho-somatic complaints, school difficulties, and feelings of jealousy and parental rejection; in two-thirds of these cases, sibling problems were still unresolved a mean of 5.5 years after treatment had ceased.

Cairns et al.[1] conducted a quantitative study to determine the more immediate impact of living with a brother or sister who has cancer. The study's findings indicated that the well children, like the sick siblings (who were used as a control group), experienced severe stress and emotional problems, such as heightened feelings of anxiety and vulnerability to illness and injury. In fact, the siblings evidenced more stress than patients in their perceptions of isolation, parental overprotectiveness and indulgence of the sick child, fear of confronting family members with negative feelings, and concern with failure.

Iles'[5] descriptive study of healthy children's perceptions of a sibling's cancer experience revealed themes of stressful change and loss permeating their family, school and social interactions. However, these changes were also noted to enhance the sibling's emotional growth, particularly gains in empathy for parents and the ill child, cognitive understanding, and self-concept.

Sourkes'[6] findings closely parallel those of Iles.[5] Insightful case study analyses from her psychotherapeutic work with siblings of pediatric cancer patients led her to identify the following thematic categories: well children expressed concern about the illness' cause, the visibility of the illness and treatment process, feelings of guilt and shame, identification with the illness, parental relationships, academic and social functioning, somatic reactions, and the mutuality of the sibling–patient relationship. Sourkes stressed the importance of the caring sibling–patient interaction that she observed; she viewed it as an enriching aspect that facilitated the adaptation of the entire family.

A more recent and multifaceted study, conducted by Spinetta and colleagues[2] found that the siblings' emotional needs were met significantly less adequately than those of other family members. Specific age-related sibling responses, in comparison to the same aged ill children included: 1) demonstrating a lower self-concept (4–6 year olds), 2) viewing parents as more psychologically distant from themselves (4–12 year olds), 3) experiencing more problems related to anxiety, depression, and maladaptive responses (6–12 year olds), and 4) perceiving their families as experiencing more conflicts and less cohesion (13–18 year olds).

METHODOLOGY

Sample Selection

The population studied consisted of healthy school age and adolescent siblings of pediatric leukemic patients who were being treated in the out-patient oncology clinic at a major West Coast medical center. Convenience sampling was used to select 11 children as research subjects. Informed consent to participate was obtained from both the well child and at least one parent. Participants were selected according to four criteria:

1. Siblings of the leukemic child must be between the ages of 6 and 16, inclusive.
2. The ill child (18 years old or younger) must have acute lymphodytic leukemia, diagnosed at least 6 months before the interview, and must never have had central nervous system involvement and or a bone marrow relapse.
3. The siblings must be part of a two-parent family, be living in the same home as the ill child, and not be under treatment for any significant health problem.
4. The parents and siblings must speak English.

Study Design

An exploratory descriptive pilot study design was used to answer the question; "How do healthy children perceive the experiences of living with a brother or sister who has cancer?" Data were obtained from one-hour private interview sessions with each well child. The sessions were structured around a Healthy Sibling Interview Guide devised and pre-tested by the author for this study. The interview guide consisted of 20 open-ended and semi-structured questions aimed at eliciting the children's perceptions of how the illness experience had affected their lives. Content validity was established by thoroughly reviewing the literature and by expert critique of the tool. The questions were specifically designed to address perceived changes within the family unit and emotional responses to those changes (e.g., What was it like for you when your brother/sister was diagnosed with leukemia? Are things different between you and your parents since your brother/sister became sick? In what ways?) All interviews were taped recorded and transcribed verbatim, to ensure accuracy and completeness. Then each interview was subjected to content analysis, which summarizes recurrent themes into descriptive categories. Interrater reliability was established by a second reader with expertise in qualitative field research.

A parent questionnaire (also devised by the author) was administered solely to collect demographic data, to account for extraneous variables that might threaten the study's validity, and to inquire about any maladaptive behavior changes noted in the well sibling since the leukemic child was diagnosed. This last item was included as an assessment measure so that appropriate help could be sought if necessary. The parent questionnaire was self-administered during the sibling's interview.

FINDINGS

Parent Questionnaire

A total of nine families participated in the study: Seven families each had one healthy sibling in the 6–16 year old range, while two families had two well children. Thus, a total of 11 siblings were interviewed. As the criteria for inclusion specified, the healthy siblings all came from two-parent families. Except for one child who was living with his natural mother and a step-father, all siblings live with both biological parents. The mean age of the parents was 37 years with a range of 25 to 47 years. The parents were above the norm in education, with an average of two years of college.

The mean age of the leukemic child at the time of the interview was 8.7 years; seven were females and two were males. The average length of time since diagnosis was 36 months; the overall range was from 8 to 66 months. The mean age of the healthy siblings at the time of the ill child's diagnosis was 7.6 years (range 2–15 years) and their mean age at the interview was 10.6 years. Five of the healthy siblings were males and six were females; seven were older than the ill child, three were younger, and one was a twin.

Healthy Sibling Interview

Qualitative analysis revealed that the healthy siblings' responses fell into two major categories: Negative Impact and Positive Impact. Each category is summarized below and analyzed using quotes to illustrate key themes.

NEGATIVE IMPACT

Coding the negative impact was extremely complex because numerous themes and subthemes emerged that were frequently interrelated. The healthy siblings experienced three major stresses as a result of their brother's or sister's illness. Each stress was further subcategorized into three negative consequences associated with sibling emotional responses. Table 19-1, which is a synopsis of the negative stresses on the healthy siblings, summarizes the components of each stress.

STRESS #1: EMOTIONAL REALIGNMENT

The first source of stress for the well siblings, emotional realignment, stems from parental preoccupation with the sick child. A triad forms between the mother, father, and ill child, while the healthy siblings are left on the periphery of family life. The well children were keenly aware of this shift in family dynamics and spoke candidly about it.

Table 19-1. Childhood Cancer in the Family: Negative Impact on the Healthy Siblings

Sources of Stress	Negative Consequences	Emotional Responses

Emotional realignment	Emotional deprivation
	Decreased parental
	  tolerance
	Increased parental
	  expectations
		Increased sibling rivalry
		Anger, frustration
		Rejection
		Guilt

Separation	Lack of information Decreased family involvement Insufficient social support	Loneliness, isolation Sadness Confusion Anxiety

Ill child's therapeutic
  regimen
	Witnessing ill child's
	  physical & personality
	  changes
	Witnessing ill child's
	  anxiety & pain
	Adjusting to changes in
	  family's usual routines
		Embarrassment
		Anger, frustration
		Guilt
		Fear, anxiety

Negative Consequences of Stress #1: Emotional Realignment
Emotional deprivation. The healthy siblings described parents as "partial to" and "favoring" the ill child, leading them to believe that perhaps their parents did not love them as much: "My parents treat him nicer because he's sick"; "It makes me think they don't care about me and don't love me." A preoccupation with the sick child was not limited to parents; other family members and friends tended to be more attentive to the sick child. The siblings tried to understand and rationalize their parents' and others' behavior by acknowledging the ill child's plight of having cancer and undergoing painful procedures. But they could not discount the ramifications of the illness affecting their own lives: "I just got really upset because nobody did anything for me or hardly took me anyplace. It was like people forgot about me. Everywhere I'd go they'd say, 'How's your sister doing?' Nobody ever asked about me." Overall, the well children felt that this lack of attention and concern was more pronounced for the first several months after the diagnosis, but gradually improved with time.

Decreased parental tolerance. The children's responses indicated that emotional realignment was also responsible for parents being less tolerant of their behavior in contrast to their permissiveness with the ill child. This decrease in tolerance of the well child's behavior was primarily evident in regard to discipline: "If Nancy did something wrong, my mother would let it pass, but if I did something wrong, my mother would really get upset and yell." Six of the informants commented on the ease with which the ill child could capitalize on his/her sick role: "Whenever we fight, she'll get the good end and I'll get the bad end." Although frustrating, this manipulation by the sick child tended to be more easily tolerated by the sibling during the several weeks immediately following the diagnosis. However, all of the well children felt that months or years later, their brother or sister was still able to influence their parents because of illness.

Increased parental expectations. The well siblings felt the extra demand of chores that the ill child was frequently excused from doing. Although this was more of a problem at the onset of the illness, two children felt that they still (9 months and 4 years post diagnosis respectively) were expected to do the majority of chores: "If something needs to be done in the house, like folding the laundry, my mom will usually tell me to do it, more so than Lisa." The other well child explained that her sister would exploit her established sick role, claiming, "she couldn't do anything because she had leukemia."

Perhaps the greatest parental expectation of the healthy siblings is that they should tolerate and understand parental permissiveness, overindulgence, and preoccupation with the ill child. Some parents openly acknowledged their behavior to the well children, admitting that they "pay more attention to the sick child because he or she may not be here as long."

Sibling Emotional Responses to Stress #1: Emotional Realignment
Increased sibling rivalry. Predictably, normal sibling rivalry became intensified as the result of one child being seriously ill. The well children specifically used adjectives like "mad," "frustrated," and "jealous" when describing how they felt about

negative consequences resulting from the situation of emotional realignment. One well adolescent remembers that when she was about 8 or 9 years old, she thought, "Hey, it might not be that bad to get leukemia." Since the symptoms of leukemia are less visible and the implications of the disease not entirely understood, a child may at times think that the special treatment and status accompanying the illness make it worth getting the disease.

Anger and frustration. In addition to resenting inequitable parental treatment, the well siblings were also frustrated with the ill child for not appreciating or recirocating considerate treatment. When one sick child told her sister that she didn't know what it was like to have leukemia, the well child, feeling as though she had been "pretty understanding," replied, "Well, you don't know how it feels to be a sister of someone who has leukemia."

The age of the healthy children at the time of diagnosis seemed to influence their reactions and comments. There was less anger and jealously voiced by two children who had been 2 and 3 years old when their ill sibling was diagnosed. They were less verbal than the older subjects and had difficulty remembering how they felt. The adolescents seemed to use their cognitive ability to both analyze and rationalize their anger and jealous feelings.

Rejection. The well children spoke of partiality and favoritism toward the ill child, of "not feeling love," "not being cared for" and "feeling like running away." Although self-esteem was not measured by this study, it seems likely that the healthy siblings are at risk for a lowered self-concept as a result of the experience.

Guilt. When the healthy children spoke of their anger, frustration, and resentment, they also expressed a sense of guilt. First, they regretted the ways in which they had treated the ill child before the illness, recalling episodes of sibling rivalry that were expressed both verbally and physically. Parents also contributed to the well children's sense of guilt: In response to a sibling quarrel, one mother reprimanded, "What do you think you're doing? Your sister is sick and could even die. Don't you feel guilty?"

Several children felt guilty because they were healthy and therefore believed they had no right to complain; they spoke of enjoying unrestricted play activities, while the ill child was often homebound due to neutropenia, thrombocytopenia, or just not feeling well. This guilt over being healthy was intensified by a fear of the ill child's death, which eight of the 11 well children openly discussed. One child, recognizing her source of guilt, worried that she "could be doing the wrong thing by not playing with her (sister) or being mean because she may not be here some day."

STRESS #2: SEPARATION

The second major source of stress identified from the healthy siblings' interviews was separation from the rest of the family. These periods of isolation occurred as a result of the sick child's hospitalizations, frequent clinic visits, and the parent's general preoccupation with the ill child.

Negative Consequence of Stress #2: Separation

Lack of information. The diagnosis of leukemia necessitates immediate hospitalization, which separates the family members and potentially interferes with communication. Many of the well siblings, who learned of the diagnosis from parents either by phone or in person several days later, felt the information was incomplete, inadequate, or misleading. In several instances, the initial information given was distorted by the well child due to misconceptions of the disease, such as thinking that the illness "was like a cold" and that "it would go away really easily."

Analysis of the subjects' response indicated that communication gaps were caused by several factors: 1) parents were busy at the hospital, feeling overwhelmed themselves as they tried to find answers to their own questions; 2) because of physical separation, parents frequently relied on the telephone to communicate with their well children; for this reason, their messages were not always as clear or reassuring as they might have otherwise been; and 3) the well children, who could not easily visit the hospital, were rarely included in the initial family conferences when the primary information was given about the disease and its treatment.

Decreased involvement with parents and the ill child. Separation also resulted in a lack of family involvement, which took on several forms throughout the illness. At the time of diagnosis the family unit was temporarily divided; the parents and ill child were together in the hospital, while the well child was "boarded out" at the homes of grandparents and close friends.

On the average, the ill child required one other hospitalization during the illness course (range 1–4). All of the mothers reported staying with their ill children in the hospital for the duration of each admission (mean length of 10 days).

Grandparents assumed the major responsibility for care of the well children in the grandparents' home. In most cases, the father had more contact with the well children than did the mother because he needed to continue working. Phone contact was the most frequent means of keeping in touch with the well children; physical contact was infrequent. The distance each family lived from the hospital (mean distance one way was 119 miles) and visiting restrictions on minors were major obstacles to periodic trips or visits to the hospital by siblings.

Even though the well children were relieved when the family was finally reunited at home, parental preoccupation with the ill child kept them from feeling like intergral family members. Frequent trips to the medical center for clinic visits also disrupted the family because school attendance prevented the well siblings from being included.

The well children specifically talked about how the illness interfered with their relationship with the ill child. Their contact with the ill child was minimal when he/she was hospitalized or feeling sick at home; five children alluded to this loss of a playmate.

Insufficient social support. Closely associated with the healthy siblings' decreased involvement in family life was the loss of emotional and social support. Because parents were frequently gone or occupied, the well children lacked family support to help them through the more difficult times: "There was nobody around to talk to really, I just kept most of my feelings inside." One boy longed to receive the support of his father by staying with him in their own home instead of being sent to his grandmother's during hospitalizations. Several siblings were reluctant to confront parents with their feelings: "I felt dumb talking to my mom and dad. They already had enough troubles on their minds."

There were also fewer opportunities for emotional and social exchanges between siblings, since the well child's relationship with the sick child was stressed by periods of separation. During this time of isolation from family members, social support from outside sources was critical. Unfortunately, the camaraderie and emotional interaction typically provided by peers was also lacking. Seven children said the illness seemed to strain their relationships with friends. When they learned of the diagnosis, many of their friends did not know how to respond and made themselves scarce. Fear of the illness being contagious was the most frequent reason offered for their friend's abandonment. However, three children believed that a temporary change in their own personalities (being "grouchy" and "irritable" because of anxiety they felt at the time of diagnosis) was partially responsible for the alienation of their friends. For most children, lack of peer support was transitory, but it occurred during the first few difficult weeks following the diagnosis when friendship was most needed.

Sibling Emotional Responses to Stress #2: Separation
Loneliness. Decreased family involvement evoked profound feelings of loneliness in the well children. They perceived themselves as "all alone" in a "dark world" with "no one around to talk to about what was happening." Suddenly, the stability of their family position seemed undermined, as one child explained, because "no one paid any attention" to them.

Sadness. The healthy siblings repeatedly used the word "sad" to describe their feelings in response to family isolation and the decreased social support they experienced. The three youngest children added that because of their sadness, they "cried a lot."

Confusion. Isolation and few opportunities to visit the hospital and/or clinic increased the well children's sense of confusion. "Not knowing what was going on" and filling in the gaps of knowledge with misconceptions were counterproductive to their adaptation.

Anxiety. Being separated from family members, as well as harboring unanswered questions, contributed to the well children's sense of anxiety. Visiting the hospital and/or clinic did help allay most well children's anxiety by providing them with first-hand information about how the ill child was doing. However, two well siblings (ages 5 and 10 at diagnosis) described their visits to the hospital as negative experiences that actually increased their anxiety. Their fears centered on the hospital environment (the intensive care unit) and the equipment (intravenous therapy), which they knew little about. Anxiety over the fear of contagion was a major concern of five children until they received reassurance from parents or hospital staff.

STRESS #3: ILL CHILD'S THERAPEUTIC REGIMEN

The third source of stress on the healthy siblings was the ill child's medical regimen. All the ill children were placed on cooperative clinical research protocols with treatments scheduled at specific times. Treatment consisted of cranial radiation, evaluative procedures (such as bone marrow aspirations, lumbar punctures, and complete blood counts), and chemotherapy. After the initial hospitalization, all children received their therapy as outpatients unless a complication required hospitalization.

The therapeutic regimen with its use of needles, uncomfortable positioning, varied side effects, the interruption of normal routines, is feared and dreaded by most children with cancer. Although the frequency of the procedures usually results in an improved tolerance (especially for the older children), the experiences are still painful and produce anxiety for the ill children and their families.

Negative Consequences of Stress #3: Therapeutic Regimen
Witnessing ill child's physical and personality changes. The most disturbing physical change the well children talked about was the ill child's hair loss, remarking that their brother or sister "looked different," even "like a stranger." The well children often saw the ill child being teased by strangers as well as peers: "People would say stuff like 'he looks ugly' or 'he looks stupid' but I didn't believe what they were saying."

Substantive gains and losses in their siblings' body weight were also upsetting to the well subjects. One well child was placed in a frustrating position when her twin sister, who had gained weight on prednisone, would remind her, "you're so skinny, I'm so fat." The well twin was empathetically torn between wanting to help her sister lose weight or gain weight herself. The healthy children were even aware of the more subtle physical changes, such as lethargy and proneness to bruising, which often interfered with sibling play. Personality changes were also apparent to the well siblings, who described the ill child as being "moody" and "hard to get along with" as a result of being ill and taking medications, especially prednisone.

Witnessing the ill child's anxiety and pain. Throughout the interviews, the subjects seemed preoccupied and disturbed as they recalled the ill child's anxiety and pain in response to therapy. The younger children seemed more preoccupied by "needles" and "IV shots." The older children reacted not so much to the fear of "needles" and "shots," but spoke more generally of their discomfort in witnessing "pain." Three children stated that observing the ill child's anxiety and pain was one of the "worst" aspects of the illness.

Adjusting to changes in the family's usual routines. The well siblings, who stayed at friends' or grandparents' homes when the ill child was hospitalized, faced altered family structure and routines. Those children who remained home when parents were at the hospital or clinic assumed new roles and responsibilities. Five children reported that giving oral medication at home became an important aspect of the daily routine, especially for two leukemic children who needed considerable "coaxing and patience." The illness and the therapeutic regimen also interfered with the family's degree of outside social activity, which, in turn, affected the well children's lives. They explained that their families "stopped doing things they used to do, " and that "in the beginning, especially, you have to give up a lot."

Fear of the ill child getting sick due to the immuno-suppressive side effects of therapy was the primary reason offered for isolation among family members: "If I'm sick, we have to be in separate rooms or sometimes I'd have to go down to my grandpa's so Cathy wouldn't get sick on top of her leukemia." Worried about a superimposed infection, parents also restricted playmate contact and large group activities. The rules were especially strict when the absolute neutrophil count was low: "We couldn't have any friends over and I couldn't really see her that much." Two children mentioned that going to the movies, where there would be a large crowd in close proximity, was worrisome to parents and, therefore, was discouraged or even restricted.

Sibling Emotional Responses to Stress #3: Therapeutic Regimen
Embarrassment. Three children admitted to feeling embarrassed about the physical changes that occurred in the ill child. Their reactions closely bordering on anger seemed to be prompted by insensitive teasing: "People looked a lot. I was embarrassed but not that much. I tried not to think about it."

Anger and frustration. Although the well siblings acknowledged that the personality changes were influenced by the medicines, they still were angry and frustrated by the ill child's behavior. They coped with the situation by trying "not to get involved," rationalizing that it was the prednisone that caused the moodiness, and recognizing that the ill child's negative behavior was partly due to "just being mad at what was happening to her."

The well children also resented the changes in family routines mandated by a rigorous treatment regimen and its potential complications. They particularly disliked the restrictions surrounding social activities when the ill child was neutropenic in addition to the family isolation they felt if they themselves became sick.

Guilt. As previously described, the well children felt both relieved and guilty over being healthy and thus spared the trauma associated with the therapeutic regimen. They also felt potential guilt over the possibility of exposing the immunosuppressed leukemic child to a complicating secondary illness: "We were all worried if Nancy caught it, she might die. Then it would be on your conscience because you got sick and gave it to her."

Fear and anxiety. Hearing about or watching the ill child undergo painful procedures was frightening. Sensing the ill child's anxiety and pain, as well as witnessing physical and personality changes, not only confirmed the reality of the illness and the threat to the ill child's life but also raised the well children's anxiety over their own vulnerability to illness.

POSITIVE ASPECTS

The effects of the leukemic illness on the well siblings were not all negative. The same experiences that engendered the negative feelings of isolation, frustration, anxiety, and resentment also brought about positive and adaptive responses in the healthy siblings and their families.

Increased sensitivity and empathy. As the healthy children talked of the ill child's anxiety, pain, and self-consciousness, they also expressed feelings of empathy and love. A 15-year old adolescent sister sensitively described her concern: "You just don't want anybody you love having to go through anything like that."

This sensitivity led to a desire to protect the ill child from the ridicule of peers and strangers. The school environment was the most common setting in which curious stares and cruel comments prevailed. Of the four children who adopted a protective role, three were older siblings and one was a twin.

The well siblings were also sensitive to the illness' impact on their parents. They spoke of not wanting to "ask for anything special for Christmas," and not complaining to parents because they "didn't want to put any more pressures on them."

Personal maturation. Several of the healthy siblings spoke of the sudden maturity prompted in them by the cancer illness. Two children (16 and 10 years old) revealed that the experience helped them to "grow up a lot," to become more tolerant of others, and to develop inner strength. Another teen explained that she and her family now "have a better, more positive attitude toward things." This same teen spoke of a second personal change, "a new perspective on life," learning to value her own good health and "to value time more—to make the most of each day."

Increase in family cohesion. Three children said that the illness had made their family closer, being "more willing to talk openly together," "to do and care for each other," and even to express their love for one another. A seven-year-old child reported that his father now "hugs me a little more," implying that he and his father share a closer relationship as a result of his sister's illness.

The three older children readily articulated positive aspects gained from the illness experience. They explained that they now could look back, having survived the chaotic period around the time of diagnosis and intensive therapy, and evaluate its impact on their life in a broader context. By sensitizing them to the feelings of other family members, the illness helped the well children to become less self-centered and more appreciative. A 16-year-old teen summed up an important lesson gained from her sister's illness: "It opens up your eyes to know that something like this can happen to your family. You never think it could happen, but things do. You really never know what can happen, so you should take what you have today and care for it."

CONCLUSIONS

When viewed collectively, each aspect and phase of the illness represents an emotionally overwhelming and stressful experience for the healthy siblings. They experienced a great deal of disruption in their lives as a result of the changes brought about by their brother or sister having leukemia; and they had to deal with these changes in the face of much uncertainty and a lack of emotional support. One teenager, when asked about the worst part of having a sister with leukemia, could not specify any one aspect; instead, she replied, "The worst thing? Probably just the trauma of the whole thing, knowing that you might lose your sister, and people treat her differently and they treat me differently, too. I guess they treated our whole family, all of us, differently."

The impact of a brother or sister's cancer illness is not short-lived. Several children, whose brother or sister had just finished or was about to finish therapy, talked about family life beginning to return to "normal." Yet, they still spoke of themselves and their parents worrying about the future well-being of the leukemic child. They also noted that lingering favoritism was unfair to the formerly ill child: "My mother doesn't want to admit that she still treats my sister special. I accept the fact. Most parents will do that. It just makes me pretty mad though because Nancy needs a chance to be treated like a normal person."

The same experiences that threatened the well children's healthy adaptation can also produce growth. The study's findings indicate that the illness increased the well sibling's capacity for empathy, enhanced with personal maturation, and promoted family cohesion. Predictably, the older children were better able to recognize and describe the subtle positive consequences of the illness; but perhaps with time the younger siblings will also be able to draw such conclusions.

It was encouraging that the positive effects identified by this study agreed with findings from other studies.[5,6,7] The illness was not viewed exclusively as a negative experience, as it provided opportunities for individual and family growth. However, it would be naive to think that the coping process develops smoothly and painlessly, with no risk of maladaption for the healthy siblings and their families.

The small, convenient sample size, representing a broad developmental age span, limits the analyst's ability to generalize about the study. Also, the *Healthy Sibling Interview Guide*, although pre-tested, is in an early phase of development. Because no control group was used, the present study does not address the relationship between the dependent variable of sibling distress and the developmental sibling issues that occur in families without a seriously ill child. This relationship could be explored in a follow-up study using age-matched control groups of healthy children whose siblings have other chronic illnesses as well as those whose siblings are well.

Despite the study's limitations, the in-depth information gleaned from the healthy siblings' interviews provides a rich foundation from which to build a better understanding. The descriptive methodology allowed the siblings to educate health care professionals in what it is like to live with a leukemic brother or sister and the singular way in which the illness affects their lives. The well children's responses were probed for information on "what has/would have helped," alluding to the key variables which influenced their adaptation and coping. Their suggestions included: 1) more frequent hospital/clinic visits; 2) more information about the disease and its treatment; 3) open and honest communication; 4) greater involvement in the ill child's care; 5) at-home care during siblings' hospitalizations; and 6) passage of time. Table 19-2 outlines general nursing interventions for supporting the well children, addressing several major issues identified during their interviews.

Overall, the study's findings reinforce the philosophy that nursing care needs to be truly "family centered." Through this kind of commitment the healthy siblings will no longer be referred to as "forgotten family members." Although it is

Table 19-2. Nursing Implications

Intervention Areas	Specific Suggestions
Initial Family Assessment	Inquire about the well children at home: Where are they staying? Have they been told the diagnosis? Do the parents need guidance in disclosing the diagnosis? What were the siblings' reactions, questions, and concerns? Provide parents with anticipatory counseling regarding the healthy siblings' role in the illness experience, their unique concerns and responses. Elicit parent's perceptions of how you might be helpful.
Sibling Involvement	Encourage siblings to be involved in the care of the ill child in the hospital and at home. Encourage phone calls, letter writing, and picture exchanges during periods of separation.
Educational Support	Encourage inclusion of the siblings at the initial family conferences. Arrange for follow-up teaching sessions (either individual or group) in the hospital or out-patient clinic at convenient times for the siblings. Employ teaching strategies: Prepare slide show presentation of procedures (i.e. bone marrows, lumbar punctures, IV chemotherapy) and use of puppet play manipulating procedure equipment.
Emotional Support	Develop an ongoing sibling support group to allow for the sharing of common concerns and feelings. Develop a "sibling network," placing well children in touch with each other by telephone or by establishing penpals.
Family Communication	Encourage honest and open family counseling. Counsel parents that sibling communication should be age-appropriate. Reassure the family that it is OK to show their emotions. Encourage parents to explore the meanings behind sibling questions and statements. Remind families that communication needs to be an ongoing process.

not feasible to think that the stresses and negative consequences experienced can be entirely prevented, it is realistic to expect that they can be openly addressed and more effectively managed.

REFERENCES

1. Cairns NU et al: Adaptation of siblings to childhood malignancy. J Pediatr 95:484–487, 1979
2. Spinetta JJ: The siblings of the child with cancer. In Spinetta JJ, Deasy–Spinetta P, eds): Living with Childhood Cancer. St Louis, CV Mosby, 1981
3. Gogan JL et al: Impact of childhood cancer on siblings. Health Soc Work 2:41–57, 1977
4. Peck B: Effects of childhood cancer on long-term survivors and their families. Br Med J 1:1327–1329, 1979
5. Iles JP: Children with cancer: Health sibling's perceptions during the illness experience. Cancer Nurs 2:371–377, 1979
6. Sourkes B: Siblings of pediatric cancer patients. In Kellerman J (ed): Physiological Aspects of Childhood Cancer. Springfield, IL, Charles C Thomas, 1981
7. Taylor SC: The effect of chronic childhood illness upon well siblings. Matern–Child Nurs J 9:109–116, 1980

20 · Factors Influencing Children's Reactions and Adjustment to Illness: Implications for Facilitating Coping

Lynda L. LaMontagne

Illness in a child can be viewed as inflicting a series of losses on the child to a degree that depends upon the type and severity of illness. These losses include, but are not limited to, loss of certain physical abilities and functions, loss of health and a sense of well-being, and to some extent, loss of self-esteem and ability to cope effectively with daily stress. The nature of the specific illness, however, may be less influential to a child's coping and overall adjustment than such factors as the child's cognitive and emotional development and the supports his or her environment provides.

This paper describes person and situation factors that are central in determining a child's reactions to his or her illness and successful adjustment to the illness situation. It also provides modes of coping that can be adopted by sick children depending upon their unique developmental needs and coping resources.

CHILDREN'S REACTIONS TO ILLNESS

From the theoretical perspective of Lazarus and his colleagues (Lazarus, 1966; Lazarus, Averill, and Opton, 1974; Lazarus and Launier 1978), the stress responses associated with any situation, such as illness, arise from and reflect the nature of the person's appraisal of the situation's effect on his or her well-being, and the resources available for mastery. That is, the person appraises the event as stressful according to his or her understanding of (1) the power of the situation to produce harm and (2) the resources available for dealing with the event. Thus, the appraisal actually determines the degree of stress. Coping, then, is defined as efforts both action oriented (e.g., information seeking efforts), and intrapsychic (e.g., defenses such as avoidance) aimed at trying to meet the demands of the situation and manage or control internal conflicts engendered by the situation.

With respect to illness and hospitalization, the most central factor influencing a child's reactions to the stress of the illness situation is the child's age in terms of his or her cognitive and emotional development. But, this is not the only contributing factor. Children may also be influenced as much by the quality of the parent–child relationship and the supports available from the extended family and the care setting as by any traumatic treatment episode. We may conclude, then, that a child's appraisal of the stresses of illness and hospitalization stems from a combination of *person* and *situation* factors that influence how he or she responds emotionally to them. In other words, stress responses must be viewed in terms of a transaction between the child and situation with the meaning or appraisal of the illness as the key issue affecting his or her overall adjustment.

Person Factors

COGNITIVE DEVELOPMENT

A child's cognitive development influences how he or she appraises and understands what is happening in a given situation. Although illness and hospitalization may be universally stressful for children, what may be appraised as stressful for one child may not be for another simply because of the level of his or her thinking.

Research has shown a cognitive developmental trend in the way children conceptualize illness (e.g., Bibace and Walsh, 1979; Perrin and Gerrity, 1981). Preoperational children (usually younger than 7 years of age) have difficulty separating themselves from the world. Because thinking is egocentric, every object and process is related to the children themselves; thinking is in terms of what they can see, so explanations are perceptual dominant. Thus, conceptions are determined to a large measure by the potency of physical attributes. Illness is understood in terms of the child's own unique experience, such as one single external symptom associated with the illness (e.g., "measles are bumps on your arm") or something or someone in the immediate environment (e.g., "colds come from cold air"). Above all, during this phase, children develop awareness of events through play, which is their major vehicle with which to experience real-life events. For the preoperational child, play has all the elements of reality and serves as the communication link with the outside world. Thus, a preoperational child's ability to understand any event, such as his or her illness, is greatly enhanced through mere play that involves not only concrete language, but imitation as well.

In contrast to the younger, preoperational child, concrete operational children (usually older than 7 years of age) are beginning to think and reason logically about objects in their environment and to perform mentally actions that previously had to be carried out in actuality. Although the child in this stage can clearly distinguish between what is internal and external to the self, the focus is still on external concrete events. That is, the child understands events in the real world in contrast to hypothetical events (e.g., what is, instead of what might be). Thinking is less egocentric and is not focused on a part to the exclusion of the whole. For instance, concrete operational thinkers have the ability to understand illness in terms of the whole state, including its physical and social aspects. The primary focus, however, is not on what happens physiologically within the body, but on what is visible in the external world. This explains why children of this age are particularly vulnerable to the stresses associated with the visible effects of the illness or treatment such as the loss of hair resulting from chemotherapy. Unlike the younger preoperational child, concrete operational children also have the ability to reverse processes, which enables them to understand illness in a reversible way (e.g., one gets well after being sick or one will feel better after taking medicine).

Formal operational children (usually beyond 11 years of age) are at the stage when there is the greatest amount of differentiation between self and world. At this stage, what the child knows is subordinate to what he or she sees in concrete reality. Therefore, these children are apt to expand their logic in conceptualizing illness. While the cause of illness may be reasoned as an external event (e.g., a bacteria or virus), illness is understood in more abstract terms such as internal physiological and psychological structures and functions, whose malfunctioning can manifest itself in multiple symptoms. Formal operational children are also capable of making hypotheses about the link between the body and environment in causing and controlling illness. This type of reasoning makes these children good candidates for self-help approaches designed to manage the illness.

EMOTIONAL DEVELOPMENT

The affective needs of a child will also influence how he or she appraises, and reacts to, the stresses of the illness. According to Erikson (1978), each of the phases of emotional development are products of interactional experiences between the child and his or her world. For instance, issues of trust and autonomy, once earlier themes, emerge again when the child faces the new world of peers in later childhood. These issues are dealt with differently but are still vital. Therefore, although each stage of emotional development will present special needs, each child progresses by carrying over the issues from previous encounters. For Erikson, it is the ego, the affective aspects of life, and the innate inner sense of self that revolve around each child's ongoing struggle to achieve control or mastery over events going on in his or her particular time and space.

Learning how to cope with anxiety and stress is essential to emotional growth. Children who are ill are also faced with the unique stresses of their illness. These stresses are related to multiple stressors such as various physical symptoms, pain, and reasons for illness. The often frequent and lengthy hospital admissions also pose an array of psychological threats with which these children must cope. For example, a very sick school-age child who cannot dress and feed himself or use the bathroom without help, must deal with loss of his developmental gain of independence. Further, any child with a serious, chronic disease has to deal with lasting physical impairments that produce certain limitations on his or her activities. The stresses of long-term illness are inevitable. A developmental task is to learn how to cope with them successfully. Helping the sick child to maintain a positive sense of self while responding to these stresses is the key to facilitating his or her emotional development and managing the stresses involved.

Situation Factor

ENVIRONMENTAL SUPPORTS

A child's reactions and ability to cope with the stresses of illness also depend on the support his or her environment provides. A child's coping capacity involves the ability not only to respond to the stressors involved, but also to influence and control the demands of the situation. A major factor contributing to a child's ability to adjust to the demands is his or her judgment that there are resources available to help him or her cope with them. Continuity of care by sensitive parents who have professional support and guidance as well as support from peers and a well-informed staff, is an essential network for helping the child to deal with the emotional aspects of the illness and hospitalization and to minimize stress.

FACILITATING COPING

It is the responsibility of adults to help sick children develop effective coping strategies to meet the demands of the illness. Sick children are usually taught some aspects of their illness, but rarely how to control or manage the stresses engendered by the illness. Yet the ability to manage these stresses is especially necessary to a child's overall adjustment.

Helping sick children to manage and reduce the stresses of illness is not easy. Children must be helped to appraise their own resources more accurately and shown how to use them more efficiently. For example, major stresses such as those associated with exacerbations of illness put strain on the coping abilities of children. Adults who communicate openly and provide comfort, support, and understanding during times of stress reinforce in the child the notion that it is okay to rely on adult support when it is most needed. This is particularly essential for older children who cognitively and emotionally have difficulty depending on adults. Further, children need help to develop effective coping modes such as problem solving, therapeutic (e.g. relaxation) techniques, and preventive strategies that enhance well-being. For instance, sick children need to develop awareness that having a chronic illness means taking extra responsibility. However, they also need to realize that they are not defined by special medical needs or physical limitations, and helped to discover what they *can* rather than what they *cannot* do. In doing so, adults must evaluate the child's developmental capabilities, set reasonable goals for achievement, and seek to provide opportunities for emotional secu-

Table 20-1. Coping Interventions

Information

Help child to understand illness by

1. Providing opportunities for child to ask questions at own pace
2. Encouraging expression of feelings
3. Giving repeated, truthful, simple, but comprehensive information about the illness, its symptoms and therapeutic concepts
4. Providing concrete experiences (e.g., play materials) to help the child master stressful situations, or creative play in which the characters, themes, and outcomes change
5. Eliciting verbal conceptions/misconceptions of the illness and adapt explanations according to child's cognitive/emotional level
6. Preparing the child for procedures and likely clinical manifestations

Communication

1. Encourage child to tell parents, doctors, nurses, and others what is happening before and during stressful episodes and exacerbations of the illness.
2. Demonstrate respect for the child by providing privacy and understanding of his or her point of view.
3. Provide predictable daily routines, including treatment routines.
4. Ensure continuity of care by seeing that explanations and plans are understood by the child, parents, and staff members.

Development of Self Responsibility

1. Family involvement: Overprotection and undue restrictions at home, at school, or in the hospital should be discouraged. Parents need instruction on how to develop in their child an age-appropriate responsibility for self-care and protection through problem solving skills:
   a. Observation: ability to see the situation or factors that lead to signs and symptoms
   b. Discrimination: ability to notice changes that indicate impending signs and symptoms
   c. Direct action: ability to make a decision to seek help or stop symptoms
2. Self-help approaches
   a. Teach relaxation techniques.
   b. Encourage positive attitude regarding ability to manage illness.

Environmental Supports

1. Provide consistent support for family. Involve parents (family) in decision making, continuity of care plan, and regular visitation.
2. Use peer educators. Involve peers who have the same or other chronic illnesses to engage the child in frank discussions, peer support, and sharing of advice on how to cope with illness.
3. Respect child's cultural background and its influence on expectations and perceptions of symptoms, pain, and attitudes.
4. Create an environment that avoids traditional care practices and routines (e.g., provide safe areas that are located away from treatment).

rity and growth. Children of all ages need to be shown how to turn problems into workable solutions. This is especially true for the chronically ill child. It may help to point out aspects of the illness or treatment regimen that he or she can be responsible for, such as avoiding foods or agents that cause symptoms and expressing feelings freely and appropriately.

Nursing interventions that assist the child to understand and cope with the stresses of the illness are presented in Table 20-1. These coping interventions are designed to help children maintain positive attitudes regarding their ability to control or manage the stresses involved. Implementation of these strategies depends on the nurse's assessment of each individual child's cognitive and emotional development, how the situation is appraised by the child (and family), and what coping resources are available. For any intervention to be effective, it must be designed to meet the needs of the particular child because, although children of the same developmental stage may be similar, individual influences that affect how they cope with stress makes them different from other children of the same age. Therefore, the interventions must be tailored to the individual child according to his or her unique developmental needs and coping resources.

REFERENCES

Bibace R, Walsh ME: Developmental stages in children's conceptions of illness. In Stone GC, Cohen F, Adler NE (eds): Health Psychology, pp 285–301. San Francisco, Jossey–Bass, 1979
Bibace R, Walsh ME: Development of children's concepts of illness. Pediatrics 66(6):912–917, 1980
Lazarus RS: Psychological stress and the coping process. New York, McGraw-Hill, 1966
Lazarus RS, Averill JR, Opton EM: The psychology of coping: Issues of research and assessment. In Coelho GV, Hamburg DA, Adams JE (eds): Coping and Adaptation, pp 249–315. New York, Basic Books, 1974
Lazarus RS, Launier R: Stress-related transactions between person and environment. In Pervin LA, M Lewis (eds): Perspectives in Interactional Psychology, pp 287–322. New York, Plenum, 1978
Maier HW: The affective theory of Erik H. Erikson. In Boehm WW (ed): Three theories of child development, pp 71–132, New York, Harper & Row, 1978
Perrin C, Gerrity S: There's a demon in your belly: children's understanding of illness. Pediatrics 67:841–849,1981

21 · Passage Through Hospitalization of Severely Burned, Isolated School-Age Children

Marilyn K. Savedra

She lay on her bed exposed, helpless, fearful, engulfed by pain, and totally at the mercy of the nurse assigned to her care. Her screams were piercing and uncontrolled. I stood in the doorway gowned and masked, wanting to turn and run, to escape the horror of what I saw and knew was to follow. The child seemed oblivious to my presence as I moved closer to the bed. The protective bed cradle had been removed. She lay flat on her back, neck hyperextended, naked except for a bandage covering her right arm and hand.

The primarily third-degree burn involving approximately 45 percent of body surface area, including anterior trunk, neck, lower face, ear, arms, hand, and part of the back, was clearly visible. Skin grafts had been placed on her neck and chin. The major part of the burn was still an open, red, oozing sore covered with dried Sulfamylon cream.

Her straight, light-brown hair was disheveled. Her face was tense and anxious. Her legs trembled and she hit the bed with her foot as the gowned, masked, and gloved nurse removed the old Sulfamylon with saline-soaked gauze. Repeatedly she cried out, "Don't hurt me, Connie. I don't want you to hurt me. Do it lightly. You're not doing it lightly. You're hurting me."

Unhesitatingly, the nurse proceeded, firmly but gently. The child was told that it was all right to scream and hit the bed with her foot, but she was not to hit the

Reprinted from Batey M (ed): Communicating Nursing Research: Critical Issues in Access to Data. Denver, Western Interstate Commission for Higher Education, 1975.

· 279

nurse. The nurse repeatedly said she did not want to hurt the child, but the procedure had to be done. The nurse acknowledged that it was painful. After 20 minutes of torture, the removal of Sulfamylon was completed and the child's request to dry before the cream was reapplied was granted. After saying she wanted to sleep, she shut her eyes, apparently physically exhausted and emotionally drained. The brief sleep would shut out the world of pain before it once more became all-pervasive.

I was relieved to leave the room. Although I had detected no odor of decaying flesh, I felt sick from what I had witnessed. I sensed the nurse was glad for a break, for she too immediately left the room. I wondered if granting the child's request to sleep was based more on the child's need or on the nurse's need. Perhaps it was both.

This was my introduction to Jane, aged 7 years, 11 months, isolated and severely burned. It was the beginning of an involvement that was to last for many months. I saw Jane several times each week starting on the 27th day postadmission. My purpose was to observe and record the behavior of a child isolated as a result of an extensive severe burn. Jane informed someone who asked about me that I was a nurse who was going to school to learn to be a better nurse. I visited, she said, because I liked her.

Jane was the first of six patients to be included in a study of severely burned, isolated children. The purpose was to provide some measure of prediction and/or explanation of behavior so that clinical practitioners could anticipate problems and be more effective and timely in their nursing interventions.

BACKGROUND OF THE STUDY

The study evolved as the result of my growing interest in the child on isolation technique. As I had cared for such children, I had become increasingly aware that some of the behaviors of the children were directly related to the fact that they were alone in an isolation room.

Informal interviews with several nurses involved in caring for children on isolation technique revealed a conviction on their part that the behavior of such children has distinct differences from that of children not isolated. When asked to indicate the differences, they were far less certain in their responses.

Research pertaining to patients on isolation technique is extremely limited. The one study relating specifically to children deals with the child's understanding of the rationale for isolation technique and the presence in the child's explanation of recausal or causal thinking (Pidgeon, 1967). Findings revealed a general lack of understanding in preschool children, while the majority of school-age children correctly understood the reason for isolation technique.

Although isolation technique has been used for centuries in caring for patients with contagious disease, it is only recently that textbooks have referred to the psychological effects of isolation on the patient. A current pediatric nursing textbook indicates that a child may experience feelings of separateness and loneliness and fear of masks, gowns, and gloves worn by those who enter the room (Marlow,

1969). Brodie and Matern (1962) discussed the aloneness experienced by the severely burned child. While acknowledging that no research has been done in this special area, on the basis of observation of the experience of adults, they assumed that fear, reduced mental efficiency due to persistent monotony of surroundings with lack of sensory input, feelings of depersonalization, and aloneness do exist. Studies of adults experiencing social isolation and/or sensory deprivation reveal great variation in subject response. In general, subjects have found the condition unpleasant and in many cases could not tolerate resultant anxiety (Marks, Ganzer, and Collins; 1968).

Thus, personal experience in caring for isolated children, discussions with clinicians involved in the care of hospitalized children, and reading in the areas of sensory deprivation, social isolation, and care of the isolated patient were the background of this study of children isolated with severe burns. The specific purpose was to identify patterns and sequence of behavior in severely burned, isolated children 6 to 10 years old during their initial hospitalization and immediately upon their return home. In the context of this study, isolation was defined as being in a single room or ward with restrictions on free movement of the patient out of the designated area and of other people into the area.

RESEARCH DESIGN

The nature of the problem, plus the dearth of research related to children or adults on isolation technique, led to an exploratory research design using participant observation as the primary method of data collection.

Selection of Subjects

Children with severe burns, second and/or third degree of 20 percent or more body surface area, were selected for the study because they are inevitably isolated, generally for extended periods of time. When cared for in a setting other than a burn unit, they frequently move in and out of isolation during their initial hospital stay. This would be helpful in identifying behaviors related to the isolation factor. Only children isolated for a minimum of two consecutive weeks were included in the study. Children 6 to 10 years old were selected because they are capable of verbally expressing feelings about what they are experiencing and because they fall within one developmental stage.

Collection of Data

The first task was to identify hospitals where severely burned children might receive care for an extended time. Eventually, arrangements were made with six hospitals to observe if a severely burned child was admitted and isolated.

The next task was to locate the patients. In none of the hospitals, including one with a burn unit, could one expect to find 6- to 10-year-old children with severe burns at any given time. Therefore, all the hospitals agreed to notify me if such a patient was admitted, but because busy hospital personnel might forget, the hospitals were visited or called regularly. In addition, if friends read or heard news reports of burned children who were hospitalized, they notified me.

Each child was visited several times a week during the major period of hospitalization. A limited number of unobtrusive observations was made. Nursing care by me, as the observer, was restricted primarily to what was initiated by the child and consisted of such activities as reading to the child, assisting the child in eating, and providing comfort measures.

As the observations extended over weeks, and in some cases months, a close relationship was developed with the children; this undoubtedly had some effect upon them and their subsequent behavior. Observations took place at varying times of the day, to coincide with mealtimes, routine care, dressing changes, visiting hours, and bedtime. A limitation of the study was that no observations took place during the night.

While the initial plan was to limit any single observation to a brief period—approximately 30 minutes—particularly when the child was alone in a room, it was not adhered to rigidly. When at all possible, observations were made at transitional points such as surgery, removal from isolation, and return to isolation after restrictions had been temporarily removed.

Field notes were recorded as soon as possible following each observation and were completed each day before beginning a second day's observation. While selectivity of observations cannot be denied, attempt was made to record as completely as possible what was seen and heard that involved the children and their interactions with all who entered their environment.

Analysis of the Data

Analysis was an ongoing process. During the early months, when only one child was part of the study, thematic behaviors exhibited by the child were identified. With the addition of other children to the study, comparison became a major focus. A total of six children were observed, including Jane, isolated alone in a room; Larry, Sherri, Kenny, and Jennifer, isolated together in a burn unit; and Julie, also isolated alone in a room. All of the children were burned as a result of their clothing catching fire. Body surface area burned varied from 20 percent to 75 percent. One child, Sherri, died 9.5 weeks postburn. See Table 21-1 for data on the children.

Data were organized in the form of case studies to share more fully with the reader the outcome of the research. The case study is one of the few documented sources of rich clinical experience. Sufficient data are presented to confirm the researcher's conceptualizations or to allow the reader to make additional or varying conceptualizations (Strauss and Glaser, 1970). The scope of this paper does not allow the detailed presentations of cases, but excerpts are provided to support the conceptualizations made.

As observations continued over several months, it was evident that isolation, the phenomenon that triggered the study, was only one variable in an extremely

Table 21-1. Data on Burned, Isolated Children

Name (Pseudonym)	Age (yr/mo) at Time of Accident	Body Surface Area Burned (%)	Degree of Burn Severity	Length of Hospitalization (Days)
Jane	7.10	45	Primarily 3rd	114
Larry	9.5	62	Primarily 3rd	118
Sherri	6.0	65–75	Primarily 3rd	73
Kenny	7.9	30	Primarily 3rd	47
Jennifer	8.9	32	2nd & 3rd	44
Julie	5.8	20	Primarily 2nd	35

complex situation. Within the research design, it became increasingly difficult to identify behaviors related solely to the isolation experience. It was the burn with its all-encompassing pain that dominated the situation.

Initial and subsequent analysis suggested that most of the data clustered around three dominant themes common to all of the children. These were categorized as aloneness, pain, and loss.

Aloneness

The selection of aloneness as a dominant concept resulted from two major factors. First, the beginning focus for the study was isolation. The literature relating to isolation invariably associates "aloneness" with being isolated. Second, during the first interaction with Jane, she said that she felt "alone."

Initially aloneness was viewed as relating only to isolation, but quickly it became obvious that it was integral to the burn experience as well. Children were hospitalized for an extended time, and several were in institutions far from home, making visits from significant others rare or nonexistent.

Jane's comment made it evident that aloneness means more than simply being without people. Aloneness can be an internal feeling resulting from circumstances irrespective of whether people are present. Sherri, too, expressed this feeling of aloneness when she said, "Stay with me, I need you." Similarly, Larry often urged, "Stay with me." His need for someone specifically relating to him was particularly great in the early weeks and when his mother was not present.

Jane commented one day several weeks postburn that she did not like to be "alone" with someone who did not like her. Her concept of whether a person "liked her" appeared to relate to several factors, including how well she knew the person and the efficiency and skill of the person if care was to be given. On my first day of observation she initially wanted me to leave when I was the only person in the room with her.

The literature indicates that, for most people, enforced aloneness is unpleasant and undesirable. Early in her hospitalization Jane stated that she did not like to be alone. Nurses in both hospitals said they felt it was not best for a child to be by himself or herself. They saw the visits of the observer as being helpful in counteracting aloneness and as being generally beneficial for the children.

At the opposite extreme, aloneness may be sought by the severely burned child. On more than one occasion, Jane wanted to be by herself. She specifically chose to exclude me following surgery when she appeared to be experiencing her greatest physical pain. It may well be that selected aloneness is sought by the severely burned child in response to an experience that is unshareable. It is, in a sense, psychological insularity against an overwhelming assault on the self. In the burn unit, Larry once stated that he wanted a private room with a private nurse. Toward the end of his hospitalization, at times he chose to have the curtains pulled around his bed.

It became evident from the data that "aloneness" as related to the burn experience falls into two classes: 1) imposed or engendered by the hospital, and 2) selected or managed by the child.

Pain

Pain was the second category abstracted. If any one factor could be designated as having the greatest influence on behavior, it would be pain. Pain was not only present as the children lay quietly in bed but accompanied almost every move they made, every nursing measure used in their care, and every therapy ordered by the physician.

Pain, although primarily related to the burn experience, is also related to the isolation experience. Like isolation, pain may be viewed as punishment. When the two occur simultaneously they may compound the child's distress. Aloneness may be sought by the child in a private room to escape additional pain inflicted by nurses in their therapeutic activity.

The most intense pain occurred with the direct care of the burn wound. Regardless of the therapy, all of the children responded, particularly during the first weeks, with hysterical screaming. Some, as time progressed, became less tolerant of the pain. Fifty-two days postburn, Jane screamed with greater forcefulness than previously observed. She said it hurt more. It was 85 days postburn when Larry screamed during his dressing change that he wanted to die. He kept repeating, "Oh God, I love you," and cried for God to heal his skin. In the last weeks before her death, Sherri not only screamed but physically resisted being placed in the tub. Previously she was somewhat controlled, screaming only occasionally.

Several strategies were used by the children to cope with the pain. Postponement was used most often. Jane frequently stated that she needed to rest when it was time for tubbing and a dressing change. At times she insisted on going to the bathroom just as she was to go into the tub. Jennifer was overheard pleading with her nurse not to be first into the tub. Sherri once wanted to wait 6 weeks before having her dressing changed. Larry tried to postpone pain-producing situations by asking if nurses were acting on doctor's orders.

Attempts to bypass was a strategy used less frequently. Jane once asked her nurse to "just pretend" to do the dressing change. Jane, Sherri, and Larry often used this strategy when routine care, including position changes, was to be carried out. Sherri once said she did not need to go into the tub. She reasoned that she did not have a bath every day at home.

Jane and Sherri used strategies to reduce the threat of pain. During a dressing change, Jane would repeat over and over, "Don't hurt me." Sherri would say in a pleading voice, "Go easy. Go very, very easy."

Jane was noted only once to use distraction to cope with pain. A nurse read a story to her while tubbing was in progress. Jane screamed only intermittently during the procedure and appeared to listen. When asked later if she had listened to a story when she was in the tub, she said she had not because she was too busy screaming. Kenny used this strategy effectively when he asked me to hold his hand and to be told what to talk about. Larry was the only child observed trying to create distance between himself and the threat of pain. Toward the end of his hospitalization, when told that his dressing needed to be changed, Larry screamed that he did not want it done because it hurt. He asked to have his covers and pillow removed so that he could get out of bed; physically, he was unable to accomplish that.

When the children needed to move, if at all possible they preferred to do it on their own. Larry made a most revealing comment, "When people help, they hurt."

Sherri associated screaming with pain and burns. Once when she heard someone scream on a television in another part of the ward, she asked if someone was being burned and if the house was on fire. When asked if she had screamed when she had been burned, she replied that she had, a little, because it had hurt.

Loss

Loss was the third category abstracted from the data. Loss as a concept was viewed as relating equally to isolation and to the burn experience. That contrasts with aloneness, which related primarily to the isolation experience, and with pain, which related primarily to the burn experience. This critical category was divided into four classes: 1) loss of the bodily self by death, 2) loss of parents through separation, 3) loss of control over self and the environment, and 4) loss of attractiveness and body integrity.

First and foremost for the severely burned children was the possible loss of self by death. Death for the school-age child in contrast to the younger child is seen as something final and personal. Jane talked extensively to a variety of people about her fear of death. Larry talked at length about the death of an elderly patient in the burn unit. He did not talk openly of the possibility of his own death, but his statement that he would not go home reflected his fear of dying.

Loss was experienced by all of the children as hospitalization and isolation brought temporary separation from parents. For four of the children, distance between home and hospital curtailed family visits for all or part of the hospitalization. Even when parents were present, the extensive nature of each child's burn limited physical contact. Gowns, masks, and occasionally gloves added another dimension of physical separation.

Loss of control over themselves and their environment was identified as a common factor in the experience of all the children. Loss of control resulted from the burn wound itself. Mobility was limited to varying degrees depending on the location of the burn and the grafting procedure. Even some of the most elemental body movements were severely restricted or precluded, constituting a special form of loss. Jane, Larry, and Sherri initially were unable to use their hands and consequently were completely dependent on others. Isolation precautions imposed controls, even when mobility was possible. Treatments for the children in the burn unit, and to a considerably lesser degree for Jane alone in a room, were carried out with little or no adjustment to the child's wishes.

Lastly, there was a deep concern over loss of attractiveness and body integrity resulting from the raw oozing burn wound. Examples of concern over body image include Sherri's statement that she would be nice again when she got her new skin, Jane's ostrichlike position to hide her face, and Larry's concentration on medical books that showed progressive changes following a severe burn.

Each of the three key categories, although seen as relating to both the burn and the isolation experience, were also seen as relating to each other. For example, separation from parents resulting from hospitalization and isolation led to a sense of devastating loss for the child. Loss of parents coupled with the unshareable pain of the burn experience was a major factor contributing to the awful sense of aloneness.

Stages of Passage

When observations were concluded on five children—Jane, Larry, Sherri, Kenny, and Jennifer—it was found that all of the events in the experience could be arranged into a social-psychological sequence consistent with chronological sequence. Three stages were discovered in the total sequence of events. The three key concepts—aloneness, pain, and loss—could in turn be examined in the light of the defined stages.

Stage I (Agony) begins with hospitalization and ends when the child senses he or she is improving and will survive. During Stage I the child is focused almost exclusively on self and pain. Relationships with others not directly related to his or her condition are limited or nonexistent. There is a need and desire for the presence of parents, particularly mother. Fear of death may or may not be verbally expressed and is related to the extent and severity of the burn.

Stage II (Hope) begins when the child senses he or she is improving and will survive. The stage ends when a fairly definite time for discharge has been designated. During Stage II the child is no longer centered exclusively on self. Relationships begin to develop with others not directly related to the burn. The child becomes involved in play activities, even if to a limited degree. Separation from mother is more readily tolerated, except at critical points such as surgery. Spirits improve and the child becomes generally more outgoing. There is an even more marked change for the child in a private room, where isolation restrictions are removed, in comparison with the child in the burn unit, where physical surroundings are not altered.

Stage III (Reorganization) begins when a date for discharge is set and ends when the child leaves the hospital for home. During this stage there is a focusing on body image and the child expresses concerns about changes in body appearance. This signifies anticipation of altered relations with acquaintances who have not "kept up" with changes in the burned child's appearance. The extensively burned child who has been hospitalized for a prolonged period begins to pull away from dependency on the hospital.

A CONCEPTUAL MODEL

The final step in the analytic process, after identifying key concepts and relating them to the sequential order, was the development of a conceptual model of the passage through hospitalization of a severely burned, isolated school-age child. The beginning point of the passage is after accident that results in a hospitalized child severely burned and isolated. The child moves through three stages toward the goal of recovery and discharge from the hospital. While recovery is the goal, death is possible in any one of the three stages, although decreasingly so. The child's behavior throughout the passage is influenced by many factors, including the circumstances of the accident, age and developmental level, personal characteristics, and past experiences, as well as interaction with parents, staff, other patients, and other persons while in the hospital. The pain, sense of aloneness, and feelings of loss experienced during hospitalization and stemming from the burn and the state of isolation, exert the dominant influence on behavior. Figure 21-1 diagrammatically represents the above description and interrelationship. The model was tentatively tested by observations of the sixth child, Julie. Although she was slightly less than 6 years old and was less extensively and severely burned than the first five children, her behavior substantially fit the conceptual model.

FINDINGS AND IMPLICATIONS FOR NURSING AND RESEARCH

The research produced a vast amount of rich and exciting data, which also prompted numerous questions needing further study.

Stages of Passage

The major outcome of the study was the conceptual model of the passage of a severely burned school-age child through initial hospitalization. Such a model could prove extremely valuable to nurses and other members of the health team who plan and implement care of the severely burned child. It should be equally valuable for parents in helping them to understand and cope with their child's behavior. Although the data indicate that the model does describe the stages of passage through which the severely burned school-age child moves, there is a need for further testing. The testing should include not only children of different ages, but children with burns of varying extent and severity. Use of the model by health personnel would depend on the results of additional testing.

Further study of the model is needed in several areas. Each child did not fit the model in every respect. Extent, severity, and location of the burn were set forth as

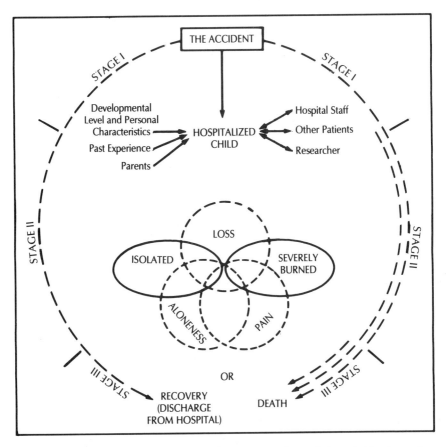

Figure 21-1. A conceptual model of the passage through hospitalization of a severely burned school-age child. Redrawn after Batey M (ed): Communicating Nursing Research: Critical Issues in Access to Data. Denver, Western Interstate Commission for Higher Education, 1975

probably explanations for the differences. Other significant variables may also account for the differences. Staff expectations could be a crucial factor. For example, in the burn unit the child was not encouraged to express feelings. It is possible that the child in such a setting would not talk about a fear of death.

Further study is needed to identify those cues that lead a child to perceive that he or she is improving and will survive, and that move him or her from Stage I to Stage II. Covering of the burn with grafts and removal of isolation restrictions were identified as signals to the child of hopeful change in the situation; yet there must also be more subtle cues that help the child move to the next stage.

While several factors were identified as having an influence on the child's behavior, no conclusive statements can be made because of the study design and the limited number of subjects in the study. A number of questions were raised as a result of observations relating to the conceptual model. They include:

1. What are the factors that influence the way nurses relate to severely burned children? More specifically, why do some nurses encourage the children to express their feelings by crying during pain-producing experiences, whereas others maintain that a painful procedure does not hurt? Furthermore, is there any difference in the length of recovery time and the emotional trauma experienced by children who are encouraged to express themselves, as opposed to those who are not encouraged to do so?
2. What conditions must exist before children will express their concerns?
3. Are severely burned children more likely to express their concerns to a person not involved in pain-producing care?
4. What factors elicit fear of death: the extent of the burn, the severity of the burn, the area involved, the reaction of others, the circumstances surrounding the accident, the nature of treatment, the amount of pain?
5. Is it desirable, even in a permissive atmosphere, to have at least one member of the health team who demands that the children control their behavior—(e.g., the surgeon who controlled Jane's behavior by threatening to stop caring for her if she screamed)?
6. Do children feel more secure when controls are placed on their behavior?
7. Are severely burned children frightened and disturbed by the gowns and masks worn by those who come in contact with them?
8. Do the severely burned children understand the rationale for the isolation precautions?
9. What process do the children who have been hospitalized for a prolonged time go through in preparation to leave the hospital and return home?

Aloneness

The data provide evidence that feelings of aloneness do exist when children are alone by themselves in a room. There is also evidence that the experience may be distasteful and cause them to use strategies to bring people to them and keep them there. This finding supports the commonly held belief that being alone is unpleasant and undesirable. The data also suggest, however, that there are times when severely burned children are not distressed by aloneness and may actually choose it. It may well be that aloneness has definite positive effects during certain phases of the passage, such as Stage I. Related questions include:

1. Are there times when aloneness has therapeutic benefit for severely burned children?
2. When and for how long does one allow such a child to choose aloneness?
3. Is the recovery time longer for children isolated alone in a room than for children in a burn unit?

Sensory Deprivation versus Sensory Overload

The observations indicated that sensory overload rather than sensory deprivation was the predominant condition for the children, particularly in Stage I and for those isolated in the burn unit. Even for the children alone in a room, the nature of the illness required many procedures and people involved in their care. Consequently, none of the children lacked contact with people. Sensory overload was also related to the intense pain that was a constant companion through much of the hospitalization. The physical environment for the children, even when alone in a room, was not devoid of visual and auditory stimulation. Television, radio, record player, mobiles, and pictures on the wall were present. The children were often deprived of touch experiences.

The question most needing an answer is, What is the relationship between sensory overload and recovery rate? Other questions include, Do members of the health team caring for a severely burned, isolated child perceive the situation as one of sensory overload or deprivation? Do they consider these factors in planning and implementing care? Is sensory overload related to the severely burned child's occasional desire for aloneness? How does the quality and quantity of sensory overload and sensory deprivation vary in each of the three stages? What strategies does the child use to cope with sensory overload?

A related problem is perceptual deprivation. It stems not only from isolation restrictions but from immobility. As with sensory overload and sensory deprivation, a question arises as to the relationship between perceptual deprivation and rate of recovery. What measures are taken to prevent perceptual deprivation? Do children find hospitalization less distressing when perceptual deprivation is avoided?

Control

All of the children in the study experienced a loss of control over themselves and their environment. This loss of control was related to both the burn and the state of isolation.

All six children were confined to bed initially, and four were dependent on others for every aspect of their care for a number of weeks. The children given some control over when and how something was to be done appeared to tolerate the situation more readily and were able to cooperate with the plan of care. Questions relating to control are:

1. What factors deprive hospitalized children of control of themselves and their environment?
2. How is control sought by severely burned, isolated children?
3. Are there similarities in the way these patients seek control compared with children with other diagnoses in other settings?
4. How do staff react to strategies used by the children to control a situation?
5. Is there a relationship between having a degree of control and the ability to cope with pain?

6. Do children with restricted mobility have a greater need to control the environment and their body functions that they are capable of controlling than do ambulatory children?
7. Do attempts for this control by severely burned children vary at different stages in the hospitalization?

Parents

In all three settings, parents were not restricted from being with their children because of the isolation precautions. Parents were cooperative about carrying out the procedures. The observations indicate there is evidence that hospitals are not warranted in restricting parents from entering isolation areas. There was no indication, as had been anticipated as a result of prior observations, that parents were distressed by or focused on the isolation aspect of their child's hospitalization. No parent was known to question the rationale for the isolation procedure.

Parents of children in the burn unit became involved with the other children and communicated freely with them. For some, the friendships continued even after the children were no longer hospitalized. There appeared to be a bond between the parents and a sharing of concerns and feelings.

Several inferences may be made about parents. The data indicate that the parents are able to function in difficult and trying situations and can assist in meeting the needs of their child. Frequently the strength and abilities of parents are underestimated by health personnel and are not used in the care of the acutely ill child. In the burn unit, children received attention from other parents as well as their own. Perhaps these children experienced fewer emotional problems as a result of interactions with other parenting adults. A study should be made of the effect of communication between parents who are experiencing similar problems. Do parents with a child in a hospital where no other burned children may be at the time need a different type of support from staff than those parents whose child is in a burn unit? There is evidence from the limited observations after discharge that parents of children in the burn unit continued to communicate with each other. Study is needed to understand the values gained from this continued relationship.

SUMMARY

The conclusion of the study of severely burned, isolated children was in essence only the beginning. Aside from the numerous questions raised that open possibilities for future research, there is the need for further test of the conceptual model. For the researcher, and hopefully for the reader, the study afforded a graphic and dramatic picture of the experience of severely burned, isolated children and their families during initial hospitalization after a truly catastrophic occurrence.

EPILOGUE

I wish to acknowledge the role that Eugenia Waechter played in this study of school-aged children hospitalized with a severe burn. Gene first and foremost was my teacher. She opened the world of theory and research and the relation of both to clinical practice in her course in the development of the school-aged child. Later she served as a member of my doctoral dissertation committee. This chapter is in part the result of her input into that research. Her thoughtful critique and guidance along with that of the other members of the committee, Betty Highley—Chairperson, Leonard Schatzman, and John Bruvold, launched my research career. Questions raised in this exploratory work have led me to examine the coping strategies of school-aged children hospitalized for a surgical procedure and more recently to study school-aged children's and adolescents' descriptions of the pain experience. Currently, I am co–principal investigator of a study to develop and test a tool for assessing pain in school-age children and young adolescents.

REFERENCES

Andreason NJC, Noyes R, Hartford CE et al: Management of emotional reactions in seriously burned adults. N Engl J Med 286:65–69, 1972
Brodies B, Matern S: Emotional aspects in the care of a severely burned child. Int Nurs Rev 14:19–24, 1967
Bullough B: Where should isolation stop? Am J Nurs 62:86–89, 1962
Burke JF: Isolation techniques and their effectiveness. In Polk HC, Stone HH (eds): Contemporary Burn Management. Boston, Little, Brown, 1971
Byerly EL: The nurse researcher as participant–observer in a nursing setting. Nurs Res 18:230–236,1969
Glaser BG, Strauss AL: The Discovery of Grounded Theory. Chicago, Aldine, 1967
Hamburg DA, Hamburg B, deGoza S: Adaptive problems and mechanism in severely burned patients. Psychiatry 16:1–20, 1953
Leiderman H, Mendelson JA, Wexler D et al: Sensory deprivation: Clinical aspects. Arch Int Med 101:389–396, 1958
Long RL, Cope O: Emotional problems of burned children. N Engl J Med 264:1121–1127, 1961
Loomis WG: Management of children's emotional reactions to severe body damage (burns). Clin Ped 9:362–367, 1970
Marks J, Ganzer V, Collins LG et al: Personal differences in perceptual deprivation. Arch Gen Psychiatr 19:146–154, 1968
Marlow DR: Textbook of Pediatric Nursing. Philadelphia, WB Saunders, 1969
Pidgeon VA: Children's Concepts of the Rationale of Isolation Technique. In ANA Clinical Sessions 1966. New York, Appleton–Century–Crofts, 1967
Prioleau WH: Psychological considerations in patient isolation on a general surgical service. Am Surg 29:907–908, 1963
Quinby S, Bernstein NR: Identity problems and the adaptation of nurses to severely burned children. Am J Psychiatr 128:90–95, 1971
Schatzman L, Strauss AL: Field Research-Strategies for a Natural Sociology. Englewood Cliffs, NJ, Prentice-Hall, 1973
Stoll CP: Responses of Three Girls to Burn Injuries and Hospitalization. Nurs Clin N Am 4:77–87, March 1969
Strauss AL, Glaser BG: Anguish—A Case History of a Dying Trajectory. Mill Valley, CA, Sociology Press, 1970
Vernon JA: Inside the Black Room. New York, Clarkson N. Potter, 1963
Ziskind E: Isolation stress in medical and mental illness. JAMA 168:1427–1431, 1958
Zuckerman M: Perceptual isolation as a stress situation. Arch Gen Psychiatr 11:255–276, 1964

22 · Dying Children: Patterns of Coping

Eugenia H. Waechter

INTRODUCTION

Until ten years ago, no systematically controlled research had been done directly with children to determine their awareness of a life threatening condition. Former conclusions about the impact of illness on children were based on observations of them and their parents and on indirect evidence drawn from anecdotal data provided by hospital personnel. Although there was general agreement that adolescents were aware of the potential outcome of their illness, and were anxious and concerned about body integrity, it was assumed that children under the age of ten years were not aware of their diagnosis or prognosis and had little or no anxiety about their bodies or the future. This conclusion was based on previous research concerned with the development of the concept of death in normal, well children which indicated that a mature concept of death is not formed in children until after the age of nine years [1,2]. These findings were based on a Piagetian framework. The reasoning then followed that children do not have concerns about future body integrity until they have reached this age of understanding. Therefore, professionals working with children with life threatening illnesses assumed that the findings with healthy children also applied to their patients and reasoned that if adults did not discuss the seriousness of their illness with them, they would experience no anxiety. This concept was somewhat supported by the fact that young children rarely questioned their caretakers directly about death.

From Wass H, Corr C: Childhood and Death. Washington, DC, Hemisphere Publishing, 1983.

THE DYING CHILD'S AWARENESS OF DEATH

Early Assumptions

Based on these studies and the derived reasoning, a widespread closed clinical approach was advocated by physicians during the 1950s and 60s to the effect that disruptions of this natural order for readiness to deal with feelings of death would be harmful to the child [3,4]. Physicians widely counseled parents to maintain a sense of normality in the family and shield children from the realization of the seriousness of their illness, and assumed a cheerful manner that things would soon be well [5,6].

Other clinicians, however, contested the practice of shielding children from knowledge of their illness giving rise to a "to tell or not to tell" controversy. It was their contention that maintaining silence was an unrealistic burden for parents which would result in greater problems for the child, since he would be able to sense this withdrawal by parents and lose trust in them.

Vernick and Karon [7] were among the first to challenge the protective approach in their observational study of older school-aged children in a leukemia ward. They suggested that all their patients were afraid and anxious despite lack of specific knowledge. They further suggested that children sense adults' discomfort with the topic of death and learn not to ask disturbing questions. This lack of trust in the veracity of caregivers in their view led to further anxiety, withdrawal and need for greater emotional support. They were convinced that, "Every child who is lying in bed gravely ill is worrying about dying and is eager to have someone help him talk about it. If he is passive it may only be a reflection of how freely the environment encourages him to express his concerns" (p. 395).

From his clinical experience, Solnit [8] also disagreed with the closed approach and observed that his young patients invariably sensed what was happening, even when deliberate attempts were made to shield them from this tragic and frightening situation. He suggested that adults are blinded to the fears of dying children because of their own anxiety.

As a result of clinical interactions with young leukemia children and their parents, Binger et al. [9] agreed with the contentions of Vernick and Karon, and reported that, "Most children above 4 years of age, although not told directly of their diagnosis, presented evidence to their parents that they were well aware of the seriousness of their disease and even anticipated their premature death" (p. 415). They suggested that these young patients attempted to communicate their concerns through behavior and symbolic questions.

FIRST SYSTEMATIC AND CONTROLLED STUDIES

The first direct, systematic and controlled study of children with life threatening illness was conducted by Waechter [10]. In order to elicit expression of the child's concerns about present and future body integrity, Waechter studied 64 children between the ages of 6 and 10 years inclusive through the use of a projective test and anxiety scale. These children were divided into four groups: 1) children with chronic disease for which death was predicted, 2) children with chronic disease with a good prognosis, 3) children with brief illness, and 4) non-hospitalized, well children. Children between groups were matched as to sex, age, race, social class and family background. Children within the fatal group fell into four categories by diagnosis: 1) leukemia, 2) other neo-plastic disease, 3) cystic fibrosis, and 4) progressive septic granulomatosis.

The study was carried out while the first three groups were hospitalized for treatment for diagnosis. The children within the fatal group were matched with subjects within the other three groups for sex, age, race, and social class.

A set of eight pictures was shown individually to each child and stories requested in order to elicit fantasy expression of the child's concern regarding present and future body integrity and functioning. Four of the pictures were selected from the Thematic Apperception Test and four were specifically designed for the study depicting hospital situations involving children and caretakers.

The stories were scored with attention to content related to threat or fear of death, body mutilation or loneliness, to the methods used in the story to cope with threat and to the problems anticipated in the reduction of insecurity. The measurement of fear was based on the same general rationale utilized in the scoring of other motives under the view that fear of bodily harm is a motive.

The General Anxiety Scale for Children as designed by Sarason and associates [11] was administered to each hospitalized child in the study. Previously determined normalized scores for well children were used for comparison with the scores received by the hospitalized groups.

A tape recorded, semi-structured interview was held with the parents of each hospitalized child in the study. The purpose of the interview was to elicit information regarding the following variables deemed significant to the amount of death anxiety expressed by the child: 1) the amount of verbal interaction with the ill child as to his diagnosis and prognosis, 2) the child's previous experience with illness and death, 3) the religious training which the child had received, and 4) the warmth of the mother–child relationship.

Analysis of the data from the General Anxiety Scale for Children indicated that the mean score for fatally ill subjects was almost double that of the two comparison groups of hospitalized children and three times the score of healthy children as presented by Sarason. This finding supported the prediction that children aged 6 to 10 years with a diagnosis for which death was predicted expressed significantly more ($p > 0.01$) generalized anxiety than did children who did not have a poor prognosis.

Analysis of the children's stories also supported the prediction that the dying children would express significantly more anxiety specifically related to death, mutilation and loneliness than other ill children. A χ square test of significance between proportions of the groups telling unrelated stories was found to be greater than 0.01. These findings indicated that the subjects were more preoccupied with threats to body integrity even though only 2 children within the fatal group had been told of their diagnosis.

The test of significance of differences of proportions of subjects using fear-related imagery in their scoreable stories indicated that the children with fatal illnesses used both loneliness and death imagery more frequently than all comparison groups at a significance level of 0.001. It seemed possible therefore that the concern with loneliness was also related to the concern about death.

Judgments were made on the basis of the maternal interview regarding the opportunities the child had had to discuss the nature of his illness with parents or professional personnel. Most parents felt very strongly about this question. A few felt that their child should know as much as possible about his illness, whereas most went to great lengths to insure that the diagnosis would not be mentioned to their child by hospital personnel. Many parents felt unable to cope with the feelings which a frank discussion about the possibility of imminent death would arouse. As previously indicated, only 2 children with fatal illness had discussed their imminent death with their parents, six had received little realistic information regarding their illness, and the remainder had been informed that their illness was temporary or trivial.

The dichotomy in the degree of awareness on the part of the child as inferred from his imagination stories and the parents' belief as to the child's awareness was often striking. Although only the two subjects had discussed their concerns about death with their parents, the percentage of death imagery in stories containing threat was found to be 63 percent. Many of the children who had not been told their diagnosis nevertheless indicated awareness of knowledge of the diagnosis or symptoms in their imaginative stories. In all of the protocols, the degree to which the characters in the story were given the subject's personal diagnosis and symptoms was striking.

The correlation between the child's opportunity to discuss his illness, and the anxiety score on the projection test was found to be $r = 0.633$ which was significant at the 0.01 level. This finding indicates that those children with fatal illness who had had a greater opportunity to discuss their fears and concerns about their future and present body integrity expressed less specific death anxiety. This finding supported the hypothesis that understanding acceptance or permission to discuss any aspect of his illness may decrease feelings of isolation, alienation and the sense that the illness is too terrible to discuss.

The findings of this study indicated that despite efforts to protect children from knowledge of their prognosis, they had considerable preoccupation with death in fantasy when given the opportunity, along with feelings of loneliness and isolation and a sense of lack of control of the forces impinging on them. It was suggested that the child perceives the threat through the altered affect in his total environment and from parental anxiety communicated in non-verbal ways. The data also suggested that adults may be blinded to the child's anxiety because of personal fears and concerns and a sense of helplessness related to the diagnosis. Further, even though the child may not have achieved a mature concept of death, the threat to body integrity was nonetheless communicated.

A study by Spinetta et al. [12] was conducted to test Waechter's conclusion about the higher level of anxiety in fatally ill, hospitalized children. This study also utilized a control group of non-fatally but chronically ill children—the two groups being matched for frequency and intensity of hospital experiences. In the study, 25 children aged 6 to 10 with a diagnosis of leukemia were matched in age, sex, race, grade in school, seriousness of the condition, and amount of medical interaction with 25 children with such chronic illnesses as diabetes, asthma, congenital heart disease, and renal problems.

The children were asked to tell stories about each of the four pictures designed by Waechter, and about each of four figurines (nurse, doctor, mother, father) placed in a three-dimensional replica of a hospital room. Each child was also given a brief anxiety questionnaire sorting out hospital anxiety from home anxiety.

This study supported the Waechter findings in that the leukemia children related significantly more stories that indicated preoccupation with threat to, and intrusion into their bodies, both in the stories relating to the pictures and the stories told about the placed figurines. The children with fatal illness also expressed more hospital-related and non-hospital related anxiety than did the chronically ill children.

Although the parents of these children maintained that the children did not know their illness was fatal, as was the case in Waechter's study, there was a significant difference in the level of anxiety that was present from the very first admission to the hospital. Spinetta also concluded that despite efforts to keep the child with fatal illness from becoming aware of his prognosis, he somehow feels a sense that his illness is not ordinary, but very threatening.

In a later study [13], Spinetta investigated the question, "Does awareness of the seriousness of their illness persist with the fatally ill children when they are not in the hospital?" Using the same instruments as in the previous study, he tested 32 children between the ages of 6 and 10 years attending outpatient clinics for treatment of leukemia and other non-fatal chronic illnesses. Again, he found a significantly greater pre-occupation with loneliness and with threat to body integrity and functioning than did the control group of chronically ill children. He also found that the younger chronically ill children had a level of anxiety relative to the outpatient clinic that diminished with age, whereas the leukemia childrens' anxiety relative to those attending the outpatient clinic increased with age at a significant level.

NEWER TREATMENT DEVELOPMENTS

Since the early Waechter study, however, the definitions and prognoses of fatal illness have altered considerably. The diagnosis of cancer no longer automatically means impending death. Because of major successes in medicine in treating some kinds of childhood cancer, more and more children with this disease have the chance to become adults. At least half of the 6000 children expected to develop cancer in the United States next year are likely to survive many years, thanks to improved radiation and chemical therapy.

These illnesses which were once acutely fatal, have now become chronic life threatening conditions. However, despite the positive success of increased life spaces, new problems have emerged in relation to the quality of life which concern parents and professionals engaged with them and their children. Parents face much ambiguity and uncertainty related to making treatment decisions, integrating the ill child into the mainstream of the community, and the child's education. Maintaining constructive peer relationships has become increasingly important as has the long term effects of treatment on the child's physical and psychosocial development. Parents are encouraged to devote their energies toward the issues of life and to hope for prolonged remission or cure. On the other hand, they must be told that death is also a possibility and that which of the two alternatives will occur may not be known for a number of years. These parents and children now sit under a modern sword of Damocles, which is, understandably, a powerful source of stress.

Despite the greater openness in our society related to death, the social stigma of cancer does not seem to have altered substantially in the past ten years. Cancer is still seen as a mysterious, often fatal disease. Parents often complain of the treatment they receive from former associates and their children are often shunned by former playmates. Such responses are still sometimes due to a fear of contagion. More frequently, they are due to a continuing unease with "what to say" and the child's uncertain future. Confrontations with life threatening illness also often evoke personal fears of mortality.

CURRENT STUDIES

In a current study, Waechter and her associate interviewed the parents of 56 children between the ages of 4 and 10 years who were under outpatient treatment. All but a few of these parents responded that they felt they should be open with their children. All reported discussing aspects of treatment with their children, although some parents, particularly those with very young children were more guarded in discussing the prognosis. However, if the child asked questions about death, no parent stated that they avoided or refused to discuss them. Most of these children were under medical care which espouses the open approach and many were included in the conferences physicians held with their parents.

Almost all parents stated that their children over 5 years of age also learned much about their illness from other children and from professionals on the wards and outpatient clinics. The amount learned and the quickness of learning appeared to be related to age, the acuteness of the illness, and the degree of openness espoused by the particular medical setting. Older children with an illness having a faster course treated in an open setting were able to answer the most questions in greater detail about tests, symptoms and diagnosis. Most of this knowledge stemmed from the induction phase of the illness. These children, however, did not necessarily also speak freely about their prognosis. Some children talked openly about their possible deaths, whereas others stated that they would rather not know too much about the future since it would cause them to worry more. Almost all children over six years of age stated that their mothers worried about them, whereas only a few felt that they could or should share all their worries freely with their parents.

Some children as young as four years of age indicated awareness of the seriousness of their illness. Although children of this age may not ask as many questions of their parents regarding causality, diagnosis and prognosis, many give behavioral clues of fears and concerns. Most mothers of four- and five-year-old children described changes in their child's behavior after the diagnosis was made even though the child was physically doing well. One mother of a four-year-old girl described her daughter's unruliness and their initial tolerance of her behavior after a diagnosis of leukemia had been made: "I think she really thought to herself, 'I must be pretty sick if I can get away with this kind of behavior.' You have an urge to do everything possible you can right now and the hell with anyone else, but as soon as you see the changes aren't good—bah, she was horrible."

In an effort to discover whether the greater hope given to parents at the time their child was diagnosed as having a life threatening illness would reduce the child's preoccupation with body integrity, the children in Waechter's current study were asked to tell stories in response to eight pictures. Four of these were drawn from the Thematic Apperception Test and four were designed for the study.

In addition to eliciting attitudes and concerns about treatment procedures, the stories also contained much imagery relating to loneliness, mutilation and death. Those children with life threatening illnesses told stories containing such imagery significantly more (p = 0.001) than did the matched children with other chronic illnesses. Thus it appears that despite the greater hope offered to parents, the children were still greatly concerned about the integrity of their bodies in the present and for the future.

CONCERNS AND COPING PATTERNS OF CHILDREN WITH LIFE THREATENING ILLNESS

Concerns communicated by children, either verbally or through their behavior are related to their cognitive preceptions of events as well as to the relationship between illness and treatment effects and the developmental tasks of the period. Concerns may also be related to the specific diagnosis and its implications and the severity of the illness. Coping patterns are also related to the child's developmental capacities as well as to innate individual differences and prior experiences.

THE PRESCHOOL CHILD

Causality of Illness

Although young children rarely ask why they have become ill, they often have their own convictions. Because of immature concepts of causality, they often assume responsibility for their illness and may feel guilt in addition to their many other fears and concerns. This was supported in the author's current study as children under six years of age tended to assign the cause of illness to some aspect of their own behavior, either of commission or omission related to obeying parental mandates.

Young children are convinced that nothing happens by chance, and that retribution follows as swiftly for "bad behavior" as it does for breaking a physical law of nature. They are also convinced that if they have been punished, it was justified by their bad behavior or thoughts. It is a small step from the concept, "I have been bad" to "I am bad." Certainly nothing can seem more punishing than abandonment and rejection by parents in the frightening, new world of the hospital and some of the procedures with which they are confronted. This is illustrated in a story told by a four-year-old: "That's a little boy just sitting there. Somebody killed a bird. He's thinking about the dead bird. The bird got killed because the bird was bad. The boy is a bad boy too—so something is going to happen to him."

Where these internal convictions are unvoiced, they may be inadvertently reinforced by adults. In attempts to protect the child from knowledge of the possible future and the purpose of painful treatment which seemingly continues indefinitely, adults convey to the child a quality of punishment which strengthens the belief in his or her own unworthiness.

When hospitalized, therefore, young children tend to blame themselves for this rejection and may respond with guilt, sadness, and withdrawal. In rejection of their own angry thoughts, they see professional personnel as also hostile to them. Young children also believe that others can read their thoughts as they themselves can, and therefore expect retaliation in further punishment. This also extends to their parents in that they are angry at them for their desertion despite their need for them.

Because of their feelings of guilt and self-blame for the punishment, "I deserve," some young children will keep their feelings inside themselves and become even more withdrawn from others. It is also frightening to be angry at people on whom they depend and cannot do without. Other children may direct the anger they feel toward their parents, to other children or adults in their hospital environment. This may earn them avoidance or disciplinary measures which confirm their wickedness.

Preschool children who are hospitalized need their parents to cope with these emotions. They must have reassurance from their parents that they have not been abandoned or rejected. Parents must also emphasize that they are not angry with the child and miss him when they cannot be with him. The child needs confirmation of his parents' love in order to regain a sense of worth.

The young child cannot cope constructively without the physical and emotional support of his parents. He is cognitively unable to understand the cause and effect relationship between his illness and treatment procedures. Nor is he able to comprehend all of the alterations in his former patterns of living and the pain he is forced to endure. Only with the support and presence of his parents will he be able to openly express his anger and resentment. It is the secure child, and self-confident child, who can express such feelings. Children who are uncertain of parental love are unable or afraid of verbalizing such feelings because of the threat of further loss of love.

Anger must be accepted and understood and the child should be reassured that such feelings are not indications of his wickedness. At the same time, the child cannot be allowed to abuse either his parents or professional staff. He will require help in channeling his resentment productively by pounding a peg board or other aggressive play which does not endanger others.

CONCERNS ABOUT THE BODY

Threat to body image may also cause distress to young children at a time when they are beginning to form a concept of self. Whereas healthy children are now becoming comfortable with the functioning of their bodies, the bodies of ill children are under constant assault. The flaws in their own body are also constantly in their attention and they may also need to deal with the side effects of treatment.

Even very young children may be quite concerned about obesity resulting from steroid therapy and loss of hair resulting from chemotherapy. Because of the egocentricity and lack of empathy of children at this age period, their playmates and other children may respond to them in a negative manner which is painful. In an interview the mother of a four-year-old boy commented, "Kids can be cruel sometimes. Like Gene for quite a while was awfully bloated. His stomach was bloated way out and his cheeks were puffed out. He looked like he had perpetual mumps. We took him to the zoo one day and he started to play on a certain toy and there was a little girl there and she said, 'No, go away you fat little boy. You can't play here.' And Gene was really hurt. He started to cry and run to Mommy. It was hard for him."

Loss of hair may be taken in stride by some four year olds, although other children in the later preschool years may be very concerned. Others may not verbalize their feelings, but withdraw from former contacts. It is also possible, that although concerns about body image may not be overtly expressed at ages three to four, such concern may surface at a later date. A mother of a 5-year-old girl reported, "Lately things have been coming up, although she isn't bald now. She'll say, 'Don't stare at me.' She wasn't concerned about being bald a year and a half ago—it's funny—like she'll be in a grocery store and there will be some girls over in the corner laughing and she'll come back to me and say, 'It's 'cause I don't have any hair.' When she did get obese and lose her hair, she was four, she wasn't too concerned about it. But now she sees pictures of herself as she was then and I know she felt a lot of people staring at her. I asked her, 'Well, if you saw somebody bald, wouldn't you look at them?' And she said, 'No, that would make them sad.' I felt, 'Wow, she must have felt bad, although I didn't know it at that time.' " Such children may be forced by such circumstances to move beyond egocentrism at a relatively early age.

Whereas some children cope with hair loss matter-of-factly, by showing their head when they are questioned, parents of other children must prepare their children, to anticipate such confrontations. Providing them with a reply often restores their confidence in meeting playmates.

CONCERN ABOUT TREATMENT PROCEDURES

Most very young children do not appreciate the therapeutic intent of professional personnel and view procedures as hostile and punishing. Because of their own feelings of anger, they also attribute such feelings to those caring for them. With their viewpoint of adults as all powerful, much of what is done to them may appear as merely the whim of the administrator of the treatment. In the current research, previously cited, young children gave significantly fewer stories where the administrator of the treatment felt positively toward the child, and more where the child saw the treatment as an attack. Further, young children told significantly more stories where the child did not know the goal of treatment, and where the child had no choices in the matter.

Young children, because of lack of knowledge as to the purpose of treatment, may fantasize the specifics of a personal attack. One four-year-old boy told the following story after seeing a picture of an intravenous infusion. "This boy has a blood problem. It's a very bad thing and he's not feeling good. The doctor put the tube in. To drain out his blood. He took a whole lot of blood. The boy dies. He gets buried. He feels unhappy because he did not want to die. He is mad at the doctor. He dunno why the doctor did that to him—'cause he wants his blood to test." In this illustration, the child's immature conception of death is also apparent—the child dies but does not cease to exist.

Young children also have vague ideas of internal body functioning, and do not realize things adults often take for granted, such as that their bodies are capable of generating more blood. Repeated withdrawal of blood may imply to them that there will soon be none left. Urgent requests for a bandaid may have the dual purpose of "keeping the blood where it belongs" and of restoring a sense of body wholeness.

Diagnostic and therapeutic procedures may become the battle ground for the child's expression of his feelings of helplessness regarding the entire series of events since a diagnosis of life-threatening illness was made. One mother of a four-year-old boy who fought everyone like a tiger when a procedure was done explained, "I think, personally, that there's so much that he's not had a say about that he uses this time to bring it all out. I think it gets bottled up inside him and he just takes it out on everybody that way and gets rid of it. I think that is it, because he's so young and he didn't have much to say. So this is the way he gets back at everybody—he's fighting the whole thing right there." A child who has developed such a pattern of coping could be described as a "defier, non-complier."

Other children, realizing the inevitability of the procedures, despite their protest, may become passive conformers, though this may increase their sense of helplessness and hopelessness. Their feelings may also surface in indirect ways. One mother of a five-year-old girl who described her daughter as "just laying down and taking bone marrows—very relaxed and calm," later also related "There is a lot under the surface with her—a lot. The other day she had a bad dream about mosquitoes and Dr. Grout sometimes teases her and says, "I'm going to give you a mosquito bite' when he's giving her a shot. Well, she had this dream about hundreds of mosquitoes. I know there is a connection there somewhere . . . they were just all around her trying to bite her. Imagine how terrifying!"

Other children may make a "differentiated protest." Though seeming defiant at the beginning of the treatment, they realize (consciously or unconsciously) that they are dependent on the administration for assistance and survival, and place boundaries around their behavior. Though they may scream, "I hate you" to their physician while he is engaged in the procedure, they may make attempts at amends when the procedure is completed. One mother described her four-year-old's behavior: "But afterwards, they are friends and he still wanted Dr. Kuay to carry him back to his room and tuck him in and give him his teddy bear and sit and talk to him for a couple of minutes. Even though he knows Dr. Kuay has to hurt him once in a while."

Parental expectations, of course, greatly influence a child's response to painful procedures. Such expectations are conveyed to children consistently after initial procedures are done on diagnosis. Some parents are more tolerant of their child's protest, seeing it as natural and expected in terms of the child's age. For example, the mother of the four-year-old who fought like a tiger commented, "Oh, I think its all right to get mad. I don't want him to hurt anybody, but I think this is good for him."

Other parents convey expectations for more conforming behavior. Not only does their child's behavior reflect on them as parents; but they must trust the medical team, and particularly, the physician to ease some of their anxiety about their child's survival. Behavior which might be seen as alienating the administrator can be threatening to parents.

Some children, as young as four years of age, cope with the procedures, their feelings of helplessness and their parents' expectations through developing a pattern of "confronting–controlling." This adaptive pattern is enhanced when professional personnel allow children whatever measures of control are possible in the situation; and when parents are perceptive in timing their preparation of the child for what is to come.

Many parents describe how even very young children prepare themselves through rehearsals, through talking and asking questions and through gathering knowledge of "what is going to happen next." One father of a four-year-old girl related, "She wants to know what days she has to come in for treatment and what days she has off. She sort of prepares herself." A mother of a five-year-old boy described even greater initiative in this process of information gathering. He stated to his parents, "We've got to have a talk and you tell me exactly what they are going to do and what's going to hurt and what to expect."

Many parents have also found, however, however, that because of the young child's immature concept of time, they have needed to pace the timing of informing their child about coming procedures in order to eliminate extensive periods of worry. Shorter periods of time allow the child to mobilize resources without great elaboration of fears with fantasy.

The manner in which the first extensive diagnostic procedures were done at the child's first hospitalization often sets the stage for what is to follow—for better or worse. If the first experiences were excessively traumatic and restricting, each new procedure may reactivate feelings of terror and helplessness. One mother related that her five-year-old daughter "was stuck four times before they could get any blood—they wrapped her in a sheet so she couldn't move. This whole kind of control thing was crammed down her throat before she met Dr. Knox. She was terrible with procedures after that. It was a totally different thing with Dr. Knox and he gave her a lot of room and she was working with him and it worked!"

Another mother of a five-year-old stated, "Well, the first time they gave her a spinal, they tried to put her under, and that was a disaster. She was half-conscious, really terrified—but anytime she feels sort of in control . . ." Other mothers have confirmed that when time is taken with the child during the period of diagnosis and first hospitalization to explain the procedures with patience, truth, and empathy at the child's level of understanding, the child is able to develop trust and a greater sense of adequacy.

The need to trust and the need to control are frequently mentioned variables in the child's response, and increasingly so as the child matures. In parents' words, "Knowing they have something involved in it—they don't feel so helpless." Control over sites of injection, timing, assisting in the procedures whenever possible and permission to express feelings often help enable the very young child to master excessive anxiety and to lessen convictions that the procedures are punitive. Further, the enhancement of the child's self-esteem may assist in coping with other painful experiences in the future.

Following procedures many young children can use some of the equipment in play in order to express their anger and frustrations and to master the feelings of helplessness through personal contact. One mother of a five-year-old related, "He loves to play doctor at home, and they'd let him take the disposable syringe home and practice on his teddy bear. Well, sometimes Pooh isn't good enough and he has to try it on Mommy, because Pooh didn't say "ouch." He'd shove that thing at me—boy he'd really let out his frustrations."

FEARS OF DYING

Although as previously mentioned, many young children do not overtly speak of their own possible death, they may nevertheless have fears and concerns. Although preschool children have an immature concept of death as incomplete and reversible, by the age of four years they nevertheless are aware that other living creatures have become nonexistent. With their frightening convictions related to guilt for past misdeeds, some children may fear that even greater retribution is to follow; that they may not go to Heaven, or that they may be left alone to face the ultimate.

Though preschool children may avoid speaking of death and seem outwardly unworried, they may show their concern in their behavior. Many parents report that their children, though not asking about death, may have nightmares or other behavioral changes, such a greater play aggressiveness, or concern about the death of others. One mother of a four-year-old stated, "I believe that she thinks a lot more than we know." Another mother of a five-year-old reported, "He's so terrified. He's never asked me, but he's got this funny laugh now."

Many other young children may not allow themselves to think of non-existence and not ask questions, suppressing their feelings. For them this is necessary until death is very near. Regression to more infantile behavior then allows them to become very dependent on their parents. At that time, they need the reassurance that they will be cared for and not left alone to face the unknown without support.

THE SCHOOL-AGED CHILD

The school-aged child has many more resources with which to cope with threat. He can communicate his thoughts and feelings verbally to a much greater degree. Although still operating very much in the here and now, he has grown cognitively and can solve problems by thinking as well as by action. He has learned about rules, and is much better able to see cause and effect relationships. He has increasing self-control and is learning cooperation in achieving a goal. Although still in need of parental support, the attitudes of his peers are of great importance and influence his behavior.

Awareness of self has become much more stable as has self assertion. Although still dealing with a sense of inadequacy, problems can be seen as a challenge which he can master with support from peers or adults. This sense of mastery increases self-esteem. On the other hand, he is vulnerable when the problem seems overwhelming, such as disease of his body, which threatens defeat.

With a sense of time as flowing from past to future, he can also imagine an unpleasant future. He is learning about death, and some healthy children become preoccupied with the meaning of this concept. Many have been taught about a hereafter, but this may not be comforting to the child who must look forward to possibly going to Heaven alone and without parental support.

COMMUNICATION OF CONCERNS ABOUT THE FUTURE

Most parents now are advised to discuss their child's questions with him as they arise; particularly at the larger medical centers. Parents reported that almost all of the children between the ages of 6 and 10 in the current study cited earlier asked questions about their future at some time. This generally occurred at the time of diagnosis or relapse and much less often during periods of remission, when the topic was most generally avoided. Some communicated their thoughts and concerns openly, some indirectly, and a few reportedly did not question their prognosis. The amount of direct communication which occurred was related to the openness of the parents to such dialogue and to the relationships within the family. One eight-year-old boy repeatedly asked his parents to tell him if and when he was going to die so that he could prepare himself. At one time he commented to his mother, "Mom, I wouldn't mind dying and going to Heaven, but I'd like to come back." At another time during a conversation with his father who had sensed his concern following a clinic visit, he commented, "I don't want to worry you, Dad. You know Dad, I won't mind dying, but I know you and Mom will miss me so much."

Other children may not be so direct in discussing their thoughts, but seek information indirectly with questions such as Dean voiced after several years of treatment for leukemia, "Am I ever going to get well?" Others speak of death jestingly to test the healer's reaction. When joshed about his talkativeness by his physician, Mark quipped, "Well, you know doctor, there's just so much you have to say in this world before you die."

With increased cognitive capacities, many children question why they were singled out for this calamity. Although some may still express self-blame and guilt for the illness, many others now are able to see external circumstances as the causation factor when the matter is explained honestly. Nevertheless, the specter of punishment still hovers near. Eight-year-old David who had had a bone marrow one day followed by a spinal tap the next day cried, "Mommie, why is God punishing me?" Later he questioned, "Mommy, why did God give this to me? You said God does everything." His mother answered, ". . . maybe, because He know you were a big and strong boy and could take it." At this, David cried and replied, "But Mommy, I'm not a big boy. I'm just a baby." This comment also illustrates a sense of vulnerability and the fear that his abilities might be unequal to the coping tasks ahead. In talking with their children, some parents have been able to elicit concerns about death in order to help their children. The mother of a seven-year-old girl stated that she was talking with her daughter, Gina, one day when her daughter said, weeping, "Momma, if I die and go to Heaven, when you come to Heaven you'll be old and I won't recognize you." The mother replied, "Honey, I'll call your name." And Gina smiled and said no more.

Spinetta and Maloney [13] studied communication patterns in school-aged children with cancer, and its relationship to successful coping. They defined coping as successful attempts on the part of the child to master troublesome situations relative to the illness, a nondefensive personal posture, closeness to parental figures, happiness with oneself and the freedom to express negative feelings within the family. It was an assumption that communication of the child's thoughts and concerns, both happy and painful, was healthier than silence. They hypothesized that the child with more open communication would score as less defensive, express closeness to family members, express happiness with the self, and be more free to express negative feelings. Parents were scored on a 4-point scale as to how much communication occurred within the family. All of the items characterizing successful coping correlated significantly with amount of communication except for freedom to express negative feelings and there was a strong trend in that direction.

Spinetta and Maloney concluded as did Waechter [10] that the choice for silence can lead to denial, and lead to a feeling of rejection and isolation in the child. In contrast, open communication can at the child's own request lead to mutual support among family members. However, Spinetta and Maloney caution that a forced openness too soon for some families can be destructive in that the additional stress may cause maladaptive behavior.

EDUCATION AND SOCIAL RELATIONSHIPS

With the increasing survival rate in the past ten years, the focus of parental concerns regarding the time the child missed from school has changed from providing normality in the child's life to the child's need for education itself in an uncertain future. The importance of school is also stressed as school is the main arena for the child's social relationships.

The need for long term medical supervision in inpatient and outpatient settings results in the loss of four to six weeks of school time within a year for many children. Academic difficulties imposed by this loss of time may be compounded by the child's reluctance to attend school because of negative changes in appearance imposed by treatment and at times, by the fear of separation both on the part of child and parents.

Although there may be teasing and negative response to the ill child by peers, this is not as evident in school-aged children who have the ability for empathy and who are assisted in understanding the reasons for physical changes. However, the changed behavior of the child after diagnosis may induce problems in former peer groups. Deasy [14] found significantly different behavior in children with cancer as opposed to their healthy classmates. These children had difficulty in concentrating, in initiating activities, in attempting new things and in participating in ongoing activities. They were also more lacking in energy, more self-conscious, and worried more. More of these problems were seen in children receiving treatment and in relapse.

Teachers require help and support in dealing with the ill child in the classroom. This experience is generally a new one for the teacher who may not know how to deal with the situation or how to respond. Information about the illness and the particular child's activity patterns is necessary in order to smooth the child's transition back into the classroom. Without information, the teacher may create dual standards for the child as opposed to his peers, thus enhancing the child's sense of inadequacy.

Problems of reintegration after a prolonged absence may be particularly difficult. Many parents are now counselled about the positive value of school in the child's overall adjustment to the illness. Yet their need to protect the child, both physically and psychologically may be in conflict with this goal. In schools where psychological consultation is available, children have less difficulty. In these instances, reintegration of the child can be facilitated by involvement of the school, the parents and the child in preparation of his return.

BODY IMAGE

The increased emphasis placed on the child's involvement with peers and school often compounds the child's concern about his appearance. More vigorous, aggressive therapy now utilized also often produces side effects of a more drastic nature than was seen formerly. Loss of hair, jaundice, stunted growth, obesity or amputation are sources of great distress for the child.

The isolation of children with cancer is a major concern of parents and helping professionals. In the author's current study, four out of five children were isolated to some extent and some were severely withdrawn to the point where they had little contact with peers and others in the community. What this can mean for emotional and social development is obvious.

Children however, can and do learn to cope with social concerns in a variety of ways. Learning to live with baldness can be most difficult, particularly with girls, yet many children do find ways to deal with their classmates' curiosity. Heffron and associates [15] report that one boy who had been given a wig discovered a technique for preventing the teasing of classmates. He would take off his wig and play catch with it! In the author's study, a grandmother described her seven-year-old grandson's response to his loss of hair and how she helped him cope.

Monday, his hair started coming out. The next day there was more and by Wednesday morning, he was completely bald, and believe me, that was trauma! That really was! So we decided a little wig would help a lot, you know. Of course, after we explained to him that it would grow back and when he saw that it didn't show too much under the cap, it wasn't too bad. But then he didn't want us to see him when I put him to bed. He didn't want Grandpa to see him. So I said, "You know, Mark, that Grandpa will not love you any less without your hair." And then I explained to him, "You know, Mark, if you will not take off that cap right away and show the kids, they're going to call you Baldy. You just take off that cap right away and show it to him and then you tell him that it was because of your radiation and your illness and so on and he'll never ask you again."

Well, the funny thing was, he's got these two little boys next door that he plays with and he just loves them. One is about two years older and the other is about two years younger. So he was playing with them and had his little cap. So when he came in to eat his dinner, he said, "Grandma, I showed Mike and Jeff my head." I said, "What did they say?" He said, "They didn't say anything. They wanted to know how come I was bald and I told them it was because I had leukemia."

Some children may use their illness to become manipulative with peers and teachers, as well as with parents and siblings. Parents always have concerns about disciplining their children with life threatening illness. Previously, when life expectancy was relatively brief, parents could rationalize indulging their ill children with the argument that they wished their child to be as happy as possible in the short time available. Even then, however, they encountered problems with their other children who tended to get caught in the cycle of jealousy and guilt, which was excerbated when relatives bestowed special presents and favors on the ill child.

Currently, when life expectancy is much more ambiguous, parents are regularly counselled at the onset of the illness to maintain normalcy for the child in order to support the child's positive view of the future, to prevent sibling problems, and to avoid creating a "social tyrant" who will have trouble in relating to others in the future.

This is a difficult area for parents, since the young cancer patient tends to be manipulative with parents because of hospital experiences and may be difficult to discipline. This difficulty is increased because of the parents' sense of guilt for the illness. Most parents are able to deal with this period of self blame. Others, however, unable to resolve their guilt and engrossed with anticipatory grief, may abdicate this parental responsibility. Severe family problems are usually inevitable. In a recent retrospective study, Gagan and others [16] reported that five or more years after diagnosis of cancer in a child who is still alive, problems with siblings included intensified rivalry, inappropriate feelings of guilt and a sense of exclusion from a significant family crisis.

In the author's current study, all but two parents reported problems with disciplining their ill child. Of those children who had siblings, all parents except one reported sibling problems ranging from mild to severe. These problems ranged from somatic complaints to difficulties with school, peers, family and other relationships. Obviously these deteriorating sibling relationships also negatively affect the fatally ill child.

FURTHER CONCERNS ABOUT HOSPITALIZATION AND PROCEDURES

School-aged children, though gaining increasing independence from parents still need them when ill and are lonely, frightened and sad when hospitalized. However, with support and with increased resources, most are able to cope. They may be angry and direct this hostility toward the treatment team, but when treated with respect and honesty, they are usually able to control themselves and cooperate in the treatment regime. When unable to trust, however, they may become depressed and withdrawn.

School-aged children are still frightened by procedures and many are supported by the presence of their parents or other familiar adults. Control over the situation as much as possible is almost a coping requirement, as is becoming familiar with the environment and equipment. The mother of a seven-year-old reported, "She tells them which finger she wants pricked, she sets up her own tray, goes right through the lab and looks at the microscope." Children of this age may also be much more assertive than preschool children in verbally communicating their opinions on the matter. The mother of the same girl reported on another occasion, "She was not about to have it in her arm, and she let them know it in no uncertain terms, and there was a fight." The administrators of the procedures are also often evaluated as to how much pain is inflicted, and one administrator may be preferred over others. After many repetitions of a procedure, some children seem to acquire the nonchalance of a veteran and will walk into a laboratory stating, "Do you want to use my finger or my arm?" Successful coping in the fact has led to a sense of mastery and enhanced self-esteem.

When hospitalized, many children have the additional concern of loss of status in the peer group, particularly if the absence is to be prolonged. They can be greatly cheered by cards, letters, and visits from their friends and reassured that they are cared about and not forgotten. Often they place these on the walls about their beds, for constant visual assurance of their importance to their friends.

THE ADOLESCENT

There is still much room for research regarding the concept of death during adolescence. Most developmentalists assume that by early adolescence most individuals have reached a level of cognitive growth at which the finality and inevitability of death are comprehensible, though they may not be accepted emotionally. This is true for many adolescents, particularly for those in the middle and late stages of the developmental period. However, it is not true for all. Many individuals have not reached the level of formal thought described by Piaget [17]. Others may have had previous experiences with death which have led to a distortion of the concept. For some, death may still be seen either as a redeemer or as an avenger that punishes for sins committed [18]. For many adolescents, who already have a tendency to feel guilty as they attempt to separate from parents, death may be seen as a confirmation of essential badness. This is reinforced by the inevitable breaking of many family and cultural rules as they test their independence.

THE SENSE OF ISOLATION

In addition to guilt and depression, the adolescent with life threatening illness is also bitter, angry and bewildered. He may know that he has broken many rules, but he is deeply shocked at the magnitude of the punishment which also implies rejection. Because he is resentful toward those people whom he still depends on and cares for deeply, his quiet depression and helplessness deepen. Many dying teenagers feel that no one can understand them, and they face death lonely and alone.

Such a sense of isolation is also a result of separation from the peer group, which has become all-important as the ties to parents and family loosen. This is particularly difficult for those adolescents who have disrupted family bonds abruptly or drastically. Teenagers who have felt deprived or rejected by parents during childhood may, of necessity, become extremely dependent on peers for direction, for support, and for the comfort of companionship. These teenagers are extremely vulnerable when faced with life threatening illness, for the group may be of little help. The serious illness and possible death of a friend is threatening to them in that it points up their own vulnerability and fraility. When body image is a major concern, they are uncomfortable with illness, mutilation or disfigurement. In order to cope with feelings they have not had to face before, they must withdraw from former close relationships.

Dying adolescents also contribute to the loosening of such ties. In defending themselves against the threat of abandonment by friends, they often deny their need for them by emphasizing their own self-sufficiency and independence. Fearing rejection by friends, they may repulse friendly overtures. Feeling very different, they set themselves apart to prevent exclusion and to avoid pity they do not want. If the teenager turns to his parents in his loneliness and need for understanding, he may feel that he is surrendering and returning to a former, outgrown, child-like state. Wanting attention desperately, he may cut himself off from all warmth.

THE BODY AND THE FUTURE

The young adolescent wants to live. Acutely aware of his body, he senses its deterioration. At a time when the whole world is opening up, he learns there is nothing for him. Understandably, the young adolescent is bitter and resentful and asks, "Why me?" "To whom can I assign blame?" Keenly living life, he can appreciate losing everything in dying. He has just come to realize what life can hold when the visions and dreams are snatched away. Not knowing where to direct his anger and bitterness, he often struggles on alone.

Death can only mean defeat for the adolescent on the threshold of mastery. The 16-year-old youth is well aware that death will take away all his physical and mental powers, will strip him of his competency and of his future. The 16-year-old young woman often, in addition, faces the deterioration, deformity, or disfigurement. It is not surprising that young people who are undergoing such major alterations of body image and destruction of hopes have self-doubts and low self-esteem, or that they withdraw from contact with others. This is cruel reality, and the adolescent will reasonably react with anger, bitterness, and helpless rage at the futility of life, because the adolescent at this age has tasted mastery and self-achievement, the deprivation is the greater.

COPING WITH THREAT

Those adolescents, however, who have become more secure in their own individuality may not need to reject their parents as violently as does the young, troubled teenager. With greater self-confidence, they no longer need to defend themselves as strenuously against ease and comfort lest they become children again. Even though they feel bitterness and rage, the need is less intense to direct such feelings against parents, particularly when communication lines have been maintained and concerns can be discussed openly. When such communication lines are closed, however, and the young person is not allowed to disclose feelings, bitter episodes of fighting between adolescent and parents may occur until the adolescent finally becomes severely depressed and withdrawn. Neither side knows how to break the silence, which may last to the end.

When communication is open, the adolescent's rage may periodically erupt against his family, but usually the older teenager will attempt to control and direct these feelings elsewhere. Explosions are usually triggered by changes in treatment procedures, lack of proper explanations, or threats to the adolescent's sense of independence—for example, not allowing him to have a voice in the decisions which concern him. When the adolescent is the last to know about a new therapy which is being considered, he rightly explodes and considers it unfair, for, after all, it is his body, "they're doing it to." Though angry and hurt, he may continue to smile at hospital personnel for fear of being further excluded from decision-making processes in the future.

In coping with the intense threat of premature death, adolescents use much denial, which often permits them to live with their illness. As time progresses, both the adolescent and his family may begin to grieve in anticipation of death. This "grief work" often allows the adolescent to accept, at last, the inevitability of his own death. As death approaches, the world of the adolescent narrows to his bed and to a few loved members of his family. Even the young adolescent is able to accept the caring of warm and loving relations. He can allow himself to be babied, as death grows nearer, as long as he is not treated disrespectfully.

In the terminal phase, adolescents usually select one or two adults to share their thoughts and feelings. Some younger adolescents may resist to the end, lonely and proud, but this is relatively rare. In many cases, as death nears, adolescents show amazing strength, comforting their parents who are in pain and providing meaning to this tragedy by teaching others the value and ideals of living.

REFERENCES

1. Nagy MH: The child's theories concerning death. J Genet Psychol 73:3–27, 1948
2. Kubler–Ross E: On Death and Dying. New York, Macmillan, 1969
3. Green M: Care of the child with a long-term, life threatening illness: Some principles of management. Pediatrics 39:441–445, 1967
4. Natterson JM, Knudson AG: Observations concerning fear of death in fatally ill children and their mothers. Psychosom Med 22:456–465, 1960
5. Evans AE: If a child must die . . . N Engl J Med 273:138–142, 1968
6. Toch R: Management of the child with a fatal disease. Clin Pediatr 3:418–427, 1964
7. Vernick J, Karon M: Who's afraid of death on a leukemia ward? Am J Dis Child 109:393–397, 1965
8. Solnit A, Green MP: The pediatric management of the dying child. Part II. The child's reaction to the fear of dying. In Solnit A, Provence S (eds): Modern Perspectives in Child Development. New York, International Universities Press, 1963
9. Binger CM, Ablin AR, Feuerstein RC et al: Childhood leukemia: Emotional impact on patient and family. N Engl J Med 280:414–418, 1969
10. Waechter EH: Children's awareness of fatal illness. Am J Nurs 71:1168–1172, 1971
11. Sarason S, Lightfall F, Davidson K et al: Anxiety in Elementary School Children. New York, John Wiley & Sons, 1960
12. Spinetta JJ, Rigler D, Karon M: Anxiety in the dying child. Pediatrics 52:841–849, 1973
13. Spinetta JJ, Maloney LJ: Death anxiety in the out-patient leukemic child. Pediatrics 56:1034–1037, 1975
14. Deasy P: The role of the school in the life of the child with cancer. Paper presented at Symposium, "Living with Child Cancer," San Diego, California, February 2, 1980
15. Heffron WA, Bommelaere K, Masters R: Group discussions with parents of leukemic children. Pediatrics 52:831–840, 1973
16. Gagan J: Treating the pediatric cancer patient: A review. J Pediatr Psychol 2:42–46, 1977
17. Inhelder B, Piaget J: The Growth of Logical Thinking from Childhood to Adolescence. New York, Basic Books, 1958
18. Reigh R, Fineberg H: The fatally ill adolescent. In Feinstein S, Giovacchini P, (eds): Adolescent Psychiatry, vol 3. New York, Basic Books, 1974

23 · The Feasibility of Home Care for the Dying Child With Cancer

Ida M. Martinson

Abstract

I studied the feasibility and desirability of a home care alternative to hospitalization for children dying of cancer at a Midwest university. During the 2-year period, 1976 to 1978, 64 dying children and their families participated in home care. This system of home care was directed by nurses with a physician consultant and did not entail extensive participation by other health professionals.

This study suggests that home care at the end stage of cancer is a viable alternative for children when made available to families, even when those families are located at considerable distance from the treatment centers. Of the 64 family participants, 58 of the children died during the 2 years. Seventy-nine percent of the children remained at home through death.

BACKGROUND

Despite encouraging advances in the treatment of childhood cancer, death remains the long-term prognosis for some children with cancer. Hospitals have traditionally provided the setting for the treatment of children with cancer. Hospitalization is, however, particularly frightening and upsetting to children. For young children a principal fear is the separation from the mother, in addition to separation from other family members, the home, and playthings. Hospitalization forces separation from the mother at the same time that it introduces the child to new people, places

Supported in part by DHEW, National Cancer Institute.

and, frequently, painful routines. The older child, in addition to the fear of separation, is preoccupied with the threat to his or her bodily integrity and functioning (Spinetta, Rigler, Karon, 1973). The child's needs for the parents increases markedly during serious illness, but hospitalization has traditionally reduced the child's access to them. At present, attempts are often made by pediatric oncologists to administer cancer treatment protocols to children on an outpatient basis. However, when these patients have exhausted treatment protocols and their cancer is still out of control, they have generally been hospitalized for the final days of their lives.

As a result of the attention directed in the late 1960s and 1970s (Green, 1962; Knudson and Nattreson, 1960; Easson, 1976; Spinetta, 1974; Waechter, 1971; Bluebond–Langner, 1978) to the child's needs while hospitalized and their understanding of their disease status, health care professionals have attempted to change their facilities to meet these needs. For instance, rooming-in is becoming available for mothers, and family members may visit at any time (Sauer, 1976; Friedman, 1977). Attempts are also currently being made to encourage family participation in the child's care when in the hospital (Ayer, 1978; Korsch, 1978; Hardgrove, 1978; Jackson, 1978). Changes in communication between the dying child, family, and health care professionals are also being encouraged. Parents and professionals are encouraged to be honest and supportive in their dealings with these children, allowing them to ask questions as often or as infrequently as they can emotionally handle.

Despite these adjustments in acute care hospitals, these facilities are somewhat at odds with the dying patient's needs. Hospital technology, protocols, and professionals function with cure or restoration as a goal. People with diseases that have failed to respond to this restorative therapy no longer appear to fit into the hospital framework of health care delivery. Hospice care is one alternative to acute care hospitalization for dying adults and children. July 1967 marked the opening of the well-known St. Christopher's Hospice in Sydenham, England (Saunders, 1975). Numerous other hospice facilities have been developed since that time (Lack, 1978; Mount, 1976; Hackley, 1978; Lamer, 1978); most are based upon the St. Christopher's model. St. Christopher's Hospice has a 55-bed inpatient facility that seeks to provide physical, emotional, social, and spiritual care to dying patients, predominantly those dying from cancer. The main objective is to provide comfort care; special attention is paid to pain control. The skills of physicians, nurses, social workers, members of the clergy, pharmacists, volunteers, and others are joined to help the dying patient. The patient's family is involved, and bereavement services are provided to assist surviving members.

Home care is an alternative method of health care delivery to the dying adult and child. Dying children usually wish to be at home, to have their parents at hand, and not to be subjected to unnecessary intrusive procedures. These wishes are not antithetical to the child's needs. Parents are the normal providers of their child's care and emotional support and may continue to give care in their own home, even when the child is dying. Home care has been central to the development of hospice services. Patients receiving home care have nursing and other services available to them 24 hours a day. Should home care be no longer desired or feasible, then the dying patient may enter the inpatient hospice facility, which strives to have a homelike atmosphere and few restrictions in visits.

Home care services have been available in the United States for adults and children since the early 1900s (Freeman, 1963), through public health and visiting nurse agencies. However, public health nursing agencies have not traditionally been structured to provide the 24-hour, 7 days-a-week comfort care model of treatment that has continued to be an important component of services offered at hospice facilities. Hospital-based home care programs have been increasing in number but have not typically provided 24-hour coverage.

PURPOSE

The purpose of this study, then, was to explore the feasibility and desirability of home care for children dying of cancer. The study was based on the premise that following the cessation of cancer cure–oriented treatment, with death the inevitable outcome, it was desirable for the child to return to the home environment, and it could be feasible for the family to provide necessary comfort-oriented care with the assistance of a home care nurse and a physician serving as a consultant.

In order to explore the feasibility of this home care alternative, the first priority was to provide and refine a model of home care service for dying children that could eventually be delivered through existing community services.

The findings of the first phase, the provision and coordination of home care, are reported in this article. Preliminary information on this phase was published by Martinson, Armstrong, Geis et al. (1978a,b). A preliminary report on the second phase, the transition of the home care services to the community, can be found in Moldow and Martinson (1980).

METHODS

Procedure

The primary goal of our model was the comfort of the dying child while at home, including, as desired, the actual death at home. We postulated that the comfort care measures needed would·be within the expertise and preparation of a nurse and that the home care nurse could be the health professional responsible for coordinating the care, with a physician available for consultation for the nurse and family. We also postulated that the parents could function as the primary caregivers and decision makers, roles that are often difficult, if not impossible, to maintain in the hospital but are entirely appropriate when the goal is comfort care of the dying child. The parents were thus considered the primary caregivers, the nurse coordinated the home care, and the physician acted as a consultant to the nurse and family.

The home nursing service components of this study were coordinated at a university school of nursing, though it remained administratively separate from existing nursing services. After a child was referred to the project by his or her physician, a nurse from the home care project staff contacted the child's parents. The nurse explained the project to the parents and secured their informed consent. If the initial referral was made by another health professional, such as a pediatric oncology nurse, the patient's physician was then contacted before any contact was made with the parents.

Owing to the limited number of research staff available to provide home care services and the geographic distribution of families, it was necessary to contract for nursing services for most of the participating families. Home care nurses were located through family recommendation, or local community health institutions were contacted to identify a nurse who would be willing to assist the family and participate in the study. A backup nurse was also secured who provided home care services when the primary home care nurse was not available. Two project nurses oriented the home care nurses to the special services they would provide and offered continued consultation.

The home care services provided by the project included the following nursing services: (1) the family's home care nurse was on call 24 hours a day, 7 days a week; (2) the nurse went to the home whenever and as often as the family requested without questioning the necessity of the visit; and (3) the nurse was available to help the family in whatever way it was deemed necessary, beginning at the time of discharge, throughout the home care period, as well as during and after the child's death. Attendance at the child's funeral was desirable, and follow-up within the first month to assess the family's situation was encouraged. If the nurse felt the family lacked adequate internal or community support to assist them through the grieving period, she referred them for additional professional assistance in their community.

In addition to the nursing services, a physician (usually the child's oncologist) served as a consultant to the family, and the nurse and was available by telephone at all times. The option of readmission to the hospital remained open at all times.

Subjects

Criteria for referral to the home care project were (1) the patient was 17 years of age or younger, (2) the patient was dying of cancer, and (3) no procedures requiring hospitalization were planned at the time of referral.

A total of 64 children were referred during the phase of the project reported here. Referrals were received from 23 different physicians from university hospitals and nine other hospitals in the state. The university hospitals were the largest source of referrals and constituted 53% of all referrals.

Of the 64 children referred, one child experienced a spontaneous remission and was subsequently withdrawn from the project. Three additional children were referred because there was no further treatment available for them; however, these three children were not appropriate subjects to be included in the research reported here since their prognosis was months or even years of life. An additional two children, who were thought to be dying at the 2-year cut-off time of the research reported here, were referred to existing community home care agencies.

Data Sources

Research data were derived from the child's medical record; forms and records completed by the home care nurse; questionnaires regarding personal characteristics that were completed by both the parents and the nurse; notes kept by the nurse coordinators of the project; and interviews with parents, physicians, and nurses after the child's death. Such interviews followed semistructured formats that consisted of predetermined questions with open-ended responses. Parent interviews were conducted in the family home at 1 month, 6 months, 12 months and 24 months after the child's death.

RESULTS

Duration of Care

Of the 58 children in the project who died, 46 (79%) died in their homes. Of the 12 deceased children who took part in home care but did not die at home, 11 died in the hospital and 1 died in an ambulance en route to the hospital. Duration of home care was defined as beginning after the child's discharge from the hospital and/or when a home care nurse was available to provide care, and ending at the death of the child. Figure 23-1 shows the duration of home care for the 58 children in the project, both those who died at home and those who died in the hospital. It shows a wide variability in duration of home care for both groups. Including both groups, 18 children (31%) were in home care for less than 1 week. Six (50%) of the children

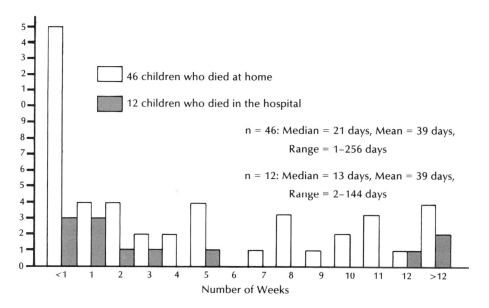

46 children who died at home

12 children who died in the hospital

n = 46: Median = 21 days, Mean = 39 days, Range = 1–256 days

n = 12: Median = 13 days, Mean = 39 days, Range = 2–144 days

Number of Weeks

Figure 23-1. Duration of home care (including days of final hospitalization).

who died in the hospital were rehospitalized for 1 day or less. The remaining six children were rehospitalized from 4 to 35 days with a mean of 10 days of hospitalization. Three children had 2 months or more of home care services before returning to the hospital to die.

Family Characteristics

In an attempt to determine which families would benefit most from the home care alternative and which families might not be suited, the personal characteristic variables of the 58 families were analyzed. The ages of the 58 children were evenly distributed across the range of less than 1 year through 17 years. The mean age was 9.3 (SD = 5.5) and the median was 9.5. The children represented a broad range of cancer diagnoses consistent with 1978 American Cancer Society statistics for the U.S. population. Twenty-four children (41%) had leukemia, 12 (21%) had central nervous system carcinomas, 7 (12%) had lymphomas, 6 (10%) had bone tumors, 5 (9%) had neuroblastoma, and 1 each had malignant histiocytosis, embryonal cell carcinoma, hepatoblastoma, and rhabdomyosarcoma.

Of the 58 families, 25 resided in metropolitan areas, 25 in cities and rural areas throughout the rest of the state, and 8 in two neighboring states. Four of the 58 families were single-parent families. The variable of socioeconomic status (SES) was computed using the Hollingshead two-factor index of social position (1975). Families represented the entire range of the index with a concentration in the middle to lower classes. Of the 57 families for whom data are known, 4 families (7%) were in Class I (the highest), 7 (12%) were in Class II, 17 (30%) were in Class III, 27 (47%) were in Class IV, and 2 (4%) were in Class V (the lowest).

With the exception of one American Indian parent, all parents were Caucasian. One parent was Spanish-surnamed. Among 55 of the 58 families, who did indicate a religious preference, both parents in 46 of the families reported the same religious preference: Protestant (29 families) and Roman Catholic (17 families). In nine other families the parents reported different religious preferences. On the basis of the mother's stated preference, six of these were Protestant families and three were Roman Catholic.

An additional family characteristic was the number of children in the family. The mean number of children was 2.8, and ranged from the dying child being an only child in four instances to one instance in which the dying child was one of 11 children. Examination of these family variables indicated that there were no obvious differences between the families whose child died in the home and those whose child died in the hospital or en route to the hospital.

Family Members as Caregivers

As stated above, the families provided comfort care to their children with the assistance of the home care nurse and physician. Each family, including the child if old enough, decided upon their own plan of comfort care in consultation with their physician and nurse. A broad range of possible comfort care measures was available at home, such as the use of intravenous fluids, oxygen administration, gavage feedings, and medications such as laxatives, corticosteroids, and analgesics. In addition, each family chose the degree of intensity of supportive treatment that they wished to provide at home. In almost all instances, the families managed the total provision of this care with minimum physical assistance from the home care nurse. To provide this care they utilized a wide variety of hospital furnishings, equipment, and supplies, including such items as hospital beds, suction machines, intravenous equipment, urinary draining equipment, and incontinence pads.

In all instances, pain control was important. Analgesics alone or in combination with antianxiety medications, or antianxiety medications alone, were used to treat pain. Table 23-1 shows that each of the 58 children received prescription medications, and all but 3 received some medication for pain control. Almost half of the 58 children received prescription narcotics and antianxiety medications to control pain. In addition to analgesics, numerous other types of drugs, such as corticosteroids, laxatives, antiemetics, antiseizure medications, sleep-inducing drugs, and antacid medications, were used for comfort.

Nurse Services

Each family received the assistance of a primary nurse and a co-primary or backup nurse. The nurse provided a broad range of services for the family, such as teaching, health assessment, procurement of medical equipment and medications, provision of physical care and technical treatment such as suctioning and catheterization, and emotional counseling.

A number of variables related to the home care nurse were examined to determine whether it was possible to identify a type of nurse who would best function in this home care alternative. The variables of nurse degree and experience were explored. The total number of different primary or co-primary nurses who provided home care was (coincidentally) 58. Only nine of these nurses had repeated involvement in the study. The mean age of the 58 nurses was 35.9 years,

Table 23-1. Medications Used for Pain Control During Home Care

Medication	Number of Children	Percentage of Total
Narcotic analgesics and antianxiety medications	28	48
Narcotic analgesics	11	19
Antianxiety medications	10	17
Nonnarcotic analgesics and antianxiety medications	3	5
Nonnarcotic analgesics	3	5
None	3	5
Sum	58	99

and they ranged from 23 to 63 years. Seven (12%) had master's degrees, 19 (50%) had baccalaureate degrees, 1 (2%) had an associate degree, 17 (27%) had hospital diplomas, 3 (5%) were licensed practical nurses, and 1 (2%) was a baccalaureate nursing student. The 57 nurses who had nursing degrees had a mean of 9 years of professional work experience; 23 (40%) had prior public health nursing experience, and 27 (47%) had prior pediatric work experience. For all but 2 nurses this was the first time in their careers that they had provided terminal care at home for a child.

One of the important measures of feasibility of home care was the ability to secure nurses who were willing to provide the services specified by this model and at distances remote from the cancer treatment center. In every case, a nurse (or supervised nursing student) agreed to provide the care, and in the 1 case in which the nurse assigned could not complete the case, another nurse was recruited.

Table 23-2 shows the amount of direct contact by the home care nurse with the family during the period from referral through the child's death. Although the nurse spent additional time coordinating and facilitating the care (e.g., conferring with the physician and arranging for delivery of equipment and supplies), Table 23-3 focuses on the number of the actual home visits, since that is the item typically used in figuring charges for home care services. Follow-up visits after the death of the child are often not reimbursable and were therefore not included in the table.

A number of nurses made daily home visits. Some home visits lasted only about a half-hour; however, others often lasted about 2 hours. In some instances, especially at the time of death, visits lasted several hours and in one instance an entire day. Nurses and families used the telephone to maintain close contact and therefore often made daily phone calls. Parents remarked that the nurses' 24-hour availability, reinforced by their ready accessibility by telephone, was very comforting and provided a sense of security during this stressful time. Emotional support was a major service provided by the nurses. In all contacts with the family, the nurses spent a large part of their time providing emotional support for the parents.

Table 23-2. Home Care Nurse Direct Contact for 58 Children

	Number Visits per Family	Total Hours per Family
HOME VISITS		
Median	7.5	23.5
Mean	11.7	29.9
Range	1–110	1–305.6
TELEPHONE CALLS		
Median	14.5	2.4
Mean	19.8	3.9
Range	0–101	0–23.5

Table 23-3. Rate of Nurse Home Visits per Day During Home Care

	Rate for 46 Children Who Died at Home	Rate for 12 Children Who Died in Hospital
HOME VISITS		
Median Rate	0.42	0.21
Range	0.06–3.0	0.03–0.67
TELEPHONE CALLS		
Median Rate	0.61	0.50
Range	0–3.67	0.07–3.0

Physician Services

Physicians were an important component of this model of home care, even though they were not as actively involved as the nurses. The physicians had in all cases been involved in the referral to home care, thus sanctioning the concept of the child dying in the home. Physician availability for consultation was very important to these families, who would call the physician, even if he or she was located at a distant referral center, to report on their child's health status. The families and nurses, therefore, used the physicians as consultants to answer medical information questions, to make medical assessments based upon the parents' and/or nurses' descriptions of the status of the dying child, and to recommend treatment such as medication adjustment and blood products for transfusions. Although the vast majority of all contacts with the physician were by telephone, 22 children were examined at an outpatient clinic or doctor's office. The number of such visits for those 22 children ranged from 1 to 19; the median was 1.5, the mean 4.0. Table 23-4 shows that some physicians also made home visits. Fourteen children were seen at home by their oncologist, and one family received 12 weekly visits from a psychiatrist.

Table 23-4. Physician Home Visits during Time of Home Care and Immediately after Death for 58 Children

Number of Visits	Number of Families
0	44* (76%)
1	9† (16%)
2	1 (2%)
4	2 (3%)
7	1 (2%)
17‡	1 (2%)

* Includes 34 home and 10 hospital deaths.
† Includes 7 home and 2 hospital deaths.
‡ Includes 12 psychiatrists visits.

Other health professionals also made home visits. Such visits were not an integral part of our model and were therefore not extensively used. A laboratory technician made visits to four families, two families were visited by an occupational/recreational therapist, two families were served by a home health aide, and one family each was visited by an x-ray technician, a chiropractor, and a homemaker. Most of these health professionals visited only one time per family, with the exception of one family who received 43 home health aide visits and another family who received 16 homemaker visits.

Feasibility and Desirability

The areas that were explored to determine feasibility were also often used to examine desirability. These areas included the following:

1. The ability of families to provide high-quality comfort care for their children at home and to keep them at home through the time of their death and the families' willingness (if they had to choose over again) to provide home care for their children
2. The availability of nurses and physicians who would agree to assist the families in providing the care
3. The ability of professional staff to obtain adequate medications and medical equipment and supplies.

Family Involvement

As previously stated, 46 (79%) of the 58 families studied kept their child at home through the time of the child's death. From the parents' vantage point, this seems to suggest feasibility. In all instances, the home care nurses felt the families provided high-quality care at home.

Parents were asked 12 months after the child's death, if they had to choose over again, would they choose home care for their child. In those families in which the child died at home, only 2 (2.7%) of 73 parents who responded expressed some uncertainty about choosing home care again.

The 12 families who returned their child to the hospital to die may have found home care or death at home undesirable. It was therefore necessary to examine the factors that may have led to their child's readmission. We therefore reexamined each case, looking at the characteristics of the families and the process of home care delivery for these 12 families. Their variables were compared to those of the 46 families whose child died at home. The reasons given by the families for the child's final admission to the hospital were also examined.

The 12 children who died in the hospital after some home care services did not obviously differ from the 46 who died at home on variables such as sex, age, socioeconomic status, rural/urban residence, religious preference, race, number of siblings, birth order, number of parents present in the home, diagnosis or duration of home care. The place of death was also not obviously influenced by when, in the process of this program's evolution, the family entered the home care program.

There were differences when the process of delivery of home care services was evaluated. Table 23-3 shows the rate of nursing visits per day, omitting those days when the child was in the hospital, and therefore would not receive home visits. The 46 children who died at home received approximately twice as high a rate of home visits and a slightly higher rate of telephone calls than did the children who died in the hospital.

There were also differences in medication usage. Children who died at home typically received a greater total number of medications than did those who died in the hospital. There were very noticeable differences in the use of analgesics and antianxiety medications. Eighty percent of the children who died at home received narcotic analgesics while only 42% of the children who died in the hospital received narcotic analgesics. Of the children who died in the home, 76% received antianxiety medications, while only 50% of the children who died in the hospital received these drugs.

In addition to medication differences there were also differences in the number and kinds of medical equipment, supplies and furnishings; once again, a larger percentage of children who died in the home received various furnishings, equipment, and supplies such as bedpans, commodes, hospital beds, antipressure devices, suction machines, and dressings, compared to those who died in the hospital. Children who died at home were twice as likely as children who died in the hospital to visit their physician's office or clinic. The variables of rate of physician home visits and home visits from other professionals were also explored, but there were no obvious differences.

In summary, it appears that there were multiple factors that influenced the return of 12 children to the hospital. Insufficient nursing services were cited in only two cases despite the differences reported above in the amount of home care services received by the 46 children who died in the home compared to the 12 who did not die at home.

Health Professional Involvement

Another indication of the feasibility of this care model was that a nurse was always recruited to assist the family. In addition, physicians indicated their support by referring patients and subsequently being available to the family and nurse during the home care period.

A further measure of feasibility was the willingness of these nurses and physicians to provide home care services again in the future. Nurses were asked if they would be willing to provide home care again. There were a total of 44 respondents to the question, "Would you be willing to be a home care nurse again?" Of those nurses, 33 (63.5%) said "yes," none said "no"; however 19 (36.5%) said "yes, but." Of the 19 nurses who answered "yes, but," 5 said they might be willing to be home care nurses in the future but they "needed time to recover," three said they wanted to get to know the family before providing home care services, two said it depended upon the situation, and two said "family needs permitting." The following explanations (each noted once) were given: would need more support and more information; moving out of the area; was pregnant now; would only serve as a backup; a number of changes are needed; new employment precluded involvement; and only with a beeper and a back-up nurse.

Of the 23 physicians who referred families to the research, 19 were interviewed. An additional 20 physicians who provided home care services to families in the study but were not the child's referring physician were also interviewed. Of the referring physicians, 10 referred one child and 13 referred two or more. When interviewed, all of the physicians said they would use home care services again. Their comments included statements such as "home care is a tremendously positive thing," "it can be a meaningful experience for the family," and "when the final end comes, the last days should not be spent in the hospital."

A further indication of feasibility was that the home care nurse or project staff were able to obtain medical equipment supplies and medications in sufficient quantities and at the time they were needed, although not always without difficulty.

DISCUSSION

The material reported in this article represents the first phase of the study, the major purpose of which was to provide and coordinate the nursing and other services necessary to support the home care of children dying of cancer. The research component focused on measuring the feasibility and desirability of the home care services provided. In addition, during this phase, research efforts provided concurrent data regarding areas of effectiveness and efficiency in the provision of home care. As a result, the home care model on which this project is based has been dynamic and evolved in response to on-going feedback provided during the study.

In more established modes of care, it is feasible to concentrate research primarily on the outcomes of the care. However, in projects such as ours, in which the objective was to develop a mode of care (and therefore in which the evolutionary changes are both important and relatively extensive), it was necessary to consider first the evolution of the process of care and then to concentrate on outcomes. Consequently, the research reported was not based on a clinical trial design in which cases were randomly assigned to groups.

Despite these methodological realities, the research has provided valuable information on the process of home care and its impact on families, nurses, and other health care professionals. It has demonstrated that a home care model could be developed that would provide home care to 58 families and thus enable 46 children to die at home with apparent satisfaction of those families at the time of death and 2 years later.

The research also suggests that in many ways this home care model is both feasible and desirable. The study has shown that physicians will refer patients, that children and parents will agree to participate, and home care nurses can be recruited. In addition, needed equipment, supplies, and medications can be secured.

No clear criteria have emerged that would rule out this home care alternative for any children dying of cancer and their families. The child who developed continuous seizures was an appropriate candidate for rehospitalization, although seizures *per se* do not preclude a child from home care services. Although the child who developed sudden pain was rehospitalized, other children have suffered pain at home that was subsequently adequately controlled. Despite the exhaustion and feelings of anxiety that many parents reported, they desired and managed to keep their children at home. In general, the home care alternative was feasible for a wide range of children who had a variety of special needs.

IMPLICATIONS FOR NURSING

This study has demonstrated that a home care program that is comfort oriented can be coordinated and directed by nurses, rather than physicians. For, although the physician was enlisted to change treatment (i.e., order a different medication), the nurse made the assessment and frequently recommended the treatment change. We believe this indicates that similar programs, utilizing nurse direction, could be developed for children dying from diseases other than cancer as well as for adults dying from a variety of diseases. Numerous practical implications have been identified. Since approximately one-third of the children died within a week of admission to home care, the home care nurses should initiate home care services on either the day of discharge or the first day thereafter. This would afford the nurse and family the time to establish a relationship and be adequately prepared for home care and death at home, if the family so chooses. The extremely high incidence of the use of medications for pain control in this study and as reported in the hospice literature (Lamerton, 1974; Twycross, 1978; Lack, 1978) indicates that the nurse caring for both dying children and adults should be prepared, on very short notice, to obtain pain medications for patients. We would recommend that home care nurses obtain orders for analgesic medication upon admission to home care and should have available the necessary syringes and other equipment to administer the medication.

Because this study identifies no particular "family type" that was either "not appropriate" or "most appropriate" for home care, health professionals should use criteria other than family characteristics in deciding who should be referred for home care. Similarly, because little difference was found in the performance of nurses on the basis of their education or experience, other factors should be considered in choosing home care nurses.

The 24-hour, 7-days-a-week on-call status was predicted to be a disadvantage to this model, but we have had so few nurses with repeated long-term involvement that we are unable to make a definitive statement. Parents' responses, however, suggest that this on-call availability was a major factor in their positive reaction to home care. Finally, although we are unable to state with certainty that the differences observed in nursing services provided to families whose child died at home and those whose child died in the hospital were a factor in hospitalization, such a possibility clearly exists. We believe that home care should be available as an alternative for families with dying children and that nurses who accept such a referral should be supportive of the family's wishes to have their child at home. Working together they can make the final days of the child's life as comfortable as possible.

REFERENCES

American Cancer Society: Cancer statistics. CA 18(1):17–32, 1978
Ayer AH: Is partnership with parents really possible? Am J Matern Child Nurs 3(2):107–110, 1978
Bluebond–Langner M: The Private Worlds of Dying Children. Princeton, Princetown University Press, 1978
Easson WM: Management of the dying child. J Clin Child Psychol 3:25–27, 1976
Freeman RB: Public Health Nursing Practice, p 19. Philadelphia, WB Saunders, 1963
Friedman GR: A comprehensive care center for children. Health Soc Work 1:158–168, 1977
Green M: Care of the dying child. Pediatrics 40:492–497, 1967
Hackley JA, Fan WC, McIntar TM: Tucson (1977)—Hillhaven Hospice. Death Educ 2:63–82, 1978
Hardgrove CB, Kermoian R: Parent including pediatric units. Am J Publ Health 68:847–850, 1978
Hollingshead AB: The Two-Factor Index of Social Position. New Haven, AB Hollingshead, 1957
Jackson PB: Child care in the hospital: A parent/staff partnership. Am J Matern Child Nurs 3(2):104–107, 1978
Korsch BM: Issues in humanizing care for children. Am J Publ Health 68:831–832, 1978
Knudson AF, Natterson JM: Participation of parents in the hospital care of fatally ill children. Pediatrics 26:482–490, 1960
Lack SA, Buckingham RW: First American Hospice: Three Years of Home Care. New Haven, CT, Hospice, 1978
Lamers W, Jr: Marin County (1976) development of Hospice of Marin. Death Educ 2:43062, 1978
Lamerton R: Opiate delusion. World Med 25(4):44–45, 1978
Martinson IM, Armstrong GD, Geis DP et al: Home care for children dying of cancer. Pediatrics 62(1):106–113, July 1978
Martinson IM, Armstrong GD, Geis D et al: Facilitating home care for children dying of cancer. Cancer Nurs 1(1):41–45, February 1978
Moldow DG, Martinson IM: From research to reality: Home care for the dying child. Am J Matern Child Nurs 5:159–166, 1980
Mount BM: Palliative care service October 1976 report. Montreal, Royal Victoria Hospital, 1976
Sauer SN: The hospital setting for the child with cancer. In Martinson IM (ed): Home Care for the Dying Child: Professional and Family Perspectives. New York, Appleton–Century–Crofts, 1976
Saunders C: St. Christopher's Hospice: Annual Report 1974–75. London, St. Christopher's Hospice, 1975
Spinetta JJ, Rigler D, Karon M: Anxiety in the dying child. Pediatrics 52:841–845, 1973
Twycross RG: The assessment of pain in advanced cancer. J Med Ethics 4:112–116, 1978
Waechter EH: Children's awareness of fatal illness. Am J Nurs 71:1168–1172, 1971

24 · Working With Bereaved Parents

Lee Schmidt

Working with bereaved parents can be a difficult, highly charged, painful, challenging and richly rewarding experience for nurses and other health care professionals. Such work requires knowledge, sensitivity, patience, commitment, and genuine warmth and caring. While most of these qualities cannot be taught *per se,* they can be developed and nurtured through learning about the issues involved in losing a child, through emphatic listening, and through practice.

THE UNIQUE NATURE OF THE LOSS OF A CHILD

The first thing to understand is that the loss of a child is the most painful of human experiences. It *wroughts* an almost indescribable devastation in the hearts and lives of the child's parents. The agony felt when a child dies is not paralleled in any other experience.

The relationship between parent and child is a powerfully unique and complex one. No other human connection is comparable in terms of endurance, ambivalence, vulnerabilities, and responsibilities. The tie between child and parent is a biological and emotional one which has its beginnings even before the birth of the child and extends beyond the present into the imagined future. The child's early utter dependency on the parents elicits a nurturing bond that the parents never are totally able to relinquish, even as they try to prepare their child for future independence.

The death of a child reverses the nature order of things. In modern American society children are not supposed to die before their parents. Parents expect to see their children grow up to be adults themselves. They expect to grow old surrounded by their children and grandchildren. The unacceptable nature of the loss of a child is underscored by the fact that no single term is attributed to bereaved parents. The terms *widow* and *widower* are used to designate the loss of a spouse. A child whose parents have died is called an orphan. No such title exists for parents who have lost a child.

Parenting is a future-oriented activity with both immediate and anticipated rewards. Parents nurture their children's bodies and minds so that they will grow into healthy, able adults, all the while dreaming of the person their child will become. When their child dies, their investment in the future is lost. Indeed, they feel that their own future is over.

Since the most basic task of parenting is to nurture and protect the child, the death of a child is often perceived by the parents as the ultimate failure of their parenting. Their emotional self-expectation is that they should be able to protect their child from hazard and harm even though their rational selves know and fear that such protection is not always possible.

When a parent's self-perceived omnipotence is shattered by the death of a child, it is often replaced with self-blame. The basis for this is frequently as unrealistic as the previously held omnipotence—at least from the point of view of the objective outsider who sees no culpability on the parent's part.

ISSUES IN WORKING WITH BEREAVED PARENTS

Nurses who work with bereaved parents must deal with several major issues: (1) their own professional goals, (2) the impact of the vulnerability of bereaved parents on their own ego, and finally, (3) the emotional costs and rewards of such work.

In considering their own professional goals nurses have to first identify what their goals usually are and then decide whether these goals are appropriate to working with bereaved parents. Since the goals of many nurses and other caregiving professionals originally derived from the medical model—which is a cure-oriented model—they frequently too are cure-oriented goals. A cure orientation calls for changing a situation, or at least as much of the situation as one can. Stitching closed a laceration, stopping the spread of infection, bringing a patient's fever down are a few of thousands of examples of changing a situation, of working toward a cure.

For bereaved parents there is no cure: Their child cannot come back to life. Their own lives will never be the same again. Regardless of the skill of the nurse, the situation cannot be fixed. No matter what the nurse or others do, the parents will *never* consider it right, just, fair, or appropriate that their child died. The application of a cure-oriented model places the professional in the frustrating situation of being helpless to effect change, and since few people tolerate feelings of inadequacy, the tendency of most nurses is to avoid contact with the bereaved.

Changing the focus from a cure to a care model, with care-oriented goals (see Table 24-1 for examples of care-oriented goals), places the nurse in a more positive, helpful position. Once the nurse decides that she cannot change what happened to the parents but that she can make a difference in helping them deal with their loss, she no longer will be helpless. That change in orientation opens up many avenues

Table 24-1. Examples: Care-Oriented Goals

To reduce the parents' sense of isolation
To open channels of communication between both parents
To encourage expression of all types of feelings
To promote the recounting of the positive things they did for
their child
To help each parent find out what feels right for him or her in
terms of their grieving process
To foster self-acceptance for the uniqueness of each parent's
own grieving style

of intervention with sensitive listening and empathic responses underlying each of them. Using a care orientation stresses the counseling, comforting aspects of the nurse's role and makes her, in effect, a nurse–counselor.

The vulnerability of bereaved parents and its impact on the caregiver's ego is another issue that confronts professionals. Bereaved parents are not psychically whole persons. Their sense of intactness has been severely compromised. It is as if a gaping hole has been left in their psyche; much of what they were is missing; it died with their child. What they are left with is raw, agonizing pain. In an effort to assuage that pain, parents frequently reach out to anybody or anything that suggests a promise of relief. The mind-numbing effect of alcohol and drugs is sometimes sought, as are the elusive promises of psychics and feel-good gurus.

When the help of the nurse–counselor is sought by bereaved parents, it is usually with the hope and belief that she possesses special knowledge and skill that will alleviate their pain. This faith in her, combined with the parent's vulnerability, places the nurse in a powerful position to help or harm. Consequently, it is imperative that she be clear about her goals and maintain a healthy balance between sensitivity and objectivity.

There are emotional costs extracted when nurses work with bereaved parents. And, there are rich rewards. Bereaved parents are not necessarily easy people to work with. Their emotional swings are predictable in their probability but unpredictable in their nature and timing. A parent may be smiling one minute when recounting a special memory and sobbing the next. Another parent may talk freely during one interaction, and refuse to talk during the next one. Consequently, the nurse must be able to handle the unpredictable and to tolerate ambiguity.

It is extremely difficult to hear the undiluted pain of another human being. Such outpouring can touch the core of the nurse's emotional self, reminding her of her own losses, disappointments, and vulnerabilities.

Listening to bereaved parents can make the nurse feel inadequate as a professional. Even if she has adopted care-oriented goals, and values the work she is doing, there are limits to what she can accomplish. She can alleviate some parental pain, but she cannot eliminate it; she can listen to the whys parents ask, but she cannot provide the answers; she can encourage communication between emotionally isolated family members, but she cannot compel it. For the nurse who is also a parent, listening to a bereaved parent can be particularly threatening. It is a reminder that no matter how vigilant a parent she is, absolute protection of her children is not possible. Children can and do die; hers could too.

Despite the costs exacted, rewards from working with bereaved parents are many and rich. There is the satisfaction of helping people who are acutely needy but for whom few avenues of help are open. To be a source of strength and comfort is extremely gratifying and most certainly congruent with the mission of nursing. There is the opportunity to relate with people who have dropped all artifices and facades. It is a uniquely rewarding experience to share in another human being's life in a deeply personal way.

The heightened appreciation for life that comes from such work is another major reward. An increased awareness of the preciousness and fragility of life can lead the nurse to savor relationships and moments that are frequently overlooked by those who take life for granted.

In addition to the professional/personal issues involved in working with bereaved parents, the nurse needs to be aware of issues specific to the child's death, particularly the child's age and the cause of death. An understanding of these issues enables the nurse to better assess parental grief and to plan intervention strategies for dealing with it.

AGE OF CHILD

Death of an Infant

Parents who lose a neonate experience an especially lonely form of grief. If the child dies *in utero,* at birth, or shortly thereafter, the parents are likely to be the only people who "knew the infant." The mother, in particular, is isolated in her grief. The life that has lived within her is gone . . . a life that no one else has experienced in the same way that she has. In many ways the death of a baby is a uniquely maternal loss.

For this reason, parents who lose a neonate often grieve in a social vacuum, receiving little, if any, validation of their loss. Instead, all too frequently they hear such comments as, "It's better this way since you hardly knew him," or "It'll be all right. You can always have another baby." Such comments discount rather than actualize their loss, leaving hurting parents to wonder what is wrong with themselves that they feel so much pain when they "obviously shouldn't."

Planning for the birth of a child is a dream-building project. Expectant parents dream about what their child will look like, who he will take after, and even what he will be when he grows up.

At the same time that a couple dream of their child-to-be, they prepare themselves for the role of parent by thinking and fantasizing about being parents. The loss of the infant arrests the development of the parental role and leaves the couple feeling frustrated and purposeless. Eleanor echoed these feelings when she said, "I have all this love stored up to give a baby. Now what do I do with it? Where do I go?"

Death of a Young Child

As the child grows out of infancy, his own individual personality evolves and his world widens. Though still dependent on his parents, he is taking his first steps away from them toward being a unique, independent person. At the same time he is establishing a firm hold on his place in the family, loving freely, fighting fiercely, and exploring endlessly.

When the young child dies parents yearn for all the special tender moments that mark the preschool years, the "owies" so quickly healed by a kiss, the excited wonder at the sight of a ladybug, the giggles and silliness over just about anything. They long for the developmental potential that they saw so briefly, for what he was and what he might have become. If the young child had been ill and hospitalized before his death, the grief of the parents may be compounded by haunting memories of the painful and frightening experiences their child may have had to endure. "I just keep remembering how scared Janey was when they put her in isolation, how terrified she was about the shots and IVs," one mother recounted. "It was a nightmare and I keep reliving it."

Death of a School-Age Child

The child's world continues to widen during the school years to include friends and their families, teachers, and people in his community. His involvement in a variety of activities, sports, clubs, scouts, and church groups multiply his contacts, and thus his death is more widely felt than that of a younger child.

Parents often find solace in seeing how many other people are affected by their child's death. Despite the shock they're in at the time of the funeral, most parents can recount in vivid detail who came to the services and how many came. Any special form of reaching out to them by their child's schoolmates and playmates often brings a sense of comfort to them.

Death of an Adolescent

Adolescence brings with it turmoil for the young person going through it and his entire family. As the adolescent struggles for the independence of adulthood, for an identity of his own, separate from his family, he creates bewilderment in his parents. They're not sure who this developing person is or how to react to him. These changes commonly create discord in the family and a sense of inadequacy in the parents.

The death of an adolescent often leaves parents beset by memories of conflict and feelings of guilt. They may repeatedly recall angry exchanges, threats of punishment and other perceived parental failures. And they are powerless to recant any of them.

Parents also feel frustrated and bitter over the time and energy invested in raising and nurturing their child only to be deprived of the reward of seeing him achieve productive adulthood. After investing so much, they are left with a devastating void. Their link to the future is gone, just short of being realized.

The sense of unfairness that parents feel is embued with a great sadness— sadness that the world will never bear witness to their child's promise and ability. Sadness that their child has been cheated out of the rewards of growing up.

CAUSE OF DEATH

While the loss of a child from any cause is painful beyond description, there are special issues related to the specific nature of the child's death. Knowledge of these issues will assist the nurse in understanding the dynamics of parental grief.

Illness

When a child dies from a brief illness, the parents are left with wrenching questions about the events surrounding the death. Did they fail to recognize symptoms earlier? If they had seen them, would their child still be alive? Did they take their child to the right physician, the right hospital? Could something have been done that wasn't? The questions are endless and unanswerable.

The long-term illness of a child poses different issues for parents. The parents may have experienced multiple losses prior to their child's death. They may have seen their child go from a happy, outgoing, healthy child to an emaciated, cranky and withdrawn one. During the month before Sandy died of leukemia, her mother stopped nurses and doctors in the hallway to show them pictures of her daughter as she once was, freckled faced, with long brown braids and a mischievous grin— pictures in sharp contrast to the wasted, lethargic child in the hospital bed.

The death of a child after an extended illness may leave the parents with difficult memories of the pain and fear their child endured and they witnessed, and of their own powerlessness to change the situation. Many parents describe these times as having a nightmare quality.

An extended illness does provide parents with the opportunity to take care of unfinished business with their child. This is particularly important in the situations that involve dying adolescents or other children for whom parents may feel some degree of alienation. For all children, predicted death gives the parents the chance to express or reaffirm love, to help their child cope with his own fears, and to say good-bye.

Accidents

The accidental death of a child provides no warnings. Parents are left with the stark incongruity of having a healthy child one moment and a dead child the next. Before they have much of a chance to comprehend what has happened, they are often asked to make painful, long-ranging decisions. Will they permit an autopsy? How can they tell their other children; their own parents? What kind of funeral service do they want?

The suddenness of the event leaves them with little or no time to take leave of their child, to say the things they always meant to say. It also may leave them with feelings of having failed their child by not predicting and preventing the accident.

During an extended illness the child and his family may get to know their caregivers quite well. This is not true in accidental death, which often involves various groups of strangers—policemen, ambulance and emergency room personnel, and the like. Experiences with these people may bring comfort or pain later on in the parents' grieving process.

The first person on the scene when Karen was fatally injured in an automobile accident was a young policeman who bore a startling resemblance to an actor Karen admired, who, ironically, portrayed a policeman on television. As Karen lay in the street, the policeman knelt beside her, held her hand and assured her that she'd be fine. Later her parents acknowledged being comforted by the thought that Karen actually believed her TV hero was at her side. They appreciated the policeman's "looks" as well as his actions.

Suicide

Parental survivors of suicide have a particularly difficult time coping with their child's death. They are left with all the normal pain of grief compounded by overwhelming feelings of shame, guilt, and anger. Their sense of shame comes from the recognition that suicide is stigmatized in our society. It is considered by many to be a socially unspeakable loss.

The suicide of a child is often perceived by parents as being the ultimate failure of their parenting. They feel responsible for their child's actions and are torn apart emotionally by questioning themselves about what they should or could have done differently. The feeling of guilt is exacerbated when the suicide occurred during a time of family conflict.

Intense feelings of anger are also felt. It is often directed at the child for having committed such a horrendous act, for rejecting the parents' love, and for leaving the parents with an unbearable load of pain. The anger may also be directed at others involved with the child: health care personnel, teachers, the child's peers, and so forth. One family expressed great rage at the psychiatrist who had been treating their daughter. They felt he should have been able to assess the lethality of her intentions and prevented her from carrying them out, even though they knew that she consistently had refused to cooperate in her treatment.

Murder

While murder is the least common reason for a child's death, it, too, leaves parents with enormous feelings of rage and guilt. The parents' anger initially is directed at the murderer. Frequently, though, it soon is directed as well toward the law enforcement and judiciary systems, which are seen as unresponsive and unfeeling. The rage parents experience is not without basis in fact. Overworked policemen and overloaded courts frequently are unable or slow to apprehend and convict those responsible for the child's death.

RESPONSES OF OTHERS

The way in which other people respond to bereaved parents can facilitate or inhibit their movement through the grieving process. The persons with the most significant impact include their spouses, their surviving children, their own parents, and their close friends. Even people more removed from the parents can have a positive or negative impact.

Spouse

One of the most widely held misconceptions about parental grief is that the experience of losing a child will bring the parents closer together. In almost all cases, nothing could be further from the truth. The death of a child severely strains marital unity and family equilibrium, as evidenced by the higher-than-average divorce rate among bereaved parents (some studies showed the rate to be as high as 70% within the 2-year period following the child's death).

Even though the loss of a child is the most mutual of all losses, each parent's primary response to that loss will be as an individual, not as a partner. Husbands and wives often grieve in different ways, and they move through the grieving process at varying and different rates. These natural differences are compounded by our cultural values, which more comfortably tolerate emotionality among women than among men. Women are expected to withdraw, to cry; men are expected to continue working, to be productive. It is not uncommon for a father to be asked, within weeks of his child's death, how his wife is doing. Yet the inquirer rarely asked the father how *he* is doing.

Individual differences and societal values are not the only agents contributing to marital strain. As one mother put it, "We (bereaved parents) are emotionally bankrupt people. We have nothing left to give anyone." This observation is not too surprising. Whatever the cause, pain constricts the sufferer's world and limits his ability to help anyone else. The anguish of losing a child, which well may be the worst kind of emotional pain a person can experience, rapidly uses up the internal coping resources of parents, leaving them little or nothing to offer a marriage.

Surviving Children

The relationships between bereaved parents and their surviving children are complex and fraught with potential problems. The child's grasp of the facts and implications of what has occurred is dependent on his own developmental level. The very young child does not understand the nature or permanence of his sibling's death. Children in the school years have the cognitive ability to recognize the ramifications of death, but they do not possess sufficient coping skills to defend themselves. The adolescent, caught as he is between childhood and adulthood, does not know whether to react as a child or an adult. He understands what has happened but rages against the reality.

Despite his age, a surviving child usually feels bewildered about the changes he perceives in his family life. He desperately wants things to return to normal and resents it when they don't. He still has his own needs, after all—and they aren't being met.

In an effort to reestablish family equilibrium, a surviving sibling may try to take on the characteristics or interests of the child who has died. Or he may try other tactics to comfort his parents such as keeping his once messy room spotless, trying to improve his school performance, and the like.

From the parents' point of view, dealing with their surviving children can be a problem or a help. Just as they have little to give each other, parents have a diminished capacity to give to their own children. They often recognize their children's bewilderment and hurt but are at a loss as how to handle them. Even if they know what to do, they have little energy to do it.

The care of surviving children, on the other hand, can be therapeutic for parents. Young children especially provide distraction for hurting parents and can promote healing by forcing parents to become reinvolved with life.

Grandparents

Grandparents are in the position of experiencing a compound loss. They grieve the loss of their grandchild. At the same time, they grieve for their own child as they witness his pain, knowing they cannot help him. Grandparents may rage against a world which has allowed a young child to die while they have lived long enough. And they may feel shut out by their own child who is too grown up to lean on them and too much in pain to help them.

Friends

Bereaved parents frequently find themselves avoided by others, even previously close friends. The reasons for this neglect are multiple. Sharing in loss makes people feel impotent and vulnerable. Friends don't know how to help and their sense of helplessness keeps them from reaching out. Often they substitute empty cliches' or insensitive remarks for patient, listening ears; or they simply leave the parents alone. Their discomfort increases when the parents continue to grieve and to talk about their dead child long after they deem appropriate. One month after Sheila's daughter died in an accident her best friend asked her if she should still be crying so much (implying, of course, that she shouldn't).

Outsiders feel threatened by bereaved parents. It is as if they consider death contagious. They may avoid contact with the family or refuse to accept belongings of the dead child for fear they are contaminated with death. John recalled with bitterness that when his 15-year-old daughter Linda was dying of cancer, his own sister refused to kiss her.

The death of a child threatens all parents. They know that if others could lose a child, so could they. They would rather shun friends than confront that painful possibility.

Friends who are able to overcome their own fears and impotence can be a source of great strength and comfort for bereaved parents. One mother put it this way: "I don't know what I would have done without Kay. She let me talk and cry—as much and as often as I needed to. She helped keep me sane. I owe her an unpayable debt."

Friends who want to help but don't know how can be guided by the nurse. It may be helpful for them to read a book like *The Bereaved Parent* or *Recovering from the*

Loss of a Child. Although both books are directed at the parents themselves, friends can gain a sensitive understanding of parental grief as well as some guidelines on how to be helpful and supportive. Another resource is the list of Do's and Don'ts compiled in Table 24-2.

Strangers

Even strangers can influence parental grief. One of the questions most frequently asked in social and business settings, as a conversational ice-breaker, is "How many children do you have?" This question creates a painful dilemma for parents. If their answer includes acknowledgment that they had a child who has died they risk breaking down in front of a stranger and putting that person in an awkward, uncomfortable position. If their answer excludes mention of their dead child, they may feel they somehow have betrayed that child by denying his existence.

Each parent must come to grips with an answer that feels most comfortable for them. One mother resolved the problem by answering, "I *had* two children." That answer, she felt, left it up to the stranger to pursue the topic or not.

Although it is relatively rare, strangers can be a source of great comfort as well. Since they are unencumbered by a shared history and anticipation of a future relationship, they may be freer to listen openly.

INTERVENING WITH BEREAVED PARENTS: GENERAL PRINCIPLES

There are some general principles of intervention that are important guidelines for the nurse to consider in working with bereaved parents.

Principle One: Grief is a universal human phenomenon that is experienced in highly unique and individual ways. The universality of grief means that many aspects of it are quite probable and predictable. On the other hand, the individual subtleties of grief render other aspects of it unpredictable and unusual. An analogy is useful in understanding these seemingly contradictory observations. Fingerprints are a universal physical phenomenon, and to the nonexpert they all appear alike. However, closer examination reveals that no two sets of fingerprints are exactly the same, just as individual experiences of grief are never identical. The types of specific grief responses are as many as there are grieving parents. The subtleties and emphasis of each parent's grief are never duplicated by another parent.

Principle Two: Allow as much grief to be expressed as the parent is able and willing to express at the moment. This principle recognizes the individual nature of grief as well as the fact that parents differ in their ability to express their grief in general, and at specific times. This principle implies that the nurse needs to be able to be equally comfortable with long periods of silence, with emotional outbursts, with nonstop talking, and with a multitude of other forms of human responses.

Principle Three: Grief has its own natural timing. One of the most commonly heard clichés about grief is that time will make it better. To the degree that *eventually* the passage of time will correspond with movement through the grieving process, the cliché is correct. However, in the short term, it is patently wrong. At first, time

Table 24-2. Do's and Don'ts for Helping Bereaved Parents

Do's	Don'ts
Do let your genuine concern and caring show.	Don't let your own sense of helplessness keep you from reaching out to a bereaved parent.
Do be available . . . to listen, to run errands, to help with the other children, or whatever else seems needed at the time.	Don't avoid them because you are uncomfortable (being avoided by friends adds pain to an already intolerably painful experience).
Do say you are sorry about what happened to their child and about their pain.	Don't say you know how they feel (unless you've lost a child yourself you probably don't know how they feel).
Do allow them to express as much grief as they are feeling at the moment and are willing to share.	Don't say "you ought to be feeling better by now" or anything else that implies a judgment about their feelings.
Do encourage them to be patient with themselves and not to impose any "shoulds" on themselves.	Don't tell them what they *should* feel or do.
Do allow them to talk about the child they have lost as much and as often as they want to.	Don't change the subject when they mention their dead child.
Do talk about the special, endearing qualities of the child they've lost.	Don't avoid mentioning the child's name out of fear of reminding them of their pain (they haven't forgotten it).
Do give special attention to the child's brothers and sisters—at the funeral and in the months to come (they too are hurt and confused and in need of attention that their parents may not be able to give at this time).	Don't point out that at least they have their other children (children are not interchangeable; they cannot replace each other).
	Don't say that they can always have another child (even if they wanted to and could, another child would not replace the child they've lost).
	Don't suggest that they should be grateful for their other children (grief over the loss of one child does not discount parents' love and appreciation of their living children).
Do reassure them that they did everything they could, that the medical care their child received was the best or whatever else you know to be *true and positive* about the care given their child.	Don't make any comments that in any way suggest that the care given their child at home, in the emergency room, in the hospital, or wherever was inadequate (parents are plagued by feelings of doubt and guilt without any help from their family and friends).

(Copyright: Lee Schmidt, RN, MN, Parent Bereavement Outreach, Santa Monica, CA) makes the pain worse instead of better. As the initial shock wears off, more and more pain is felt. Bereaved parents find themselves feeling much more pain 2 months after their child's death than they did at the time of the funeral. Generally, parents report that between 2 and 6 months their pain is almost constant. The only relief they experience is when they are asleep or are able, however briefly, to be totally distracted, such as when they are engaged in an involved project at work.

Many parents find that sometime between 6 and 8 months after the death they hit a new emotional low.

"It was as if the bottom dropped out from under me," Carol explained. Seven months after her son had died from a brain tumor she thought she was coping well. "I had days when I wasn't thinking about Scotty every minute. Friends had begun to comment on how much better I looked. Then, wham! I could barely get out of bed, much less function on the job."

There are several explanations for why grief gets worse. After the initial shock has worn off parents attempt to cope with their child's death using whatever coping strategies had helped them deal with past losses. These strategies simply don't work. The loss of a child is the worst tragedy that can happen to a person. Coping with previous losses is not an adequate rehearsal for handling the loss of a child.

Another, interrelated explanation, is that the parents simply are letting go after a long period of emotional control. When the child's death is still new there are things the parents must attend to, including planning the funeral, dealing with the bureaucratic details of a death (e.g. hospital bills, coroner's report, autopsy results, and the like), and comforting others. Initially they are surrounded by family and friends who seek to console. As the months pass, though, there are few distractions and less offers of emotional support. What has kept them going either no longer works or is not available anymore. Whatever the explanation, the experience is upsetting and confusing, particularly since it is contradictory to the assurances they've heard that time will make it better.

The principle that grief has its own natural timing also refers to the fact that grieving cannot be rushed, but it can be impeded. Ironically, well-meaning outsiders often try to hurry parents through their grief only to elicit the opposite result.

A classic and extreme example of this fact came to the attention of one bereavement counselor who received a call from a 74-year-old woman. Forty-three years before, the woman's 6-year-old daughter had died after a short illness. The mother tried to talk about her grief with three different people, two friends and a physician. Each of them told her, in so many words, that she was young and ought to get on with her life. She resolved then never to speak to another human being about her pain. She kept that vow for four decades until her own impending death reactivated the unresolved pain of that long ago loss.

Movement through normal grief was best put by one mother who said, "I guess I'm just going to have to walk through this." The nurse–counselor's most basic role, then, is to facilitate the "walking through."

THE INTERVENTIONS

There are six interrelated and equally important things that nurses can do to help bereaved parents:

1. Help them accept the reality of their loss
2. Assure them they *can* survive their loss
3. Facilitate the identification and expression of their feelings
4. Interpret their feelings and behaviors for them
5. Help them find sources of continuing support
6. Interpret "recovery" for them

ACCEPTING THE REALITY OF THE LOSS

The first reaction parents have to the death of their child is a sense of unreality. This reaction occurs even when the child's death was expected. In order to *start* to accept the reality of their loss, parents must recognize that they will not see their child again, at least in this lifetime. This process of actualization is a slow and painful one. It may be many months before the parents are able verbally to acknowledge, "our child is dead and we won't see him again."

There are many illustrations of this sense of disbelief. Mothers frequently report that they find themselves waiting expectantly at 3:30 for their child to come home from school, only to realize, with a start, that the child is dead. Or, they catch themselves setting the dinner table for four instead of for the family of three they now are. Fathers tell of arriving home at night and listening for their child's running footsteps and cries of greeting, "Daddy! Daddy!" only to be met with silence.

The most important activity that facilitates actualization is talking. Parents need to be given the opportunity to talk about their child, what happened, how they found out, what was said to them and by whom, what they felt at the time. They need to be able to share the nightmare qualities of their child's death as well as the good and special memories they have of their child. Most parents need to review over and over what happened before they can come to the full recognition that their child actually is dead. Talking about the death and events surrounding it gradually helps to defuse the situation for the parents by expending the emotional energy the death triggered. To understand the need to talk, the nurse only needs to recall her own memories of hearing shocking news and the urgency she then felt to tell everyone who would listen the minute details of where she was when she heard the news, what she was doing, and how she felt.

In order to help bereaved parents, the nurse–counselor must be a good, patient listener. She needs to help the parents talk specifically about the circumstances of the child's death. Questions such as "What happened?", "Who was with your child at the time?", "How did you find out?", "What did the doctor say?" all help the parents to focus on the specific circumstances. The nurse needs to provide a safe, nonjudgmental, accepting environment in which parents can share their thoughts and feelings.

Surviving the Loss

When the anesthesia of shock dissipates and the pain of the loss begins to penetrate, some of the first questions most parents ask are "How can I possibly survive this pain?", "How can I continue living without my child?", "Will I be able to go on?" A related question soon follows, as if in answer to the first questions: "Do I even want to?"

Initially, the effective nurse–counselor should listen to these questions without feeling compelled to suggest answers. Later, she might help the parents find their own answers by exploring with them their strengths and remaining hopes for the future.

While it is not unusual for parents to say they would rather die than live without their child, the competent nurse–counselor should always assess the parents' suicide potential. She needs to explore the extent of suicidal thoughts, that is, whether the parents view suicide as a solution and, if so, what means, if any, have they considered. When asking these questions, the nurse–counselor should not hesitate to be direct. In evaluating the answers she should know that the greater the specificity of the answers, the greater the risk of suicide.*

Facilitating Identification and Expression of Feelings

Recovery from the loss of a child is contingent upon the parents' allowing themselves to feel and work through the pain of their grief. While the nature and intensity of their pain are experienced individually, there is no healthy way to avoid the pain altogether. Loving a child and losing that child is the quintessential reason for emotional pain.

The feelings engendered by the loss of a child are many and varied, anger, guilt, and sadness being the predominant ones. All of these feelings are unpleasant to experience. To avoid the discomfort these feelings arouse, parents may attempt to deny or repress them. They need to be helped to identify and express these feelings in order to achieve an effective resolution.

ANGER

Anger is a common reaction of parents to the death of their child. It is also a confusing emotion for them. They expect to feel sad and depressed but they don't usually anticipate the intense anger they feel. They may be angry at a world in

---

* For an excellent reference on suicide, see Harron CL, Valente SM: Suicide: Assessment and Intervention, 2nd ed. Norwalk, CT, Appleton–Century–Crofts, 1984.

which a child is allowed to die, their spouse, their other children, the doctor and nurses who cared for their child, the driver of the car, who killed their child, or anyone and anything deemed responsible for their child's death. Parents also feel angry at their child for dying, though they are often reluctant to acknowledge it. They may be angry at their child for contributing to his own death, or they may simply be angry at him for dying and leaving them.

Whatever the target, the anger needs to be acknowledged and expressed. The parents need to be helped to identify who they are angry with and what they are angry about. Then they need to be encouraged to express that anger in a safe, effective form—whether by pounding their fist on the table, screaming in the car, beating their pillow. Bereaved fathers, in particular, often report that on the way to and from work, they roll up the car windows and scream. Mothers more often stand in the shower when no one else is home and yell and yell.

SADNESS

Not surprisingly, the most predominant feeling that bereaved parents express is one of profound sadness. The natural way to express sadness is to cry. Crying is healthy and therapeutic. In fact, there is evidence that the tears shed in grief are not idle tears (Frey, 1980). Instead, they are different biochemically from other types of tears in that they contain more toxins. This suggests that bereaved parents quite literally are releasing poison from their bodies with each tear shed.

Since crying is such an important means of releasing sadness it is particularly unfortunate that not crying is frequently equated with "being strong." Parents often report that they are trying to be strong. When asked to explain what that means, they say it means suppressing their tears in public and carrying on.

While crying alone is useful, it is generally more healing to be able to cry with someone else who can hear the sadness being expressed and offer support. The nurse needs to be able to listen, to tolerate the flow of tears and then help the parent identify the meaning of the tears, knowing that the meaning will change as grieving progresses. When parents are allowed to release their grief through crying, they usually end their crying episode with a loud sigh. The sigh seems to signal a feeling of quiet relief.

GUILT

Bereaved parents are highly vulnerable to feelings of guilt. They believe that they should have been able to protect their child from harm and that, since they didn't, they are failures as parents.

Initially parents need to be able to talk about their guilt, why they feel guilty, what they could have done differently, how badly their guilt feels. Often just the opportunity to express guilt feelings enables parents to test reality by asking questions that review their actions in a sequential manner. This type of review usually enables parents to come to grips with the fact that they did all they could do under the circumstances.

While talking and crying are important means of releasing grief, they are not the only ones, nor are they appropriate for every bereaved parent. Some parents simply are not able to verbalize their pain. Others find talking helpful but not a complete outlet. Such parents may need to channel their grief through some sort of work or creative activity. One father described chopping wood by the hour. As he chopped, he alternately cried and screamed at fate. Another man, whose son died of leukemia, set about raising funds for cancer research. A year after his son's death he had raised over $200,000. Many parents report keeping journals in which they pour out their feelings and record their memories of their child.

Other parents find exercise a helpful outlet for their grief, particularly fathers who have difficulty expressing feelings. Not only does strenuous activity permit the release of conscious feelings, there also is evidence that exercise causes the release of biochemicals that are antidepressive in nature.

Interpreting Their Feelings and Behavior

Grief causes a great deal of cognitive and emotional confusion. Bereaved parents often report that they are experiencing difficulty concentrating and find themselves unable to make the simplest of decisions. This is bewildering and frightening in that they fear they are losing their minds. Their fear is not surprising, since many of the signs of normal grief are also indications of mental illness: cognitive confusion, depression, acute anxiety, and hallucinations.

The fear of bereaved parents may be underscored by the comments and suggestions of family members and friends about how they should be feeling and acting. Such statements as, "Don't you think you ought to be pulling yourself together by now?" and "Maybe you need professional help since you don't seem to be able to get on with your life," support the parent's fear of losing their minds.

Parents need to be assured that they are not going crazy. They need to be told that their feelings and behavior are normal. Parents who have been mentally healthy in the past are at *extremely* low risk of decompensating or becoming psychotic as a result of their loss.

Another normalizing intervention the nurse can do is to discuss with parents how normal it is to grieve in different ways and at different rates. If parents are helped to relinquish the myth of automatic cohesion, they then will be better able to give each other permission and room to grieve in their own unique manner.

Reassurance also can be offered about the constricting effects of the pain each parent is experiencing. One useful method is to point out to the parents that if they were both hospitalized with an acute illness or severe injuries, they would not be put in the same room and told to take care of each other!

Provide Sources of Continuing Support

Since normal parental grief takes so long to work through, there is a great need for continuing support. The nurse–counselor can facilitate on-going support in two important ways: (1) she can serve as a source of that support over the most difficult

Table 24-3. Books to Help Bereaved Parents

Donnelly K Fair: Recovering from the Loss of a Child. New York, Macmillan, 1982

Friedman R, Grandstein B: Surviving Pregnancy Loss. Boston, Little, Brown, 1982

Miles MS: The Grief of Parents: When a Child Dies (booklet). Oak Brook, IL, Compassionate Friends, 1980

Panuthos C, Romeo C: Ended Beginnings—Healing Childbearing Losses. South Hadley, Massachusetts, Bergin & Garvey, 1984

Peppers LG, Knapp RJ: Motherhood and Mourning. New York, Praeger, 1980

Schiff HS: The Bereaved Parent. New York, Crown Publishers, 1977

times during at least the first year following the child's death, using the principles discussed in this chapter, and (2) she can refer parents to other useful resources.

One major resource consists of books written for bereaved individuals, including ones directed specifically at parents. Some of the books currently available are listed in Table 24-3.

The most potent resource available, however, are specific support groups for bereaved parents. Compassionate Friends, Parents of Murdered Children, Share, and Parent Bereavement Outreach are all examples of bereaved parents support groups (specific addresses for each group are listed in Table 24-4). These groups, and others like them, provide an invaluable service to grieving parents by putting them in contact with other parents who are going through a similar experience. At group meetings parents can cry, talk, express anger, and even laugh without fear of being judged. Their outpourings will be heard by the most understanding of ears: parents who are there or who have been there.

The following quotes from mothers and fathers who have participated in a support group* highlights the value of the group experience:

"The value of the group has been that no one knows what it is like to lose a child unless they have been through it. The group doesn't take away the pain but the shared tragedy is somehow comforting."

"It was comforting to be able to confess the feeling of coming apart at the seams and to find that other parents feel the same way."

"The group helps us to be more comfortable with the unpredictability of our grief. It helps, too, to be able to allow ourselves to laugh and have fun again without feeling guilty."

"Everybody has his own mountain to climb in dealing with grief. . . . Whatever the problem, the group provides acceptance and understanding."

Interpreting "Recovery"

The ultimate goal of working with bereaved parents is to help them incorporate the loss of their child into their lives so that they can go on living in healthy,

---

* Parent Bereavement Outreach.

Table 24-4. Support Groups for Bereaved Parents

AMEND (Aiding Mothers Experiencing Neonatal Death)
4324 Berrywick Terrace,
St. Louis, MO 63128

Compassionate Friends
P. O. Box 1347
Oak Brook, IL 60521

National Foundation
Sudden Infant Death
5401 West 95th Street
Los Angeles, CA 90054

Parent Bereavement Outreach
535 Sixteenth Street
Santa Monica, CA 90402

Parents of Murdered Children
1739 Bella Vista
Cincinnati, OH 45237

Share (deals with infant loss)
St. John's Hospital
800 East Carpenter
Springfield, IL 62769

productive ways. Recovery takes a long time; longer than most parents and inexperienced professionals might predict. Typically it takes parents 1½ to 2½ years to "recover" from the loss of a child.

Nurse–counselors and bereaved parents alike need to understand that recovery does not mean that the parents will totally and always be free of pain. Instead, recovery means learning to live in a world that no longer contains the loved child. It means that the occurrences of pain will decrease first in frequency and later in intensity. Nonetheless, as long as the parents live part of them will always hurt over the death of their child. The hurt, though, will become a muted sadness rather than a wrenching agony. Bereaved parents eventually learn that life will never be the same again, but it can be good.

REFERENCES

Frey WH: Not-so-idle tears, Psychol Today, 8(13):91–92, 1980
Hagan J, Gemma P: A Child Dies—A Portrait of Family Grief. Rockville, Maryland: Aspen Systems Corporation, 1983
Hansen JC (ed) Death and Grief in the Family. Rockville, Maryland: Aspen Systems Corporation, 1984
Worden JW: Grief Counseling and Grief Therapy. New York, Springer-Verlag, 1982

Commentary

Reflections on Dr. Eugenia Waechter's Contribution to Knowledge for Nursing Practice

Bonnie Holaday

The purpose of this commentary is to examine the scholarly work of Dr. Eugenia Waechter, and to consider her contribution to parent–child nursing's theoretical base for nursing practice. In the past decades, much attention has been given to identifying nursing's scientific foundations for practice. A consensus now exists that an effective approach to this process is to examine central concepts of the discipline of nursing: person, environment, health, and nursing (Flaskrud and Halloran, 1980). Recently, Meleis (1985) proposed that nursing has seven conceptual domains. These are identified as the nursing client, transitions, interaction, nursing process, environment, nursing therapeutics, and health. Meleis proposes that "the nurse interacts (interaction) with a human being in a health/illness situation (nursing client) who is in an integral part of his sociocultural context (environment) and who is in some sort of transition or is anticipating a transition (transition): the nurse/patient interactions are arranged around some purpose (nursing process) and the nurse uses some actions (nursing therapeutics) to enhance, bring about, or facilitate health (health)." This typology of theoretical domains serves as a useful framework to examine one nurse researcher's work. This commentary will focus on Dr. Waechter's work in two of these domains—the nursing client and nursing therapeutics.

RESEARCH APPROACH

The nursing client is concerned with theoretical issues that pertain only to the client. The focus is on such areas as client characteristics in health and illness, patterns of interaction with the environment, patterns of adaptations, the phenomena that arise as the result or threat of illness, or the phenomena that arise from contact with the health care system. Dr. Waechter's research focused on how to best care for children and to promote their well-being and growth. Her research was naturally linked to and dependent upon knowledge of how children grew and developed normally. Therefore, it is not surprising to find that Dr. Waechter used a developmental model as a way of organizing human phenomena into categories appropriate for scholarly examination from a nursing perspective. Dr. Waechter's comments on the use of the developmental model identify the general goals of her research, and the interdisciplinary thrust of her work (1974):

Current developmental theory is allied to many other fields in the study of the human individual, in that its goal and purpose are to delineate broad principles which can be utilized for the accurate description, explanation, and prediction of behavior. It differs from other theoretical formulations in that it stresses continuity of behavioral patterns throughout the life cycle and is concerned with sequences of events. It also emphasizes the unitary nature of the developmental process and the constant interaction of the organism with its psychological, social, and physical environment. Whereas most disciplines stress concepts which are germane to the particular prevailing theoretical stance or mode of thinking, researchers using developmental theory strive for a wider understanding of the developmental process by scrutiny of behavior from various perspectives and by reorganization of previous knowledge.

   The purposes of the study of developmental theory are threefold. The first is to illuminate the causality of behavioral characteristics in particular individuals. Through continuous study and systematic investigation, the boundaries of "normal" or "average" rates of development and behavior are being established, an achievement which contributes perspective in the evaluation of the individual. However, the ultimate goal in this field is not merely to produce a series of portraits of the child and adult at successive steps in development, but to clarify the process of change involved in such transformation. Knowledge of normal limits within stages, nevertheless, is necessary to evaluate current or past physical, intellectual, emotional, or behavioral abnormalities or any problems in one or more of the developmental stages or areas. Understanding of the factors affecting each area of development (physical, social, emotional, intellectual) in terms of the process of change also offers clues for the amelioration of problems and modification of behavior through direct therapeutic intervention, manipulation of environmental variables, or support of available internal and external strengths. The prediction of one variable from another often becomes possible within reasonable margins for error, and the scientific understanding of causality can lead to alterations and controls within the environment of the individual.

   Knowledge of norms—of process and variables involved in the transformation of one phase to another—may then serve not only for diagnosis, but also in the outlining of treatment plans. The therapist who is knowledgeable regarding the elements necessary for healthy development and functioning will have a broader basis for alertness to the possible results of insufficiency or distortion in one of these areas.

   However, the thesis of multiple causality must always be kept in mind. Limitations imposed by inadequate or insufficient knowledge within the discipline or incomplete understanding of the history of the individual under evaluation may result in inappropriate therapeutic intervention.

As a summary, therefore, the study of normal developmental theory is an important end in itself; but, in addition, knowledge so derived can have important practical applications in the understanding and prediction of the behavior of particular children—and of adults and of group phenomena—in forming the basis for therapeutic plans and also in the formation of hypotheses which point the way for further investigation of variables important to developmental outcomes.

In general, research proceeds in stages from the exploratory to the descriptive to the analytical to the experimental. In the first stage, the aim is to develop insights so that a potentially unlimited range of characteristics can be narrowed to make it possible to observe them. Some of Dr. Waechter's work from this first stage is available from her student papers and notes; however, much must be inferred from her later work. It is evident that her ideas came from her own experiences, the literature, personal contacts, teachers, and encounters with other scientists. Her subjective impressions were probably also useful in formulating her strategies and approaches. Material is available to examine Dr. Waechter's second (descriptive) and third (analytical) phases of research. In her early descriptive studies, there were no hypotheses, but variables of interest were specified. In the third stage, there were specific hypotheses or research questions about the relationships among observed events or characteristics. Her experience was validated by data, and data subsequently supplemented experience in making decisions about patient care.

Thus, Dr. Waechter's study of children with a life-threatening or chronic illness and their families began with an understanding of the general and unique problems and stresses posed by these types of illnesses. Illness-related problems and stresses would be expected to intersect with other developmental, social, and psychological factors to affect the child's development, influence the child and family's patterns of response, and ultimately lead to adaptive or nonadaptive responses. Within these parameters, the major classes of problems and stresses studied by Dr. Waechter and her students include physical symptoms, treatment regimens and procedures, impact on development, and life-threatening illness. As a guide for subsequent discussion of nursing therapeutics, the general nature of the findings are summarized here. The findings are not necessarily unique to Dr. Waechter's work or that of her students. However, along with the work of other scientists, they represent a contribution to our knowledge about these clients.

DESCRIPTION OF THE NURSING CLIENT

Physical Symptoms

Depending on their disease, children with chronic or life-threatening illness endure various physical symptoms. Frequently, these symptoms cannot be prevented, but must become a part of day-to-day life if a normal life-style is to be maintained. Individual illnesses vary considerably with respect to the affected organ system, the nature and degree of physical symptoms and pain, and the way life functioning is disrupted by disease-related symptoms (Waechter, Phillips, and Holaday, 1985).

For example, Dr. Waechter's work illustrated that many children did not experience severe physical symptoms but that other children, such as those with renal disease or cystic fibrosis faced daily reminders of the physical symptoms of their disease. The physical symptoms also influenced the development of the child's self-concept and sense of competency (Crittenden, Waechter, and Mikkelson, 1977; Mikkelson, Waechter, and Crittenden, 1978; Waechter, 1971).

Some chronic or life-threatening illnesses include a constellation of symptoms that may also represent a source of anxiety. Much of Dr. Waechter's research focused on the examination of death anxiety in children with a chronic or life-threatening illness, and this will be discussed in a later section of the paper.

Procedure and Treatment Regimens

Only a small portion of Dr. Waechter's research addressed the issue of the chronically ill child and family's response to hospitalization, diagnostic procedures, and treatments. However, the topic was addressed in some depth in her text *Nursing Care of Children*. The diagnosis and management of a chronic or life-threatening illness presents a multifaceted crisis that requires the child to adapt to the loss of normal functioning, tolerate and comply with medical procedures and treatments, and struggle with feelings about the meaning of the disease and its treatment (Waechter, Crittenden, Mikkelsen, and Holaday, 1986).

The diagnostic and treatment regimens involved actual or imagined assaults to bodily integrity, autonomy, and sexuality, and these in turn threaten body image and self-concept (Waechter, Phillips, and Holaday, 1985). These treatment regimens were found to involve periodic or regular visits to the hospital, which added the additional stresses of separation, loss of familiar routines, and absence from school.

The treatment regimens at home affected the balance of interpersonal relationships within the family. In some cases, they led to problems of parental overprotection and dependency, interpersonal conflict between parent and child and parent and siblings, and problems with noncompliance. Treatment regimens imposed burdens on the parents in terms of time, energy, finances, career, and negotiations of the parental role (Waechter, 1977).

Impact on Development

Illness-related impairments can limit the child's physical activity, capacity to function at school or play, and independence. Although many children with a chronic illness can expect a good quality of life for extended periods, those with other conditions such as end-stage renal disease and myelomeningocele can experience physical immobility and social isolation. Moreover, the advanced stages of disease such as cystic fibrosis and cancer can lead to losses of physical skills and activities, as well as cause a troubling change in personal goals. These changes in physical status require exceptional coping patterns for the child and the parents (Waechter, 1978).

Hospitalizations, clinic visits, and changes in treatment regimens required the child and family members to adjust to new schedules or new environments. This sometimes resulted in emotional problems and led to disturbances in academic and social settings. These transitions are important areas for nursing intervention.

Life-Threatening Illness

Life-threatening illnesses pose unique psychological problems for children (Waechter 1971). The majority of Dr. Waechter's research focused on the variables that affect the amount and quality of expressed anxiety in children with chronic and life-threatening illness. Her studies indicated that children with fatal illness demonstrated significantly greater anxiety than other groups of children. The children with fatal illnesses expressed more anxiety related to death and told stories containing more references to death, loneliness, fear, and sadness. However, one of the most significant of the findings indicated that children who had had an opportunity to discuss their illness, diagnosis, and prognosis expressed less anxiety than did the other children with fatal illness who had not had such an opportunity ($r = .63$; $p = .01$) (Waechter, 1972).

These findings suggested that, contrary to the supposition that children below the age of 10 years who have a poor prognosis are not concerned with impending death, these children, although not directly informed of the nature of their illness, did indicate considerable preoccupation with death in fantasy, loneliness, and isolation. They also suggested a sense of lack of control of the forces impinging on them, along with a sense of incapacity to affect the inner and outer environment. There was also a great dichotomy seen between the parents' perception of the children's awareness of their prognosis and anxiety surrounding the concept of death expressed by the children. This finding suggests that children do perceive the threat through the altered affect in their total environment and from the parents' anxiety communicated in nonverbal ways. It also suggests that adults were perhaps blinded to the child's anxiety because of their own fears, concerns and sense of helplessness related to the diagnosis (Waechter and Blake, 1976).

Summary

Dr. Waechter's scholarly work related to the nursing client originated in the real world problems or issues in the lives of children and their families. Her focus of inquiry and concern was directed to relatively complex issues—children's understanding of death, death anxiety, parental response to chronically ill or terminally ill children. A major result of her sustained focus on substantive problems was her decision to use an applied versus a basic perspective in her research. If a full understanding of the nature and sources of developmental growth and change in chronically ill children was to be attained, one had to move beyond the confines of the laboratory setting and the experimental method. I believe that the use of an applied perspective was also related to Dr. Waechter's interdisciplinary background (nursing, developmental psychology, education). Dr. Waechter believed that when focusing on complex topics, other disciplines provided challenging information and ideas.

Several orientations that provide the underpinnings for nursing therapeutics are evident from a review of Dr. Waechter's work. First, understanding developmental concepts and phenomena from a milestone approach aids in understanding the client and health. The milestone approach has as its main thrust an orientation toward providing effective interventions at different developmental levels when the child or family might be thought at-risk for certain problems. Milestone approaches have a great potential for influencing behaviors that occur at predictable junctures during development. Thus, Dr. Waechter's efforts to describe fatally ill children's awareness of death at different ages, to identify patterns of expression of death anxiety at certain ages, and to identify patterns of parental response to children with a congenital defect will help nurses recognize important developmental patterns. Parent–child nurse researchers need to continue to clarify their concept of these developmental patterns because they underlie many of the problems that nursing clients might face.

The second orientation evident in Dr. Waechter's work is a problem-focused approach. This approach examines children and families who are at-risk for difficulties or whose circumstances place them at higher risk. The thrust of this approach is for the nurse to focus on the special needs and circumstances of these children and their families. Therefore, studying chronically ill or terminally ill children and their families proceeds with an orientation toward the needs and problems of these groups. This approach is useful because it often identifies phenomena, perhaps unique to this population, that require some type of nursing actions. This includes such phenomena and concepts as pain, death anxiety, body image disturbances, and grieving.

NURSING THERAPEUTICS

The domain of nursing therapeutics is defined as "all nursing activities and actions deliberately designed to care for nursing clients" (Barnard, 1980). As mentioned previously, an understanding of the nursing client is of critical importance in determining the contents and goals of nursing actions. This is the domain in which we draw from our scientific knowledge base about the nursing client, and prescribe specific actions to fit the special requirements of the client. This domain represents the ultimate objective of the science of nursing—prescription.

My concept of nursing actions, identified by Dr. Waechter, that assisted children and families with the management of the psychosocial effects of chronic and life-threatening illness, is presented here. The task was a challenge because Dr. Waechter did not identify a general approach to explain her ultimate goal. Based on my analysis of Dr. Waechter's work I believe her ultimate goal was to prevent severe behavior problems associated with chronic and life-threatening illness. Specifically, her goals of intervention included (1) mastery of anxieties related to illness; (2) integration of the illness into family life; and (3) adaptation to the illness, treatments and hospitalizations. I have grouped these various goals under the general category of "prevention."

Given the unsettled dispute among theorists as to the definition of prevention, I have provided a definition for this article. Prevention is defined as helping a vulnerable high-risk individual or group by taking actions to avoid the onset of a disturbance and/or to enhance the client's level of adaptation. A preventive intervention may occur shortly after a problem develops, as in a crisis such as the birth of an infant with congenital anomalies (Waechter, 1977), or after the diagnosis of cancer is made. These events are likely to have a severe impact on the person unless he undergoes preventive treatment (Waechter, Phillips, and Holaday, 1985).

Living with a chronic or life-threatening illness presents additional problems. Nursing is still in the process of defining the client, and therefore we still have difficulty in predicting psychosocial malfunctioning before it appears in these groups. Currently, we work to spot early manifestations of problems so we can take actions to prevent more serious ones later. This can also be viewed as intervening shortly after a problem is diagnosed, preventing further problems.

Prevention interventions with clients with chronic illness also involves "long-term" action. Efforts are made prior to the development of would-be problems because this is an at-risk population. These efforts are continued over the life span to promote and support the desired psychosocial and developmental outcomes (Waechter, 1985).

Dr. Waechter's *Nursing Care of Children* recommends many specific nursing actions, such as preparation, teaching, or stimulating, that can be taken to prevent problems from developing. However, behind these specific actions Dr. Waechter had a set of organizing principles for taking a preventive stance in dealing with psychosocial problems. These included

1. A family-centered focus
2. Mutual participation by child and family
3. A developmental perspective
4. A focus on coping and competence
5. Active participation by the nurse.

The use of these principles will be highlighted in the following section.

PREVENTIVE INTERVENTION

Family-Centered Focus

For Dr. Waechter, a family-centered focus meant the inclusion of family members and subgroups in the child's care in ways that involved the family in problem solving, decision making, and management of illness-related stress (Waechter and Blake, 1976). Since Dr. Waechter considered the quality of the parent's relationship critical for the child's development and coping, it was identified as a focal point for the nurse's contacts with the family. The successful management of a chronic or life-threatening illness required a delicate balance between support and overinvolvement. The nurse worked with all family members to achieve this balance.

Florence Blake (1954), Dr. Waechter's teacher, colleague, and friend, identified the importance for the child and family to see themselves as active partners rather than passive recipients of care. Dr. Waechter concurred and urged nurses to structure their contacts with the family to facilitate open discussions about their perceptions of the illness and their concerns about treatment and about the impact of the illness on the family and the child's development. Dr. Waechter's research (1971, 1986) has found that it is important to create an atmosphere in which the children's and families' perceptions are believed, and in which families and children are given clear feedback on the course of the disease. Children and families who felt that they were listened to and believed seemed to be more likely to adhere to treatment regimens and to provide feedback to health care personnel regarding the child's status.

Planned family-centered care suggests a concept of nursing care that embraces the family in its entirety during the total experience of illness and hospitalization and has as its goal the enhancement of the family's well-being. The unique role of the pediatric nurse in family-centered care is determined through the blending of appropriate cues from the child and other family members. This is made more complex by the additional incorporation of cues provided by the dynamic functioning of the family as a whole. The nurse's task is to move all family members forward during the illness situation by incorporating the present experience into the family's concept of a meaningful experience. Through carefully planned therapeutic intervention techniques, the nurse stimulates personal development and emotional growth so that the potentially disruptive occurrence of illness or hospitalization is a positive experience (Waechter, Phillips, and Holaday, 1985).

Developmental Perspective

For Dr. Waechter, a developmental perspective was critical in establishing the approach to interventions. For the child, the intervention must be related to developmental capabilities if it was to be successful. A child's understanding of his or her disease, emotional concerns, and expectations for management and outcome varied considerably with age and level of developmental maturity. The nurse must structure the intervention to emphasize developmental expectations, and evaluate the child's progress over time to determine subsequent interventions. The goal is to prevent the occurrence of developmental delays or emotional disturbances.

The stress of chronic and life-threatening illness is intertwined with family developmental issues. The nurse must consider the family's functioning, and whether the family is at a critical transition point in its development, such as the birth of a baby or a child starting school or experiencing the onset of puberty (Waechter, 1978). The nurse's intervention must consider the family's developmental needs if a supportive environment for the ill child is to be maintained.

To protect the child's growth potential to the fullest, the nurse must take into account to the situation of the parents, not only because they make up the most important part of the their child's environment but also because they are important people in their own right. Parents, too, are in the process of development. They require help (1) in working out constructive relationships with each other and with their children (2) in acquiring satisfaction and competence in child rearing, and (3) in learning to cope with their feelings and responsibilities when their children are ill or handicapped. To a great extent intrafamily relationships make the child what he or she is. They will also influence to a considerable degree the kind of adjustment the child will make to health problems and the necessary treatment (Waechter and Blake, 1976).

Coping and Competency

Prevention as competency suggests that the intervention should do more than accomplish the short-term avoidance of problems. This approach suggests that the nursing interventions should add to the child's and parents' growing collection of skills, and that both should experience an increase in abilities to solve problems, make decisions, and manage problems, and that competency-building interventions teach important behaviors or skills that will directly enhance current functioning and thus prevent future problems. It is assumed that enhanced functioning resulting from skill acquisition will ultimately be preventive for any number of reasons. For example, individuals will be better able to deal with stress, be more adept in dealing with repeated hospitalizations, have greater self-confidence, or have more adaptable parenting patterns. (Waechter, Phillips, and Holaday, 1985). The emphasis on building strengths communicates a sense of hope and optimism to chronically ill children and their families. Coping and competency interventions that focus on the stressful, yet manageable, prospect of living with a chronic or life-threatening disease suggest that mastery is possible.

Active Participation by the Nurse

Effective preventive interventions require active participation by the nurse. The child and family identify problems, but the nurse is equally responsible for identifying current or potential problems. Preventive interventions require that the nurse assume the initiative in working with a family with a child with a chronic or life-threatening illness. Thus, the nurse is expected to structure opportunities for the family and child to express feelings and to provide feedback and additional information about the disease and its management. To function in this role, the nurse must have a thorough knowledge of the disease and its treatment, and an understanding of expected versus deviant psychological reactions. With this background the nurse can help most families view their stress reactions as legitimate ways of coping, and therefore view themselves as mastering the situation.

Dr. Waechter (1985) addressed this active approach when she discussed anticipatory guidance. She believed that nurses used their knowledge base to anticipate the types of problems emerging at different ages. For example, the newly diagnosed leukemic child will experience death anxiety. In anticipatory guidance, the nurse informs the parents about this phenomenon, tells them what to look and listen for, and explains actions that they can take.

It is exciting and informative to examine the contributions of one individual to nursing's knowledge base for practice. As Dr. Steckel (1981) noted, "Nothing breeds success like success so, let us recognize what we have achieved and increase our odds of achieving even more in the future." The challenge for all of us is to continue with the development of an organized body of knowledge for nursing practice.

REFERENCES

Barnard KE: Knowledge for practice: Directions for the future. Nurs Res 29:208–212, 1980
Blake FG: The child, his parents and the nurse. Philadelphia, JB Lippincott, 1954
Crittenden M, Waechter EH, Mikkelson C: Taking it one day at a time. Child Today 6(3):4–6, 1977
Flaskerud JH, Halloran EJ: Areas of agreement in nursing theory development. Adv Nurs Science 3(1):1–7, 1980
Meleis AI: Theoretical nursing: Development and progress. Philadelphia, JB Lippincott, 1985
Mikkelsen C, Waechter EH, Crittenden M: Cystic fibrosis: A family challenge. Child Today 7(4):22–26, 1978
Steckel SB: Reach out and touch success with someone. (NR newsletter 12(3):3, 1981
Waechter E: Developmental correlates of disability. Nurs Forum 9(1):1970
Waechter E: Children's awareness of fatal illness. Am J Nurs 71:1168–1172
Waechter E: Bonding problems of infants with congenital anomalies. Nurs Forum 16(3):298–315, 1977
Waechter E: How families cope: Assessing and intervening. Paper presented at the Children's Health Center, University of Minnesota, Minneapolis, Minnesota, 1978
Waechter E, Blake FG: Nursing Care of Children, 9th ed. Philadelphia, JB Lippincott, 1976
Waechter E, Phillips J, Holaday B: Nursing care of children, 10th ed. Philadelphia, JB Lippincott, 1985
Waechter E, Crittenden M, Mikkelsen C, Holaday B: Concomitants of death imagery in stories told by chronically ill children undergoing intrusive procedures: A comparison of four diagnostic groups. J Pediatr Nurs 1(1):2–11, 1986

Commentary

A Compassionate Scholar

M. Colleen Stainton

I met Dr. Eugenia Waechter when I enrolled in the first course of a child development series she was offering for graduate students at the University of California,
San Francisco. As a maternity specialist, I felt it was prudent to study the infant.
What I discovered was a nurse, highly qualified in child development, who used
her knowledge and experience as a medium to stimulate thinking in ways never
before available to me. As a result, I continued to take the whole series of courses
through to adolescence, a decision that has proved highly valuable many times
since. Gene's love of children and her deep understanding of their thinking, needs,
and development not only motivated my increased awareness of children and their
needs, but improved my sense of people in general.

Gene continued to be my friend and mentor after I finished the Masters'
program in 1971. She died just after I entered the doctoral program in 1981. I have
missed Gene very much. It is therefore a particular privilege to have the opportunity to comment on some of her papers as they provide the access to her thinking,
and the stimulation of mine.

This commentary will take the form of a thematic analysis of the unit as a
whole. It is hoped that those new to the field will find this approach helpful as a
guide to reading the included works with greater understanding and appreciation
of how they link together and the contribution they make to science and practice.
For those more seasoned in the field, this analysis can provide a springboard for
discussion and debate—a scholarly activity in which Gene delighted.

This last unit, devoted to caring for dying children and their families, reflects
Gene's compassionate scholarship. Her careful attention to the cultural and family
context of dying came from a deep understanding of dying and its meaning to
families. This knowledge was acquired in the style of a clinical scholar—by study
of theoretical components in the research literature, interaction with the few

colleagues interested in dying as a phenomenon, and then, without peers for most of her career, systematic from the nursing perspective study of the process of a child's death.

Gene's pediatric clinical practice, research, and theory building was rooted in study of the care of children with Florence Blake, a person she admired and credited throughout her career as being a continuing source of insight and inspiration. Later, in a doctoral program, she focused on child development under the direction of Pauline and Robert Sears at Stanford. From this unique background, Gene developed penetrating research questions combining clinical and developmental components of a child's living and dying that led to a series of studies by her graduate students and by some others acknowledged in the papers.

For me, one of the highlights of this unit is Gene's own description of her dissertation and the subsequent research it generated. This is a rare treat from one so humble about her own prowess in a field of inquiry. Her work is an example of the eclectic theoretical stance of the nurse clinician. The question around which her dissertation was built emanated from an apparent discrepancy between the commonly held beliefs associated with dying children that guided practice—that children under age 12 years did not have an awareness of dying—and the cognitive and emotional development of the school age child. The subsequent creative and courageous research design she developed, the difficult work of acquiring the necessary data from dying children, and the analysis that followed resulted in a classic work that broke new ground in science and challenged the work of senior scholars. This work stands, therefore, not only as important in the fields of pediatric nursing, child development, and thanatology, but also as an exemplar of the important contribution original clinical nursing research makes to science. Gene's continuing research and that of her proteges, several of whom are contributors to this unit, underscores the importance of the beginning she provided by opening up the field of inquiry through dissertation work.

Gene's skills as a compassionate and scholarly clinician enabled children and their families undergoing one of life's most painful experiences to express themselves to her. Her analytical skills applied to the acquired data identified concepts, processes, and theoretical notions important for nursing and other disciplines. As a result of this intensive and difficult work, nursing has the gift of theoretically grounded nursing interventions designed specifically for care of the dying child and family members.

The unit opens with Gene's interpretation of the lived experience of dying in the better known adult terms and eloquently describes how nurses can provide meaningful caring in relation to that lived experience. She then further interprets the experience of childhood death using her own work and illustrations from the raw data woven in a manner that adds a special poignancy to Gene's conceptualization.

Gene describes the grief experience of the parents and the dying child in nontraditional terms. She does not set out a trajectory of phases or stages. Instead, as always, Gene, sets the experience within the framework of the child's understanding of the world, cognitive ability, and basic needs. The interventions described are based on her systematic study of various ways parents and their child coped with the issues facing them. Again, detailed clinical data support the theoretical notions derived.

Some of the suggestions to increase our sensitivity to the child are traditional, such as, "stay with and listen to the patient." Gene does not suggest only that we be sensitive, however. She guides our thinking into levels of sensitivity specifically directed to the experience of dying during childhood. Her repeated reminders to separate the child's *living* from the child's *dying* is based on her deep knowledge of the experience the child and family have during various conditions of the child's living while dying.

Gene's social learning orientation with the emphasis on positive reinforcement was paramount in her interaction with people in general and is apparent in her descriptions of nursing care of the dying child and the family. Continuous reference is made throughout this unit to fostering positive experiences for the family members within the desperate situation of a child's dying. She reminds us that pleasure and growth are still appropriate and attainable. Clear suggestions are made of ways the nurse can foster individual and family mastery and development under the often overwhelming conditions of their situation. It is part of Gene's great understanding of children that she can provide us with this necessary reminder of the child's needs for living. Chapter 22, outlining patterns of coping, is particularly helpful in providing guidance to those having the opportunity to make a difference to the way the fatal illness of a child is experienced by all involved.

The developmental approach to the presentation of both awareness behavior and coping styles of the children studied is the hallmark of Gene's work. Her specific analysis of the experience from the child's developmental perspective was and continues to be unique.

The family orientation Gene gave to her work was unusual at the time. We may read it with complacency unless we realize that nursing was highly individual-centered when her work was done in the 1960s. Her respect for the father's experience and role in situations involving parents and parenting was virtually unprecedented. Her fascination and inquisitiveness also included concern for siblings. Again, she linked developmental theory with clinical data to identify specific areas of young children's experience with the dying and death of a sibling. As with the dying child, Gene set goals for the outcomes of care directed toward fostering potential for the growth of other children and the parents.

At times, Gene admonished us with examples of care that was less than it could be. It was done without tirade and in the parents' or child's own words. Balancing the child's view of the disease process with his well self, which needs touch, parental love, definitions of socially acceptable behavior, interaction with peers, and acknowledgment of growth and developmental processes, enables the nurse to think holistically in a clinical situation that may otherwise seem without future goals. Gene brings us up short at times, reminding us that we need to care, not only for the pathological aspects of the child, but for the whole person who has a fatal illness and the family members who know the child better as a well person. The child's own words are used to illustrate the salient points and to obviate any element of doubt of her interpretation of the experience.

A major area of controversy and stress in caring for the dying child is the question of talking to the child about the experience of dying. Gene addresses this question clearly and, using empirical data, provides guidance to the clinician who must confront this issue. We are given documented evidence of the outcome of a child's being allowed to express feelings about the dying with parents.

One of the more difficult areas of nursing practice is pediatric oncology. The experience of the child and the family is excruciating in the loss, not only of a loved member of the family, but also of all the potential and expectations of a future not to be achieved. Current readers of this book will be clinicians, graduate and undergraduate students, parents and perhaps even some dying children. It is important to keep in view the changes that have taken place in the field of pediatric oncology and chronic illness. All of Gene's subjects died—a factual and difficult part of doing this research. Today, treatment modalities have changed the trajectory of the disease processes, modified the life-style of the child with a fatal illness and the family, and rendered the outcomes of specific disease entities less certain. Continued replication of the original study and extensions of the questions need to be done in order to retest the theory generated within the unstable context that medical science creates. The nursing interventions postulated require rigorous testing against the changing careers of illnesses in which death is no longer predictable. Periods of remission may be long, short or potentially permanent. Little is known about families in which the prognosis is unclear and uncertain. The sick/well cycle of some childhood diseases resulting from advances in health care and management modalities create new zones of concern and anxiety for the child and family members. With the bombardment of technology during acute crises and increased home administration of chemotherapy, dialysis, and other treatment modalities, nurses are faced with interrupted contact with potentially fatally ill children and family members. The body of knowledge that Gene Waechter's research generated was a beginning to understanding children's experience of living with a fatal illness.

The themes Gene identified in the clinical phenomenon of the dying child remain critical to the on-going development of the body of knowledge so important for all who encounter the phenomena. The papers in this unit show her work to be characterized by a holistic blend of conceptualizations from child development, family dynamics, grief and grieving, death and dying, stress and coping, social support, nursing process, and the social and cultural context.

The special value of Gene Waechter as a nurse, teacher, and scholar was the pervasive respect she had for all human conditions. She cherished human behavior, and took considerable pleasure in understanding it. Those of us fortunate enough to have been her students know her interests ranged far beyond the study of dying children. She formed a colleagial relationship in the quest for knowledge with students studying many aspects of child health care. She enjoyed sharing the puzzles as well as the insights. Gene seemed always to be searching for a better question and did so with a sense of perspective, good humor, and intellectual wisdom.

I have thought about what Gene would think of this book being undertaken and how she would guide me in this commentary. I know she would take considerable pleasure in seeing the work of many of her students included, and knowing of the on-going doctoral research of others, such as Ki Moore, would please her very much. Her advice would undoubtedly include a reminder to stress the importance of using the current state of the art in nursing, child development, and other adjacent bodies of knowledge in conjunction with clinical data to provoke the most ardent and incisive questions possible, and then, letting the child and family tell the story.

Gene was a significant model for me of the compassion required of the clinician and the scholarship demanded of science. She was a compassionate scholar. In a short time, she gave us all so much. The foundation has been provided by Gene. The rest is up to us.

Afterword

Dr. Eugenia Waechter:
A Committed Theorist

Afaf I. Meleis

THE THEORIST

Theorists are researchers or clinicians with visions that connect research and clinical practice to a wider field of investigation. They conceptualize each research project as only a part of a whole, and they conceptualize the relationship between their field of investigation and the larger disciplinary concerns. They have visions of the forest even when they focus on one of the trees, and in focusing on one of the trees they answer questions that affect both the trees and the forest as a whole. Theorists are innovators, they question the status quo, they are visionaries, risk takers, and systematic builders. They are persistent and focused. Dr. Eugenia Waechter's theoretical work exemplifies these characteristics.

Eugenia Waechter created something that continues to make an impact on nursing knowledge; she created insights that have outlived her. Her contributions began, where most theorists' ideas begin, by being open and by questioning some assumptions that have been firmly held and adhered to by researchers and clinicians. The assumptions were grounded in developmental theories and previous research. The theory was that children younger than 10 years of age are not aware of impending death and therefore do not fear it or experience any anxieties related to it.

Dr. Waechter manifested risk-taking behaviors at different levels. Her inquisitiveness began in the 1960s when only a handful of clinicians and researchers were discussing death and the dying experiences. Death, for the most part, was a taboo subject. Researchers stayed clear of it and clinicians pretended it was a family affair and shunned discussions related to it. Even those who transcended these values were open to considering adults' dying experiences as a subject of discussion, but did not entertain children's experiences as worthy of exploration. This reticence was based on the notion that one might induce fear and anxiety in the child where none existed before. Waechter opened up both for discussion and

360 ·

exploration, and she further supported the notion that discussion of fears and anxieties surrounding death is nursing's business. Notwithstanding the restrictive climate surrounding the death of children, she was able to recruit subjects into her research study and to help the children and parents in communicating their fears of the illness and of death to each other.

She innovatively designed a picture projective test that consisted of eight pictures designed to use with the 6- to 10-year old children. Of the eight pictures, four were from thematic apperception tests and the other four were specifically designed for her studies. The newly designed pictures represented scenes from the hospital and included personnel frequently encountered in the hospital. She also interviewed parents to ascertain their perceptions of children's awareness of death. Her innovations were extensively used by other theorists and researchers (Malone, 1982; Spinetta, Rigler, and Karon, 1973). The use of different modalities in collecting her data emerged from strong conceptual bases, such as the level of cognitive and emotional development of children, and the effectiveness of the methodologies she used was well supported by appropriate statistical analysis to ascertain their validity and reliability.

For theories to develop and provide explanations for some set of phenomena, they require a committed and persistent individual or group of individuals. Waechter focused on one area of investigation during the scientific phase of life. She rendered some support to her hunch that the 6- to 10-year-old group are aware of death and have anxieties and fears. She also supported a further hunch that, by providing a cognitively and emotionally congruent approach to levels of development, children can be encouraged to communicate their fears, and they often are able to express their concerns and anxieties. The next logical question for a nurse–theorist to ask was, could nurses develop a nursing therapeutic to decrease the impact of these fears. To provide answers to this question, further explorations of the relationship between parents' attitudes about communication and levels of children's anxieties and fears were needed. Waechter proceeded to explain a new but related set of phenomena. Two characteristics of theoreticians were thus demonstrated: a vision of the whole and a persistence in developing cumulative knowledge.

THE NURSING DOMAIN

Nursing is concerned with responses of people and environment to health and illness, and the relationship between a person and his/her environment. Nursing theories address central domain questions and describe central nursing concepts. There are several indications of this focus in Waechter's work. Her research emanated from implicit and explicit assumptions that are congruent with shared assumptions in nursing. Additionally, she focused on questions that revolve around the crux of nursing domain.

Though Waechter did not specifically identify all the premises upon which her ideas were developed, her theoretical work could very easily be analyzed in terms of agreed-upon and shared assumptions of the domain. (See the listing on page 362.) When comparing domain assumptions with Waechter's implicit assumption,

Major Assumptions of Domain

1. Human responses to health and illness are repetitive, orderly, organizable, predictable, and unified; they reflect mind–body integration.
2. Health and illness are experiences perceived and understandable through the meanings that individuals, groups, and societies place on them and through scientific advances of the time.
3. Nursing deals with human and environmental experiences and responses to health and illness.
4. The goals of nursing actions are maintenance and enhancement of a sense of wellbeing, providing care for effective transitions and the treatment of illness responses.
5. Nurses act to preserve and promote the rights and dignities of their clients.
6. Nursing actions are provided within the sociocultural context and have the potential of influencing the quality of environment and a person's life.
7. Practice is central to the discipline.

Meleis AI: The Domain of Nursing: Visions and Revisions. November 1985

we find that she considered perceptions and the levels of awareness of children of their fatal illness because she assumed such experiences could be generalizable to larger populations of 6- to 10-year-old children who are confronting their own death. In addition to those domain assumptions that are adhered to by Waechter implicitly, she had other explicit assumptions, two of which are related to children. She maintained that (1) children "are often closely protected" from their diagnosis and prognosis, and (2) their cognitive and emotional development are not yet mature.

Waechter's development of theoretical aspects of nursing focused on children (clients) and their mothers (environment) and on ways by which nurses can promote the well-being and maintain a quality of life of the children and their mothers' health as they try to cope with fatal illness. She dealt with clients undergoing a major transition, that is, a diagnosis of illness with a poor prognosis. Thus, her work lends further support to the centrality of the concepts of client, environment, transitions, and health in nursing.

STRATEGY FOR THEORY DEVELOPMENT

Several strategies for theory development have been identified in the literature (Walker and Avant, 1984; Meleis 1985). A review of Waechter's life's work indicates that she used a practice–research–theory approach. She began her research expectations from a firm grounding in pediatric nursing. The phenomenon of telling children the truth about the diagnosis and prognosis of fatal illnesses became a nagging clinical question. Instead of attempting to deal with her discomfort with these questions by using experiential ready-made answers, she formulated a set of investigative questions. Had she attempted to answer the questions by surverying parents and nurses, she would not have answered the fundamental questions relating to levels of awareness of children of their prognosis or types of concerns and fears that children have that heighten their anxieties of the impending death. She reformulated the question "should children be told the truth about their diagnosis?" to "do they know the truth?", "what is truth?" and "what do children with life-threatening illnesses tell us about their fears, concerns, and anxieties?" In answering these theoretical questions about the children's fears, concerns, and anxieties, Waechter also answered other, related questions. One such related question is, "are parents' perceptions of their children's awareness of the impending death congruent with the children's perceptions of their own awareness." By demonstrating the discrepancy in perceptions, she was supporting the need for nurses to include children in their assessment as well as parents.

Analyzing Waechter's approach retrospectively, a reader could identify many of the theory development tools that were discussed in the literature after her death. She relied on her observations to identify a clinically significant problem, on her knowledge to rephrase the question, on her intuitions to question existing theory, and on other theories to develop appropriate methodology to answer the questions. While formulating her first research project, she completed an extensive review of the literature. Such careful analyses of the state of the art in research related to cognitive and emotional development of children, death anxiety, and ways of coping with impending loss due to fatal illness allowed her to support the significance and rationale of her life's work and provided guidelines for the different approaches to develop her ideas.

The process of theory development in nursing mandates the close connection between theory, practice, and research. Waechter's publications exemplify these relationships. Her research emanated from a clinical base and was promptly communicated to clinicians (Waechter 1971). New questions emerged from previous findings and from nurses' focus on nursing therapeutics. Therefore, the questions of whether open communication help in decreasing children's fears of fatal prognosis and what are the most effective ways for opening communication about death formulated her concern with nursing therapeutics.

Waechter used a contemporary thinking approach to theory development. Although quantitatively inclined, she attempted to describe the experience of mothers and children as they lived it and as they experienced it. She also considered hospitalization, diagnosis, and prognosis not as they are but as experienced within the context of a milieu that didn't encourage expression of awareness of the presence of a fatal illness and the fears and anxieties that may be associated with this awareness. Therefore, she described the values and norms that govern that milieu, the perceptions and meanings that parents impose on their children's behavior.

As a researcher, she meticulously answered each question; as a theorist she put the answers together with other answers and described and explained perceptions, awareness, and experience by clarifying the context. In doing so, she may have been anticipating the 1980s dialogs surrounding the need for using quantitative and qualitative approaches in developing knowledge in nursing.

Eugenia Waechter, a nurse–scholar, explored central questions in the care of terminally ill patients. She was a risk taker and a persistent researcher who systematically attempted to explain and describe children's awareness and fear of death and parents' mechanisms in protecting children from their diagnosis. Her work exemplifies an approach to theory development that is congruent with nursing, its assumptions, and its domain. She was a theorist who had a clear vision of how to develop knowledge. She left a road well-mapped so that others can complete what she had begun. Dr. Waechter's work provided a significant beginning to a theory of responding and coping with fatal illness. Others will need to complete what she began.

REFERENCES

Malone MM: Consciousness of dying and projective fantasy of young children with malignant disease. J Devel Behav Pediatr 3(2):55–60, 1982
Meleis AI: Theoretical Nursing: Development and Progress. JB Lippincott, 1985
Spinetta J, Rigler D, Karon M: Anxiety in the dying child. Pediatrics 52(6):841–845, 1973
Spinetta J, Maloney L: Death anxiety in the outpatient leukemic child. Pediatrics 56:1034–1037, 1975
Waechter E, Crittenden M, Mikkelsen C, Holaday B: Concomitants of death imagery in stories told by chronically ill children undergoing intrusive procedures: A comparison of four diagnostic groups. J Pediatr Nurs 1:2–11, 1986
Waechter E: Children's responses to life threatening illness and death. (unpublished manuscript).
Waechter E: Children's awareness of fatal illness. Am J Nurs 71(6):1168–1172, 1971
Walker LO, Avant KC: Strategies for theory construction in nursing. New York, Appleton–Century–Crofts, 1983

Afterword

Dr. Eugenia Waechter:
A Clinical Perspective

Bonnie Holaday, Tamar Krulik, and Ida Martinson

Dr. Waechter made her major contributions as a teacher, theoretician, and re-searcher—but in all of these activities, the child, his family, and the nurse practi-tioner were the final focus. It was her wish to bring improved care to those in need through humanistic and scientific nursing. She was also aware of the nurse pro-viding that care, and the many problems that she encountered in the process of caring.

The major messages to the practitioner to be found in Dr. Waechter's work are the essence of conscious existence, the integral role of nursing in the life process of children and families, commitment of the practitioner to recognize problems and seek answers, awareness of self in the caring process, ethics of professional in-volvement, and the utilization and valuing of clinical experience by teachers and researchers.

THE HUMAN ESSENCE

Eugenia Waechter's work grew out of a deep and basic trust in the individual human being. She believed not only that human beings are able to find and employ inner resources to cope with harsh reality, but that they can also make a concen-trated effort to do so. Harsh reality may include the need to face and contend with the dark side of human experience—anxiety, loneliness, and death.

This belief implies an additional credence not only that human beings are willing and able to face their own deep-seated anguish, but also that they are able and willing to share with each other in giving and receiving help. Human beings need one another in the depths of their sorrow, their loneliness and fears; they need each other in facing death.

THE HUMAN ESSENCE: AN INTEGRAL PART OF NURSING

Eugenia Waechter believed that nurses in their human capacity are willing and able to share these experiences of the dark side of life. She believed that their professional capacity enables them to find answers to the needs of suffering individuals. This professional capacity rests upon the desire to learn and grow, upon a deep creative potential and knowledge. Experience, creativity, and knowledge are the sources from which nurses can develop their caring—caring that becomes effective by adapting it to the specific needs of the other individual in pain, in despair, or in the face of death. According to Eugenia Waechter, nurses learn to develop interventions taking into account individual differences, levels of individual and family growth and development, and the specific problems different disease entities pose at different stages.

THE COMMITMENT OF THE CLINICIAN

Eugenia Waechter's nursing philosophy expects a genuine commitment of the clinician—a commitment to ask questions and seek answers in areas of emotional threat, in areas that are socially sensitive, such as grief, loss, loneliness, and death. Her own research on death anxiety in children at a time when it was believed that young children could not possibly experience death anxiety is a testimony to her commitment. She also demands a commitment to competence: in knowledge and in the development of cognitive skills of integration of various areas. Waechter demanded the development of means of turning intuitive reactions into planned and effective interventions. These interventions, which have predictable outcomes, were the force underlying her work in the area of assessment and research tool development.

Commitment to the human essence and to competence is joined by the demand for commitment to relevance. Eugenia Waechter's commitment as a clinician changed and remained relevant over time. While ahead of her time in addressing the issues of death and the terminally ill child, she also advanced with the development in medicine and technology. Responding to a changing reality, she then focused her major work upon children facing life-threatening disease and later on chronic illness in childhood.

THE NATURE OF THE CLINICIAN'S INVOLVEMENT

Awareness of self is Eugenia Waechter's first request of the clinician. What are her own reactions to loss, impairment, and death? Parallel to this awareness comes a painful and neverending process of working through her emotions. A clear division of one's own needs as a person and clinician and the diverse needs of the child and of the different family members is a ground rule for remaining involved.

Knowing one's own strengths and weaknesses as well as those of the clients is a crucial attribute of effective intervention. Monitoring involvement and letting go are crucial skills of professional involvement.

THE NATURE OF PROFESSIONAL CLINICAL INTERVENTION

The basic assumption underlying Eugenia Waechter's work is the great potential for effective nursing interventions. Eugenia Waechter was very clear that in order for interventions to be effective, their goals must be clearly defined. Short-term, medium-term, and long-term goals must be distinguished and measures of outcome—successes and failures—have to be developed.

Clinical intervention is in essence a shared endeavor and a shared responsibility. All goals and decisions must result from the interaction among the nurse, the child, and the family and often also involve other professionals. Decisions must be joints reached and must be acceptable to all involved.

Especially in the area of intervention, Eugenia Waechter was mainly concerned with issues regarding loss and death. In these areas clinicians may face dangerous pitfalls. Their knowledge and experience, as well as the fact that the emotional impact of the situation is not the nurse's personal pain, may result in the nurse's taking over parental roles. Although short periods of carefully planned taking over may be justified, the pitfall expressed by the phrase "we know best" must always be avoided.

TEACHING AND LEARNING

To address Eugenia Waechter's important role as an educator is beyond the scope of this afterword, but we would do the clinician injustice if we did not even mention the basic maxim in her teachings: Use clinical material! Use the wealth of knowledge in clinical experience that, through inductive analysis, becomes our major source of knowledge.

SEEDS OF FUTURE DEVELOPMENT

Eugenia Waechter recognized the vital importance of concepts such as self-care, symptom control, social support, body images, and the care–cure relationship, long before they were "discovered" as major areas of interest in nursing. She saw and planted the seeds for a wide array of future developments.

Eugenia Waechter laid the foundation in her research and education for the growth and development of an entire generation of nurse clinicians and researchers. And her work goes on. . . .

Appendix A

Waechter's Adapted Picture Test

A

B

C

From Morgan CD, Murray HA: A method for investigating fantasies: The TAT. Arch Neurol Psychiatr 34:289–306, 1935. Reproduced with permission.

D

E

From Morgan CD, Murray HA: A method for investigating fantasies: The TAT. Arch Neurol Psychiatr 34:289–306, 1935. Reproduced with permission.

F

G

From Morgan CD, Murray HA: A method for investigating fantasies: The TAT.
Arch Neurol Psychiatr 34:289–306, 1935. Reproduced with permission.

H

From Morgan CD, Murray HA: A method for investigating fantasies: The TAT.
Arch Neurol Psychiatr 34:289–306, 1935. Reproduced with permission.

Appendix B

Projective Pictures: Scoring System

Eugenia H. Waechter

The framework of the scoring system is based on anxiety as expressed by the ill and hospitalized child; the methods the child uses in coping with this stress, and the problems he anticipates in reduction of his insecurity about present and future events. The major interest in analyzing the content of the stories is in terms of the type of anxiety expressed, and the pictures are chosen to elicit a wide range of imagery related to these different types of anxieties with which children deal when they are ill. These threats to security, or fears, may be related to loneliness or separation from meaningful adults, to body intrusion, or to mutilation or death. Clues in the picture relate to the place of threat, to body image, to darkness, or to activities aimed at regaining body integrity or functioning.

The anxiety aroused in children by illness and hospitalization activates different adjustive mechanisms. The second major area of analysis, then, is directed toward delineation of these mechanisms as illustrated in the content of the stories.

Other subcategories in the scoring system note problems and obstacles that the child indicates as blocks to security, affective states experienced, and anticipations of the future.

PROCEDURE OF ADMINISTRATION
Description of Pictures, Giving Code Letter and Source

Form A: Two boys in adjoining beds (designed for the study)
Form B: Small child in hallway outside closed door to ICU (designed for the study)

Form C: Boy in front of mural depicting operation (TAT 8 BM)
Form D: Small child in bed, nurse nearby with back turned (designed for the study)
Form E: Figure outlined in open window (TAT 14)
Form F: Child in bed, parents and doctor outside door (designed for the study)
Form G: Woman entering room, face on hand (TAT GF)
Form H: Small child sitting in doorway of cabin (TAT 13 B)

Procedure

Pictures are to be shown to each child individually by the experimeter. Instructions are to be given as follows: "Tell me a story about this picture. Make the story as exciting or as interesting as you can. Include in the story:

1. What is happening in the picture?
2. What has happened before?
3. What are the people thinking, feeling, wanting?
4. What will happen? How does the story end?

If the child persists in describing the picture, a tactful reminder is to be given to the effect that the story is to test their imagination.

Should the child mention an intrusive procedure such as an injection or operation, the experimenter will ask, "How does he (she) feel about that?" The purpose of this probe is to form a basis for the decision whether the imagery is related to anxiety regarding body mutilation or to instrumental activity aimed at reducing insecurity. While showing Form B, the experimenter will read the words *intensive care unit* to all children, but will make no interpretation of the meaning of the term.

CATEGORIES AND SUBCATEGORIES IN SCORING
Threat Imagery

(Fear-related imagery. Criteria for scoring story.) The story must contain reference to a threat to body integrity or to physical or psychological security (loneliness). There must be some actual threat in the story, or action taken to avoid a threat, real or unreal. Someone in the story is threatened by disease from within or by environmental threat to body intactness (accidents, fire, etc.). Any imagery in the story involving concern regarding separation (negative affect), or statements of loneliness, illness, mutilation, or death is sufficient to score the story. The threatened individual in the story is concerned with getting well, going home from the hospital, avoiding an accident; there is fear related to dying or not getting well or negative affect related to body integrity. Negative affective states such as sadness unrelated to body integrity or loneliness are not sufficient to score the story. A direct statement of fear about internal or external threat or a statement about threat to security is sufficient to score the story. All imagery is scored from the viewpoint of the threatened individual. Stories related to threat of, or to actual harm to, animals is to be scored. One statement in the story may be scored in several subcategories as indicated by the content.

Separation of Fear or Threat Imagery

Loneliness or separation imagery, mutilation imagery, and death imagery are to be separated to provide for later analysis of major content of fear of threat in the stories.

Mutilation

A statement directly expressing or implying body intrusion, bleeding, or breaking of skin is scored as mutilation. Broken bones or falls from which bruising is probably the result or crippling conditions are not to be scored as mutilation. If there is no statement in the story that the injection or operation was wanted, it is scored as mutilation.

Loneliness, Mutilation or Death Thema

These themes are scored separately. The purpose of this is to determine the predominant expressed fear of the child telling the story. The main theme of the story is related to loneliness or separation, mutilation, or death and dying. The entire story revolves around a theme of separation, mutilation, or death. A story is to be scored only once for thema.

METHODS OF DEALING WITH ANXIETY: ADAPTIVE MANEUVERS
Wish Fulfillment Fantasy

The imagery is related to a wish to retain or regain body integrity. Someone in the story wishes for or wants to get well, to go home from the hospital, or for something to remove the threat to body intactness or reduce fear or insecurity about body integrity or loneliness. The threatened character in the story wants or wishes for something to remove the threat of injury or death. Wishing to go home from the hospital is interpreted as a wish to be well enough to go home. A wish or want to go *to* the hospital (direct statement) is interpreted as instrumental activity, in that the imagery signifies a personal cooperation (even if only thinking) that has as its function the regaining of body integrity or reduction of insecurity and anxiety. The activity is deemed instrumental by the narrator in regaining body integrity.

A desire for regaining body integrity, or imagery that can be interpreted as indicative of this, such as going home, or a desire for recovery of body functioning and health is scored as wish-fulfilling fantasy.

Thinking of going home as a definite projection into the future as a certainty is to be scored as goal anticipation, and not as wish fulfillment. Examples:

"She just keeps laying there and mumbling that she wants to get well."
"She wants to go home."
"He's wishing he could go home."

Instrumental Activity

(I+, I−, I?) The main character in the story performs or thinks of performing an act, the function of which is to reduce or remove the threat to body integrity, anxiety, or insecurity about body intactness or functioning. Someone goes to the doctor, asks for medication, and so forth. The person in the story who is threatened must do the act himself: think, problem solve, act, cooperate, and so on, to remove blocks to body integrity, which is a function toward achieving his goal. The threatened person must instigate some action or think of instigating some action aimed at direct removal of threat or in obtaining help in removing the threat or in reduction of anxiety or insecurity.

Statements such as "had to go to the hospital" are not scored.

Separation of Imagery Related to Instrumental Activity

Imagery related to instrumental activity is to be scored separately in terms of whether the action instigated by the threatened individual is successful, unsuccessful, or doubtfully successful in achieving the goal of reducing threat to body integrity or psychological security. Examples:

"He asks the nurse if he can have an appointment for Monday night."
"He's thinking about getting a book that will teach him how to walk."

Dependency

Someone in the story cares for, gives advice and sympathy, provides relief from pain, gives comfort, or assists in maintaining or regaining body integrity or in reducing fear or threat from internal or external sources. Assistance may include aid in escaping from a dangerous situation that could lead to body mutilation. Dependency is scored from the viewpoint of the person in the story who is threatened with loss of body integrity. Being visited by someone while in the hospital is scored as dependency. Aid must be directed toward regaining or retaining body integrity or toward reducing fear or anxiety.

Care or aid of doctors and nurses is scored as dependency if such help is not actively solicited by the person threatened. If the function is actively solicited, or there is a statement of cooperation in order to achieve a goal, such as "wanting a shot," "doesn't mind the shot," and so forth, it is also scored as instrumental activity. A statement directly implying "giving" in the form of definite treatment is scored, even though the hero states he does not want the treatment, if it results in cure. All visiting implying care or sympathy is scored. Examples:

"The doctor tried to make them well."
"They take his temperature."
"His mother rushed him to the hospital."
"I think the nurse is getting her food ready."
"The nurse gets him a book about walking."
". . . and the nurse is taking care of him."

OBSTACLES OCCURRING DURING PROGRESSION TOWARD GOAL
Block, Environment

Something in the environment prevents someone from getting well after the disease process has begun or the original body mutilation has occurred. Environmental or human agents prevent going home from the hospital or regaining body integrity. An environmental situation in which the course of events indicates that the possibility of further personal injury or death exists or is probable will be scored. Anything interfering with the successful mastering of threat, reduction of fear, or regaining of body integrity that emanates from the environment will be scored. Examples:

"They didn't have any material to make a leg, so he stayed forever."
"And there wasn't any cure for the disease."

Block, Personal

Something within the person prevents the regaining of body functioning or integrity, prevents mastering the threat, or reducing anxiety and fear. He does not have the will to live or fight to regain body integrity; resists the assistance of someone else to such an end, or internal body functioning fails in the fight toward the goal of achieving security. There is some block within the person in the smooth progress toward the goal of regaining body integrity and in reduction of threat. Examples:

"And later he had a heart attack."
"He just didn't want to live."

AFFECTIVE STATES EXPRESSED
Positive Affective State (Self)

Statements that the threatened individual is happy about going home, getting well, avoiding an accident, and so on, are to be scored as positive affective state, self. Also scored are direct statements of objective benefits gained by achieving the goal beyond the goal itself, such as, "He got well and could go out and play." The statement must specify that the person enjoys the activities; or imply such, as "plays." Example: "Soon he walked so good that he can climb a hill or a mountain, and he never quits walking."

Negative Affective State (Self)

Statements of experiencing pain, fear, or sadness related to present body functioning or integrity or related to the course of current events from the viewpoint of the hero are scored as negative affective state. Negative affect is not to be inferred from the mere statement of receiving injections or undergoing operations or from an anxiety outcome less specifically stated. Negative affective states should not be inferred if not explicitly stated. Examples:

"And she was afraid."
"She is thinking that it is going to hurt."

Positive Affective State (Other)

The narrator reports that an individual in the story other than the threatened individual is experiencing positive affect in relation to the hero. Hospital personnel or visitors are happy about the threatened individual's regaining of body integrity, etc. Examples:

"And his mother was happy that she was feeling better."
"The nurse was glad that he could walk again."

Negative Affective State (Other)

Someone in the story other than the threatened individual is experiencing sadness, unhappiness, anger, and so forth, related to the threat to the hero's body integrity or security. Examples:

"And his mother was very sad when she died."
"His nurse was angry that he got up."

Delineation of Content of Affective States (Self and Other)

The scorer will also designate on the scoring sheet the content of the feeling expressed, both in terms of the threatened individual and to others in the story, for both negative and positive affective states (anger, fear, pain, dejection, defeat, despair, resignation; or happiness, indifference, empathy, etc.).

ANTICIPATORY GOAL STATES
Positive Anticipatory Goal State

Anticipations have a future reference. There is a definite statement of anticipating the future with positive affect. Someone in the story anticipates going home from the hospital, thinks that he will get well and avoid mutilation or loneliness. These statements are not related to problem solving. The person is thinking about getting well or expecting to get well as a definite projection into the future. Wanting treatment "so he could get well" is scored. There may be two anticipatory goal states within a story. Example: "She is thinking that when she gets well, she can go out and play again."

Negative Anticipatory Goal State

Statement of fear or anxiety about not getting well as a definite possibility for the future is scored as negative anticipatory goal state. There is a statement of thought of the main character that he might not or will not get well and go home, or will die or need to return to the hospital. There is anxiety over survival or deepening of the illness or threat. There is a statement of fear of unsuccessful outcome of events or fear of potential harm or loneliness. A statement of returning to the hospital for outpatient treatment as a projection into the future is not scored under this category, which is seen in a positive light by the narrator.

Doubtful Anticipatory Goal State

Statements of uncertainty about the future. Examples:

> (Negative) "The body is thinking that he might die."
> (Doubtful) "She hopes she gets well and doesn't get sicker than she is now."

PERCEPTION OF CAUSALITY: SOURCE OF THREAT

Imagery in the story may indicate directly the child's perception as to the source of threat to body functioning integrity. The child may ascribe responsibility for the threat to the actions of the hero in the story. Body mutilation or internal malfunctioning may be self-inflicted or may be a direct result of the child's own actions. This self-action resulting in body mutilation or causing internal malfunctioning may have been enacted either with prior knowledge of results or unknowingly on the part of the child. Thus, either disobedience to adult injunctions or unthinking behavior may be seen as resulting in the child's insecurity in body integrity. Fear of separation in hospitalization and threats of bodily mutilation or death may then be perceived consciously or unconsciously as just retribution for behavior or as punishment.

On the other hand, the threat from within may be exteriorized in imagery and displaced to a generalized threat from without. The inner sphere of threat may be changed to an outer sphere. The environment itself may appear menacing, or environmental circumstances or objects may be expressed in imagery as the source of the threat to the hero.

When such imagery in the stories is spontaneously expressed, the stories will be scored in terms of perception of the causality of the threat. Stories will not be scored for a mere statement that someone is ill, even though diagnosis is mentioned, without direct reference to causality as emanating from the individual himself or from the environment. Causality is to be scored in terms of the major threat, it there is more than one in the story.

Internal Causality (Self)

The hero in the story has enacted some behavior in the past that directly or indirectly results in body mutilation or malfunctioning. When this category is scored, a determination is to be made as to whether the action that results in threat to body integrity or insecurity emanates from physical, psychological, or undetermined sources, within the threatened individual. Examples:

> "She got hit by two cars . . . She went on the red. It was her fault she got hit."
> "She committed suicide because she was so sad."
> "She fell from the treehouse. She just lost her balance."

External Causality

Someone or something in the environment has caused body mutilation or malfunction or has engaged in behavior that results in a threat to life. The source of threat is outside the person threatened, that is, emanates from the objective or human environment. Source of threat may also be perceived as supernatural. A supernatural agency or deity has directly desired or ordered the illness or body mutilation or desires the death of the character within the story. This will of the deity is not linked with the actions of the individual in a manner suggestive of retribution or punishment for individual human sin. If human behavior is seen as resulting in divine retribution, it will be scored as self-causality. Examples:

> "He was walking in the field and got bit by a rattlesnake."
> "He was out hunting and some other men were out hunting, and they accidentally shot him."
> "God wanted her to come and live with him."

OUTCOME

Relief Outcome

The threatened individual in the story gets well, goes home from the hospital, successfully avoids an accident or body mutilation, or experiences relief from loneliness. There is a positive end to the story. Examples:

> "And she gets out of the hospital, and she gets well."
> "Soon he walked so good that he can climb a hill or a mountain."
> "She gets to come out of the hospital in about a week. She can go out and play again."
> "When she got well, she never had to go to the hospital again."

Anxiety Outcome

The threatened individual in the story dies: never goes home from the hospital, succumbs to the accident, or never regains body intactness. There is a negative ending to the story. External or internal forces continue to operate that will result in the person being worse off in the future. Examples:

> "And then she dies, and the mother and father are sad."
> "He does jump out of the window and kills himself. . . . They had to bury him at a place . . . a cemetery."
> "They didn't have no material to make a leg, so he stayed forever."

Doubtful Outcome

Statement of uncertainty or ignorance as to whether a character in the story maintains or regains body integrity, whether he can go home from the hospital, or whether he will ever get well. Doubtful outcome will also be scored if the narrator changes the outcome of the story while telling the story from the viewpoint of the threatened individual, or if no certain ending to the story is given. Example: "I don't know if she ever got well."

SCORING

The scoring system, utilizing the form reproduced below, is designed to determine both total amount of preoccupation with threat to body integrity and functioning

	Unrelated Imagery	Imagery: Loneliness	Imagery: Mutilation	Imagery: Death	Thema: Loneliness	Thema: Mutilation	Thema: Death	Causality: Internal	Causality: External	Wish fulfillment	Inst. act. +	Inst. act. −	Int. act. ?	Dependency	Obstacles: Block, environment	Obstacles: Block, personal	Affective states Self: Positive	Self: Negative	Others: Positive	Others: Negative	Anticipatory goal state: Positive	Negative	Doubtful	Outcome: Relief	Anxiety	Doubtful	Story scores
Form A																											
B																											
C																											
D																											
E																											
F																											
G																											
H																											
Column totals																											Total score

Formal aspects

	Affective states positive: Self	Others	Affective states negative: Self	Others	Causality Internal: Phy.	Psych.	Undet.
Form A							
B							
C							
D							
E							
F							

Scoring manual for the achievement motive.

and to provide comparative data on specific aspects, such as causality, exteriorization of threat, and perceived patterns of adaptation.

Many of the categories employed are an adaptation from the scoring manual for the achievement motive as outlined by McClelland et al (1958). The general behavior or sequence followed differs somewhat in that the focus of the present system relates to analysis of threat and adaptive maneuvers. These adaptations were found to be necessary because of the generally more complicated aspects of fear motivation related to threat to body integrity and continued functioning or existence.

Each theme is scored only once per story, despite the fact that other imagery may appear within a story. Each category of imagery, however, is also scored only once per story. If no imagery is present, related to a threat to body integrity or security, it is scored as unrelated imagery, -1, and is not scored further. Each thema is to be scored $+1$, and threat imagery and each subcategory are also scored $+1$. The total score represents the number of times threat imagery and each of the subcategories listed above are scored in the record of a particular subject. This total score is designated the fear related motivation score. The total score is thus an indication of gross preoccupation with threat.

Actual words should be present whenever possible for scoring a category. The story is also scored from the viewpoint of the person or persons threatened with loss of body integrity.

Outcome is scored only once per story. If the outcome is changed during the story, for instance from death to recovery, the outcome is scored as doubtful.

Formal Aspects

Attention will also be directed toward the formal aspects as indications of anxiety while the narrator is telling the story. These include breaks in the story line, changing the outcome of the story, unusual delays, blocks, or unusually brief stories. Notation will be made of any behavioral indices of anxiety during the time the projective test is being administered.

SAMPLE PROJECTIVE TEST

Subject: A 7-year-old girl with cancer of the brain

Form A

Two boys in adjoining beds.

This is about two boys and they're not sleeping. They're coloring in bed. They're at home. They're thinking about the pictures. They ate dinner before— they had hamburgers. These boys like to play with cars and trucks. This is at night time. Then they fall asleep. Their Mommy comes in to see them. They're not asleep yet, and they talk to her. They say, "Hi Mommy." Tomorrow they will go to school. They will learn to read and write.

Form B

Small child in hallway outside closed door to ICU.

It's a little girl. She's holding on to the bannister. She's sick and she's in the hospital. She has a cough. A girl gave it to her—it was the other girl's fault. So she had to come to the hospital. She's wondering what's behind the door. There are doctors behind the door. She's about to come in alone because the doctor's going to fix her up; give her some medicine. She wanted to go to the hospital and get the medicine. She gets well and goes home. She's happy about that, 'cause she can go out and play again.

Form C

Boy in front of mural depicting operation. TAT 8 BM.

This looks like at the doctor too. They're cutting him open, to take something out of him—maybe something he swallowed that got stuck. He didn't want the operation because it hurt, and he didn't know if it was going to help him. Then they gave him some pills to go to sleep. The other looks like a boy. He's waiting for his father to get his operation. The other is the doctor who's going to get the thing out that he ate and got stuck. The man on the table is thinking that it's going to hurt. The man gets well and goes home and he's happy about that.

Form D

Small child in bed, nurse nearby with back turned.

It's at a doctor's place, 'cause that's the nurse. It's a hospital. And that's a little girl—she's sick. She had the flu—her head hurts her bad. She had a lot of pain. She's thinking that she hopes she gets well. She's afraid she might die. The nurse is looking at a little table—she helps the little girl. They have to put stitches in the little girl's head. She didn't want the stitches because it hurts. They take care of the little girl. Her mother comes to see her. This little girl doesn't get well—she keeps on having pain in her head like me. But she doesn't die. She gets well after a very long time. She goes home, but she had to keep coming back for treatment and x-rays to her head.

Form E

Figure outlined in open window. TAT 14.

A man is going out the window. He's jumping. He's trying to commit suicide. He's trying to kill himself. He's very sad because his wife died. So he's real sad, and he wants to die too. He's thinking that he wants to die. He jumps off the window and he does die. Then he gets buried next to his wife.

Form F

Child in bed, parents and doctor outside door.

This girl is asleep. And the people are talking. They're some friends of hers, and the girl's father who's asleep. She's in her room in the hospital. She had a bad accident. Something happened to her head. They had to operate, and take her to surgery. They took something out of her head. She wanted them to do this, so she could get better, and not die. She's dreaming here about herself—that she gets well and doesn't die. After the operation, she had stitches in her head. She was very sick. They gave her medicine and took care of her. Finally they took the stitches out, and the bandage off. She didn't die, but she got better, and went home. She was very happy, but she did have to come back to the hospital often for treatment.

Form G

Woman entering room face on hand. TAT 3 GF.

It's somebody's mother. She's tired. She's coming into the room to lay down. She has some children—American children. She's so tired because she's been working too hard. She gets sick because she's so tired. She doesn't have to go to the hospital because her husband's a doctor. He gave her some pills. Her head hurts. She's just thinking about she's sick and she wants to get well. She wanted some medicine and her husband gave her some. She does get well and she's happy.

Form H

Small child sitting in doorway of cabin. TAT 13 B.

It's a little boy. He's waiting at an old house. He's barefooted, and sitting down in the doorway. It's a real old house. That's where he lives. He's waiting for his father. They're very poor. He's thinking about his Daddy. He's very lonesome all by himself. He's wishing that his Daddy would hurry up and come to be with him. He's scared too, to be so alone. The little boy just stays there, and finally his Daddy comes.

REFERENCE

McClelland D, Atkinson JW, Cleark R, Lowell EL: A scoring manual for the achievement motive, Chapter 12. In Atkinson JW (ed): Motives in Fantasy, Action, and Society. Princeton, NJ, D Van Nostrand, 1958

Index

Numbers followed by an *f* indicate a figure; *t* following a page number indicates tabular material; *b* denotes material in a box.